INSIGHT G

PORTUGAL

APA PUBLICATIONS

Part of the Langenscheidt Publishing Group

INSIGHT GUIDE
PORTUGAL

Editorial
Project Editor
Pam Barrett
Managing Editor
Emily Hatchwell
Editorial Director
Brian Bell

Distribution
UK & Ireland
GeoCenter International Ltd
The Viables Centre, Harrow Way
Basingstoke, Hants RG22 4BJ
Fax: (44) 1256 817988

United States
Langenscheidt Publishers, Inc.
46–35 54th Road, Maspeth, NY 11378
Fax: 1 (718) 784 0640

Canada
Thomas Allen & Son Ltd
390 Steelcase Road East
Markham, Ontario L3R 1G2
Fax: (1) 905 475 6747

Australia
Universal Publishers
1 Waterloo Road
Macquarie Park, NSW 2113
Fax: (61) 2 9888 9074

New Zealand
Hema Maps New Zealand Ltd (HNZ)
Unit D, 24 Ra ORA Drive
East Tamaki, Auckland
Fax: (64) 9 273 6479

Worldwide
Apa Publications GmbH & Co.
Verlag KG (Singapore branch)
38 Joo Koon Road, Singapore 628990
Tel: (65) 6865 1600. Fax: (65) 6861 6438

Printing
Insight Print Services (Pte) Ltd
38 Joo Koon Road, Singapore 628990
Tel: (65) 6865 1600. Fax: (65) 6861 6438

©2004 Apa Publications GmbH & Co.
Verlag KG (Singapore branch)
All Rights Reserved
First Edition 1992
Fourth Edition 1999
Updated 2004

CONTACTING THE EDITORS
We would appreciate it if readers
would alert us to errors or out-
dated information by writing to:
Insight Guides, P.O. Box 7910,
London SE1 1WE, England.
Fax: (44) 20 7403 0290.
insight@apaguide.co.uk

www.insightguides.com

ABOUT THIS BOOK

This guidebook combines the interests and enthusiasms of two of the world's best known information providers: Insight Guides, whose titles have set the standard for visual travel guides since 1970, and Discovery Channel, the world's premier source of non-fiction television programming.

The editors of Insight Guides provide practical advice and general understanding of a destination's history, culture, institutions and people. Discovery Channel and its Web site, www.discovery.com, help millions of viewers explore their world from the comfort of their own home and also encourage them to explore it first-hand.

How to use this book

The book is carefully structured to convey an understanding of Portugal and its culture and to guide readers through its sights and attractions:

◆ The **Features** section, identified by a yellow bar, covers Portugal's history and culture in lively, authoritative essays written by specialists.

EXPLORE YOUR WORLD®
DISCOVERY
CHANNEL

◆ The **Places** section, with a blue bar, provides full details of all the sights and areas worth seeing. The chief places of interest are coordinated by number with specially drawn maps.

◆ The **Travel Tips** listings section provides information on travel, accommodation, restaurants and other practical aspects of the country. Information may be located quickly using the index on the back cover flap, which also serves as a bookmark.

The contributors

This new edition was edited by **Pam Barrett**, building on the original book put together by **Alison Friesinger Hill**.

The history chapters were written by Harvard graduate **Thomas Hill**, while **Ruth Rosengarten** described Art and Architecture. The cuisine section was the work of **Jean Anderson**, author of *The Food of Portugal*, and **Scott Carney**, a New York wine expert contributed the chapter on wine. **Katherine Barrett Swett** wrote about travellers' accounts of their journeys to Portugal.

Sharon Behn contributed the chapters about *pousada* accommodation and on the Algarve, and **Martin Symington** wrote about Portuguese boats. Other regional chapters were written by: **Marvine Howe** (Lisbon and area); **Deborah Brammer** (Alentejo); **Jeremy Boultbee** (Trás-os-Montes; the Beiras); **Jenny Wittner** (Coimbra and surroundings); **Nigel Tisdall** (Madeira).

This edition was updated by **Brian and Eileen Anderson**, authors of several books on Portugal. They wrote a new chapter on *Natural Portugal*, and also contributed the features on *Port*, *Azulejos, Crafts* and *Festivals*. **Pat Underwood** updated the chapters on Madeira, and **Andreas Stieglitz** updated the Azores. They were aided by **Paul** and **Denise Burton**, based in North Portugal, who updated Travel Tips. The entire book was updated in 2004 by **Roger Williams**.

Many of the photographs are by **Tony Arruza** and **Bill Wassman**, who are both regular contributors to Insight Guides. Thanks go also to **Penny Phenix** who proofread and indexed the book.

Map Legend

▬ ▪ ▬	International Boundary
▬ ▬ ▬	Province Boundary
▬ ▪ ▬	National Park/Reserve
▬ ▬ ▬	Ferry Route
Ⓜ	Metro
✈ ✈	Airport: International/ Regional
🚌	Bus Station
Ⓟ	Parking
❶	Tourist Information
✉	Post Office
⛪ † ⸶	Church/Ruins
†	Monastery
☾	Mosque
✡	Synagogue
▟ ⌂	Castle/Ruins
∴	Archaeological Site
⋂	Cave
⚑	Statue/Monument
★	Place of Interest

The main places of interest in the Places section are coordinated by number with a full-colour map (e.g. ❶), and a symbol at the top of every right-hand page tells you where to find the map.

INSIGHT GUIDE
PORTUGAL

CONTENTS

Maps

A map of Portugal is on the
inside front flap, and a map
of Lisbon Transport is on the
inside back flap

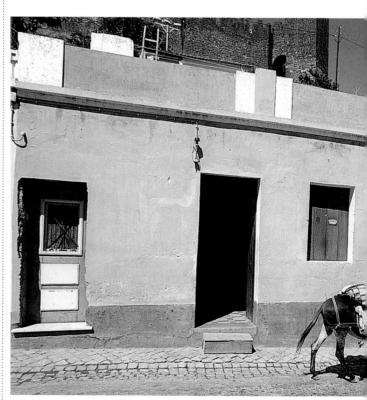

Introduction

Diverse, Delightful Portugal **15**

History

Features

A quiet
afternoon in
the Algarve

Insight on ...

Information panels

Places

BARCO RABELO

WHERE LAND ENDS AND SEA BEGINS

Portugal's diverse landscapes as well as its history and culture set it apart from the rest of Europe

Portugal is a land on the edge, "where land ends and sea begins" as the 16th-century epic poet Luís Vaz de Camões put it. At the western periphery of Europe, it is also caught between traditional living – fishing and farming – and the technology that has made the world smaller, more integrated, more complex.

It is a cosy country, encompassing an area of 92,100 sq km (33,550 sq. miles – a bit bigger than Austria), but has a stunning diversity of lovely landscapes: long white beaches and pretty coves; ranges of rolling hills and mountains – the central Serra da Estrela ("Mountains of the Stars") being the highest; numerous rivers and, in the southern central area, Alentejo's broad plain which is patched with cork oaks and olive plantations.

Crowning Portugal's natural beauty for much of the year are blue skies and a glowing light: an agreeable climate of hot summers and chilly but never freezing winters. It's a temperate country, in mood as in weather, and its people (numbering about 10½ million) are for the most part gentle, courteous, hospitable to visitors, fatalistic and immensely tolerant.

The traveller is welcome in every corner, from the discos and *boîtes* in Lisbon, open for dancing until the early hours, to the most obscure village in Trás-os-Montes, with its simple ways of baking, spinning and farming. Sample whatever is to your taste, perhaps try a little of everything.

This guide will start you off with a lesson in Portugal's long and fascinating history, followed by a brief introduction to its people – insofar as it is possible to sum up any nation of individuals. Next, the book's features section will familiarise you with Portugal's foods and wines, its wonderful *pousada* inns and manor house accommodation, and with its glorious art and architecture. Finally, the Places section will take you on a tour of the entire country. It's a trip well worth making. ❏

PRECEDING PAGES: Porto, seen from the south bank of the Douro; the cavalry parades in Belém, Lisbon; a reluctant worker; Cup Final day.
LEFT: Portugal is famous for its tiles *(azulejos)* and its port boats *(barcos rabelos)*.

1147

1227

1497

1762

1385

1834

Decisive Dates

EARLY DAYS

9th–6th century BC Phoenician and Greek traders establish settlements.
5th century BC Carthaginians in control of the Iberian peninsula.
130 BC Roman conquest. Bitter fighting between them and the Lusitani, strongest indigent group, which gave the country its early name, Lusitania.
60 BC Julius Caesar makes Olisipo a major town in the province of Lusitania.
4th century AD Christianity spreads throughout the

Roman Empire. Bishoprics are established at Braga and Évora.
AD 419 The Germanic Suevi spread into Lusitania, but during the next half century are vanquished by the Visigoths.
711 Moors from Africa occupy Iberia.
718 A victory by the Christians over the Moors at Covadonga in Asturias starts the reconquest.
868 Porto reconquered; Coimbra 10 years later.
883 Area between the Douro and the Minho is recognised as Portucale. Remains under Spanish control but with increasing power and autonomy.
11th–12th century A complex round of civil wars occurs as Henri of Burgundy and his cousin Raymond battle for supremacy.

RECONQUEST AND NATIONHOOD

1143 Afonso Henriques is declared first king of Portugal, but is not recognised by Pope Lucius II.
1147 Aided by Crusaders, Henri's son Afonso Henriques captures Lisbon.
1179 At the age of 70, Afonso Henriques is finally recognised by Pope Alexander III as king.
1189 Silves in Algarve is captured by Sancho I but lost again to the Moors.
1249 The Moors are finally expelled from Algarve.
1260 Afonso III transfers capital from Coimbra to Lisbon.
1279–1325 Reign of King Dinis, great reforming king and castle builder; married Isabel of Aragón.
1297 Treaty of Alcañices with Castile establishes borders of Portugal.
1348 Plague – the Black Death – ravages Lisbon.
1355 Inês de Castro is murdered.
1373 First Anglo-Portuguese Alliance signed with John of Gaunt who had married a Spanish princess.
1385 Defeat of the Castilians at the Battle of Ajubarrota. João I becomes king and founder of the second dynasty, the House of Avis.
1386 Treaty of Windsor is signed (and remains unbroken to this day).
1387 João I marries Philippa of Lancaster, daughter of John of Gaunt.

THE AGE OF DISCOVERIES

1415 Ceuta, on north African coast, is taken by a Portuguese force including Henry the Navigator. Madeira discovered.
1427 Azores discovered.
1434 Gil Eanes discovered West African lands beyond Cape Bojador.
1460 Death of Henry the Navigator.
1481 João II comes to the throne.
1487 Bartolomeu Dias rounds the Cape of Good Hope.
1492 Around 60,000 Jews are expelled from Spain and take refuge in Portugal.
1494 Treaty of Tordesillas: Portugal and Spain divide up the New World.
1497–98 Explorer Vasco da Gama opens a sea route to India.
1500 Pedro Alvares Cabral discovers Brazil.
1510 Conquest of Goa establishes Asian empire.
1519–22 Ferdinand Magellan circumnavigates the globe.
1536 Holy Inquisition is introduced.
1557 Trading post is established in Macau.
1580 Portugal falls under Spanish rule. The third dynasty, the Habsburgs, commences.

WARS AND REVOLUTIONS

1640 The Spanish are overthrown; the Duke of Bragança becomes João IV, commencing the fourth dynasty, the House of Bragança.

1662 Catherine of Bragança marries England's King Charles II.

1668 Treaty of Lisbon, under which Spain recognises Portugal's independence.

1703 Methuen Treaty signed, giving England dominance in the wine industry.

early 1700s Gold is discovered in Brazil which boosts Portuguese economy.

1755 The Great Earthquake devastates Lisbon. The Marquês de Pombal, granted emergency powers by the king, sets about rebuilding Lisbon.

1777 Maria I becomes queen, Pombal dismissed.

1807 Portugal invaded by the French; royal family leave for Brazil.

1808 The Peninsular War. Portugal invokes the British Alliance. Sir Arthur Wellesley (later Duke of Wellington) leads British forces.

1820 Liberal revolution.

1822 New liberal constitution lasts only two years, but ends the Inquisition. Brazil proclaims its independence.

1829–34 Miguelist Wars between factions led by the brothers Miguel and Pedro. The latter wins and becomes Pedro IV in 1834.

1834 Religious orders expelled from Portugal.

1834–1908 Rise of political parties, Septembrists (liberals) and Chartists (conservatives). Power alternates between them through the reigns of successive monarchs

1908 King Carlos and the Crown Prince are shot dead in Lisbon. Manuel II ascends the throne.

1910 Portugal becomes a republic; Manuel II exiled.

1910–26 A period of political turmoil, military coups and assassination.

SALAZAR AND AFTER

1926 Military coup overthrows democratic government and brings General Carmona to power.

1928 Carmona appoints Dr António de Oliveira Salazar as finance minister.

1932 Salazar becomes prime minister and rules Portugal as a dictator until 1968.

1936–39 Salazar defies League of Nations and secretly aids Franco in the Spanish Civil War.

PRECEDING PAGES: the evolution of Portugal's flag.
LEFT: Fernando, the Duke of Bragança.
RIGHT: as the venue for Expo '98, Lisbon received a boost to its ego as well as its coffers.

1939–1945 World War II: Portugal is neutral.

1955 Portugal allowed to join the UN.

1961 Angolan uprising brutally crushed. Wars in Africa continue. Goa lost to Indian control.

1966 Suspension bridge over the Rio Tejo opens.

1970 Death of Salazar. Marcelo Caetano becomes prime minister.

1974 Young Captains' Revolution restores democracy to Portugal. Armed Forces Movement, founded in 1973, governs until 1976. Banks and insurance companies nationalised; monopolies and estates taken over. African colonies granted independence.

1976 Mario Soares, socialist, becomes prime minister. New constitution upholds democracy.

1979 Coalition of the right takes power.

1986 Portugal, together with Spain, becomes a member of the European Community (EC).

1994 Lisbon becomes Europe's Capital of Culture.

1995 António Guterres becomes prime minister.

1998 Lisbon hosts Expo '98.

1999 Portugal joins the EU single currency. Macau reverts to Chinese control.

2001 Porto, European Capital of Culture.

2002 Euro becomes official currency. Centre right government elected.

2003 Forest fires sweep across southwest Portugal. Damage estimated at one billion euros.

2004 Portugal hosts the 12th European football championships.

ANCIENT LUSITANIA

For centuries, successive waves of invaders swept over the peninsula. The Moors held on longest, even after Afonso Henriques became Portugal's first king

Portugal is something of an anomaly on the map of Western Europe. It is separated from Spain, a neighbour five times its size, not so much by natural frontiers but rather by the dictates of historical destiny. Geographically, almost every region of Portugal corresponds closely to a region across the border. The northern Minho district is similar to Spanish Galicia; the southern Algarve and Alentejo districts bear a resemblance to Andalusia. The Tejo and Douro rivers and the mountains of the Beiras extend from Spain. In fact, the natural division of the Iberian peninsula would not be east from west, but north from south, separating the Atlantic culture and climate from that of the Mediterranean.

Yet Portugal, with borders already established by the 13th century, is one of the oldest nations in Europe. It has discovered and lost an empire, relinquished and regained its cherished autonomy and, since the 1974 revolution that ended decades of dictatorship, has formed new ties with former possessions.

Cultural diffusion

A rich prehistoric culture has left its traces throughout Portugal. There is evidence of the earliest stages of human evolution and a large number of megalithic sites. The variety and quantity of these finds have led many scholars to a theory that cultural diffusion came primarily from overseas. Opponents of this notion point out that most of the megalithic sites are far from the coastline. They think the population grew via natural land routes of settlement which, unsurprisingly, correspond to the paths invaders have taken throughout Portugal's history: across the Rio Minho from the north and over the Alentejo flatlands from the south.

In any case, by the 2nd millennium BC, social organisation consisted of scattered *castros* – garrisoned hilltop villages that suggest warfare between tribes. The people subsisted on goatherding and primitive agriculture, and clad themselves in woollen cloaks. Some of their constructions are still standing, for example at the Citânia de Briteiros near Guimarães.

In the south, tribes came under the influence of Phoenician trade settlements in the 9th-

century BC, and Greek ones in the 6th-century BC, both on the coast and inland, where metals were mined. It is only at this late point that there is evidence of a significant fishing economy among the indigenous people. Perhaps before then the rough-hewn and storm-beaten Atlantic coast was too intimidating for their small boats. During the 5th century BC, the Carthaginians wrested control of the Iberian peninsula from these earlier traders, but lost it to the Roman Empire in the Second Punic War.

Wars of conquests

The Romans called the peninsula Hispania Ulterior. Here, as elsewhere in the empire, they

LEFT: Roman milestones in north Portugal.
RIGHT: prehistoric settlement at Citânia de Briteiros in the Minho region of northern Portugal.

combined their economic exploitation with cultural upheaval. They were not traders, after all, but conquerors, who set about the business of founding cities, building roads, and reorganising territories. They also implemented governmental and judicial systems.

The locals resisted. The largest and most intransigent group were the Lusitani, who lived north of the Rio Tejo (Tagus), and after whom the region was called Lusitania. Bitter guerrilla fighting was intermittent for two centuries. The most renowned rebel was a shepherd named Viriathus, who led uprisings until he was assassinated in 139 BC by three treacherous com-

south. Lisbon became an important administrative centre, at the hub of the Romans' local road network, linking all the major population centres. These centres and routes have waned in importance, but many today – most notably the capital Lisbon – are still geographic focal points. Before their empire eventually fell, the Romans had infused the area with their language, legal system, currency, agriculture and, eventually, with Christianity. The organisation of *latifundios* – great, landed estates – was particularly significant as it brought large-scale farming to the area for the first time.

With the conversion of the late Roman

rades who had been bribed by the Romans. It was during these wars of conquest that Roman troops are said to have refused to cross the Rio Lima, believing it to be the *Lethe*, the mythical River of Forgetfulness. Their commander, the story goes, had to cross the river alone, then call each soldier by name to prove that the dip had not affected his memory. The death of Viriathus took the heart out of the revolt, although the Lusitanian uprisings were not finally quelled until 72 BC.

In 61 BC, Julius Caesar governed the province from Olisipo (Lisbon). Cities were established and colonised at Évora, Beja, Santarém, and elsewhere. Roads linked the north and

emperors (Constantine, who issued an Edict of Tolerance in AD 331, was the first Christian emperor), the tenets and organisation of Christianity spread throughout the fading empire. Bishoprics were established in a number of cities, Braga and Évora among them. As the church expanded it usurped the administrative power that had been developed by the empire at the height of its strength.

Heretical Christian doctrines held sway in Portugal during the 3rd and 4th centuries. In the early 5th century various groups of barbarians occupied the land. The Alani and Vandals each settled for a short time, but by 419 the Suevi were in sole, if not steady, possession of

Galicia, and from there they conquered Lusitania and most of the Iberian peninsula. The Suevi apparently assimilated easily with the existing Hispano-Roman population, but the tide turned with the fall of Rome and the arrival of the Visigoths.

For the next half century, military conquest meant religious conversion. In 448, Rechiarius, the king of a diminished Suevi empire, converted to Catholicism, perhaps hoping to elicit aid from Rome in battling against the Visigoths who were nominally Christian but clung to vestiges of heretical beliefs. When Rechiarius was killed in 457, the Suevi kingdom survived, led by Masdra. In 465, Masdra's son Remismund renounced Christianity, probably hoping to appease the Visigoths. But by 550, the growing power of the Catholic Church had produced a new round of conversions, led by St Martin of Dume. The remnants of the Suevi were politically extinguished in 585.

Invaders from the south

Visigoth rule, under an elective monarchy, was not seriously challenged until the Moors arrived on the southern coast in 711 and began their expansion northwards. The Moors were following the instructions of their leader, the Prophet Mohammed (who died in 632), to wage a holy war *(jihad)* against non-believers. However, like the Christian Crusades that followed *(see pages 25–26)*, their advances were increasingly concerned with empire building.

The Visigoths were defeated at the Battle of Jerez, and Lisbon soon fell into Muslim hands. Southern Portugal became part of Muslim Spain, loosely organised under the Córdoba caliph – caliphs were successors of the Prophet, regional rulers created under the Umayyad dynasty (650–749).

To the Moors, this land was known as Al-Gharb (the West), from which was derived the modern name Algarve. The Moors soon ruled all Portugal, and Christianity was forced north of the Minho where it lay gathering strength for the reconquest – the *Reconquista*.

LEFT: a sculpture found in Lisbon's Roman theatre.
RIGHT: the Temple of Diana at Évora.

A nation in prospect

Stirrings of the *Reconquista* were believed to have started as early as 718 at Covadonga. Here in Asturias, the Christians defeated a small force of Moors. Galicia became a battle-ground over the next century and a half. The kings of Asturias-León made ever-increasing excursions into Galicia and beyond. Slowly, towns fell before the Christian armies: Porto in 868, Coimbra in 878, and by 955 the king of León, Ordona III, had engineered a raid

on Lisbon. Most of the victories below the Douro, however, were transient ones, amounting to nothing more than successful raids, as the territory was seldom held for more than a season or two. Under the Emir of Córdoba, Muslims in Portugal lived in relative peace, introducing irrigation systems and water mills as well as wheat, rice, oranges and saffron. Shipbuilding was active, copper and silver mines were exploited, Roman roads expanded and towns were planned. There was religious tolerance and the arts flourished. Muslim stucco work and glazed tiles, called *azulejos*, were a lasting contribution to the nation's architectural style.

> ### OMAR KHAYYÁM
>
> The most famous Sufi poet was Omar Khayyám (1048–1120), whose *Rubaiyat*, in which women and wine are given mystical significance, was translated into English by the Victorian poet Edward Fitzgerald.

Although the local culture was strong, the authority of Córdoba began to wear thin and small kingdoms called *taifas* gained local control. Decentralisation led to internal dissent, partly caused by the rise of the Sufi religious sect. Sufism was considered a subversive and heretical kind of mysticism, but it gained popularity in reaction to the rationalism of conventional Islamic beliefs. These internal divisions allowed Christian forces to push the frontier lines down from the north, but they also permitted radical Muslim military groups such as the Almoravids and the Almohads to rise rapidly to power.

The Almoravids, who had built an empire in Africa, spread northwards. After helping the Islamic rulers in the peninsula to force the Christians back, they unified the *taifas* under their own rule. By 1095 they had succeeded in installing an austere military system and harsh government. They were soon followed by the still more fanatical Almohads and the simmering *Reconquista* took on the aspect of a Holy War for both Christians and Muslims.

The split with Spain

Portugal's separateness from Spain has been attributed to various causes, from the original borders between indigenous tribes to the land held by the Suevi against the Visigothic advances. However, it was during the Christian reconquest of Iberia that Portugal first truly asserted its independent stance and its leaders gained their sense of national destiny.

Late in the 9th century, the area between the Lima and Douro rivers, a territory which became known as Portucale, was divided under unstable feudal states, and came under the control of the Kingdom of León.

Fernando I of León was the great consolidating force in northern Spain during the 11th century. As part of his policy of centralising authority, he tried to diminish Portugal's power by dismantling it and dividing it into different provinces under separate governors. When Fernando's successor Alfonso VI took over the kingdoms of León, Castile, Galicia and Portugal, he declared himself "emperor", putting himself above kings. It may have been the lure of the title "king", which the emperor had unwittingly made available, that inspired Afonso Henriques, in the 12th century, to battle, deal and connive for the autonomy of his particular *terra*, Portugal.

Feuding cousins

Afonso Henriques was the son of Henri of Burgundy and his wife Teresa. Henri was among a number of French knights who had arrived in the late 11th century to fight the infidels. They were mostly second and third sons, who, under the prevailing system of male primogeniture – which meant that the eldest son inherited property and titles – were left with no real inheritance. If they wanted land and riches, they usually had to travel abroad to win them.

Henri's cousin Raymond, who, like Henri, was a fourth son, also came south. After proving his heroism in battle, Raymond married Alfonso VI's eldest daughter Urraca, and was granted the territories of Galicia and Coimbra. When Henri married Teresa, who was Alfonso's favourite (although illegitimate) daughter, he was given the territory of Portugal. With the death of Raymond and Alfonso VI, Urraca inherited that crown, but her second marriage, to Alfonso I of Aragon, also set off a complex round of civil wars.

During this period, Henri of Burgundy made significant strides towards gaining autonomy for the state of Portugal. The most important of these was the support he offered to the archbishops of Braga in a dispute with those of Toledo, the principal see of Spain.

In 1126 Urraca died and her son, Alfonso Raimundez, became Emperor Alfonso VII. When Henri died, his widow, Teresa, ruled Portugal as regent for her son, Afonso Henriques. Without wasting much time in mourning, she took a Galician count, Fernão Peres, as a lover, displeasing some of the nobility as well as her son. Continuing her husband's policies, Teresa schemed successfully to maintain Portugal's independence, but in 1127 she submitted to Alfonso VII's dominion after her army was

Treaty of Zamora was signed between the two cousins, wherein Alfonso VII gave Afonso Henriques the title of King of Portugal in exchange for feudal ties of military aid and loyalty.

Afonso Henriques sought to fix the title more firmly by seeking recognition from Rome. Pope Lucius II refused, keeping to a policy of supporting Iberian union in the hope of stemming the tide of Islam. It was only in 1179 that Pope Alexander III, in exchange for a yearly tribute and various other privileges, finally granted recognition of the Portuguese kingdom. By that late date, papal acceptance served only to formalise an entity that was not only well-estab-

defeated. A year later 18-year-old Afonso Henriques led a rebellion against his mother, ending her rule at the battle of São Mamede, near their castle in Guimarães.

A king is crowned

Over the next decade, Afonso Henriques vied with his emperor cousin for ultimate control of Portugal. After a brilliant military victory over the Moors in the Battle of Ourique in 1139, he began to refer to himself as king. In 1143, the

LEFT: Afonso Henriques, first king of Portugal.
ABOVE: an 18th-century engraving showing Afonso rallying his troops at the conquest of Lisbon in 1147.

MILITARY ORDERS

The crusades produced an unusual kind of soldier – that is, those belonging to the military orders created by St Bernard of Clairvaux in 1128. The Knights Templar was the first such order, based in Jerusalem, which had been captured in the First Crusade (1096–99). They were followed by the Knights of St John (the Hospitallers), established in Rhodes, and by the Teutonic Order and the Spanish Knights of Calatrava. Originally, their role was to fight for the true faith while obeying monastic rules of poverty, chastity and obedience. Soon, however, the spoils of war became more important for many of the knights than the spread of Christianity.

lished but growing. Afonso Henriques had enlisted the aid of crusaders and beaten back the Moors, adding his conquests to the emerging nation. Santarém and Lisbon were both taken in 1147; the first by surprise attack, the second in a siege that was supported by French, English, Flemish and German crusaders who were passing through Portugal on their way to the Holy Land, to fight what we now know as the Second Crusade.

The inestimable assistance of these 164 shiploads of men was extremely fortuitous; it very nearly fell through when Afonso Henriques pronounced that he expected them to

fight only for Christianity and not for earthly rewards. This was not the way the crusaders believed holy wars should be fought. The English and Germans walked out, and the king quickly compromised, offering loot and land in exchange for military service.

The western crusade

The bishop of Braga also offered aid in recruiting foreign crusaders, providing theological assurance that their enemies in the south would be heathens, and therefore no different from those they would be fighting in the Holy Land. However, Afonso Henriques's confessor questioned the diversion of troops from the crusade,

and the story is told that on the way to Santarém – with crusaders in tow – the king, believing his confessor to be right, was besieged by guilt. He was also, understandably, anxious because of the Moorish stronghold's reputation for impregnability. To soothe his torment, he vowed that he would build an abbey at Alcobaça (some 90km/55 miles southwest of Coimbra) in the Virgin's honour if the attack was successful. The battle was won, and Afonso Henriques laid the foundation stone of the promised building the following year. The abbey still stands *(see page 247)*.

Convincing crusaders that one batch of infidels was as good as another was crucial to the *Reconquista*. One result of the crusades (which began in 1096 and lasted for more than 150 years) was the founding of military-religious organisations such as the Knights Templar and the Hospitallers *(see previous page)*. These orders were rewarded with land grants in exchange for chasing out the Moors, and grew wealthy and powerful – the Templars, in fact, became prestigious bankers.

In 1170, Afonso Henriques fought his last battle, at Badajoz. The powerful Almohads had enlisted the aid of Fernando II of León, who felt that the Portuguese were recapturing not only the Moorish-held land, but territory that was by right a part of León.

The most renowned of Afonso Henriques's military cohorts was Geraldo Geraldes, a local adventurer dubbed O Sem Pavor ("The Fearless") for his brilliant raids into Muslim territory. This popular hero had won a string of epic victories, but at Badajoz the combination of Moorish and Leonese forces was too much for both Geraldes and his king. The aging Afonso Henriques broke his leg and was captured. His release came only after he had surrendered hard-won castles and territories to enemy parties. His retreat allowed the Moors to entrench their forces along the battle zone.

The founding king of Portugal's days of victory were over, with the *Reconquista* still a century away. Yet, with Henriques' monarchy, a country was born. Whether it was through an act of political will or not, the independence and individuality of the Portuguese nation was forever determined.   ❏

LEFT: the early crusaders, out to subdue the infidels.
RIGHT: an ancient royal coat of arms.

DOM IOAO III REY
DE PORTVGAL

A NATION IS BORN

*With the final expulsion of the Moors, Portugal steadily established
a kingdom under the House of Burgundy*

For a century after the death of Afonso Henriques in 1185, the first order of business was the slow riddance of the remaining, and still feisty, Moors. The *Reconquista,* now virtually sanctioned by the Church with various papal bulls and indulgences as a "western crusade", was still very much under way.

The Knights Templar had arrived in Portugal when they stopped on their way to Palestine in 1128. They were soon followed by other military-religious orders – the Hospitallers – and the Knights of Calatrava and Santiago, who all clung to the religious justification for their war-mongering and for their massive accumulation of land and loot. However, the western crusade remained controversial. In Palestine the dividing line between Christians and infidels was clearly drawn, but southern Iberia had intermingled Muslim, Christian and Jewish people in economic, cultural and political spheres. In 1197, papal indulgences were even promised in a war against Alfonso IX of León, a Christian, though at that time an ally of the Muslims.

The war proceeded steadily, if slowly. The first kings of the Burgundian line after Afonso Henriques continued to press the borders southwards. Under Sancho II, the eastern Algarve and Alentejo were incorporated in the burgeoning nation. By 1249, during the reign of Afonso III, the western Algarve and Faro fell. By 1260 Afonso had moved the capital south from Coimbra to Lisbon. These boundaries – much like today's – were finally recognised by Castile in the Treaty of Alcañices in 1297.

Social transformation

The *Reconquista* brought Portugal fundamental social transformation. The lands of the south, having been reclaimed, now had to be populated. In order to do this, the Burgundian kings needed to balance their centralised, essentially military power with popular and financial support. The need for such support forced successive kings

to consult the *cortes*, local assemblies of nobles, clergy and, later, mercantile classes. At the *cortes* of Leiria (1254), Afonso III conceded the right of municipal representation in taxation and other economic issues. For the most part, the *cortes* were gathered whenever the king needed to raise money. When later monarchs used trade

and their own military orders to reap great and independent profits, the *cortes* fell into disuse.

Another result of the *Reconquista,* with the expansion of properties and the need for labourers who were willing to resettle, was an increase in social mobility among the lower classes. Distinctions fell away among the various levels of serfs as farm workers became a scarcer and so more valuable commodity. Another, more general, effect was the early amalgamation of the divergent cultures of north and south. The south was a culture of tolerance, marked by refinement and urbanity, while the northern culture had a rough arrogance, the attitude of invaders. Differences between the two remain even today.

LEFT: King Dinis, depicted in a 17th-century screen.
RIGHT: the 13th-century cross of Sancho I.

The church rode the *Reconquista* to riches. The various military-monastic orders were granted vast areas of land in return for military assistance. Furthermore, the church and clergy were free from taxation, and were granted the right to collect their own tithes from the population. Their power was such that it soon threatened the monarchy. Afonso II was the first ruler of Portugal to defy the church by attempting to curb its voracious acquisition of property. His efforts generally failed, as did those of his successor, Sancho II, who was finally excommunicated and dethroned in 1245 for his insistence on royal prerogatives.

The poet king

It was the reign of Dinis, who was known both as "the farmer king" and "the poet king", that truly cemented Portuguese independence and the power of the monarchy. After briefly joining Aragon in war against Castile, Dinis ushered in a long period of peace and progress. He encouraged learning and literature, establishing the first university in 1288; initially in Lisbon, this was transferred to Coimbra. Portuguese, having distinguished itself from its Latin roots and from Castilian (which would become Spanish), was established as the language of the troubadour culture, and the official language of law and state.

The troubadour culture – poetry and music spread by peripatetic minstrels – was greatly influential. Drawing upon the French tradition and Moorish influences, the Portuguese troubadours created a native literature. These song-poems of love and satire were often written by nobles, among them, of course, Dinis the poet king. Other forms of literary expression lagged far behind poetry.

Dinis's rule also brought political progress. Landmark agreements were made to seal peace with Castile (the Treaty of Alcañices, 1297) and the clergy (the Concordat of 1289). The latter agreement was a major victory for royal jurisdiction in matters of property. Dinis also fortified the frontier with the construction of some 50 castles.

Economic advances

By now a monetary economy was well established, internally as well as for international trade. Agricultural production was more and

THE STORY OF PEDRO AND INÊS

Betrothed to Constanza, a Spanish princess, Pedro, son of Afonso IV, fell in love with her lady-in-waiting, Inês de Castro, a member of a powerful Castilian family. She was banished in 1340, but returned upon the death of the princess in 1345. The threat of a Castilian heir was intolerable to Afonso, so, under pressure from three of his noblemen, he agreed to her assassination, then immediately withdrew consent. In 1355, taking matters into their own hands, the nobles murdered Inês in the grounds of what is now Quinta da Lágrimas (House of Tears) in Coimbra *(see page 260)*.

Pedro was inconsolable. Two years later, when he assumed the throne on his father's death, he tracked down his lover's assassins, caught two of them, and had their hearts torn out. He then ordered the exhumation of Inês, who was dressed in royal robes and placed next to him on the throne. Each member of the court was forced to pay homage by kissing her decomposed hand. She was finally entombed in Alcobaça Monastery along with Pedro, who insisted their tombs were placed foot to foot so that, on the Day of Judgment, the first thing they would see would be each other. Both tombs carry the same inscription *Até o Fim do Mundo* – "Until the End of the World".

This dramatic story of love and revenge has been an inspiration to generations of writers and poets.

more geared towards markets, although self-sufficient farming did not disappear. Indeed, Dinis encouraged the expansion of the economic system with large fairs, trading centres that encouraged internal trade. Dinis was responsible for chartering 48 such fairs, more than all the other Portuguese kings combined. This concentration of trade also, not coincidentally, allowed for more systematic taxation.

The only section of the economy to lag during this period was industrial production. Dinis,

FARM REFORM

In his role of "farmer king" Dinis reformed the agricultural system and initiated programmes that encouraged the export of olive oil, grain, wine and other foodstuffs.

wealth within the country and prevent the Church from appropriating it. In 1317 he founded the Order of Our Lord Jesus Christ, which was granted all the former possessions of the Knights Templar, under royal control.

Plagues and crises

Afonso IV succeeded Dinis. His administration was less secure, and hostilities with Castile waxed and waned. More significantly, his reign was burdened with the Black Death. The first bout devastated the country, particu-

LEFT: the Convento do Cristo, in Tomar.
ABOVE: the tomb of Pedro I in the monastery at Alcobaça.

and later kings, were counter-productive in their resistance to the idea of corporations. Craftsmen tended to work on their own, and thus confined themselves to local markets and limited quantities. Some goldsmithing, shipbuilding, and pottery was done in commercial quantities.

Perhaps the most significant of Dinis's accomplishments was the disbanding of the Knights Templar in 1312. The order was under fire throughout Europe, and its demise was imminent. Dinis's triumph was to retain its

larly the urban centres, in 1348–49. Throughout the next century the pestilence returned again and again, causing depopulation and despondency. Concurrently, various demographic and economic crises were undermining the nation. The attraction of the urban centres left the interior underpopulated, causing inflation in food prices. Monarchs tried to regulate population movements but were ineffectual. Economic stagnation, whose dreary influence extended to literature, religion, and every element of daily life, dragged on until the coming of the maritime empire.

Politics of this period were motivated largely by fear of Castilian domination. In fact, continual intermarriage between the two royal families did keep the possibility of unification open. But the Portuguese were committed to maintaining total independence, and this, coupled with general social unrest, caused turbulence for Pedro I and his son Fernando, and finally brought down the House of Burgundy.

The reign of Pedro I was marked by peaceful coexistence with Castile. Social and political growth flourished as the country recovered from the convulsions of the Black Death. However, the increasing power of the nobles, the clergy and the emergent bourgeoisie, all represented in the *cortes,* would later break

loose in active social discontent during the reign of his son, Fernando I.

Fernando tried to unite Portugal and Castile, engaging the country in a series of unpopular and unsuccessful wars. France and England joined the turmoil, using the Iberian peninsula as a theatre for the Hundred Years' War. In 1373, Fernando signed an Anglo-Portuguese alliance with John of Gaunt, who had married a Spanish princess *(see page 34).* The same year, Enrique II of Castile attacked Lisbon, burning and pillaging the city. To add to the confusion, the "Great Schism" divided the Catholic Church under opposing popes from 1378, and Fernando changed loyalties frequently. Wars ravaged the entire country, leaving the populace tired and angry.

Fernando further alienated his subjects with his unpopular marriage to Leonor Teles, who was perceived to represent the landed gentry. Riots broke out at the wedding and again in 1383 when Fernando died, leaving his widow (aided by her lover, the Galician count, João Fernandez Andeiro) to rule as Queen Mother.

Andeiro was assassinated within weeks by João, illegitimate son of Pedro I. In the ensuing civil war, Leonor had the support of most of the nobles and clergy, while João relied upon that of the middle class. He depended upon the deepening resentment the people felt towards Castile – where Leonor had fled after Andeiro's death – and rode this growing wave to victory. The final military conflict was the Battle of Aljubarrota (1385), a decisive victory for João's troops, despite being outnumbered.

The subsequent rule of João I, founder of the House of Avis, one of the military-religious orders, represented a new political beginning. The disputes with Castile continued, but they were winding down. The unsteady Anglo-Portuguese alliance was cemented by the Treaty of Windsor in 1386, a document cited as recently as World War II, when Britain invoked it to gain fuelling stations in the Azores.

João I brought stability, but the change of order was not a social revolution. New political representation was established by the mercantile class, but in time it became clear that only the names had changed. The landed aristocracy still held the real power, and the new dynasty was much like the old. ❑

THE BATTLE OF ALJUBARROTA

A number of stories surround the Battle of Aljubarrota. Nuno Alvares Pereira, captain of João's army, was ravaged by thirst when leading his forces into battle, and swore that no traveller would ever go thirsty there again. Since 1385 a pitcher of water has been placed daily in a niche of the Aljubarrota chapel of São Jorge. João, too, made a vow: to build a church in the Virgin's honour if his vastly outnumbered army was victorious. As the enemy turned tail and fled, João hurled his lance into the air to pick the spot where the monastery of Batalha would be built. He must have had a very strong arm, because the battlefield is 16 km (10 miles) from the monastery.

LEFT: a portal in João I's monastery at Batalha.

Castles in the Air

It is said that there are 101 castles in Portugal. In fact there are more, many of them either built or rebuilt between the 12th and 14th centuries. King Dinis (1279–1325) alone began the construction or expansion of more than 50 fortresses during his reign. Perhaps he should have been called "the king of the castle" along with his other titles: "the poet king" and "the farmer king". Dinis's labours can be seen throughout Portugal, but he concentrated his efforts along the eastern boundary. He strengthened the towns of Guarda, Penedo, Penamacor, Castelo Mendo, Pinhel and others, attempting to secure the area from the threat posed by Castile. He was well rewarded: the Treaty of Alcañices, signed in 1297, initiated a period of peace and stability between the neighbouring countries.

Dinis provided the money for the castles, and even specified the exact measurements of the walls and towers. Those initiated by him were of a particularly fine construction, with decorations and designs not found on other buildings. Some of the towers were slender and elegant; many balconies were elaborate, with detailed machicolations. Dinis often gave a specific character and grandeur to the structures, as in the 15 towers he had built at Numão, or the Torre do Galo ("Rooster Tower") at Freixo de Espada à Cinta, with its beautiful and unusual seven faces.

Many castles – built by Dinis and others – were on the sites of earlier forts: Moorish, Visigothic, Roman, or even earlier. It is interesting to note the developments in warfare as they are reflected in physical features of Portugal's castles. Long wooden verandahs, for example, were attached to the castles' walls in early days. Later these verandahs were covered with animal hides to prevent, or at least inhibit, them being burned by flaming arrows, but these too were abandoned at the end of the 13th century.

By this time, the carved stone balconies were being used for defensive purposes, with machicolations which allowed the defending forces to repel attackers as they attempted to scale the castle walls. (Machicolation is the name given to a space between corbels, or in the floor of a balcony, from which boiling oil or other substances could be poured or dropped onto the enemy.)

The most significant change came with the advent of gunpowder and artillery. The heavy cannons required thicker walls, sloped to resist the more powerful projectiles. Thicker walls also meant that the ramparts, running along the tops of the walls, could be wider, and enabled the castles' heavy artillery to be perched on top. Arrow slits, a common feature in castles, were rounded to accommodate the new artillery, then abandoned as impractical.

All Portugal's castles – many still sound, some in semi-ruin – are dramatically sited. Among the best are Lamego, in the Douro Valley *(see page 288)*; Almourol, perhaps the most romantic of all,

set on its own tiny island in the Rio Tejo (Tagus) and the subject of many myths *(see page 242)*; and, of course, Guimarães, the birthplace (*circa* 1110) of Portugal's first king, Afonso Henriques. Guimarães is one of Portugal's oldest castles, having been built in the 10th century, and restored many times since. Early in the 19th century the castle was used as a debtors' prison. It underwent extensive renovation in the 1940s *(see page 304)*.

Most castles are open to visitors; some have been converted to hotels, while others stand ignored in empty fields. Solid though their construction may have been, do be careful when visiting the semi-ruined ones; it wouldn't do to end your visit under a piece of falling masonry. ❏

RIGHT: the romantic island castle at Almourol.

THE ENGLISH CONNECTION

An English queen for Portugal, military alliances, and mutually beneficial
trade have all helped cement the Anglo-Portuguese relationship

In 1147 a band of crusaders – English, German, French and Flemish – broke their Atlantic journey in Porto en route to the Holy Land (some by choice, while others may have been shipwrecked). They were persuaded by the new king of Portugal, Afonso Henriques, to join him in an expedition to seize Lisbon

from the Moors. Chronicles of the time praised the beauties of Lisbon as first seen by the British crusaders. Its fertile countryside, lush with figs and vines, epitomised the seductive pleasures of the south, and encouraged many Englishmen to settle there. The first Bishop of Lisbon, Gilbert of Hastings, was English.

The 17-week siege of the city ended in victory for the Christian forces, but this was neither the first nor last of such stopovers for the crusaders, although it was the most celebrated. Much later it became the subject of a poem by William Mickle, the 18th-century translator of Luís de Camões *(see page 45)*, who is now considered Portugal's greatest poet:

The hills and lawns to English valour given
What time the Arab Moors from Spain were
* driven,*
Before the banners of the cross subdued,
When Lisbon's towers were bathed in
* Moorish blood*
By Gloster's Lance – Romantic days that
* yield*
Of gallant deeds a wide luxuriant field
Dear to the Muse that loves the fairy plains
Where ancient honour wild and ardent
* reigns.*

The Portuguese themselves had less happy memories of the crusaders from the north, whom they generally considered a loud and drunken lot, given more to piracy than to piety. But the British, with their superior numbers and martial skills, would long feel a condescending pride in their Portuguese achievement, expecting gratitude and more than a little deference from their allies to the south.

Treaties and alliances

Kingdoms were there for the taking. In 1371, John of Gaunt, Duke of Lancaster, hoped to ensure one for his own family by marrying the ex-Infanta Constance, the elder of two surviving daughters of the murdered King Pedro the Cruel of Castile. Gaunt then firmly believed himself to be the rightful king of Castile. To double the family's claim to the crown, his brother married Constance's younger sister. There remained one problem, however: the incumbent king of Castile needed to be convinced. John of Gaunt enlisted the help of King Ferdinand of Portugal, and after rounds of courtship, lavish entertaining and the bestowal of favours, an alliance was signed in 1373 by which these two allies agreed to help one another against all enemies.

In 1386, the new and youthful Dom João ascended the Portuguese throne with English help, and John of Gaunt felt the time was right to go to Castile to invoke the alliance and establish his royal claims. Along with his wife Constance and two daughters – 26-year-old Philippa from his first marriage, and the younger Katherine – a couple of his illegitimate children and an army, John of Gaunt set up court in the north, in Santiago de Compostela. He met the king and the earlier alliance was formalised as the Treaty of Windsor. In return King João was offered the hand of the devout and virtuous Philippa. They married in Porto and the city celebrated lavishly.

The English queen

Philippa was a remarkable queen judged by any standards. By surrounding herself in court with an essentially English retinue, she encouraged merchants from England to come in pursuit of trade. Admired by the Portuguese, generous, kind, high-minded Philippa brought a virtue to the marriage which slowly transformed the king himself. João, a notorious womaniser, strayed no more and his only bastard children remained the two born before his marriage. He ended his days translating religious books.

Children were born of the marriage at regular intervals, six in all, alternately given English and Portuguese names. All five princes were highly gifted and excelled during their lifetimes. Henry, known later as Henry the Navigator, became the most famous of them all through his contribution to Portuguese exploration of the world. Philippa died of the plague in 1415, at the age of 51, and was mourned throughout the country.

Wellington rides in

Contact between these two Atlantic nations remained close. Following the period of Spanish domination of Portugal, the old alliance with England was reinstated, with Charles I (1642), Oliver Cromwell (1654) and finally by the Treaty of 1661, by which Charles II married Catherine of Bragança. Combined Anglo-Portuguese armies were not unusual: they were in action on a number of occasions, fighting each other's battles. The most heavily recorded is the Peninsular War in the Napoleonic era. Sir Arthur Wellesley, who became the Duke of Wellington, commanded the British troops and built the famous defensive Lines of Torres Vedras which effectively repelled the French and won the war for Portugal.

LEFT: the tomb of João I and his English queen.
RIGHT: *barcos rabelos* still bear the names of British port wine dynasties, such as Sandeman.

The wine trade

Throughout the long history of trade between these two countries, cotton and woven cloth made its way to Lisbon and Porto, but there was usually wine in the hold on the return trip. During the second half of the 17th century, more and more factors of British firms settled in Viana do Castelo, Monção and Porto, and selected the wines for shipping home. Porto soon became the main centre of the wine trade and British firms increased in number (*see page 109*). Names like Taylor, Croft, Cockburn, Symington, Sandeman and Graham became established and by the 19th century these fam-

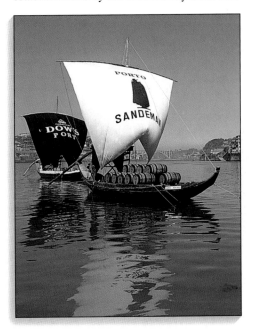

ilies were busy buying their own *quintas* (manor houses) along the banks of the Douro.

The trade in port wine flourished through wars, civil dissent, and fierce regulation, and the British made a valuable contribution, especially through people like Baron Joseph James Forrester, who helped improve safety standards in the port, and also mapped every twist and turn of the Rio Douro, in which he eventually drowned in 1862.

Born out of mutual need, the Anglo-Portuguese friendship has been touched by romance, passion, piety, greed, hope and despair, and yet has endured more or less intact for almost a millennium. ❑

EMPIRE BUILDING

Under the House of Avis, Portugal matured as a nation. The golden age of discoveries began, bringing untold wealth to the church and the king

João I ruled from 1385 to 1433, fending off the demands of a resurgent nobility by installing his legitimate sons Duarte, Pedro, Henry, Fernão and João in powerful positions as the leaders of military-religious orders. (Henry the Navigator, for example, headed the wealthy Order of Christ.) It was under João I that Portugal first began to look across the seas for solutions to internal economic and political problems. Trade and exploration, it was thought, would serve both to occupy the nobility and to boost commerce.

João's successor, his eldest son, Duarte, initially continued with overseas expansion, but drew back after a disastrous failed attack on Tangiers in 1437. The following year Duarte died, precipitating a brief civil war to determine who would act as regent to his young son, who became Afonso V.

Two of Afonso's uncles were particularly trusted advisers: Henry the Navigator, who was in the forefront of exploration and conquest, and yet another Afonso, the Duke of Bragança, leader of the newly strengthened nobility. Each was granted a large share of independent power. King Afonso himself remained above the administrative fray. He was not particularly inept, but he was a chivalric leader in an era where politics had been sullied by the growing power of mercantilists and low nobility, and he was out of tune with the times. Afonso concerned himself largely with martial glory, which he found crusading in North Africa. In 1471 he took Tangiers. Another of his accomplishments was the minting of the first *cruzado,* the gold coin that became a symbol of the wealth flowing in from the voyages.

In 1475 dispute over the crown of Castile led to civil discord. Afonso decided to marry his niece, Joana, one of the claimants, and thus unite Portugal and Castile under his monarchy. He invaded in support of his wife's claims, and

occupied León, but failed to hold his ground. Defeated by the forces of Ferdinand of Aragon and Isabella of Castile, he tried to enlist the aid of King Louis XI of France in support of his claims to the Castilian throne, travelling to France to make a personal plea. He arrived in the midst of Louis XI's tumultuous rivalry with the Duke of Burgundy and proved to be a hapless diplomat, quickly alienating both sides.

Frustrated, he announced his intention of abdicating his throne to go on a pilgrimage to the Holy Land, but even this quixotic voyage was thwarted. Louis prevented him from embarking, and the despondent Afonso was sent back to his homeland. His son, the future João II, allowed Afonso to resume his nominal position, and rule was shared until the older man's death in 1481.

Overseas expansion

The 15th century was the era when overseas expansion began in earnest, but no one had any

LEFT: a Japanese screen commemorates the arrival of Portuguese traders.

RIGHT: a statue of Henry the Navigator in Lagos.

idea of the empire that was to come. The existing policy was a strange mixture of crusading ideals, romantic curiosity, and, of course, the profit motive. Charting the world was a secondary matter to João II – less important, for example, than the acquisition of spices, or the search for the odd figure who was known as Prester John.

A mythical priest and king, Prester John was supposed to have been the leader of a vast and powerful Christian empire located somewhere in the African interior. His legend was elaborated with tales of a kingdom that was an earthly paradise peopled with a bizarre

lims wherever they could be found gave the voyages all the benefits of a crusade: the effort was legitimised, and the church lent its financial resources along with spiritual support. The sanctions of Rome, like the papal bull of 1455, would become an important factor when maritime competition intensified.

Economic and social needs undoubtedly motivated the voyages. There was a shortage of gold all over Europe, and without it, coinage was severely debased and the growth of commerce retarded. Gold from Africa, America, and India eventually did find its way into the coffers of Lisbon, but it also proved to be a

menagerie of chimeras and mythical characters. Strange as it seems, this tale had an enormous influence on early exploration of Africa. In fact, in 1455, after the Portuguese had established their dominance all along the northern coast, a papal bull granted them the sole right to discovery and conquest of all Africa except those parts ruled by Prester John. It was only later, by the early 16th century, that Portugal's explorers began to realise that spice and gold were more tangible goals, and the voyages in and around Ethiopia were replaced by more profitable itineraries.

Another goal of the seafarers was the still-popular slaughter of the infidel. Attacking Mus-

debilitating obsession, diverting attention from surer if less spectacular sources of profit. These lesser goals were nevertheless an impetus for exploration from the start. Fishing ships had circled further and further out in search of more richly-stocked waters. Moroccan grain, sugar, dye-stuffs, and slaves were all highly prized. These commodities were eventually joined by the pungent spices and rare woods of India and the Orient.

Henry the Navigator

Before any exploration could begin, of course, the technical aspects of navigation had to be mastered and improved. Navigators familiar with the Pole star, dead reckoning and the compas began to establish their position with the quadrant, the astrolabe adapted for sea use, and a simple cross-staff from which they calculated latitude. Celestial tables and so-called *portolano* charts, basic maps, became ever more detailed. Ships, too, radically changed – neatest of all was the nimble caravel, derived from the heftier cargo-carrying *caravela* of the Rio Douro. Prince Henry, who was born in Porto, would have known it well.

The Prince was dubbed Henry the Navigator and is credited with masterminding the discoveries from his school of navigation in Sagres at Cabo de São Vicente in Algarve, where he surrounded himself with expert astronomers and shipbuilders. His financial sponsorship and enthusiasm made him a profound influence, and the research material he assembled was unrivalled at the time (much of it contributed by his brother, Pedro, a true wanderer who sent Henry every relevant map and book he could find). But discovering the world – the Portuguese were the first Europeans to find two-thirds of it – was beyond the scope of any one man, and there must be other, unsung heroes.

With many hands at the tillers, the enterprise was not always well-coordinated. The main goal was to press the crusade forward and eventually to reconquer Jerusalem. Maps were accurate enough to suggest that there were islands in the unknown Sea of Darkness, and land beyond it, but it needed courage and determination to sail into oceans that legend had filled with fearsome monsters.

Prince Henry's primary goal was the taming of the North African coast, which meant the banishment of the Moors. He never travelled further than Morocco himself, where he had taken Ceuta in 1415, and gained his lifelong interest in discovery and conquest. The chronicles portray Henry devoting most of his time to squeezing profits out of his various tithes, monopolies and privileges. Only later in life, they suggest, with increasing reports of wondrous and far-off places to inspire him, did he give the discoveries his full attention. Yet he ploughed much of his profits back into the enterprises, which were a costly business, and died in debt.

LEFT: Pedro Alvares Cabral lands in Brazil.
RIGHT: the Monument of the Discoveries in Lisbon.

Epic voyages

It is easy to see why popular history might accord undue credit to an individual like Henry. The Age of Discoveries was a time for heroes and adventurers, and also a time for the rebirth of chivalric ideals. Fearless mariners sailed off into unknown realms. Their voyages were imbued with noble intentions: the greater glory of the church, the advancement of knowledge, and the benefit of their nation.

Popular history also makes unverifiable, but plausible, claims that Portuguese mariners were the first Europeans in America. Among explorers who sailed from the Azores were members

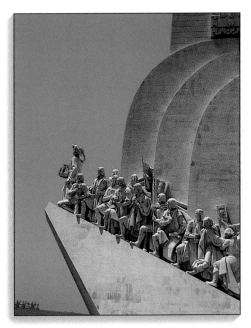

ISLAND OUTPOSTS

It was expeditions initiated by Henry the Navigator that, quite accidentally, discovered Madeira and the Azores. In 1415, two ships were blown off course and landed on the uninhabited island which they named Madeira (meaning "wood") because it was thickly forested. The first of the nine Azores (Açores) islands was discovered a dozen years later, the others over a period of 25 years. Henry proved to be an efficient and able coloniser, introducing wheat, vines and sugar cane to Madeira, and organising the settlement of the Azores, which later became recognised ports of call for sailors en route to and from the New World.

of the Corte Real family who explored the North American coast in the 1470s. One of them, Miguel, may have been marooned there.

The first hero of the discoveries was Gil Eanes. Madeira and the Azores, along with the north of Africa, had been charted. The islands had begun to be colonised. The fabulous tales of the edge of the world and the various horrors of the southern seas were soon connected with the stormy promontory of Cape Bojador, on the west coast of Africa. It became the boundary.

Finally, in 1434, Gil Eanes, a pilot commissioned by Henry the Navigator, broke the barrier. He found more coastline and safe waters, and returned to Portugal triumphant, bringing wild plants plucked from the land beyond. The next year he led voyages further down Africa's coast, and the way was opened for the many who followed. They searched primarily for the legendary Rio do Ouro (River of Gold). Eventually some of the precious ore was found.

In 1482, Portuguese ships explored the mouth of the Congo. Five years later, Bartolomeu Dias rounded the Cape of Good Hope. So intense did the competition between Spain and Portugal become that in 1494 papal intervention resulted in the famous Treaty of Tordesillas, which divided the newly discovered and the still unknown lands between the two countries. It granted Portugal the lands east of a line of demarcation 592 km (370 miles) west of the Azores, which put Brazil (then unknown, but discovered by Pedro Alvares Cabral in 1500) within Portugal's sphere.

In 1497–99, Vasco da Gama sailed to Calicut (Calcutta) in India and back (with great loss of life), immediately throwing Portugal into competition with Muslim and Venetian spice traders. In 1519–22, Fernão de Magalhães (anglicised to Ferdinand Magellan), a Portuguese in the service of Spain, led the first voyage to circumnavigate the globe, although he died before it was completed.

The expeditions opened the seaways, but there were battles to be fought to establish trading posts in Africa and the Indies. Arabs, protecting their own trade interests, fought the Portuguese wherever they could. The Portuguese, of course, were still intent on eradicating such infidels from the face of the earth. So although Portugal originally had no intentions of land conquest, by simply striving to establish and maintain a monopoly of the high seas, they were constantly at war.

Colonies

The great leader of these campaigns of discovery was Governor Afonso de Albuquerque, a brilliant strategist and, in essence, the founding father of the empire in Asia. His victories allowed garrisoned ports and fortresses to be built in key locations. Goa, in India, conquered in 1510, became the centre for all operations. Malacca (now in Malaysia) fell in 1511 and served as the East Indies hub, while Ormuz came under Portuguese control in 1515, proving the ideal seat from which to dominate the Persian Gulf. Later, in 1557, Macau was established on a kind of permanent lease with China, extending Portugal's reach to the Far East.

Albuquerque administered these new holdings under a basic policy of colonisation rather than exploitation. All the major cities, Goa in particular, were converted by architecture and government into European towns. Inter-racial marriages were encouraged and Catholic missions established.

> ### FISH FROM AFAR
>
> The Portuguese began fishing for cod *(bacalhau)* in Newfoundland's Grand Banks shortly after Columbus's voyage of discovery. It soon became a very popular dish.

The growth of Goa was extraordinary. By 1540, there were 10,000 households of European descent and the town was the seat of a bishopric. However, these few much-changed cities and the battles of the Indies were in marked contrast to the general policy of peaceful coexistence that Portugal adopted wherever it could. In Africa, Brazil, and the various islands and archipelagos, they tried to set up trading stations without interfering with local customs or politics.

It is, however, the exceptions that proved the most interesting. In the Congo, for example, where a number of missions were established, son took the name Afonso, and from that point until the 17th century the land was ruled by a succession of native Henriques, Pedros, and Franciscos.

Although it provided both ivory and slaves, the Congo was not of central economic importance. The Portuguese ships were too busy reaping bounty elsewhere to pay much attention to cultural matters: spices were carried from the Indies, gold was found in the Sudan and other parts of Africa, sugar and wine were brought from Madeira, while sugar and dye-stuffs came from Brazil.

The wealth reaped overseas made for a stable

the people were quite taken with their European visitors, though they could provide little of interest to the traders. The Portuguese had begun by overestimating the political and cultural sophistication of these people, and once the Congolese were exposed to certain Western practices, they embraced them rapidly. They took to Christianity, and imitated the manners and fashions of the Portuguese. Their first Christian monarch dropped the title "Nzinga a Nkuwu" and renamed himself João I. His

LEFT: Vasco da Gama stands tall in Sines.
ABOVE: Afonso de Albuquerque, painted by an unknown artist, *circa* 1509.

economy, but it did not make Portugal rich. Enterprising individuals and the monarchy – taking its royal fifth of all trade revenues – flourished, but even they eventually found it difficult to build or hold on to their fortunes.

At its beginning, the "empire" demanded little from its diminutive fatherland. Like other small trading centres in Italy and the later Dutch empire, organisation and central authority were more important than mere size. Furthermore, the early expeditions required little manpower. It was only later, when they found themselves trying to enforce the worldwide trade monopoly, that the sparseness of Portugal's population began to tell. It has also been suggested that a crucial deficiency was Portugal's lack of a middle class. Quashed by royal and noble dominance of commerce, it might have provided qualified and educated planners, pilots and administrators.

In explaining the empire's failure, some have pointed to widespread corruption or to the foreign control of profits garnered from Portuguese expeditions. How great an effect they had is arguable. Certainly the religious efforts that went hand in hand with Portuguese voyages did not make the wheels of commerce spin any more freely. Whether fighting Muslims, or trying to force Christianity down the throats of local populations, the Portuguese wasted time and diverted their focus from the business at hand. Whatever the causes, potential benefits of the burgeoning overseas trade were not being reaped. Deflation in Europe stifled trade. Domestic agricultural production, hampered by a lack of manpower, lagged, occasionally causing serious shortages of meat and grain. Even the Crown was in debt, as the cost of the trading empire rose higher than its revenues. It was, of course, many years before these flaws and inadequacies truly sank the empire. Trade was to continue for several centuries, although it steadily deteriorated.

Domestic life

Before the slide began, the lucrative age of empire did bring sufficient peace and prosperity for Portugal to sustain truly great eras of artistic and humanist achievement. João II had taken over from his father, the unreliable Afonso V, in 1481. Revitalising the throne, he managed to take up where Henry the Navigator, who died in 1460, had left off. João turned away from the nobility, minimising their rights and calling upon the *cortes* for support. A conspiracy soon gathered against the king, but he learned of the central traitors soon enough to strike back. In 1484, the Duke of Bragança was briefly tried and beheaded. When other members of the nobility fled the country, their titles and holdings reverted to the Crown.

The Duke of Viseu, who was both cousin and brother-in-law to the king, unwisely mounted a second plot, and was stabbed by the king himself. Another group fled the country, and João II was left in full command.

THE JEWS IN PORTUGAL

As money-lenders, tax collectors, bankers, physicians and astronomers, the Jews had lived peaceably in Portugal for a thousand years or more. In 1492, when Spain had rid itself of the Moors, it was equally determined to expel the Jews. Some 60,000 were allowed to settle in Portugal.

The contribution of the Jews to the economy and progress of the country was already invaluable, and their influence was increasing. It was the Jews who opened Portugal's first printing presses, and the first 11 books published were all in Hebrew. Abraham Zacuto, astronomer and mathematician, published the *Almanach Perpetuum*, which contained tables enabling mariners to determine latitude by declination of the sun. The *Almanach* was translated into Latin and became the basis of a system used by the Portuguese for many years.

When King Manuel married Princess Isabella of Spain in 1497, he was forced as a condition of marriage to act against the Jews. Realising their value to the country, he was reluctant to expel them so he offered the option of baptism as "New Christians", with a 20-year period of grace before their faith would be tested. Many refused, and those who accepted soon found that they were not treated as equals. Prejudice and intolerance was soon to burgeon into full-scale repression as the Inquisition took hold.

The prestige and authority that these tactics bestowed on the monarchy would stand undiminished for centuries. However, João's successor, Manuel I, who came to the throne in 1495, had to find a balance between the ferocity of his predecessor and the confused idealism of Afonso V. This was accomplished through diplomatic and far-sighted administration. The estates of the noble families were largely restored, though this did not restore their political power. Judicial and tax reforms worked to bring authority to government on both the national and local levels. The postal system was instituted. Public services such as hospitals were centralised. Essentially, Manuel lifted the power of the monarchy above both the nobles and the *cortes,* launching the first era of enlightened absolutism.

The importance of education

Manuel also fostered contacts with proponents of Renaissance humanism, which was then spreading throughout Europe. There were many trading, religious and cultural contacts with Italy, in particular, and young Portuguese men began to seek education abroad, at universities in France or Spain. Manuel actually tried to buy Paris's renowned Saint Barbara College, and although he failed it became a centre for Portuguese students. By 1487 a printing press had been established in Lisbon. Portugal entered the 16th century with a rush of new cultural currents and ideas.

New colleges and educational reforms were basic elements of the new century's progress. Teaching methods were modernised and the curriculum expanded. The students were drawn from a larger pool, including aristocrats and members of the wealthy bourgeoisie, in addition to young men from the religious orders.

These changes were not without crises. The University of Lisbon had a cultural and political influence that threatened the Crown. It was difficult to impinge on its traditional autonomy, but Manuel, as part of his process of centralisation, tried to force change through economic and legal pressure.

Finding great resistance, he turned to the idea of founding a new university elsewhere, without success. João III, who came to the throne in 1521, on his father's death, continued these efforts, later giving control of national education to the Jesuits and moving the university to Coimbra, where its permanent home was established. It was a victory for the monarchy. There would be no university in Lisbon until 1911.

Nonetheless, the century inspired a broad-ranging intellectual vigour. Some of the works produced were directly attributable to the expeditions of discovery. Travel books, with both scientific and cultural themes, were a rich vein: Tomé Pires, for example, wrote *Suma Oriental* in 1550, describing his voyages to the East.

Portugal's main contributions to the intellectual ferment of the Renaissance were in science, particularly in navigation, astronomy, mathematics and geography. This was not the mere accumulation of facts from foreign places: they amounted to a kind of sceptical empiricism, a science based on experience. Having disproved a dozen theories about the shape, limits and contours of the earth, Portuguese intellectuals felt free to question the other dogmas of antiquity.

New writers and new sciences were emerging but there was no real Reformation in Portugal, where there was an antipathy towards Germanic philosophies. Nevertheless, the

LEFT: the library at Coimbra University.
RIGHT: João III, in a portrait by Cristovão Lopes.

Counter-Reformation cast a pall of religious conformism over learning and creativity. In addition, the political threat to Portuguese autonomy – the future union with Spain was already an undercurrent – hung over all these academic achievements. In fact, Luís de Camões, Gil Vicente (the 16th-century father of Portuguese theatre) and many others wrote about half of their works in Castilian (Spanish).

Portuguese Inquisition

João III ruled from 1521 to 1557. He continued Manuel's expansion of the trading empire and of royal authority, but his most significant

act was the establishment of the Inquisition in Portugal. The Inquisition had by now become established in Spain, where it had been enforced with vigour after the Moors had been expelled in 1492 by the "Catholic Monarchs", Isabel and Ferdinand. The papacy knew there was no real need for it, no menaces to the unity of faith, so resisted its introduction. But João III was more fanatical than the pope and he used every diplomatic intrigue at his disposal to get his way. Finally, in 1536, he won approval for a limited version of the Inquisition, but within a dozen years these limitations had been lifted and its full force arrived.

João III had turned away from the current humanist influences of Europe towards religious fanaticism, and the power and the bureaucracy of the Inquisition expanded rapidly. Its main target was the converted Jews known as New Christians. What had been intended as a tool of the monarchy soon took on a direction and authority of its own. The Inquisitor-Generals, who took their orders from Rome, had the right of excommunication and, utilising the spectacular *autos-da-fé,* the public burning of heretics, soon wielded an influence far beyond their legal authority.

The influence of the Inquisition, with its rigid orthodoxy, vengeful judiciary and general intolerance, was deadening to both culture and commerce. Many of the bourgeois leaders of trade were targets.

The Inquisition's power continued under King Sebastião, who came to the throne in 1568, when he was 14 years old. An unstable and idealistic king, with a dangerous streak of misplaced chivalry, Sebastião took upon himself a crusade against the Moors of North Africa. A lack of funds prevented him from undertaking the task for many years. In the meantime he surrounded himself with cohorts no older and no more sensible than himself, dismissing the warnings of older, more prudent statesmen. Finally sensing that the time was right, he spent every *cruzado* he could raise on mercenaries and outfitting his troops. He set sail for Morocco in 1578, appointing his great uncle, Cardinal Enrique, regent in his absence.

Sebastião was as bad a military leader as he was an administrator, dismissing stratagem and planning as cowardice. He refused to consider the possibility of retreat, and therefore had no plan for it. Outnumbered and outmanoeuvred at the Battle of Alcácer-Quibir, his army of 18,000 men was destroyed. Some 8,000, including Sebastião and most of Portugal's young nobility, were slaughtered. Only 100 or so escaped.

With this debilitating disaster, the way was open for Spain to step in. From 1578 to 1580, Cardinal Henrique ruled the country, occupied primarily with raising the ruinous ransoms for the captured soldiers of Alcácer-Quibir. In 1580, Philip II of Spain invaded and within a year was installed as Philip I of Portugal. ❑

LEFT: heretics are led to their death by fire in an *auto-da-fé* procession.

Luís de Camões

L uís Vaz de Camões (1524–80), Portugal's greatest poet, never reaped fame or riches during his lifetime. He was born poor, and he died poor, but the life he led – of passion and adventure – enthrals the Portuguese almost as much as the epic, eloquent phrases in his works, which many people can quote at length even today.

After attending the University at Coimbra, the young poet's prospects were good. But many twists of fate lay ahead. An affair with one of the queen's ladies-in-waiting caused his banishment to North Africa, where he lost an eye in military service. Returning to Lisbon, Camões was involved in a skirmish that wounded a magistrate. He ended up in prison and then was banished again, in 1553, this time to the colony of Goa in India.

It was 1570 before he returned to Lisbon. Having written poetry and plays for many years with some success, he published *Os Lusíadas* in 1572. The poem's worth was recognised immediately, and Camões received a small royal pension. His final illness, however, was spent in a public hospital, and he was buried in a common grave.

The title *Os Lusíadas* means "The Sons of Lusus", the mythical founder of Portugal: symbolically, then, it means "the Portuguese". Echoing classical models, the poem chronicled the voyages of Vasco da Gama, before a panorama of strangely mixed Christian and pagan images.

Os Lusíadas has been hailed throughout Europe (Lope de Vega and Montesquieu were among early admirers), sometimes to the detriment of the rest of Portugal's extensive literature. Under Salazar *(see page 61)*, *Os Lusíadas* became an icon of Portuguese nationalism. Speeches and propaganda were peppered with quotes from it, providing a mythology for imperialism that failed to differentiate between the 16th and 20th centuries.

The 18th-century verse translation by W.J. Mickle, quoted below, though tinged with the lyrical romanticism of that era, captures the proud spirit of the poem from the opening lines:

Arms and the heroes, who from Lisbon's shore,/ Thro' seas where sail was never spread before,/ Beyond where Ceylon lifts her spicy breast,/And waves her woods above the watery waste,/With prowess more than human forc'd their way/To the fair kingdoms of the rising day.

RIGHT: Luís de Camões.

In the second canto the Muslims – the "faithless race" – prepare to attack:

On shore the truthless monarch arms his bands,/ And for the fleet's approach impatient stands:/ That soon as anchor'd in the port they rode/Brave Gama's decks might reek with Lusian blood:/Thus weening to revenge Mozambique's fate,/ And give full surfeit to the Moorish hate...

In the world of the great Portuguese discoverers, the enemy forces take their strength from the netherworld:

As when the whirlwinds, sudden bursting, bear/ Th' autumnal leaves high floating through the air;/ So rose the legions of th' infernal state,/Dark

Fraud, base Art, fierce Rage, and burning Hate:/ Wing'd by the Furies to the Indian strand/They bend; the Demon leads the dreadful band,/And in the bosoms of the raging Moors/All their collected living strength he pours.

At Vasco da Gama's request, the chronicler aboard his ship retells Portugal's history, and recounts the "glad assistance" brought by the crusaders who helped take Lisbon from the Moors:

Their vows were holy, and the cause the same,/To blot from Europe's shores the Moorish name./In Sancho's cause the gallant navy joins,/And royal Sylves to their force resigns./Thus sent by heaven a foreign naval band/Gave Lisboa's ramparts to the Sire's command. ❑

O DIABO COXO

O DIABO CORSO

O Gato Francez destruindo a Religião   emblemas   a Serpente e a Hyena

Como o Leaõ rugindo, e o Urso grunhindo assim o perverso Mandarim trata o pobre povo Prov. Cap. 28

...ção das Armas de Napoleão q̃ por si se fes Imperador agora o açoute d' a Europa cortando o bar̃.º da tranquilid.º o Globo...

...de Inglaterra e Suecia a mão e adaga p.ª Espanha dá a entender os seus designios por entre o fumo se divisão seus Estandar...

...ilho o seu nascimento o Cocodrilho, a mão sanguinolenta, o Coração negro, e a Golotina, mostrão as suas traições e tirani...

...ts q̃ mandou fazer perto de Jaffa a 800 indefezos Turcos prizioneiros.

...ter emvenenado os seus proprios Soldados doentes no Hospital de Jaffa.

...icidio do Duque Enghien.

...Padre a vir a sua coroação e pondo na sua propria cabeça a coroa de ferro com huma mão e com a out...

...Igreja Catholica a sua Cabeça. || 6. a morte do Capitão Wright por não querer ser traidor á su...

THE CONQUERORS ARE CONQUERED

Portugal was under Spanish rule for 60 years, until a popular uprising against the Habsburgs put the country back in charge of its own destiny

Throughout their rule over Portugal, the Spanish Habsburg kings faced many challenges to their authority. Not the least of their problems was that King Sebastião kept rising from the grave. After the massacre at Alcácer-Quibir in 1578, a devastating blow to national pride, there arose a popular belief, known as *sebastianismo*, that the lost Portuguese king would rise again. Consequently, a number of false Sebastiãos tried and failed to reclaim the throne.

At the root of the Iberian Union was the support it provided for merchants and traders. The Netherlands and France were strongly challenging Portuguese shipping, slicing into vital profits. It was supposed by the bourgeoisie that by combining Spanish and Portuguese interests, the maritime empire could be reclaimed. The "alliance" with Spain would also open up inland trade. In any case, there were few options: in 1560 the Casa da India, the national trade corporation, had gone bankrupt and Portugal's treasury was empty.

The three Philips

After Alcácer-Quibir, a number of candidates had aspirations to the Portuguese throne. Though the genealogical claim of Philip II of Spain was more tenuous than those of his competitors, he was the grandson of Manuel I, and a far more viable ruler than any of his rivals. The majority of the populace was opposed to the Spanish king, but the relatively impoverished nobles, clergy and upper bourgeoisie saw that Philip could provide fiscal and military stability. Ironically, the most powerful group to resist the union were the Spanish ruling classes, who saw the danger of untrammelled Portuguese trading within their traditional markets.

Part of Philip's appeal was that he promised to maintain Portugal's autonomy: no Spanish representation in Portuguese legislative and judicial bodies; no change in the official language; the overseas empire would still be ruled by Portugal; no grants of Portuguese assets to non-Portuguese; and so forth. Philip took up residence in Lisbon. In 1581 he summoned the *cortes* to declare him King Philip I.

After the years of mismanaged government,

the efficient bureaucracy of the union was a relief. However, with the succession of Philip II (Philip III of Spain) in 1598, the Spanish began to press their powers too far. The new king lacked his predecessor's diplomatic savvy, relations between the two countries were bungled, and the Spanish tried to correct their mistakes through force. Resistance grew. Under Philip III (IV of Spain), who succeeded to the throne in 1619, the union continued to erode. Spain was weakened by its involvement in the Thirty Years' War with France. Portuguese troops were forced into battle and taxes increased.

The 60 years of union with Spain did nothing to protect Portugal's empire. Between 1620 and

LEFT: a 19th-century cartoon satirising Napoleon.
RIGHT: Antão de Almada, one of the movers and shakers of the Restoration.

1640, Ormuz, Baia, São Jorge da Mina and many more trade centres fell. In 1630 the Dutch established themselves in Brazil; in 1638 they took Ceylon. There were still ports and territories controlled by Portuguese traders, but the monopoly of the seas was an era quickly fading from memory. What's more, to a country that had once been intent upon ridding the earth of the last vestige of the infidels, it was devastating to surrender their missions to the Dutch, purveyors of heretical Protestantism.

For the Portuguese, each of the three Philips

RESTORATION DAY

Restoration Day on 1 December is still celebrated in Portugal as a national holiday to commemorate the 1640 coup in Lisbon.

was worse than his predecessor. Philip II did not even deign to visit the country for years after his coronation. Philip III systematically breached all the guarantees put in place by his grandfather. The incipient revolution was aided by secret diplomatic agents sent by the French, who were still embroiled with Spain in the Thirty Years' War.

The Bragança regime

On 1 December 1640, a coup in Lisbon reflected the growing revolutionary fervour. The palace was attacked, and the reigning Spanish governor, the Duchess of Mantua, was deposed and arrested, while her strongman,

Miguel de Vasconcelos, was defenestrated. Though he had been reluctant to lead the revolt, the Duke of Bragança, was declared King João IV. So began Portugal's final royal period: the House of Bragança would hold power until the 20th century.

Most of João IV's 16-year reign was occupied in hapless efforts to form diplomatic ties in Europe. France, England, Holland and the Pope all refused to confirm Portuguese independence. Only Spain's preoccupation with other battles, some heroic Portuguese military stands along the frontier, and a well-organised national administration enabled the country to retain its restored independence.

When he ascended the throne in 1656, Afonso VI (João's son), who suffered both physical and mental handicaps, was still a minor. Later, married off to a French princess, he associated with criminal elements and, worst of all, proved to be impotent, a fact elicited from the public inquiry needed to annul his marriage. He was eventually usurped by his brother, who ruled as Pedro II.

War with Spain waxed and waned from 1640 until 1665. In 1654, a treaty of friendship and co-operation was signed with England, a useful link, but also the first step down a path that guaranteed Portugal's economic subservience to Britain for centuries to come. The alliance was sealed by the marriage of Princess Catherine to the English king, Charles II, in 1662. Included in her dowry gifts were Tangiers and Bombay. In 1661 a treaty was signed with Holland. These moves sparked a new round of battles with Spain. In 1665 a decisive Portuguese victory at Montes Claros ended the fighting and three years later, in the Treaty of Lisbon, Spain offically recognised Portugal's independence.

Pedro II became prince-regent to his brother in 1668 and ruled from 1673 until 1706. His long reign, although stable, was deeply marked by an unrelenting economic depression. The spice trade had slipped almost entirely out of Portuguese hands, while trade in sugar and slaves went through periods of competition and crisis at a time when Portugal could ill afford such instability.

On the mainland, olive groves and vineyards offered good profits, but they were largely controlled by British interests. The Treaty of

Methuen (1703) established British dominance of the wine industry and served to stifle industrialisation in Portugal. Grain shortages were common throughout the era – perhaps because investment went into vines instead of wheat.

Two of Pedro's finance ministers, the Count of Ericeira and the Marquês of Fronteira, helped plan numerous factories. Glass, textile, iron, tile and pottery industries were all supported by the state in an effort to balance national trade deficits.

Going for gold

The mercantilist approach made some headway, but what finally dispelled the economic gloom was the discovery of gold in Brazil. But the constant stream pouring in from across the Atlantic was not invested in the infant industries, which spluttered and halted. The Count of Ericeira committed suicide, while Fronteira renounced his previous economic philosophy.

Even before gold, Brazil had offered a number of valuable commodities: sugar, cotton and tobacco, as well as some spices and dyestuffs. The husbandry of cattle started slowly, but by the end of the 17th century was providing lucrative exports of meat and leather.

The Jesuit missionaries were extremely influential in Brazil, as both explorers and settlers. Among other things they held the brazilwood monopoly for over two decades (1625–49). More importantly, they were successful in winning over the native populace to Christianity, and in large part preventing their enslavement. But the abundant colonial economy naturally had a great need for native labour, and the Jesuits were pressured to step aside, even though they had the clear support of Rome in the form of a Papal Bull (1639) that threatened excommunication for the trading of natives.

João V, who succeeded Pedro II in 1706, spent the Brazilian gold with a vengeance. Taking his cue from the French court of Louis XIV, he quickly earned the nickname "The Magnanimous". Palaces, churches and monasteries were erected, and support was granted to the arts and to education. Along with this extravagance came a moral profligacy. Convents around Lisbon were converted from religious houses into aristocratic brothels. Among the royal constructions were palaces to house João's numerous bastard sons, born of various nuns.

When João died in 1750 he was succeeded by his son José, who proved to be more interested in opera than in matters of state. The full power of the crown was entrusted to a diplomat, Sebastião José de Carvalho e Melo, who eventually earned the title by which he is better known: the Marquês de Pombal.

Enlightened absolutism, as typified by the ministry of Pombal, represented both a beginning and an end. The Enlightenment ideal of

rationalism meant a leap towards modernity, while the concomitant republican ideal of social equality meant royal absolutism was on its last legs. Pombal's insistence on exercising royal prerogative sounded a death knell for the political power of nobles and clergy alike, and allowed the bourgeoisie to take over administrative and economic control. His was an oppressive, dictatorial rule, though he was careful never to claim any personal power.

The great earthquake

In 1755, on All Saints' Day – just as Mass was beginning – Lisbon was destroyed by a massive earthquake. Estimates vary, but at least

---

LEFT: Pedro II, a more effective king than his brother.
RIGHT: a scene in Lisbon harbour during the Great Earthquake of 1755.

5,000 people were killed in the initial impact, many while attending morning services. Many more died later. Fallen church candles quickly ignited the wreckage around them. Survivors rushed toward the safety of the Tejo, only to be met by a huge tidal wave.

In the subsequent weeks infected wounds, epidemics and famine increased the death toll, which may have been as high as 40,000. The Jesuits tried to fix the blame for what they saw as divine retribution upon Pombal's wayward and "atheistic" policies. He weathered both their criticism and their plot to assassinate him. The Jesuits' power throughout Europe was dis-

solving, and in 1759 they were officially disbanded and exiled from Portugal.

The catastrophe that shook the country's faith allowed Pombal's policies of secularisation and rational government to take firm hold. He took absolute control, and with the order to "close the ports, bury the dead, feed the living", began reconstruction. José granted his minister emergency powers (which were not rescinded for some 20 years) and Pombal used them to rebuild Lisbon according to a neo-classical plan, both neatly geometric and functionally sound. The social and legal distinction between "Old" and "New" Christians (the latter being Jews who had converted at the end of the 15th

century) was abolished. Pombal's economic reforms helped Portugal remain stable when Brazilian gold production waned in the middle of the century and he managed to rebuild Lisbon without depleting the treasury.

As Pombal's sponsor-king, José, neared the end of his reign, the Marquês plotted to force the crown-princess Maria to renounce her rights so that her son, another José, and a disciple of Pombal, could continue the policy of despotism. These efforts failed and Maria, a pious but unbalanced woman with no sympathy for Pombal's methods of rule, took over in 1777. She immediately had Pombal tried for crimes against the state and, when convicted, confined him to his estate rather than to prison, out of deference to his age.

Though she revived religious elements in a government and culture that had become increasingly secular, Maria allowed most of Pombal's essential economic and administrative reforms to stay in place. Her reign was a conservative one, with steady, if slow, economic progress.

Both Maria's political and personal health were badly shaken by news of the French Revolution. In 1798, long after her behaviour had become an embarrassment, she was declared insane. Her son João, an awkward, nervous man, took over as regent, becoming king after Maria died in 1816.

The Peninsular War

The Portuguese monarchy and nobility feared that the fervour behind the French Revolution of 1789, and to a lesser extent, the American one the previous decade, might be contagious.

POMBAL'S LEGACY

Anyone visiting Lisbon should know a little about the Marquês de Pombal, in order to better appreciate the city. Under his direction, the whole of the devastated Baixa area was rebuilt in neo-classical style, laid out in an orderly grid system. The upper parts of the city – the Bairro Alta and Alfama – had been spared the worst effects of the tremors. In the centre of the great Praça do Comercio he erected a statue of his king, José, astride his horse. Pombal's own statue was erected much later, high on a column in the square that bears his name, and looking out over the new city which, under his guidance, rose like a phoenix from the ashes.

They were particularly wary about possible insurgency in Brazil. In 1793, Portugal sent troops to fight revolutionary France, further aligning itself with Britain and against French-controlled Spain. In 1801, Spain invaded in the War of the Oranges. Portugal ceded various political concessions, and lost forever the town of Olivença.

In 1807, Napoleon delivered an ultimatum to Portugal, in which he demanded that Portugal declare war on Britain, and close its ports to British shipping. But Portugal could not turn on its long-term allies, and Napoleon was defied. While the royal family speedily sailed to the safety of Brazil, the French General Junot marched into Lisbon. Initially, the Portuguese government offered no resistance.

In July 1808, Britain came galloping to the rescue under the leadership of the master military tactician, Sir Arthur Wellesley (1769–1852), who became the Duke of Wellington. The Peninsular War, sometimes called the War of National Liberation, lasted two years, expelling the French but devastating the country. Three waves of attacks were halted by Portuguese victories at Roliça, Vimeiro, Buçaco and the famous Lines at Torres Vedras. The wars left the country in a rocky state. Since the flight of the royal family, Portugal's capital was effectively located across the ocean in Rio de Janeiro and the nation's general weakness fostered Brazil's claims for autonomy. In 1822 Brazil was declared a kingdom on an equal footing with Portugal.

The regency in Lisbon showed very little political intelligence or common sense, governing with uncoordinated despotism and completely ignoring the burgeoning democratic groundswell. The monarchy's blindness to contemporary political ideas fostered the revolution that would break out in 1820.

The British military occupation, under the leadership of Marshal William Carr Beresford (1768–1854), although necessary and sometimes appreciated, further undermined Portuguese self-determination. British control had been growing throughout the 18th century. In the 19th, it became stronger. In 1810, Portugal was forced to cede to Britain the right to trade

LEFT: the Marquês de Pombal, an enlightened despot. **RIGHT:** the Duke of Wellington, who led the British troops into battle against Napoleon.

directly with Brazil, eliminating its own role as middle-man. Portugal was taking on the aspects of a British protectorate, with William Beresford wielding dictatorial control.

The liberal revolution

The roots of the liberal uprising of 1820 lay in the French Revolution, its influences disseminated by military and secret societies, especially a Masonic lodge called Sinédrio. A plot against British rule by one of these clandestine groups proved to be a catalyst. A dozen conspirators accused of plotting to assassinate Marshal Beresford in 1817 were summarily tried

and executed, a brutal reprisal that heated Portuguese resentment and fostered support for the liberal movement.

In 1820, the Spanish liberal movement won control of their government, providing further inspiration, as well as political support, for Portuguese liberal forces. When Beresford left for Brazil on a diplomatic mission to discuss the growing problem, his absence sparked the Portuguese military into revolt. The uprising began in Porto, and eventually forced João VI to return from Brazil. By the time he arrived, the new constitutional ideology had gained ground. A constitution was adopted in 1822. The document was ahead of its time, with broad guarantees of individual liberties and no special pre-rogatives for nobles or clergy. It lasted only two years, but succeeded in ending the Inquisition.

Conspiracy and confusion

Portugal's profoundly conservative streak made the revolution a simple split between republicans and absolutists. New charters and new efforts to restore full-bodied monarchy kept the country unsettled throughout the first half of the century. In 1824, João VI resisted a conspiracy of royalist extremists led by his own wife Carlotta and his son Miguel.

João's queen was the Spanish princess Car-chose to stay in Brazil, abdicating the Portuguese throne to his seven-year-old daughter, Maria. Pedro intended her to marry her uncle, the exiled Miguel, who would rule as regent under a moderate constitution.

Miguel had other ideas. Upon his return he abolished the constitution and invoked a counter-revolutionary *cortes* to name him king. There was considerable popular support for these moves, but enough sympathy for constitutional ideas remained for Pedro, who had abdicated power in Brazil, to return and eventually defeat his brother in the Miguelist Wars.

Pedro IV reigned until his death in 1834,

lotta Joaquina, who epitomised the old regime. She tried her best to make a Versailles of her palace at Queluz, surrounding herself with absolutists and engaging in outrageous decadence, producing children by various lovers. Her flamboyant leadership of the absolutist cause made her popular, but the failure of her conspiracy to dethrone her husband in favour of her son Miguel – who was then banished to Brazil – marked the end of her influence.

The politics of the next 50 years were endlessly complex. In 1826 João VI died, leaving the throne to Pedro, his eldest son, who was still in Brazil. After failing to unite the two kingdoms through political manoeuvres, Pedro when his daughter, then 15, finally took the throne as Maria II. She reigned until 1853, during which time the first political parties developed. The liberals, victorious over absolutism, divided into conservatives and progressives. The Septembrists, named after their revolutionary victory in September 1836, came into power first. They initially restored the constitution of 1822, but then adopted a more moderate one. They were opposed by Chartists who took their stand, and name, from the conservative charter of 1826.

The Chartists came to the fore in 1839, when, supported by the queen and led by António da Costa Cabral, they took power. Costa Cabral's government was authoritarian, and, though it provided stability, became more and more corrupt and autocratic. In 1846 a popular uprising demanded his downfall. Maria II tried to replace him with the equally conservative Duke of Saldanha, a grandson of Pombal, and the country stood on the brink of civil war. English and Spanish intervention prevented mass violence, but resulted in Costa Cabral being returned to power. In 1851 he was (peacefully) ousted for good and Saldanha took his place.

The early period of Saldanha's rule was a period of transformation out of which came the political divisions that would exist throughout the century. Saldanha introduced a compromise that allowed his new party, Regeneração, to encompass both the old Chartists and the moderate progressives. The amendments to the constitution allowed for direct elections and an expanded electorate. A still more radical faction, initially a small group, became known first as the Históricos, and then the Progressistas.

In 1853 Maria II died in childbirth. Her husband, the German Duke Ferdinand of Saxe-Coburg-Gotha, ruled as regent until their son, Pedro V, came of age in 1855. Pedro died six years later and was succeeded by his brother, who became Luís I.

Literary Luís

The best constitutional monarchs are those who avoid politics, and the change from the meddling Maria to the literary Luís was a clear victory for the republican government. Among his other accomplishments, King Luís translated Shakespeare into Portuguese.

Arts and literature were greatly influenced by politics during this period. The energies of both liberal and conservative intellectuals were focused on rebuilding their nation. The best Portuguese prose was in essay form, the best poetry and drama was in satire, and historical writing flourished. Among the celebrated literati of the era were Alexandre Herculano (1810–77), who wrote historical fiction and a monumental history of Portugal; and the brilliantly versatile Almeida Garrett (1799–1854), best known for his drama, but also the author of poetry, novels and essays.

LEFT: citizens rallied in the streets for the liberal revolution of 1820.

RIGHT: the throne room at Queluz, Carlotta's Versailles.

The reign of Luís lasted until 1889 and was a period of relative peace. Conservatives and liberals alternated in controlling the legislature. Portugal's external affairs were more or less dictated by England, their protector under the Congress of Vienna's partitioning of small countries under major powers, in 1814–15. But Portugal was tenacious in holding on to many of its colonial claims and territories in Africa. The high expense of maintaining those colonies was a burden on the rickety national economy, but it would stand the country in good stead when the holdings finally did pay off during the 20th century. ❑

CULTURAL QUESTIONS

The influence of the rest of Europe on Portugal's cultural development in the 19th century was strongly felt. Intellectual conflicts were encapsulated in the "Coimbra question". Two groups of university scholars stood divided: the older group advocated the virtues of the status quo, while the "Generation of 1870", as they became known, called for revision of intellectual and spiritual values. Like their counterparts in other European countries, they were rationalist, anti-clerical, and anti-monarchist. In their writing could be heard the first strains of emerging socialism. Their daring critiques, however, were suppressed by the government in 1871.

REVOLUTION AND EVOLUTION

Republicanism failed to restore Portugal's former glory. Political turmoil followed
by dictatorship hindered growth and modernisation until the 1980s

The end of the 19th century saw Portugal's finances in complete disarray. The havoc wrought by the Peninsular and Miguelist wars, on top of the loss of Brazil, was insurmountable. In 1889, Carlos I became king, setting African expansion as his primary goal, but his efforts were unsuccessful. In 1892, Portugal declared bankruptcy.

Still dreaming of restoring the empire, Carlos could do little to defuse the growing anti-monarchical sentiment. Socialism and trade unionism were growing influences. The legislative *cortes* had degenerated into a powerless assembly that became full of obstructive and self-promoting debate. Corruption and inefficiency were rampant.

In 1906, struggling to maintain some form of control, Carlos appointed João Franco as prime minister, endowing him with dictatorial powers. He quickly dissolved the useless legislature. In 1908 unknown parties, either members of a republican secret society or isolated anti-monarchical fanatics, assassinated Carlos and his son, Luís Filipe, heir to the throne. In the assault on the royal carriage, Manuel, the king's second son, was wounded but survived.

Over the next two years Manuel II tried to save the monarchy, offering various concessions, but the assassination had fortified the republican movement. The long-decrepit House of Bragança finally crumbled to dust.

The rising tide

The rising tide of republicanism could not be stopped. The democratic ideal was combined with a nationalistic vision, a shift it was hoped would return Portugal to its long-lost glory. The national anthem adopted in 1910 echoed the theme: "Oh sea heroes, oh noble people... raise again the splendour of Portugal... may Europe claim to all the world that Portugal is not dead!"

The assassination of Carlos sealed the victory of republicanism, but it took time for the

various parties and coalitions to sort themselves into a workable government – practically speaking, they never did. Between 1910 and 1926 there were 45 different governments, with most of the changes being brought about by military intervention rather than parliamentary procedures. The early leadership pressed their

radical anti-Church and social reforms too hard, causing a reaction that revived the influence of the Catholic Church. Labour movements sprang up with the best intentions, but often paralysed industry. First and foremost, the republicans were unable to deliver promised financial reforms and stability, both through their own ineptitude and, later, because of the international depression of 1920s. It was their economic failure that most significantly eroded their popular support.

Afonso Costa rose to leadership of the republican factions, but the hard stance of his anti-clericalism caused too much ill feeling to allow stability. Coups became standard. General

LEFT: the first republic was proclaimed in 1910.
RIGHT: an allegory of the 1908 elections.

Pimenta de Castro grabbed control briefly, but democratic forces deposed him. Sidónio Pais formed a dictatorial government in 1917, but was assassinated the following year.

Portugal, initially neutral, joined the Allies under Britain's influence in 1916. The causes behind World War I meant little to the nation but cost thousands of lives, in Europe and Africa, and brought further financial upheaval and political unrest. In 1918 President Sidónio Pais was assassinated in Lisbon. Three years later, António Machado Santos suffered the same fate. In 1926, the democratic government of Bernardino Machado was overthrown by

military forces and the constitution suspended. Leadership passed through various hands and finally to General Oscar Carmona. He would remain as president until 1951, although it was not his leadership but that of his most influential appointee that made stability possible. In 1928, Carmona appointed António de Oliveira Salazar to the post of finance minister, with wide-ranging powers. By 1932, Salazar was effectively prime minister.

Salazar's New State

Salazar immediately set about reorganising the country's disastrous financial morass, mostly through the narrow-minded austerity which

reflected his own character. Having achieved what no leader had been able to do for a century, Salazar used his political capital to form a dictatorship, taking Mussolini's Italy as his model for national order and discipline.

The "New State", though nominally a corporative economic system under a republican government, was a fascist regime, with the National Union its only political party. It was authoritarian, pro-Catholic, and imperialist. A state police organisation, the PIDE, was notorious in its suppression of subversion. A rigid and effective censorship settled like a thick fog over art, literature and free speech. Nothing negative or critical could find its way into print. A formerly lively journalism withered away. In blatant doublespeak, the government often referred to itself as a dictatorship without a dictator.

There was some resistance. In reaction to the powerful militaristic control of the country there were numerous attempted coups and an underground communist party that grew in power, leading the clandestine opposition. However, Salazar's leadership was never strongly challenged.

Putting self-preservation ahead of ideology, Salazar pretended to adhere to the League of Nations' non-intervention policy during the Spanish Civil War (1936–39) because he could not afford international censure, but actually sent a legion of some 20,000 soldiers to aid General Franco's Nationalist forces. Franco's victory served to validate the authority of Salazar's own regime.

The republican era had seen a minor cultural resurgence, when democratic ideals encouraged efforts at mass education, a proliferation of journalism, and a few writers of modern fiction and poetry. But this was slowed by political upheavals, and effectively quelled by the New State. The greatest writer of the period, the poet Fernando Pessoa (1888–1935), had one major work, *Mensagem*, published in 1934, but it was not until after World War II that most of his works were published.

Few others transcended the romantic nationalism of the era, as formidable barriers to the larger currents of European culture were created. The censorship of the New State slowed original thinking to a trickle, and most of that was devoted to political subversion rather than artistic endeavour.

After World War II

During World War II, the New State concentrated on self-preservation. Though Salazar admired Hitler, Portugal's traditional political and economic ties with Britain demanded neutrality, at least. However, Portugal did supply the Axis with much needed wolfram (the ingredient necessary to alloy tungsten steel), almost until the end of the war. On the other hand, the Allies were granted strategic bases in the Azores. In fact, the war's main effect – though it was not widely advertised – was to replenish Portugal's coffers, as the government did business with both sides.

The defeat of the fascists should have given a signal to Salazar, a warning to mute his totalitarianism, but he was by now firmly entrenched. The changes over the next decade served primarily to protect the dictatorship still further from democratic insurgency.

In the 1950s, opposition to the New State solidified into two blocs. The legal bloc took advantage of the relaxed censorship in the month preceding the 1951 elections (the state's way of giving the impression of some democratic freedom), to run independent candidates. Members of the other, furtive, bloc organised various protest actions and engaged in what propaganda they could. These means kept resistance alive, forcing Salazar's hand. Their actions provoked new rounds of repression, deceit, and constitutional changes which eroded both Salazar's authority and popularity.

In 1958, General Humberto Delgado, a disenchanted member of the regime, stood for president, announcing among other things that he would use the constitutional power of that position to dismiss Prime Minister Salazar. Despite the mass demonstrations in his support, the official count declared that Admiral Américo Tomás, a Salazar loyalist, had been elected instead. Afterwards, constitutional decrees were enacted to prevent the repetition of such an event. The president was to be elected not by popular vote, but by an electoral college of the National Assembly, which was

OPPRESSIVE TRADITION

Censorship was nothing new to a country dominated for so long by the Inquisition. In the 500-year history of publishing in Portugal, little more than 80 years have been free of censorship.

Salazar-controlled. Delgado was assassinated in 1965 by state police, while attempting to cross the Spanish border into Portugal.

The empire strikes back

Portugal's entry into the United Nations was prevented by the Soviet bloc and by opponents of Salazar's imperial colonialism, until 1955. Membership was finally granted not because of any real change, but by a successful diplomatic effort to whitewash his despotism. Salazar would not change his poli-

cies because, despite the increasing cost of maintaining military rule in the colonies, they were very profitable for the homeland. Subsistence crops were increasingly neglected in favour of products like cotton, which fed the mills of Portugal while the Africans went hungry. The policy of *assimilado* – claiming that the goal was to assimilate the ethnic culture into the Portuguese one – allowed Portugal to exploit these "citizens" as virtually free labour.

Salazar's imperial intransigence led to serious consequences in the post-war world, where the old empires were rapidly crumbling. An explosion of African nationalism was set off by the violent 1961 Angolan uprising, which was

---

LEFT: Salazar addresses the faithful.
RIGHT: parading military pomp in Belém at the annual anniversary of the 1974 Revolution.

brutally crushed by the Portuguese. Throughout the 1960s, the government became more and more involved in maintaining the colonies, which had been renamed "provinces" in a 1951 decree that semantically underscored the insistence on a permanent Portuguese settlement.

Meanwhile, the stagnation of Portugal's home economy grew more oppressive. Hydroelectric power projects were successful, but industry and agriculture fell farther and farther behind international standards. Emigration, a national issue for more than a century, once again began to take a serious toll on the country's demographic resources.

As many young men were conscripted for the wars in Africa, popular support waned rapidly. Angola continued to be an economic boon, but the other colonies were a drain. Salazar increasingly trusted fewer members of his regime, taking on more direct responsibilities himself for continuing the wars. He also relaxed his policy of fiscal austerity, and increasingly relied on foreign credit to finance the overseas operations.

The end of an era

In 1968, the 79-year-old dictator suffered an incapacitating stroke, and the long awaited suc-

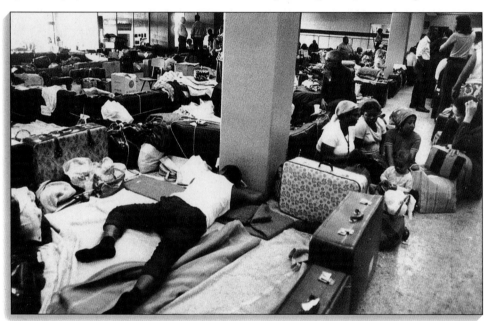

AN UNWILLING RETREAT

Despite international pressure, and increasing agitation within the colonies, Salazar's regime fiercely resisted any incursions on its colonial outposts, taking this resistance to ridiculous lengths. In 1961, the territory of São João da Ajuda, a tiny enclave surrounded by the country of Dahomey, consisted only of a decrepit fortress and the governor's estate. When Dahomey became independent from France, and delivered an ultimatum to Lisbon to return Ajuda, the Portuguese governor was forced to comply, but he waited until the last possible moment to surrender this tiny and useless sliver of territory, then spitefully burned down the buildings before departing.

cession had arrived. Because Salazar – who was unwilling to face his own mortality – had made no provision for a successor, major upheavals were expected. But the transition to power of "Acting Prime Minister" Marcelo Caetano was relatively smooth. Salazar lived his final years in seclusion and died in 1970.

Caetano, once a protégé of Salazar, had resigned seven years earlier over conflicts with his superior. Now called upon to resolve the national crisis, he saw the need for balanced change and stability, but he was not bold enough. Though many of the gravest injustices of the old regime were righted, other changes were superficial, and the colonial issue was not confronted. When his early efforts at liberalisation failed to appease opposition unrest, Caetano returned to oppressive hostility.

Discontent among all ranks of the military over the continued ineffective colonial wars led to the formation of the Armed Forces Movement (MFA) in 1973. The following year, General António de Spínola published *Portugal and the Future*, a stinging and comprehensive critique of the current situation, which recommended a military takeover to save the country. The book's messages had been voiced before, but never by so powerful a source. Many factors built towards the revolution, but this pub-

less coup began in Lisbon. Involving General Spínola and his fellow General Costa Gomes, it was conducted by angry "young captains" who commanded the 27 rebel units that seized key points throughout the city.

Caetano and other government officials took refuge in the barracks of the National Republican Guard. The formal surrender came after a young officer threatened to crash a tank through the gates. The rebel takeover was quickly accepted throughout the country. The revolution, taking the red carnation as its symbol, sparked nationwide celebration culminating in joyful demonstrations on 1 May.

lication lit the fuse. Caetano himself felt its importance, saying later that he began reading it in the late evening and "did not stop until the last page, which I read in the small hours of the morning. And when I closed the book I understood that the military coup, which I could sense had been coming, was now inevitable".

Bloodless coup

Two months later, on 25 April 1974, after a handful of premature uprisings, a near-blood-

The initial government was a National Salvation group of military men, designed to give way to a constituent assembly as soon as it was practical. A provisional government was soon in place, and negotiations with African liberation movements went ahead. There were divisions about overseas policies, and an odd coup-within-a-coup developed, with Spínola attempting to wrest control from his opponents. It was unsuccessful and liberal forces continued to divest Portugal of its colonies. Guinea-Bissau, Mozambique, the Cape Verde Islands, São Tomé and finally Angola were granted independence. One result of decolonialisation was a mass return of Portuguese nationals to

LEFT: *retornados* pour into Lisbon as the colonial wars come to an end. **ABOVE:** Prime Minister Mario Soares signs Portugal into the EC in 1988.

their homeland. As many as 500,000 people flowed into Lisbon and other urban centres, many with little more than the clothes on their backs. Angola and Mozambique were abandoned to civil wars, while East Timor was devoured by Indonesia.

As the economy careered into an abyss, the political pendulum swung the other way, and there was huge social unrest. In 1976 the socialist leader Mário Soares became prime minister, but over the following decade governments frequently came and went.

MILLIONS ABROAD

The Portuguese continue to seek their fortunes abroad. Around 4.3 million Portuguese live abroad, 10 times the number of foreigners living in Portugal. Their remittances make up 10 per cent of the GDP.

Socialist experiments were attempted as an antidote to years of Salazar. Land reforms were initiated, breaking up *látifundios*, the vast and long-established agricultural estates, particularly in the Alentejo, but these reforms have not proved successful.

In 1982, a long-awaited revision of the new constitution arrived. The democratic alliance and the far right were determined to rid the document of its Marxist taint. They were partially successful, but only after a period of nationwide demonstrations, strikes, and resignations. The Council of the Revolution was eliminated, and the hope for a truly classless society remained an unrealised goal.

In the next few years, the country witnessed a shift away from socialism towards capitalism. Although the veteran socialist leader Mário Soares was elected president in 1986 (the first civilian to hold the post in over 60 years) and re-elected by a landslide in 1991, the capitalistic social democrats, under youthful economist Aníbal Cavaco Silva, won an overall majority in July 1987.

In 1991, after a campaign based largely on his own forceful personality and on his claims that his government had wrought nothing less than an economic miracle, Cavaco Silva won another resounding electoral victory.

Joining the European club

Such stability allowed Portugal to emerge from being the most backward economy in Europe to becoming, by the early 1990s, one of the most buoyant. In 1986, it joined the European Community and in 1992 took its turn at assuming the presidency of the EC.

Among Cavaco Silva's most successful programmes was the reprivatisation of many companies and industries nationalised by the communists after the revolution.

In 1997, the Portuguese economy, then one of the fastest growing in Europe, met the requirements for the country to join the single currency, along with 10 other qualifying European Union states. Major public works projects such as the new bridge over the Tejo in Lisbon, and the continued expansion of new roads, had already culminated in the successful hosting of Expo '98, and this, even more than monetary union, was seen by many Portuguese as the final confirmation of their country's arrival as a modern, thriving European economy, poised to meet the challenges of the new millennium. A slowing down of the economy wrong-footed the Socialist government elected in 1995, and in 2002 Durão Barroso became Prime Minister of a centre right government. The country still benefits from its membership of the EU, and inward investment is evident, from the new Metro in Porto to the beautiful stadia built around the country for the 2004 European football championships. ❏

LEFT: The Stadium of Light, a spectacular new football ground for Lisbon's home team, Benfica.

Salazar

António de Oliveira Salazar, who led the country for 40 years, was the dominant figure of 20th-century Portugal. A country boy, born in 1889, he took the strict conservative values of his father far beyond the small rural world that formed them, ultimately transforming the whole nation into his image of what it should be.

As a professor of economics at Coimbra, Salazar was an active polemicist for the right. He made his first political impact as the youthful leader of the Centro Académico da Democracia Cristã (Academic Centre for Christian Democracy), a Catholic intellectual group that opposed the anti-clerical and individualistic philosophy of the republic. He made a brief foray into national politics but only accepted a political position when he could be assured of complete control.

This came in 1928, when the prime minister, General Carmona, offered Salazar the role of finance minister with absolute power over national finance. In 1932, he was appointed President of the Council of Ministers – which was another name for prime minister. Although there was opposition, dissent, and various plots against his life, Salazar's pervasive influence on Portugal would not truly lift until the April revolution of 1974, six years after a disabling stroke, and four years after his death.

Salazar imposed his own character upon the nation. He was austere, introverted, and he seldom travelled outside Portugal, perhaps taking pride in this as a mark of cultural purity. He steered his country through international affairs with as much neutrality as possible.

Portugal accepted Salazar's fascism as a kind of defensive posture in the face of the worldwide technological explosion of the 20th century. His conservative and at times reactionary attitudes toward industrialisation, agricultural reform, education and religion kept Portugal apart from the turbulence of the age. His attitude that Portugal was a naturally poor country – good for living in but not for producing anything – was widely held. Catholic cults, like that of Our Lady of Fátima, were encouraged and turned into propaganda for the regime.

Salazar also drew upon the romanticised history of Portuguese exploration and trade, inculcating a generation of schoolchildren with the self-aggrandising idea of Portugal's manifest destiny as an "empire". The country turned inwards, though still holding on to its colonies for as long as possible, and tried to ignore the changing face of world politics. It was a comforting but debilitating attitude. Portugal, in the end, would be obliged to catch up.

Salazar lived quietly, taking modest vacations by the sea or in his beloved Beira countryside. He remained unmarried, though he had a close but apparently celibate relationship with his lifelong housekeeper, Dona Maria de Jesus Caetano.

On 3 August 1968, in his fortress sanctuary in Estoril, Salazar suffered a stroke that left him an

invalid. He left no designated heir, but with surprisingly little turmoil, Marcelo Caetano, a brilliant lecturer but a rather weak politician, was made prime minister.

For the remaining two years of Salazar's life, he received few visitors and was given very little public attention. Those close to him chose not to tell him the truth about the succession of Caetano. Instead, they fabricated an image of Portugal still led by the old dictator.

When Dona Maria tried to convince him to retire, he refused and, in a last pathetic boast, claimed that he had no choice but to remain, because there was no one else. He died, aged 81, believing that he was still in control. ❏

RIGHT: at the end of his regime, Salazar's portrait adorns the cover of a biography.

THE PORTUGUESE

A rare passion for coffee and cakes is a national characteristic to which visitors can instantly relate. Other traits are a little more complex

Defining a national character is never easy. The Portuguese are often portrayed as easy-going, smiling, patient, good-natured but imbued with an inner *saudade*, a feeling variously defined as nostalgia or melancholy. Certainly the Portuguese offer a relaxed welcome to foreigners seeking sunny beaches, medieval architecture, the beauties of the countryside, and the local food and wines.

For the visitor in a hurry, the worst Portuguese character flaw seems to be a lack of awareness of time, although no discourtesy is intended when appointments are not kept. But the Portuguese have faced more serious criticism. Writing in the 1930s, the great modern poet Fernando Pessoa criticised their "provincialism", meaning their naively uncritical appreciation of all things "modern": big cities, new fashions, and so on.

Paul Descamps, a Frenchman writing in the 1930s, isolated permissive child-rearing as a key to understanding national characteristics. This may seem a specious argument, but its conclusions make sense. Portugal is a matriarchal and child-centred society, and people who have been spoiled by their mothers learn to operate by cajolery rather than diligence, to favour patience over perseverance. Raised with a lot of personal freedom, they grow up without great self-discipline, with only a vague sense of time constraints, and with a streak of independence and an unsinkable self-esteem.

Internal differences

Generalities are great liars, however. Ten and a half million individuals live in this country, from whose ancient roots (its national boundaries are the oldest in Europe) a modern European nation has emerged. Portugal had the fastest expanding economy in the European Union 10 years after joining, but its GDP per capita remains around 75 percent of the healthier EU economies and growth has slowed. Nevertheless, progress is everywhere to be seen.

In the bucolic backways of Trás-os-Montes and the Beiras, however, among the windmills, the cobbled roads, and horse-drawn

farmers' carts, you may well feel that you have stepped back in time. Rural people generally distrust Lisbon and all that it stands for: social turmoil, taxes, bureaucracy, centralised education. They would rather keep their distance. Able to sustain themselves by their harvests, they are fully aware of EU grants but have little interest in inflation or trade deficits. They are self-reliant.

In both city and country, there are ingrained social classes, but there is also a broad sense of equality. All men expect to be treated with dignity. Manners tend to be elaborate, especially in forms of address. Handshakes are exchanged at every encounter.

PRECEDING PAGES: at work in the Quinta da Eira Velha, in the port wine district of Pinhão; children out for a walk in Grandola.
LEFT: a leaping dancer in the Douro valley.
RIGHT: a couple on a working day in Aldeia Solveira.

Women, however, are on a separate footing. Feminist ideas are only now beginning to be heard. Some urban women hold important jobs, and the lifestyle of many younger ones in the cities is similar to that of their counterparts in other European countries, but despite legal equality, attitudes are slow to change, particularly in rural areas, where most people live. Changes are coming, however, and sometimes they can be quite shocking, as, for instance, with the arrival of some 300 Brazilian sex workers in the fairly remote town of Bragança in 2003. Outraged women saw their men hanging out in strip clubs and even visiting the new brothels,

hailed as the seminal Portuguese work not only for its beauty and literary influence, but for its paeans to the discoveries and to national pride. In fact, this aspect of Portuguese identity – as explorers, colonisers, a world power – has resulted in a tendency to look overseas for answers to internal woes rather than to seek a solution at home, a problem which is only now being overcome.

Work

Unemployment is relatively low and young people seeking first jobs are likely to be preferred over older people, as they will accept

but their complaints were often met with the charge that they should try to make themselves more attractive to keep their men at home.

If in many ways the rhythm of Portuguese life is slow and habits cautious, this is less to do with Latin temperament or the sunny climate than with the effects of the Salazar era and its aftermath; many people returning from the colonies, had a deeply traumatic time in the clashes between new left and old right. Their children, however, face a more prosperous and much more settled world.

Beneath the face of contemporary life lie the proud contours that comprise Portugal's history. Camões's *Os Lusíadas (see page 45)* is

COMING HOME

Long-term emigration caused strange demographics for many years, as the very young and the old were left behind while wage-earners went abroad to work and send home wages. But about half the estimated 800,000 who worked in France, Germany and other industrialised countries have now returned. And as EU capital brought new life to the country, many professional workers – doctors, lawyers and so on – arrived from Brazil and elsewhere, bringing with them their different tastes and lifestyles. With growing prosperity, Portugal itself is now receiving migrant workers from Eastern Europe – an interesting reversal of earlier times.

lower wages. Minimum wages paid by shops are around €300 a month. Well over half the population, around 65 percent, lives a rural life but villages are rapidly depopulating. Some are inhabited only by elderly widows and prospects for the newly born are dim.

In industry and commerce there are a few conglomerates; the large majority of companies are small- and medium-sized businesses employing, for the most part, fewer than 10 people; textiles and shoes are the top manufactured products and excellent value for tourists. There are no huge shopping chains, and the biggest department stores in

eucalyptus an ecological issue), with cork still a major harvest. Port wine from the Douro valley is among Portugal's most famous products, but table wines from many newly designated areas are reaching new peaks of quality. Tourism contributes a high proportion of foreign earnings and around two-thirds of the work force is in the service sector.

Salaries, although rising, are about a third of the European average, and despite recent growth Portugal remains near the bottom of the list of Europe's poorest countries with nearly one in five of the population living in poverty, the highest rate in the EU.

Lisbon are the French-owned Fnac and El Corte Inglés owned by the Spanish.

With a long coastline, fishing remains strong but it is not a high-paying industry. Agriculture has never been more than basically productive, despite the country's rustic image. Portugal's olive oil production, for example, just meets its own needs. About 10 percent of the work force is in agriculture, which produces less than 4 percent of the GDP. Forestry is profitable (the spread of

Family ties

Home and family life is a strong, stable framework of all Portuguese society. At the top everyone knows everyone, even across political boundaries. Families, especially in the north, tend to be large, as might be expected in a Catholic country. The extended family is extremely common, as grandparents help care for the children, and young adults – without access to any other housing option – often live at home until they marry.

Portugal is predominantly Roman Catholic, with a few Protestant communities, and a few Jews and Muslims, too. One interesting group is the so-called *Marranos*, Jews who converted

FAR LEFT: a carrier in Caria.
LEFT: time out for the latest gossip.
ABOVE: graduation day at the University of Coimbra.

during the 16th- and 17th-century prosecutions, and who retain some Jewish rituals, sometimes in combination with a nominal Catholicism.

The Portuguese are sympathetic to unmarried couples living together. They adore babies and small children, as you will see in restaurants and in the streets. It was therefore particularly upsetting when a paedophile scandal involving senior politicians and policemen rocked the country in 2003.

Deep superstition is a part of the culture: wax images in churches and herbalist witchery in villages are commonplace. They love a rude

joke and earthy gossip. With books, cinema and the arts in general accessible only to a small minority, television is the common cultural experience. A shared language gives them access to, among other things, Brazilian soaps, and they have easy access to an astounding range of good music from Brazil, the Cape Verde Islands and from Africa.

A changing society

Tolerance might be considered Portugal's prime virtue – capital punishment for civil crimes was abolished as long ago as 1867, and violent crime is rare. But behind the wheel of a car the easy-going nature turns too often to

dangerous bravado. The urge to overtake has given the Portuguese the dismal distinction of having one of the highest accident rates in Europe, though there's no doubt that greatly improved roads have led to better driving conditions.

You will also see – and certainly hear – numerous motorbikes and under-powered, overladen scooters. Laws, in theory, forbid high levels of noise or small children on bikes. These laws are frequently ignored by traffic police, but they may well charge you steeply for not wearing the mandatory seat belt.

Education has been thoroughly modernised but still has some way to go. Pre-school is an option for 3- to 6-year-olds, while there is free compulsory education for children between the ages of 6 and 15. Competition to enter university has become intense as secondary school graduates have increased. Adult literacy stands at about 93 percent, but is much lower in remote inland areas.

Infinite variety

To the Portuguese, their nation is an entity calling for a proper patriotism. Their *terra*, or homeland, is the place they truly love. A Lisboeta cannot believe there is a city more beautiful than lovely, hilly Lisbon. The citizens of Porto dote on their own granite city on the banks of the Douro.

The country displays surprising variations from region to region, and in particular between north and south. There are also some physical differences in the people: in the north the basic Iberian strain – dark, thick-set – has been leavened with Celtic blood, while in the south, Jewish, Moorish and African ancestors are evident. The north is generally more conservative, both politically and culturally, and is the bastion of Portuguese Catholicism. The south has a tradition of liberalism and adaptation. The two temperaments – the warm Mediterranean and cool Atlantic – wash over each other. The people are as varied as their land. There is a saying that "Coimbra studies while Braga prays, Porto works while Lisbon plays". Nothing is that simple, but it is true that travelling here unveils not only a beautiful landscape but a rich panorama of humanity. ❏

LEFT: Euro-toting tourists at Nazaré market.
RIGHT: all dressed up for a Viana do Castelo festival.

SAINTS, MIRACLES AND SHRINES

Religion in Portugal touches all aspects of life. Every town and village has its own saint, which is a cause for celebration at least once a year

In the middle of the 6th century a young monk named Martin arrived in Mondoñedo, in northwest Spain, where he founded the abbey of Dume. His mission then took him to Braga, the former Roman city that had become the political and religious stronghold of the Suevi, a barbarian tribe that had adopted Arianism, a heretical form of Christianity. Martin, who had been inspired at the shrine of St Martin at Tours, was determined to convert their leaders to true Christianity.

In 559, he succeeded in converting the Suevi king, Theodomirus. Within the next decade, Martin was appointed archbishop of Braga. He found a further challenge, however, among the general population. Although they had been Catholics since their conversion under the Roman Empire, the people had incorporated many local beliefs and customs into their religion. To Martin, this amalgam was unacceptable, and in a written sermon entitled *De Correctione Rusticorum (On the Correction of Peasants)*, he called for an end to the use of charms, auguries and divination, of the invocation of the devil, and of the cults of the dead, of fountains and stars.

In this St Martin did not succeed, nor have 14 centuries of similarly inclined zealots and reformers. All these unorthodox elements are present to this day as an obstinate strain within Catholic traditions.

Naturally, there is still much wrestling over these issues between the church hierarchy and the parishes. The bishops have banned a certain Padre Miguel, a priest from an isolated northern mountain parish who was supposed to have healing powers. Yet, though frowned upon by the orthodox church, spontaneous, independent Catholicism should not be seen as a form of superstition or magic; rather, it is evidence of a vigorous religious tradition.

What are some of these still-current beliefs? When a newborn child proves healthy, it is said that it was conceived when the moon was waxing. The states of the moon are believed to be very influential in the way all living things grow – vegetables, animals and human beings. Similarly, certain fountains are reputed to have

particular healing powers. And under many of these, Moorish princesses are said to be hiding, watching over treasures.

A variety of beliefs function to reassure people during the most frightening moments of the human life cycle. For instance, many practices have evolved that are meant to protect children as they gestate in their mothers' wombs, or just after they are born. Thus, to protect it against the "evil air" a newborn should not be taken out of the house during certain hours; its father's trousers should be placed over the cot to frighten away witches; and the mother should not eat at the same time as she is breastfeeding, or the child may grow up to be greedy.

PRECEDING PAGES: the shrine of Fátima draws thousands of pilgrims and worshippers.
LEFT: a Good Friday procession in Braga.
RIGHT: kissing the crucifix on Easter Sunday.

Around midnight

One of the more dramatic folk practices is the Midnight Baptism. This happens when a pregnant woman is prone to miscarriages or when her previous child was stillborn. The "baptism" takes place at midnight in the middle of a bridge that divides two municipalities – a powerful spot that is neither one place nor another, at the moment that is neither one day nor the next. Certain bridges, such as the Ponte da Barca in the Minho, are famous for this.

When everything is ready, the child's father and a friend, armed with sticks, stand guard at the ends of the bridge. They are there to ward returned to the church, it is a symbol of the new life shared by the whole community.

Similarly, on All Saints' Day and All Souls' Day (1 and 2 November), the celebrations at the parish cemetery are attended by everyone. Lamps are lit, tombs are cleaned and decorated with flowers. The whole parish celebrates this strongly felt sense of continuity with the past, praying together for their dead.

Perhaps the strongest evidence that the feeling of community extends beyond this life is the common belief in the "procession of the dead". Certain people claim that they have the power to hear or see a procession of the ghosts

off cats and dogs – potentially witches or the devil in disguise. The first person who passes after the church bells strike midnight must perform the rite. He or she pours river water over the expectant mother's belly and baptises the child "in the name of the Father, the Son and the Holy Ghost…" but the final "Amen" must not be uttered. This must wait until the child is born and properly baptised by a priest in church.

The church is the central meeting place of the whole parish. At Easter, the cross that represents the resurrection of Christ is taken from the church and carried to all the households. It is kissed as it enters each house, and when it is of those parishioners who have recently died. This procession is seen leaving the cemetery, with a coffin in its centre. When it returns, the ghost of the parishioner who will be the next to die will be in the coffin. Thus these seers predict how many people are going to die imminently – but they cannot reveal the names if they themselves want to remain alive.

Patron saints

The use of religion to establish a communal identity is most clearly shown by the celebrations for the local patron saint. An organising committee busies itself all year collecting money, planning decorations, arranging events.

The importance of these celebrations is immense. They represent and solidify local pride. The *festa* is a joyful occasion heralded by firecrackers and by music blaring from loudspeakers placed on the church tower. The pivotal event is the procession after Mass, when the image of the patron saint is carried with great pomp on a brightly decorated stand in a traditional, roughly circular path.

After that, the secular celebrations begin. These usually involve dancing to traditional brass bands, folk-dance groups and, nowadays, rock and pop bands. A great deal of wine is consumed and the festivities are a focus for young people, who use these opportunities as social mixers. Not surprisingly, it is this aspect of the celebration that some priests oppose.

Popular attitudes to saints differ from church doctrine not so much in content as in emphasis. The people place great importance on material benefits and personal, reciprocal relationships with saints. They pray to specific saints for specific problems – St Lawrence if they have a toothache, St Brás if suffering from a sore throat, St Christopher when going on a journey. Our Lady of the Conception, naturally, helps with problems of infertility, and the Holy Family is asked to intervene in family problems, and so on. People will also address personal prayers to particular saints. If the believer's prayer is answered, this proves that the particular image is a singularly sacred one, a favoured line of communication. In this way shrines develop, whether individual, family, or even national, with images famous for their miraculous powers.

The notion of the miracle in popular religion is also more loosely interpreted than in the church. Essentially, a miracle is considered to have taken place every time a specific prayer is answered. The believer must then "pay" the saint whatever he or she had promised.

Wax offerings

When a prayer to St Anthony asks for a specific favour – that a loved one, or even a pig or sheep, recover from a bout of ill health, or an offer of marriage be accepted – a promise is made to give the saint something in return. A wax heart might be given for a successful engagement, or a wax pig if the animal has fully recovered. If the promise is not fulfilled, punishment may follow.

If you visit churches in northern Portugal, you will often see these *ex voto* offerings hanging on the walls alongside other gifts such as bridal dresses, photographs, written testimonies or braids of women's hair. Shrines of great importance such as Bom Jesus and Sameiro, near Braga, have large displays. At Fátima *(see below)*, the best known shrine in the country, wax gifts accumulate so quickly that special furnaces have been installed to burn them.

OUR LADY OF FATIMA

Fátima, near the town of Leiria, is one of the largest shrines in Western Europe *(see page 244)*. On 13 May 1917, the Virgin is supposed to have appeared to three children (two of them died young; the third, Lucy, became a Carmelite nun in Coimbra). The event is said to have been repeated on the 13th of the subsequent five months, and each time the Virgin spoke about peace in the world. Fátima became a rallying point for the revival of Catholicism in the 1930s and 1940s. Today, from May to October the roads around Leiria are lined with pilgrims, many of whom have come great distances on foot to "pay" the Virgin for her favours.

LEFT: lighting candles for the dead, All Saints' Day.
RIGHT: St Anthony, Lisbon's unofficial patron saint, is celebrated in the streets of the capital in June.

There is also another kind of gift: a personal sacrifice. The church has been strongly critical of this, but until the late 1960s, it was firmly encouraged. If you visit the shrine of São Bento da Porta Aberta (St Benedict of the Open Door), in the beautiful mountain landscape of Gerês near the dam of Caniçada on 13 August, you will find men and women laboriously circumambulating the church on their knees.

This scene is even more striking because these people are surrounded by others celebrating the day with singing, dancing, eating and drinking. But those on their knees are cel-

ebrating, too – because the saint has answered their prayers.

Another kind of payment to patron saints has all but disappeared due to strong church opposition. In the parish of Senhora da Aparecida in Lousada, for example, before the main procession leaves the church there is another one in which 20 or more open coffins – containing living people, their faces covered with white handkerchiefs – are carried through the streets. Those who ride in the coffins are offering a false burial to the saint who saved them from having to participate in a real one. The occasion, therefore, is a joyful one, although it sounds macabre. There is plenty of light-hearted banter,

and the participants mingle with the other parishioners afterwards, drinking and dancing.

Cults and compromises

The cult of the dead, another morbid religious tradition, and one of the targets of St Martin during the 6th century, remains an object of popular fascination today in northern Portugal. Very occasionally, a body is buried but does not undergo the normal process of decay. Such people are often considered to be saints. There are a number of such grim shrines where the corpses are exposed. The Church nearly always opposes these cults at first, but eventually tolerates them as they grow in popularity – three such are the Infanta Santa Mafalda in Arouca, the São Torcato near Guimarães, or the Santinha de Arcozelo near Porto. Even in an unlikely spot like the small urban cemetery of the elegant neighbourhood of Foz in Porto, a shrine to one of these "saints" can be found.

Along rural roads one will frequently find pretty little shrines, but these are intended to protect travellers, and are not connected with the cult of the dead. They contain images of Christ or the Virgin or a popular saint. At the base, little moulded flames surround figures which represent the souls of sinners suspended in Purgatory.

Portuguese history is full of examples of the continuing conflict between the spontaneous and all-embracing religiosity of the less educated classes, and the more restrictive attitudes of the theologically-minded – and the ways in which the two have learned to coexist. From the early days of the Western Crusade in the 12th century, and the power of military-religious orders like the Knights Templar and the Hospitallers, to the dark days of the Inquisition, religious and secular authorities have vied with each other for power, and used each other to the best advantage. Imperialism, like the early exploration and discoveries, was seen as a form of religious crusade: each victory along the way was considered a miracle. And Salazar's regime actively encouraged the cult of Our Lady of Fátima, even managing to present its policy of neutrality during World War II as being based on the soothsayings of the Virgin. ❑

LEFT: plaques affixed by grateful supplicants.
RIGHT: a floral offering to the Virgin in Lamego's Cathedral.

CENTRO SOCIAL JOÃO PAULO II
(2ª FASE)

TRAVELLERS' TALES

There were some distinguished names among early visitors to Portugal,
and they left with strong impressions

English visitors to Portugal have long believed themselves to be discoverers of the one exotic land left in well-visited, well-described Europe. In 1845, Dorothy Quillinan, daughter of William Wordsworth, wrote, "There is, I believe, no country in Europe that is less thoroughly familiar to me". A century

later, Evelyn Waugh thought it was still a well-kept secret, and wrote: "There is no European capital of antiquity about which one hears so little". But English travellers have been going to Portugal, and writing about it, for some time.

Eighteenth-century opinions

The most flamboyant of the 18th-century visitors to Portugal was William Beckford, who set up a sumptuous house in Ramalhoa near Sintra in 1787. He inspired Byron's *Childe Harold*, whose first stop on his pilgrimage to Portugal was to wander through Sintra conjuring Beckford's ghost and meditating on the brevity of life and pleasure.

Beckford first visited the peninsula in 1787, shortly after the publication of his Gothic novel *Vathek*. The unorthodox Englishman, who had left England in the wake of a homosexual scandal, caught the fancy of the pious Marquis of Marialva, who hoped to convert Beckford to Catholicism. But Beckford, as we learn from his diary, was desperate not for the salvation of his soul but for an introduction to the court of Queen Maria. England's ambassador Sir Hugh Walpole refused to perform this service for his disgraced countryman. The Marquis guaranteed an introduction if Beckford would convert, but the writer had no such intention and he left, petulant and thwarted. By the time he was finally presented at court in 1794, poor Maria had long been insane.

Beckford's *Sketches of Spain and Portugal* give an idiosyncratic, slighty bitchy but sensitive view of Portugal's art, music, nature and society. Beckford's is a land of the senses: he describes the *modinha*, a haunting, erotic song, and the luxuriant beauty of the vegetation. His journals provide a brilliant, if haphazard guide to Portugal's art and climate.

On his first visit to Portugal in 1796, Robert Southey, a Romantic and the future English Poet Laureate, expressed disapproval of the filth of Lisbon, the discomfort of the country inns, and the corruption and superstition of the priests. But on a subsequent visit, four years later, although he still mourned the lack of "genial company", he fell in love with the country, and delighted in the sensual orange groves, long lazy days and lush, fertile fields.

William Mickle, the 18th-century poet and translator of Luís Camões' works, was an unqualified admirer of Portugal's "genial clime" and contrasted the "gloomy mists" of England to the "sun-basked scenes... where orange bowers invite".

Lord Byron

These writers offer a pleasant alternative to the vitriolic portrait of Portugal left by the 19th century's great promoter of European travel,

George Gordon, Lord Byron. The poet left two accounts of Portugal, neither favourable: one in his letters home during his visit there in 1809, the other in Childe Harold's pilgrimage, *Canto I*. His hatred for the Portuguese has mystified and disturbed scholars and admirers of Portugal since the latter work first appeared in print in 1812. There is no record of any encounter during his brief stay there that would have led to such dislike. The most likely explanation for his anger is that the Portuguese felt resentful rather than grateful to the British for their help in expelling the French invader, "Gaul's locust host", from their country during Napoleon's Iberian campaign. Byron, like many of his countrymen, may also have been ashamed that at the Congress of Sintra, Arthur Wellesley (later the Duke of Wellington) allowed the defeated French to carry off their booty, including many of Portugal's treasures.

Some of Byron's criticisms reveal a typical Anglo-Saxon ambivalence toward the south, but while he admired the southern spirit in Italy, Spain or southern France, his image of Lisbon is of a faithless harlot of a town, a siren who glitters beautifully from the water but who reveals, on closer contact, only filth and treachery:

But whoso entereth within this town,
That, sheening far, celestial seems to be,
Disconsolate will wander up and down,
Mid many things unsightly to strange see;
For hut and palace show like filthily...
Poor paltry slaves! yet born midst noblest
scenes.

Borrow's travels

That ingratitude of the Portuguese towards their northern liberators is testified to by another Englishman, George Borrow. Travelling in 1835, on a mission for the Bible Society, he complains that the English "who have never been at war with Portugal, who have fought for its independence on land and sea, and always with success, who have forced themselves by a treaty of commerce to drink its coarse and filthy wines... are the most unpopular people who visit Portugal." But, unlike Byron, Borrow attributed this not to the Portuguese nature but to "corrupt and unregenerate man".

LEFT: 18th-century writer, William Beckford, set up home near Sintra.
RIGHT: Lord Byron, no great admirer of Portugal.

Borrow's account of Portugal, less famous than Byron's stanzas, is an original, entertaining and evocative description. He is a great reporter of human eccentricity, and is also enthusiastic about the beauties of Portugal. Lisbon, he claims, "is quite as much deserving the attention of the artist as even Rome itself". Sintra, which captivated all travellers and was praised lavishly even by Byron, is "a mingled scene of fairy beauty, artificial elegance, savage grandeur, domes, turrets, enormous trees, flowers, and waterfalls, such as is met with nowhere else under the sun". It is truly, Borrow writes, "Portuguese Paradise". ❏

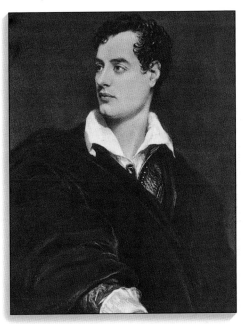

SPEAKING TO THE NATIVES

George Borrow is a wonderfully comic traveller, erratic and egoistical, and nothing like as pious as one would expect of a Bible Society missionary. His self-confidence is typified by his belief that after just two weeks he could speak fluent Portuguese. He refused to accept that much of the time people could not understand what he was saying, and his advice to novices speaking a foreign language offers the sort of wrong-headed lesson that some tourists seem to take to heart even today.

"Those who wish to make themselves understood by a foreigner in his own language should speak with much noise and vociferation, opening their mouths wide."

TRADITIONAL BOATS

Portugal's colourful boats used to be vital to the country's wine, weed and fishing industries, but most are now used for sport and pleasure

On his return to Lisbon after discovering the sea route to India in 1498, Vasco da Gama proclaimed *"Somos a gente do mar"* ("We are the people of the sea"). Using small, light, high-prowed caravel sailing ships based on an ancient Mediterranean design, 15th-and 16th-century Portuguese explorers voyaged the world and Portugal became the greatest maritime nation on earth.

A generation later Portugal lost its superior position and driftwood was all that was left of the caravels. Nevertheless, the numerous sea-faring traditions which history had thrust on the country were still in place. And as Portugal retreated into centuries of introspection, some of the boat-building techniques and traditions left by ancient mariners were absorbed in the rivers and inland waterways.

Port boats

Best known are the flat-bottomed, square-rigged *barcos rabelos*, which are a familiar sight in Porto. A flotilla of them lines the quay-side of the Rio Douro at Vila Nova de Gaia opposite the city, their sails emblazoned with the motifs of the port-wine firms whose warehouses are scattered around the wharfs. The boats have become a symbol of the product with whose destiny they have been entwined for hundreds of years.

Not always appreciated are the similarities in design with Viking longships that sailed along the Portuguese coast from the 9th to the 11th century on their way to the Mediterranean. In traditional *barco rabelo* building the hull's shell is laid first, then the ribs are placed. This is the Nordic "clinker building" method which may be a direct Viking legacy. A comparison between the bare hull of a *rabelo*, and that of a reconstructed longboat in Oslo's Viking Museum, shows striking similarities.

PRECEDING PAGES: sailing boats in a realistic mural. **LEFT:** the port of Lisbon painted in the 1940s by José Almada Negreiros, one of Portugal's greatest 20th-century artists. **RIGHT:** racing *moliceiros*.

Other features of the *rabelo*'s design evolved in the early 17th century, the nascent period of the trade in port wine. Ever since then the grapes for the fortified wine have been grown in the upper reaches of the Douro valley, from where the port is transported to Vila Nova de Gaia for shipment abroad. The adapted indigenous boats

of the Douro were constructed in large numbers and put to this use on the treacherous river, stacked with casks or "pipes" of wine. Flat bottoms were needed to shoot the rapids, negotiate the shallows, and also to achieve high loading ratios. A tall platform at the stern gave the helmsman a clear view over the rows of pipes and a huge steering oar, or *espadela* – effectively a rudder – was needed to change course rapidly. The rudder also had to be capable of being levered out of the water to avoid smashing in the rapids and rocky shallows. Intrepid boatmen slept and ate on board, suspending cauldrons from a beam and boiling their traditional dishes of pungent *bacalhau* (dried cod).

Racing *rabelos*

The damming of the Douro for hydroelectric power brought to an end the era of the *rabelo*'s interdependence with the port trade. Or so it seemed. Although for nearly 30 years port has made the journey down from the Upper Douro by road, the *rabelo* has proved to be an irrepressible symbol of the product. Boats are still constructed, at great expense, to compete in the annual race of *rabelos* owned by the various port-shipping firms. The regatta, enthusiastically contested but without much store set by winning or losing, is held on 24 June – the festival of São João (St John the Baptist and

the wind, and need at least a dozen crew members. Payloads are up to 65 pipes, each one holding 522 litres of port.

The São João regatta provides proof that the boats are more than simply advertisements for the wares of their owners.

Weed boats

Fewer visitors to Portugal come across the *moliceiro*, another craft of ancient ancestry which has been adapted for specific commercial use. *Moliceiros* are the seaweed-gathering boats of the Ria de Aveiro, a great lagoon which is linked to the Atlantic by a narrow breach in

Porto's patron saint) when the city erupts in revelry. The boats set off from the mouth of the Douro, with the race climaxing at the double-decker Dom Luís I bridge.

What *is* taken absolutely seriously is the set of rules ensuring that the *rabelos* are constructed precisely according to the specifications evolved during their heyday. The craft have to be built in boatyards along the banks of the Douro, with the hull constructed from maritime pine, forests of which cloak the north coast of Portugal, and laid down by the shell-first "clinker building" technique. The largest *rabelos* are around 24 metres (80 ft) long by 5.5 metres (18 ft) wide with 80 sq metres (860 sq ft) of sail billowing in

the dunes and spreads over the misty, marshy wetlands of the Beira Litoral province.

The seaweed, or *moliço*, which grows in profusion along the shallow bed of the Ria, is used as fertiliser on the fields of the Beiras. The high curling "swan-neck" prows of the *moliceiros* emerge soundlessly from the marshes, where the stillness is broken only by the splash of a flock of waterfowl, or by a boatman's cry.

Moliceiros are 10–15 metres (33–50 ft) long, and usually crewed by two men. At the stern is a vast rudder operated by means of ropes, and at the centre a mast on which a white, trapezoidal sail of about 24 sq metres (260 sq ft) is rigged. Hefty oars are also kept on board, but when the boat is becalmed or in reeds, a punting pole is preferred. Boatmen stand on the prow, which is painted with motifs of flowers, saints, bulls, or mythical heroes, and thrust the wooden pole into the mud that is never far from the surface, deftly propelling the boat through the reeds. The weed is scraped from the floor of the lagoon by multi-pronged rakes known as *ancinhos*, and deposited on the bottom of the boat. The harvest is then taken ashore to be dried and sold to farmers.

MOLICEIRO REGATTA

An annual regatta keeps alive the skills of *moliceiro* sailing and brings redundant boats out of retirement. The event is held in Torreira at the Romaria de São Paio in early September.

ven by oars, and have arch-shaped hulls built to ride the Atlantic swell. Designs vary, but typically the boats are about 5 metres (16 ft) long with their prows tapering up to a peak. A common motif is the pair of eyes painted on to the bows to ward off evil spirits, like those found on fishing boats in Malta.

Traineiras, the wooden trawlers based in Portugal's major fishing ports, also have a long pedigree. These are deep-sea fishing boats which for centuries have voyaged to distant

The number of *moliceiros* has dwindled. In the first half of the century over 1,000 worked the Ria, but artificial fertilisers have largely replaced *moliço*, leaving only enough demand to sustain a handful of working *moliceiros*.

Off-shore trawlers

More high-prowed boats are found on the beaches of Praia da Mira west of Ria, and along the coast of the Beira Litoral and Estremadura. Instead of having flat bottoms and sails, these off-shore fishing boats are dri-

waters in search of cod which, dried, becomes *bacalhau*. Some believe that *traineiras* from Cascais reached America in 1482, and that it was thanks to the ensuing rumours that Christopher Columbus made his discovery a decade later. Today's *traineiras* are 10–25 metres (32–80 ft) long and are fitted with diesel engines. Those going great distances have radios and radar, too, but most are no more than 12 metres (40 ft) long and stick to Portugal's coastal waters. These extended for 320 km (200 miles) out into the Atlantic when Portugal joined the EU. Now there is pressure, particularly from the Spanish, for the distance to be reduced to 20 km (12 miles). ❏

LEFT: gaily painted *moliceiros* are a source of pride.
ABOVE: hauling a *traineira* home.

PORTUGUESE FOOD

If you like fresh fish, succulent pork and hearty soups, laced with plenty of garlic, you'll find Portuguese food to your taste

To dine in Portugal is to taste the presence of other countries, other cuisines. It is to conjure up images of empire: Brazil, Angola, Mozambique, Goa and Macau. These and others all belonged to Portugal once and, in a manner of speaking, foods from four continents helped to stir the pot.

The period of Portuguese empire, when this small nation reached out across the terrifying "Green Sea of Darkness", as the Atlantic was called, has long passed. Yet Portugal, left with only the Azores and Madeira, has preserved the flavours of other cultures in its cooking.

Prince Henry the Navigator, less than 30 years old when he began to promote exploration, was a true scientist in an age of superstition. He ordered his explorers to bring back from new lands not only riches and wild tales, but also fruits, nuts and plants. In 1420 he sent settlers to colonise the newly discovered island of Madeira. With them went plants he believed would thrive in Madeira's volcanic soil and subtropical climate, including grapevines from Crete and sugar cane from Sicily. Even more significant for Portuguese cooking was Vasco da Gama's discovery of the sea route to the east in 1497–98, only five years after Christopher Columbus's discovery of the West Indies.

Spices of the orient

Black pepper was what Vasco da Gama sought, but cinnamon, which he also found in Calcutta, would soon become equally precious to Portuguese cooks. Indeed, one boatload of cinnamon sticks fetched enough money to pay for an entire expedition to India. Cinnamon is perhaps the most beloved spice in Portugal today, certainly for the famous egg sweets *(doces de ovos)*. Spaniards, on the other hand, prefer vanilla for their puddings and flans. There's good reason for this: it was the Spaniards who

PRECEDING PAGES: an elegant place to eat – at the Hotel Palace Buçaco, near Coimbra.
LEFT: the colourful market in Funchal, Madeira.
RIGHT: Portuguese sardines are plump and succulent.

found Montezuma sipping vanilla-spiked hot chocolate in Mexico and learned the trick of curing vanilla beans, the seed pods of a wild orchid. Perhaps this is why chocolate, too, is more popular in Spain than in Portugal.

The Portuguese fondness for curry powder is another legacy of Vasco da Gama's voyages.

In the beginning, only the rich and the royal could afford the precious yellow powder, which pepped up even the blandest dish, and also retarded spoilage.

Today, curry powder can be found in *supermercados* everywhere. Its function, rather than to set food afire, is to mellow and marry the other ingredients, and add a muskiness to a large repertoire of soups and stews. The spiciest Portuguese dishes, incidentally, are not found on the mainland but in the Azores and Madeira. These islands were ports-of-call for the early navigators, who would barter with the natives, offering spices in exchange for fresh fruits, vegetables, meat and the local brew.

New food for old

During Portugal's lavish Age of Empire, its navigators became couriers, bringing New World foods to the Old and vice versa. Mediterranean sugar cane, for example, was cultivated in Brazil. Brazilian pineapples were introduced to the Azores, a colony established under Prince Henry. They still flourish there in hothouses, ripening under wafting wood-smoke. Azorean pineapples, chunky, honey-sweet and tender to the core, are teamed today with rosettes of

> **A CUP OF CHAR**
>
> The Portuguese word for tea – *chá* – is almost identical to the Cantonese one – *ch'a* – from which comes the colloquial English term "char".

were African coffee, transplanted to Brazil, which today produces about half of the world's supply; Brazilian cashews, which landed in both Africa and India; and Oriental tea plants, which were taken to the Azores.

All this fetching and carrying of seeds, leaves, barks, roots, stems, stalks and cuttings by Portuguese explorers across oceans and continents dramatically affected Portuguese cooking. New World tomatoes and potatoes came to Portugal about the same time as they did to

Portugal's mahogany-hued, air-cured *presunto* (prosciutto-like ham) and served as an elegant appetiser in fashionable Lisbon restaurants.

Tiny, incendiary Brazilian chilli peppers took root in Angola, another important Portuguese colony, early on, and became so essential to cooks there that today they're known by their African name, *piri-piri*. Since Angola ceased to be a Portuguese colony in the mid-1970s, the subsequent influx to Lisbon of thousands of Angolan refugees, has meant that *piri-piri* sauce (an oil and vinegar mixture strewn with minced chillies) is as popular a table condiment in mainland Portugal as salt and pepper.

Other exchanges, thanks to the Portuguese,

Spain, in the 16th century. Portuguese cooks might drop a few garlic cloves into the soup or stew along with the tomatoes and potatoes, or tuck in a stick of cinnamon.

A la Portugaise

It's unlikely that anyone grows nuttier, earthier potatoes today than the Portuguese. Indeed, along the New England coast in the United States, where so many Portuguese families have settled, there's an old saying: "If you want your potatoes to grow, you must speak to them in Portuguese." Tomatoes respond to the Portuguese touch, too, and those harvested in the vast Alentejo province, east of Lisbon, are as juicy, red and tasty as any on earth. Not for nothing does the phrase found on French menus, "*à la Portugaise*", mean a dish that is richly sauced with tomatoes.

Onions and garlic, indispensable to any respectable Portuguese cook, were probably introduced by the Romans, who are believed to have brought wheat here, too. They aimed to make the Iberian peninsula the granary of Rome. They also probably introduced olives (a major source of income today) and grapes. From shards found in Alentejo, it is known that the Romans were making wine there as early as the 2nd century AD.

The Moors, who occupied a large chunk of Portugal from the early 8th to the mid-13th centuries, enriched the pot even more than the Romans. The southern provinces were the Moorish stronghold – the Algarve and Alentejo, in particular – and many traces of North Africa can still be seen.

It was the Arabs who dug irrigation ditches, who first planted rice (it now grows up and down the west coast), and who also covered the Algarve slopes with almond trees. The Algarve's almonds were ground into paste, sweetened, and shaped into delicate miniature fruits, birds and flowers displaying intricate detail that are still produced today.

The Moors also introduced figs and apricots to the Algarve, together with the trick of drying them in the sun. They planted groves of lemons and oranges and, as was their custom, they combined fish with fruit and fruit with meat.

It was the Arabs who invented the *cataplana*, a hinged metal pan, a sort of primitive pressure-cooker shaped like an oversize clam shell that can be clamped shut and set on a quick fire. The food inside – fish, shellfish, chicken, vegetables or a medley of them all – steam to supreme succulence. What goes into a *cataplana* depends on the whim of the cook (and on what's available), but the most famous recipe is *amêijoas na cataplana,* clams tossed with rounds of sausage and cubes of ham in an intensely garlicky tomato sauce. This unlikely pork and shellfish combination was supposedly created at the time of the Inquisition as a test of true Christianity. Pork

and shellfish, of course, were forbidden to Jews and Muslims alike.

There is no shortage of examples of Portugal's culinary ingenuity. Thrifty Portuguese cooks with an eye on their *escudos* made bread a main course by layering yeast dough into a pan with snippets of chicken and sausage and two kinds of ham – a classic from the remote northern Trás-os-Montes which is called *folar.* And when times were hard they would crumble yesterday's bread into shrimp cooking water and come up with the Estremadura favourite, known as *açorda de mariscos.* Less economical but equally inventive is the Serra da Estrela

recipe, which involves braising duck with bacon and rice; or smothering red mullet, the Setúbal way, with tiny tart oranges; or scrambling flakes of salt cod with eggs and shoestring potatoes, as is done all over the country.

Cod country

Dried salt cod, or *bacalhau* (pronounced buckle-yow), is a purely Portuguese invention. António M. Bello, first president of Portugal's gastronomic society, wrote in his *Culinária Portuguesa,* published in Lisbon in 1936, that the Portuguese were fishing Newfoundland's Grand Banks for cod within just a few years of Columbus's discovery of America.

FAR LEFT: sausages spice up many soups and stews.
LEFT: chillis and garlic are essential ingredients.
ABOVE: *bacalhau à Gomes de sá,* a classic dish.

The cod-fishing continues today, with the men putting to sea in spring and not returning until autumn. Sometimes, of course, they do not return; to see their widows dressed in black, some of them barely 20 years old, is to understand why so many of Portugal's poems, stories, folk sayings, and *fado* songs focus on the nation's bittersweet seafaring tradition:

> *O waves from the salty sea,*
> *From whence comes your salt?*
> *From the tears shed on the*
> *Beaches of Portugal.*

It was in the 16th century that Portuguese fishermen learned to salt cod at sea to make it last the long voyage home, and to sun-dry it into board-stiff slabs that could be kept for months then soaked in cool water before cooking.

Cod is still sun-dried on racks in the old way on the beach at Nazaré, although much less of it is available now. The Grand Banks have become so over-fished that the Portuguese have taken to importing *bacalhau* from Norway just to be able to meet their annual demands. This of course prices salt cod – once an inexpensive staple of the national diet – beyond the reach of the very people it sustained for centuries.

Someone once said that the Portuguese live on dreams and subsist on salt cod. They do

SARDINE SEASON

Nearly as popular as salt cod are the sardines netted off the Atlantic coast. These are what the fishermen of Nazaré go out looking for day after day – although the men are less likely now to wear their traditional tartan, and the flat-bottomed boats have mostly given way to motorised craft. Portuguese sardines are considered the sweetest and fattest in the world, and local women grill them right on the streets in every town and village, using little terracotta braziers. But you will only see this going on in spring, summer and early autumn, the "sardine season". As every right-minded Portuguese knows, sardines are too bony to eat from November to April.

claim to know 365 ways to prepare it, one for each day of the year. The best and most famous dishes are *bacalhau à Gomes de sá* (cod cooked in a casserole with thinly sliced potatoes and onions, garnished with hard-boiled eggs and black olives), *bacalhau à brás* and *bacalhau dourado* (two similar recipes composed of scrambled eggs, onions and shoestring potatoes), *bacalhau à Conde de Guarda* (salt cod creamed with mashed potatoes) and *bolinhos de bacalhau* (cod fish balls, a very popular hors d'oeuvre). All these once-humble recipes are served today in the most expensive restaurants. Prepared properly they are delicious but if too little care is taken they can be very salty.

King carne

If salt cod and sardines share top billing as the favourite fish, pork reigns supreme as the king of *carne* (meat). Portuguese pork is incomparably sweet and tender because of the pigs' agreeable diet and life of leisure. In the northerly Trás-os-Montes province, they say that if you want good pork in the autumn you must feed your pigs twice a day in August. Some farm women even go so far as to cook potatoes for their animals.

Small wonder the hams *(presunto* and *fiambre)* and sausages *(salsichas)* are so highly prized here (the best of all are said to come

with baby clams, still in the shell. The clams open slowly under the gentle heat, spilling their briny juices into the ambrosial red mixture. The secret behind achieving the distinctive nut-like flavour of Alentejo pork is that the pigs are turned loose each autumn to forage among the cork oaks. Here they nibble on acorns and wild herbs, as well as the occasional truffle.

Sausage-making is also highly-prized in the Alentejo, and this region's garlicky *chouriços, linguiças, farinheiras* (sausages plumped up with cereal) and chunky, smoky *paios* are without peers. As one of Portugal's food authorities, Maria de Lourdes Modesto, writes in

from Chaves). Small wonder, too, that *charcuterie* figures so prominently in the regional soups and stews. Cooks here will wrap freshly-caught brook trout in slices of *presunto,* then bounce them in and out of a skillet so hot the ham is transformed to a crisp, deeply smoky sort of pastry.

But Portugal's most famous pork dish comes from the Alentejo. It's *porco à alentejana,* for which cubes of pork are marinated in a paste of sweet red peppers and garlic, browned in the fruity local olive oil, then covered and braised

Cozinha Tradicional Portuguesa, "The grand destiny of the pig in the Alentejo is to become sausage".

Here, every part of the pig is used – ears, snout, tail, feet – even, it would seem, the squeal. At carnival time, for example, the centrepiece of each banquet festa is *pezinhos de porco de coentrada,* dainty pigs' feet braised with onions, garlic and fresh coriander.

Another province famous for its pork is the coastal Beira Litoral, particularly the little town of Mealhada, which is not much more than a wide place in the road about 20 km (12 miles) north of Coimbra. Here both sides of the highway are lined with restaurants that make suck-

LEFT: the fish market in Setúbal.
ABOVE: *carne de porco à alentejana.*

ling pig *(leitão assado)* a speciality. The piglets are rubbed with secret blends of oil and herbs, skewered from head to tail, then spit-roasted over white-hot hardwood coals until their skin is as crisply brittle as an onion's and their milk-white flesh so meltingly tender it falls from the bones at the touch of a fork.

Cabbage patch

The Portuguese national dish, ironically, is built neither upon salt cod nor pork. Its key ingredient is cabbage, specifically a richly emerald, tender-leafed variety *(couve galega)*. The dish itself is called *caldo verde,* a bracing, jade-green soup which is brimming with potatoes, onion, garlic and filament-thin shreds of green cabbage. Sometimes the soup may be fortified with slices of *chouriço* or *linguiça,* although in the humblest Minho versions (it's here that the recipe originated), it often contains nothing more than water, potatoes, onion, garlic, cabbage (of course) and perhaps a tablespoon or two of robust olive oil.

To some people, "robust" may seem a bit of a euphemism. Portuguese olive oil, *azeite,* is richly aromatic – and far too strong for some unaccustomed palates. The distinctive flavour comes from the harvesting methods. The festive

December olive harvest is a casual event. The olives, once beaten down from their branches, are left to age lying on the ground for a week or so. That, in addition to the hot-water pressing methods, accounts for their intense flavour.

Every Portuguese province now calls *caldo verde* its own, and it's not unusual to find kettles of it steaming in every kitchen. Indeed, *caldo verde* is such a staple of the Portuguese diet that plastic bags of minutely shredded *couve galega,* ready to drop into the pots of potato broth bubbling at home, can be bought at Lisbon's Mercado da Ribeira and other markets – the ultimate in convenience food.

The preparation of *couve galega* is something every country girl learns by the time she's grown head-high to the kitchen table. The trick is to shred it with the speed of light: the leaves are stacked, perhaps five or six deep, rolled into a fat cigar, then literally shaved as a razor-sharp knife is whisked back and forth across the end of the cabbage roll so fast the movements are scarcely visible. The fineness of the cut is what makes a bowl of *caldo verde* resemble molten jade; also the cabbage is tossed into the pot just minutes before serving so that its colour intensifies but does not turn to a paler shade.

Soups and stews

The food of Portugal has often been referred to as the food of farmers and fishermen. Fishermen brew giant drums of *caldeirada* (literally, "kettle of fish") on the beaches at Sesimbra, Nazaré, Albufeira and Sagres, beginning with water (sometimes sea water), adding tomatoes, onions and garlic, then white and oily fish in roughly equal proportions, and if their catch has been especially good, squid or octopus, too. No two *caldeiradas* are ever alike. One of the pleasures of visiting a deserted beach in Portugal is the chance of running into a group of fishermen cooking their latest catch. They're nearly always willing to share.

Farmers' soups and stews are ever-changing, too, as country women improvise with odds and ends – a bit of chicken from the Sunday dinner, a few *favas* (beans) left over from lunch, a handful of carrots, a sprinkle of rice, some crumbs of yesterday's bread, and maybe some freshly minced coriander. This is the way many of Portugal's great recipes were created.

Next to *caldo verde,* Portugal's most famous soup is probably *açorda à alentejana,* a coriander-strewn, bread-thickened, egg-drop soup seasoned, as someone once remarked, "with enough garlic to blow a safe". The soups and stews of Portugal – whether they're made of chick-peas and spinach (another Alentejo classic), of tomatoes and eggs (a Madeira speciality), of pumpkins and onions (a Trás-os-Montes staple), or of dried white beans and sausages (the universally beloved *feijoadas*) – are frugal and filling, nourishing and soul-satisfying. All they need for accompaniment are a glass of wine, a chunk of cheese and a crust of bread.

LEFT: making bread the traditional way in the Algarve.
RIGHT: sweet fried dough is sold on street corners.

Bread and cheese

Does any country bake better bread than Portugal? The simple country breads usually contain only the usual four ingredients – flour milled from hard wheat, water, yeast and salt – but they're kneaded until their dough fairly springs to life. And because they're baked in wood-stoked brick or stone ovens, they have a faintly smoky flavour. There are fancier breads, to be sure, notably the sweet festival breads, the *pão doce* of Easter and the fruit-studded *bolo rei* of Christmas. There are huskier breads, too, the rough round barley breads and, most famous of all, the *broas* – yeast-raised corn-

breads of the Minho that are sold by the truckload at the market in the river town of Barcelos.

Barcelos' country market is Portugal's biggest and best. Held every Thursday in a vast tree-shaded square, it's divided into quadrants: one for breads, cakes and other baked goods; one for fresh produce (everything from potatoes to poultry); one for farm and wine-making equipment; and the fourth for the lace tablecloths, fancifully painted brown pottery and exuberantly decorated ceramic roosters of the region.

Cheeses can be bought at country markets everywhere. The queen of them all is the ivory-hued *queijo da serra,* a cheese so strictly demarcated it can be made only from the milk of sheep grazing on the wild mountain herbs of the Serra da Estrela. At the peak of its season – winter – a properly ripened *serra* is as biting, buttery and runny as the finest Brie.

Portugal also produces a number of other cheeses that are a match for the world's best: the nutty, semi-dry *serpa* from the Alentejo town of the same name, which connoisseurs rank as the nation's second best (it's cured in caves and brushed regularly with paprika-laced olive oil); *beja,* a buttery semi-hard cheese from Beja, near Serpa; *azeitão,* lovely little rounds

of gold cheese, tangy and creamy, that come from the village of Azeitão on the Arrábida Peninsula just across the Tejo from Lisbon. Finally, there are the *queijos frescos*, snowy, uncured cheese much like cottage cheese, which calorie-conscious Portuguese sprinkle with cinnamon.

Egg sweets

The Moors are thought to have introduced egg sweets to Portugal during their 500-year occupation. But it was the 17th- and 18th-century nuns of Portugal who glorified them – one reason, no doubt, why so many egg sweets bear such names as "bacon from heaven" *(toucinho do céu),* "nuns' tummies" *(barriga-da-freira)* and "angel's cheeks" *(papos d'anjo).*

Regardless of their names, what the dozens of different egg sweets have in common is a prodigious use of egg yolk and sugar. Many are flavoured with cinnamon, others with lemon or orange or almonds, and each is shaped in its own traditional way: like little bundles of straw, for example, miniature haystacks, or even lamprey eel. The Portuguese so love this ugly river fish they make golden egg effigies of it for festive occasions. A ritual practised at nearly every Portuguese restaurant, whether simple or sophisticated, is the pastry cart, a glittering double-decker trolley laden with *doces de ovos* brought round at the meal's end.

Usually there are half a dozen choices – sunny little hillocks bathed in clear sugar syrup, flans decorated with cinnamon, individual goblets of rice pudding *(arroz doce)* as radiant as molten gold, flat yellow sponge cakes twirled around orange or lemon custard fillings, tiny translucent tarts *(queijadas)* and a snowy poached meringue ring known as *pudim molotov* (one of the few egg sweets made out of the whites). All are beautifully presented.

The egg sweets look irresistible but most of them are excruciatingly sweet and far too rich for contemporary non-Portuguese palates. The Portuguese, on the other hand, find that nothing complements – or follows – an egg sweet so well as a silky, syrupy wine – a vintage port, or a madeira.

But if you do choose a *doce* from the cart, you can bypass the wine, because you'll always be assured of a good cup of coffee to cut the sweetness. Coffee houses are a national institution, a gathering place morning, noon and night, which is not surprising in a country whose former colonies – Brazil and Angola – still produce some of the finest coffee beans in the world. The choice may be a *bica,* a powerful espresso-type brew, or a *café,* which is closer to standard percolated or filter coffee. Or you can order *carioca,* which is half-*café,* half-hot water; it will still be pretty strong and very good. Be aware, though, of regional variations: there are different ways of ordering coffee, depending on where you are. ❏

Left: Café A Brasileira in Lisbon.
Right: preparing the ubiquitous *caldo verde.*

WINES OF PORTUGAL

Wine-making is moving into an exciting phase. New favourites are
supplementing old reliables, and many smaller quintas *are producing quality wines*

Port wine is virtually a national emblem, and for many years the only wine (except Madeira) that many people associated with Portugal. But things are changing fast: the country's scintillating *vinhos verdes* have gained a well-deserved reputation, and there is an expanding range of excellent wines available. Under European Union (EU) regulations, closely supervised by the Instituto da Vinha e do Vinho (Vineyards and Wines), wine areas are "determined" or "demarcated" under the initials VQPRD (Quality Wines Produced in Demarcated Regions). Twenty-eight newly determined areas mean that fanciers familiar with classic Bairrada or Dão wines can look with fresh interest to *zonas vinícolas* like the exhilarating Douro, to Tomar in the Ribatejo, or the always popular Alentejo. The scene is an exciting one, but port still leads the field.

Port wine

Port wine begins life in the Upper Douro, a demarcated region whose boundaries cling to the banks of the Douro and its tributaries. A wide variety of grapes grow here: preferred reds include Tinta Roriz, Tinta Francesa (a descendant of the French Pinot Noir), Touriga Nacional and Bastardo; among the whites are Malvasia, Esgana Cão and Rabigato.

Come October, the silence on the great terraced slopes is broken when the harvest – *vindima* – begins. Groups of grape pickers, mainly women and girls, are specks in a vast landscape. Men stride the terraces carrying 50-kilo (112-lb) baskets of grapes to waiting containers. At night, in some wineries, platoons of bare-legged treaders reduce the grapes to a purple must, accompanied by an accordion and encouraged by watching, dancing girls. In other wineries, rows of shining auto-vinificators silently perform the same function.

PRECEDING PAGE: *barcos rabelos*, the clinker-built port wine boats, are still raced on the Douro.
LEFT: casks must be tended with skill and care.
RIGHT: tawny port is aged in wood for seven years.

As new vineyards are planted, modern techniques – bulldozing and dynamiting – have made expansion economically feasible. Virtually all the new area has been forged upriver, in the valleys of the Douro tributaries: the Pinhão, Tua, Torto and Távora. The regions producing the finest ports presently centre around

Pinhão, some 20 km (14 miles) east of Régua, and extend to the Spanish border.

The famous shipping firms all have their *quintas* (manor houses) in the hills of the Douro. It is here that the fermentation process takes place in autumn, interrupted by the addition of grape brandy, to create the raw, fortified wine. Young port then spends the winter at the *quinta*. In springtime, it is transported to the port lodges in Vila Nova de Gaia by truck, where it is blended and matured into a variety of styles.

In times past, the port was shipped to the lodges in the lovely *barcos rabelos,* flat-bottomed, clinker-built boats with large square sails, very similar in construction to the Viking longboats *(see page 85)*. Restored versions adorn the Douro's southern bank at Vila Nova de Gaia. During the São João *festas* in June they are raced in a lively regatta.

Vila Nova de Gaia, facing Porto, has more than 80 port lodges; many of them are open to the public. It is here that you can learn the basic differences of port styles, aided, delightfully, by sampling the product itself.

Vintage port

The most famous and most expensive of the ports is the vintage variety. Representing only

two percent of the entire annual port production, it is the jewel of Portuguese wines. It is produced from the grapes of a single harvest and is "declared" only in years when the quality is deemed extraordinary. Vintage port is bottled after just two or three years in wood. This is what distinguishes vintage from all other ports: the majority of the ageing process takes place in glass, rather than wood. From a legal standpoint, vintage port must identify itself as such – stating the name of its producer and the year of the vintage – and must carry the governmental seal. For example, the great 1963 vintage must, by law, have been bottled between 1 July 1965 and 30 June 1966.

As bottle ageing progresses, vintage port "throws" a heavy sediment as heavier particles in the wine succumb to gravity. So it is important that the wine is stored correctly: horizontally, yet at a slight incline, wine in contact with the cork. When vintage port – or any ageing red wine, for that matter – is then opened, its contents will be decanted, a simple procedure whereby the clear wine is poured away from the accumulated dregs. A properly stored bottle will facilitate this procedure.

Vintage port may be drunk as soon as 10 years after its vintage date, but most wines hit their stride after about 15 to 20 years. Classic wines were produced in 1963, 1977 and 1994; 2000 was a particularly good year when several shippers "declared". Taylor, Graham, Croft, Noval and Ferreira are some of the best-known names among a host of eminent port wine makers.

Crusted port

Crusted port differs from vintage port in that its grapes need not come from a single year, or vintage, but is mostly created from two or three different harvests. Crusted port spends extra time in wood, accelerating the maturation process. This extended ageing makes for a lighter-bodied wine. Like vintage port, however, it throws a sediment and needs to be decanted.

Late bottled port

Late bottled vintage (LBV) sees even more time in wood – from four to six years. As its name implies, the wine comes from a single year's harvest, but is much lighter in colour than vin-

---

CONFUSING *COLHEITAS*

There is a confusing offshoot of the vintage-dated wines, called "Port of the Vintage" or "Port with Date of Vintage". These wines come from a single year, but will have been aged in wood for no less than seven years. The bottle will often say *Colheitas* (which means "vintage") and give the year; it will show the date of bottling and some indication that the wine has been aged in wood.

The house of Nierport has a wonderful stock of these *Colheitas*. They are the first step into tawny ports, but the fact that they are from a single vintage prevents them legally being so titled under the strict regulations which control all aspects of port making and marketing.

tage port and need not be decanted. Both the date of the vintage and the date of bottling must appear on the label. When buying, it is worth remembering that shippers generally do not offer late bottled vintage in the same years as they offer real vintage port.

Wood ports

Wood ports are the bread and butter of the port trade. They are blended wines – using grapes from several harvests – that are matured in casks until they are ready for drinking. Because they are

TASTING AND TESTING

One good place to sample various port wines is at the Solar do Vinho do Porto (near Palácio Cristal in Porto). Here you can taste port wine of almost any age and type.

usually older, and certainly more expensive.

White ports are also matured in wood. They can come from either red or white grapes: a clear wine can be obtained from red grapes by separating the juice from the skins during fermentation before the colour has been extracted. Wine-makers have tried to popularise whites by fermenting out the sugar, adding brandy, and marketing them as dry aperitif wines.

Last, but by no means least, there is tawny port, a special blend of port wine from different

blended, it is the goal of the shipper to define his style through this wine so that year after year the customer can confidently expect a consistent product. The three main types are ruby, white and tawny.

Ruby is young and hearty, not complex and not expensive. To a port drinker, it is the staple wine, attractive for its full, overt flavour. It is aged for two or three years in cask before bottling. One offshoot of ruby port is called "Vintage Character" port. It will have the same general features but will be of a higher quality,

LEFT: traditional wicker baskets are used at harvest time. **ABOVE:** treading grapes to make white port.

vintages which sees many years in cask. Through the more rapid oxidisation process within the barrel, this wine matures rather more quickly. Tawny port is thus more mellow in style than the "vintage-dated" ports, but it is refined, with a rich tawny colour and fabulously scented bouquet.

Old tawnies are rather expensive, priced in correlation to the long years the wine has spent ageing in barrel. They should not be confused with the cheap tawny port available abroad, which owes its existence to the strong world demand for a less concentrated but drinkable port wine. The port shippers have handled this demand by concocting a blend of ruby and white port. The product is a simple wine of pinkish hue, in contrast to the fading russet of a true tawny. It will have none of the complexity that real tawny port gains through long ageing. Since the name "tawny" can apply to either wine, the consumer must rely on colour and price to distinguish between the two. Real tawny is not cheap; cheap tawny should never be expensive.

Among a wide choice, Ferreira, Noval and Taylor 10-, 20- and 30-year-olds are fine examples of tawny port. Only the "real thing" will reveal why this is the wine which many port houses most prize and which many

Light and refreshing with an alcohol content of only 8 to 11 percent, *vinho verde* is made from fully matured grapes from varieties that include Azal, Trajadura, Alvarinho and Loureiro for the whites, and Brancelho, Pedral and Tinto Cão for the reds. The taste is dry, with many subtle shadings. The fizz – known as *pétillance* to wine connoisseurs, *agulha* to the Portuguese – is not added, but appears naturally during the making.

First, the grapes are fermented to convert their natural sugars into alcohol. Then a secondary fermentation, called the malolactic, takes place. Induced by naturally occurring bac-

blenders enjoy as an all-day drink (and have even been seen to add ice cubes to).

Vinho verde country

The lush, green Minho is the country's oldest and most intensively cultivated wine area, the region of *vinho verde*. The vine seems to be everywhere – along narrow roads, framing houses with pretty bowers called *ramadas,* across new, neat plantations of *cruzetas,* crosses with wire supports a tractor can reach, and still, in places, clinging to tall trees – though *vinho verde* does not, as a cheerful promotion had it, grow on trees. Nor, as its name suggests, is *vinho verde* a green wine.

teria, this converts malic acid to lactic; a harsher, rather unpleasant acid into a milder, more palatable one.

While this secondary fermentation is common to wines made in many countries, the *vinhos verdes* are distinguished by their retention of the fermentation's by-product: carbon dioxide. From this comes that characteristic sparkle in the wine, which can vary, depending upon age, technique and storage, from a light tingle on the tongue to a spritely carbonation, the hallmark of *vinhos verdes*.

The *vinho verde* region was demarcated in 1908, and has six sub-zones. The differences

Much admired among single-estate wines is the Palácio da Brejoeira *vinho verde* produced from a single grape variety, Alvarinho, in Monção. It is also the most expensive. You can, though, taste a good, and cheaper Alvarinho made by the Adega Cooperativa of Monção.

Wine regions

Truly superb wines, a few eccentric and many sublime, are to be found in Portugal. From the once-cherished Dão area, which in recent years has tumbled from its pedestal, comes Caves São João's good red Porto dos Cavaleiros (its Reserva among the very best Dão wines) or the

in the wine's taste from grower to grower reflect location and climate, as well as the grape itself, but also result from the increasing number of single-estate producers in recent years.

Notable estate-made *vinhos verdes* come from over 50 members of the Association of Producers and Bottlers of Vinho Verde who must produce wine only from their own grapes (not buy them, as bulk producers do). The result is a range of wines produced in small quantities but with individual characteristics.

LEFT: grape pulp from an auto-vinificator in Pinhão.
ABOVE: a rich harvest of grapes on their way to becoming *vinho verde*.

Sogrape Dão Reserva; and, from Sogrape's technologically advanced winery, the old favourites Grão Vasco and Terras Altas.

Bairrada, a small area north of Coimbra, has held its reputation for classic wines, more than 80 percent red, mainly from the Baga grape. The whites include a pleasant espumante, or sparkling wine. Good Bairrada wines are made by Sogrape, Messias and Caves Aliança.

For something really special, head for the bizarre and extravagant neo-Manueline Palace Hotel do Buçaco *(see page 267),* whose cellar of its own Buçaco wines, dating from the 1920s, is virtually a national treasure. Reasons to visit this unusual palace are numerous – the forest is enchanting, historical aspects intriguing, and you can stay in the suite occupied by the last king of Portugal. But if wine is your pleasure, and you have the resources, you can luxuriate for days eating classy food and sampling 30-year-old whites and 40-year-old reds.

You can also taste perfectly good Bairrada wines at the cluster of down-to-earth roadside restaurants that can be found in nearby Mealhada, all offering the local speciality, *leitão*, suckling pig.

The Douro is the source of many of Portugal's finest table wines (even in the port region only 40 percent of the grapes go into port).

Ferreira, a distinguished port wine producer, also makes the renowned Barca Velha, probably the finest of all Portugal's red wines. Other Ferreira reds include their Reserva Especial or the more accessible Esteva. Top-ranking Douro wines also include those under the Quinta do Cotto label – Grande Escolha is one. As in other areas, Sogrape are conspicuous – Planalto is just one of their good Douro wines. Adriano Ramos Pinto produce the really excellent Duas Quintas red.

Closer to the capital

From nearer to Lisbon comes a variety of good wines – the white from Bucelas is a consistent favourite. Pleasant wines, too, come from the Colares area, just beyond Sintra, which is particularly interesting as its rootstocks are among the few survivors of the phylloxera plague *(see below left)*.

To the south of Lisbon two major wineries, confusingly with very similar names, are in Azeitão, near Setúbal (both are open to the public). One, José Maria da Fonseca, makes a very popular red Periquita and the excellent dry Branco Seco. If you care for sweet muscatel dessert wines, you might like to try the Moscatel de Setúbal.

The second and more modern winery is J.M. Fonseca International, widely known for its very successful Lancer's red, white and rosé, sold in their distinctive clay jars. Two eminent wines from the Setúbal area are João Pires, and the deep red from the Quinta de Bacalhoa, both developed by the skills of Australian oenologist, Peter Bright.

Wines from Portugal's southernmost province, Algarve, are largely consumed on the spot but they should not be dismissed and many are improving. Look out for a souvenir bottle of Vida Nova ("new life") from Sir Cliff Richard's Quinta do Moinha, launched in 2001. A range of good quality wines are made in the eastern Alentejo in such towns as Borba, Reguengos and Vidigueira, which produce a very good white *reserva*. Look, too, for the deep red and distinctive Esporão. In good Lisbon restaurants you will very likely be recommended an Alentejo red, rather than the more usual white, if you choose any variety of *bacalhau* (salt cod). ❏

PHYLLOXERA

Phylloxera was a devastating disease which hit European vineyards in the last quarter of the 19th century. It was caused by an unpleasant louse, which found its way to Europe from America, where it bred and fed, unseen at first, on the roots of the vines, which gradually withered and died. The disease wiped out many vineyards and caused severe hardship to growers. Eventually, it was found that grafting indigenous vines onto imported American stock – which was resistant to the louse – would ensure healthy plants, and the industry began to recover. Today's rootstocks are the American ones, and there has been no recurrence of the disease.

LEFT: Sir Cliff celebrates the first vintage of his Vida Nova wine.

Port Dynasties

In a technological age there are few trades where heritage and family ties are a matter of pride. Port is one of them, a commerce with its roots in the wild upper reaches of northern Portugal's Douro valley, a wine region that has had virtually the same frontiers since the Marquês de Pombal defined them in 1756.

At the time, the reforming Pombal, who felt a hearty dislike for the British and their leading role in Portuguese trade, was determined to restrict the hold they had had on the area ever since the Methuen Treaty of 1703 had established their dominance of the industry. In subsequent centuries, port has improved immeasurably in quality and the profits are more evenly spread. But although snobbish exclusivity is long gone, the British are still very much part of the port scene.

The British association with port is long and eventful – although these days the French buy more. British buyers enthusiastically explored the Douro valley in the 17th century. George Sandeman instructed the Duke of Wellington's troops on the finer points of port.

One of the pioneers, cartographer Joseph James Forrester, a Scot, fought tirelessly for high standards and mapped every inch of the river. He was made a baron in 1855 for his efforts. It was regarded as a national tragedy when, in May 1862, Forrester's boat overturned and he drowned in the Douro. He was travelling between various wine-growing *quintas*, paying the farmers in gold coins, and it is said that it was his money-belt, heavy with gold, which helped to drag him down.

A survivor of the tragedy was another outstanding personality in the saga of port: Dona Antónia Adelaide Ferreira, whose vineyards covered huge areas of the Douro.

These and other colourful characters are familiar to everyone in the business. The founders of the port wine trade are ever-present, their faces and names on port wine labels. Many rival companies have inter-family links. Their names, however, can be deceptive: for all its English ring, Cockburn Smithes has had a Portuguese managing director for many years.

But at Taylor, Fladgate & Yeatman (founded in 1692), the managing director is descended from

a Yeatman, and the company's taster has Fladgate ancestors. The company also owns Fonseca Guimaraens whose technical director is David Guimaraens, sixth generation of the founder of the firm. Delaforce and Ferreira both have eighth-generation family members closely involved in the business.

Inescapable since the 1800s is the name of Symington. The family owns and manages a distinguished list of companies: Warre's (founded in the 1670s), Silva & Cosens (whose brand is Dow), Quarles Harris, Smith Woodhouse, and Graham's. In the 1990s two generations and eight members of the Symington family were still involved in man-

agement, production, sales and marketing of the fine ports made by these independent companies. The family has, more recently, become prominent in promoting the re-emergence of much under-rated Madeira wine.

The wine shippers still meet at lunch on Wednesdays in the Feitoria Inglesa or 'English Factory House' in Porto to discuss business and sample a good vintage following the meal.

Efficient modern methods are used in the wine industry these days but technology blends smoothly with tradition. Even the Symingtons' Gaia offices hold echoes of port's memorable past: they are in Travessa do Barão Forrester, in the very house where Baron Forrester once lived. ❑

RIGHT: Francisco Olazaba of Ferreira, with traditional baskets of harvested grapes at Quinta do Seixho.

FESTIVALS FOR ALL SEASONS

You can't go far in Portugal without stumbling across a festival – colourful occasions which demonstrate a national talent for celebration

On almost every weekend throughout the year there will be a festival taking place somewhere in Portugal. Saints' days are the biggest single stimulus for holding a *festa*, and every village and town in the country enjoys the protection of a patron saint. *Romarios* are generally more sober affairs with a greater religious dimension. Plenty of these take place too, especially at Easter time.

There are other causes for celebration, some of them distinctly pagan, but there will invariably be a strong religious element, even if this is lightened, as it usually is, with feasting and decidedly secular revelry.

All these events involve a vast amount of work and planning. Committees must be formed, fund-raising events held, and local authorities involved. Routes must be planned, traffic diverted and streets colourfully decorated. When the big day arrives, it all seems worthwhile. Crowds gather to watch the parades starting out from the local church. Flower-decorated religious tableaux, saints, virgins and icons are carried in solemn procession with music provided by local bands. With the procession over, celebrations start in earnest, with eating and drinking, music and dancing and general merrymaking. A fitting climax, bringing everything to a close, is usually provided by a spectacular and very noisy firework display.

◁ **ALTE, ALGARVE**
This May Day folk festival in Alte features processions and dancers in regional costumes.

△ **VILA FRANCA DO LIMA**
At the Festas da Senhora das Rosas, richly costumed women carry huge constructions of rose petals and flowers on their heads.

◁ **STREET DISPLAYS**
Lavish street decorations raise the profile of any good *festa*. These, in Serpa, Alentejo, are in honour of Nuestra Senhora da Guadaloupe.

△ **AUGUST CELEBRATIONS**
Nossa Senhora da Agonia in Viana do Castelo, one of Portugal's biggest festivals, celebrates the Virgin Mary with a colourful display of national costumes.

REGIONAL CELEBRATIONS

It is not a question of see one festival and you've seen them all. Many are unusual and unique to a particular region. At Miranda do Douro, Trás-os-Montes, stick dances are performed to the music of bagpipes, cymbals and drums (15 August); and in Amarante (early June) young men offer phallus-shaped cakes as tokens of love to the young ladies in celebration of São Gonçalo, the patron saint of love and marriage. Others are simpler affairs, where the fringe activities, such as biscuit-eating competitions *(above)* are as popular as the main attraction.

Lisbon hosts several lively festivals: one of the biggest is Festas dos Santos Populares in June, which celebrates Saints Anthony, John and Peter, and takes place in Alfama. The liveliest night is 12 June, when thousands gather to eat sardines, drink vast amounts of wine and join in the singing and dancing until late.

▷ **FESTAS DAS CRUZES**
The Festas das Cruzes in Barcelos commemorates the Miracle of the Cross each May, with much pomp and ceremony.

▷ **FIREMEN ON PARADE**
The whole community takes part in local *festas*, especially in smaller villages. In Almoçageme the *bombeiros*, the voluntary fire brigade, parade in full dress uniform.

▷ **MONÇAO**
Corpus Cristi celebrations in Monçao in mid-June start with a procession led by a "blessed ox" and finish with a lively skirmish between good and evil which is reminiscent of the battle of St George and the dragon.

THE HISTORY OF ARCHITECTURE

Some of Portugal's finest architecture is found in its religious buildings,
but the wealth from the Age of Discoveries also left a legacy of fine palaces

Portugal's unusual geographical position, cut off from Europe by Spain on one side, facing the New World on the other, is reflected in its architecture. The country's architects have always looked outside for influence and affirmation, and local traditions have blended harmoniously with imported ideas.

Romanesque

The story of Portuguese architecture really begins in the Romanesque period of the 12th century, when nearly all buildings of any importance were religious ones. This was the time when the kingdom was founded, when Portugal was (largely) reconquered from the Moors, and Christianity was strongly felt. The construction of cathedrals followed the path of reconquest from Braga to Porto, southwards to Coimbra, Lamego, Lisbon and Évora.

In the north, Romanesque-style churches continued to be built well into the 14th century, when the Gothic style was already spreading throughout the rest of the country. Portuguese Romanesque is an architecture of simple, often dramatically stark forms, whose sturdiness is frequently explained by the need for fortification against the continued threat of Moorish or Castilian invasion. This fortified appearance is enhanced in the cathedrals of Lisbon and Coimbra by the crenellated façade towers.

Most of these buildings are of granite. The hardness of this material renders detailed carving impossible, thus favouring a simplicity of form. In areas where the softer limestone abounds, such as the central belt of the country (including Coimbra, Tomar and Lisbon), carved decorations are more common.

These Romanesque churches share a certain robustness; a method of construction based on semi-circular arches and barrel vaults; a cruciform plan; and a solid, almost sculptural sense

of form in the interior which allows for a play of light and shade. This sobriety is accentuated by the paucity of decoration, which is frequently reduced to the capitals of columns and the archivolts surrounding the portals. When the tympana are not bare, the simplified carvings are usually stylised depictions of Christ in

Majesty, or the *Agnus Dei* (Lamb of God), or simply of a cross. In some cases, animals and serpents climb up the granite columns, as in the *Sé Velha* (Old Cathedral) of Coimbra or in the unusually richly decorated principal portal of the early 13th-century church of São Salvador, in Bravães in the Minho.

Gothic

In France, new methods of construction involving pointed arches and ribbed vaults allowed for lighter, taller architectural forms. As the main weight of the building was now borne outside at fixed points by flying buttresses, the walls could be pierced at frequent intervals. The

---

PRECEDING PAGES: exquisite ceiling in the Igreja dos Paulistas, Bairro Alto, Lisbon.
LEFT: the Unfinished Chapel at Batalha.
RIGHT: the Romanesque Old Cathedral in Coimbra.

light filtering into these Gothic interiors became a metaphor for Divine Light, replacing the Romanesque emphasis on Mystery.

The first building in Portugal to use these new construction methods was the majestic church of the abbey of Alcobaça, commissioned by Afonso Henriques. With its great height and elegant, unadorned white interior bathed in a milky light, Alcobaça is one of the most serene and beautiful churches in Portugal. Begun in 1178 and consecrated in 1222, it is almost purely French in inspiration: its plan echoes that of Clairvaux, the seat of the Cistercian Order in Burgundy – a nave and two side aisles of almost the same height, a two-aisled transept, and an apse whose ambulatory fans out into chapels.

The apogee of the national Gothic style came after the Portuguese armies defeated the invading Castilians at the Battle of Aljubarrota. In fulfilment of a religious vow made prior to the battle, King João I commissioned the construction in 1388 of the Dominican Monastery of Santa Maria da Vitória (St Mary of the Victory), better known as Batalha, which simply means battle.

The stylistic influence of Batalha is seen in various churches throughout the country, such

as the cathedral at Guarda and the now-ruined Carmo church in Lisbon, which were both begun at the end of the 14th century.

Generally speaking, Portuguese Gothic leaned towards temperance rather than flamboyance, a reflection of the austerity imposed by the mendicant orders and, perhaps, the sombre streak in the national character.

BUILDING BATALHA

Batalha's construction can be divided into three stages.
1. The first phase ran from 1388 to 1438, when the central nave, with simple ribbing supporting the vault, was built. The Founder's Chapel and the chapterhouse vault have a greater refinement and elegance, influenced by English Gothic. Contact with England was close at this time as João I's wife, Philippa of Lancaster, was the daughter of John of Gaunt.
2. During the second stage, which lasted until 1481, a second cloister was built.
3. The third, Manueline, phase culminated in the Arcade of the Unfinished Chapels and the Royal Cloister.

The Manueline style

The exhilaration of Portugal's overseas discoveries had a marked effect on art, architecture and literature. The term "Manueline" was first used in the 19th century to refer to the reign of Manuel I (1495–1521), during which Vasco da

Gama reached the coast of India (1498), and Afonso de Albuquerque conquered the Indian city of Goa (1510). The term is now used more often to refer to certain stylistic features predominant during the Avis dynasty (1383–1580), especially in architecture.

Manueline architecture does not have major innovative structural features – the twisted columns, such as those at the Church of Jesus in Setúbal, perform the same function as do plain ones. Rather, Manueline can be seen as heterogeneous late Gothic, its real innovation lying in its stone decoration, the exuberance of which reflects the optimism and wealth of the period.

nave. Perhaps the most notable feature of Manueline architecture is the copious carving that surrounds portals and semi-circular windows. The imposing southern portal of Jerónimos, together with the window of the chapterhouse at the Convent of Christ in Tomar, well deserve the acclaim that they both receive. Construction on the Tomar window began much earlier, in the 12th century, along with the Templar Charola – a chapel with a circular floor plan. During the 16th century, the convent buildings, including four cloisters, were added. The lavish Manueline decoration of the church culminates in the famous window,

Inspired by the voyages to the New World, it is ornate and imposing, uniting naturalistic maritime themes with Moorish elements and heraldic motifs: during the reign of Manuel I, the king's own emblems are usually included – as they were in the churches built in the newly discovered overseas territories.

The Monastery of Santa Maria de Belém in Lisbon, which is better known as Jerónimos, is one of the great hall churches of the period – that is, a church whose aisles are as high as its

which is designed with two great ship's masts on either side, covered with carvings, topped, like the southern portal at Jerónimos, by the cross of the Order of Christ.

Manueline architecture also adopted and modified certain Moorish *(morisco)* features. At the Palácio Nacional at Sintra, for example, restored during Manuel's reign, *morisco* features include the use of tiles, merlons, and windows divided in two by columns. Another important *morisco* feature is the horseshoe arch, which can be seen in the chapterhouse of the Convent of Lóios in Évora. In Alentejo, many provincial palaces have *morisco* decoration, including lattice-work ceilings and chimneys.

FAR LEFT: a portal in the lovely Gothic abbey at Alcobaça. **LEFT:** Manueline archway at Monchique. **ABOVE:** the graceful cloister of Jerónimos Monastery.

Renaissance and Mannerism

The Renaissance has been described as a narrow bridge crossed the moment it was reached. This was certainly the case in Portugal. In their art and architecture, the Portuguese shied away from Renaissance rationalism, instead inclining towards naturalism or towards the drama of the baroque.

The Renaissance in Portugal, then, was best represented by foreign artists. Foreign sculptors were frequently invited to decorate the portals and façades of Manueline buildings, introducing elements of Renaissance harmony and order within the general flamboyance of

in Tomar, Torralva's Great Cloister at the Convent of Christ evokes the balance and harmony of Palladian classicism. Many years after Torralva's death in 1566, this majestic cloister was completed by the prestigious Italian architect Filippo Terzi, a specialist in military architecture who had been invited by Philip II of Spain (who became king of Portugal in 1581).

Azulejos

Azulejos, the painted ceramic tiles so familiar to visitors to Portugal, were one of the major features of the 17th century. First used in the 15th century, they gained ground during the next 100

the Manueline decorative scheme. The coincidence of Manueline and Renaissance influences, and later of Renaissance and Mannerist forms, explains the hybrid style prevalent during this period. Mannerism uses elements of Renaissance classicism but the sense of an ordered, harmonious whole gives way to an exaggeration of these elements.

The Spaniard Diogo de Torralva is thought to have been responsible for one of the finest examples of Renaissance design in the Iberian peninsula – the Chapel of Nossa Senhora da Conceição (Our Lady of the Conception) in Tomar (*circa* 1530–40), with its simple exterior and diffusely lit, barrel-vaulted interior. Also

years, and by the 17th century, when economic conditions permitted extensive restoration and reconstruction, they were virtually indispensable. Vast decorative schemes of tiled panels filled churches and palaces, but the *azulejos* were put to good use in humbler settings, such as kitchens and stairways, as well.

In addition to murals (for which *azulejos* were most commonly used), there were small floral panels, or single tiles adorned – in the Dutch style – with birds, flowers and human figures. The Paláçio of Queluz (*see page 181*) is a fine example of the use of *azulejos* in garden design. (See pages 170–71 for a special feature on *azulejos*.)

Baroque

The baroque is considered to be the stylistic range which, although it uses a basic classical vocabulary, strives for dissolution of form rather than definition. Emphasis is given to motion, to the state of becoming rather than being. This obliteration of clear contours – whether by brushstrokes in painting or as an optical illusion in sculpture and architecture – is further enhanced by a preference for depth over plane. These features all stress the grand, the dynamic and the dramatic.

The first truly baroque Portuguese church is Santa Engrácia in Lisbon, with its dome and undulating interior walls. This building, begun in 1682, was not completed until 1966. The richness of the coloured marble lining the walls and floor, the dynamic interior space, and the general sumptuousness of the edifice are typical of construction during the reign of João V (1706–50), known as João o Magnânimo.

The wealth from Brazil and the extravagance of João V made the early 18th century a period of great opulence. He was the king who commissioned the Chapel of St John the Baptist at the Church of São Roque in Lisbon. The entire chapel was built in Rome, blessed by the Pope, shipped to Lisbon and reassembled in the church, where it shines with bronzes, mosaics, rare marble and precious stones.

In the north of the country the major centres for the development of the baroque were Porto and Braga. Here, the influence of the Tuscan architect-decorator Nicolau Nasoni, who came to Portugal in 1725, predominated. He introduced a greater buoyancy and elegance, and rich contrasts of light and shade. He incorporated local characteristics as well: his elliptical-naved Church of Clérigos in Porto had no successor. But his secular buildings, such as the Freixo Palace in the same city, with their interplay of whitewash and granite, established a large following.

The gleaming Basilica da Estrêla in Lisbon, dating from the 1780s and commissioned by Maria I, was the last church to be built in the baroque Grand Style. By then, architectural styles had moved on and, with the dissolution

of the monastic orders in 1834, religious architecture lost its privileged position in Portugal.

Rococo

In the rococo style, drama was replaced by fantasy, and an emphasis on flourish, sensuality and ornament. The chapel of Santa Madalena in Falperra is a good early example of the style. Rococo was also marked by a growing interest in landscaping. The type of church represented by Bom Jesus in Braga became popular: surrounded by gardens it sits atop a hill and is reached by a sweeping succession of stairways which at a distance seem to cascade downward.

FAR LEFT: the baroque church of Nossa Senhora dos Remédios in Lamego (1750–60).
LEFT: *azulejos* adorn a façade in Alfama, Lisbon.
RIGHT: Rua D'Oura Totta, part of "Pombaline Lisbon".

In Lisbon the rococo was more sober than in the north. After the earthquake of 1755, Carlos Mardel designed many of the city's public fountains in a toned-down version of rococo, including those of Rua do Século and Largo da Esperança. Mardel was also responsible for part of the Aguas Livres Aqueduct, which withstood the earthquake, and is still a familiar landmark.

Neo-classicism

Although it took place at much the same time, the Pombaline style of the reconstruction of Lisbon – named after Marquês de Pombal *(see page 119)* – is closer in many respects to clas-

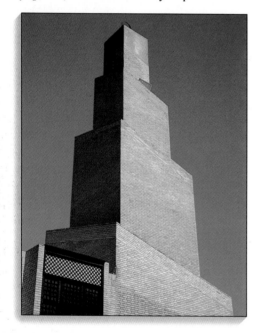

sical models than to the rococo constructions in the north. The neo-classical style proper, with its emphasis on Greco-Roman colonnades and porticoes, was introduced to Lisbon in the last decade of the 18th century. It received court approval when used for the Royal Palace of Ajuda (begun in 1802 and never completed), after a fire destroyed the wooden building that had been the temporary royal residence since the earthquake.

After the construction of this palace, perhaps the only noteworthy public building to be built in Lisbon in the first half of the 19th century was the Theatre of Dona Maria II (1843), with its white Greco-Roman façade. The dissolution of the monasteries had a negative effect on the development of large-scale public buildings, as well as on religious architecture.

The middle-class ambience of Porto proved fertile ground for conservative neo-classicism to take root. It was favoured by the English community connected with the port industry, perhaps because of its affinities with the work of Scottish architect Robert Adam (1728–92). The British consul, Sir John Whitehead, commissioned the Feitoria Inglesa in Porto, and the Hospital of Santo António, perhaps the finest neo-classical buildings in the country.

Romanticisim

If neo-classical art and architecture represented an escape from the turmoils of the present into a restrained, harmonious classical ideal, another form of escapism was an important ingredient of Romanticism. It was typified by flights into medievalism and orientalism, or into altered-states of dreams and madness.

The most extraordinary architectural manifestation of this was the Pena Palace in Sintra (commissioned by Prince Ferdinand of Saxe-Coburg-Gotha, consort of Maria II, in around 1840). The building is a strange mix of medieval and oriental forms, including Manueline, Moorish, Renaissance and baroque, and incorporating parts of the site's original structure – a 16th-century monastery. The result is a pastiche of English Gothic revivalism.

Modern styles

One of the best examples of Portuguese architecture from the first half of the 20th century is the art deco Casa Serralves in Porto (now a museum); while a distinctive post-war style commenced with the construction of the Gulbenkian Museum in the 1950s. More recently, Porto architects such as Fernando Távora and Alvaro Siza have established solid reputations: the rebuilding of the Chiado district after Lisbon's 1988 fire was entrusted to the latter. The post-modernist work of Tomás Taveira is also notable in Lisbon, particularly his office towers at the Amoreiras. And Expo '98 produced some stunning modern pavilions, many of which have become government offices. ❑

LEFT: Portugal has major modern landmarks, too, such as the mosque in Lisbon's Avenidas Novas. **RIGHT:** the flamboyant Pena Palace, Sintra.

PORTUGUESE ART THROUGH THE AGES

From 15th-century altarpieces to modernist masterpieces, the country's museums, galleries and churches cover the artistic spectrum

The 15th century was the first great age of Portuguese painting. Almost no paintings from the 12th to 14th centuries have survived, although frescoes were certainly painted in churches. One interesting, rare example of an early 15th-century fresco is a surviving fragment from a secular painting – the allegory of justice entitled *O Bom e o Mau Juiz* ("The Good and the Bad Judge") in a Gothic house in the town of Monsaráz.

The most notable surviving religious fresco of the same period is the *Senhora da Rosa* in the sumptuous Church of São Francisco in Porto. It has been attributed to an Italian painter, António Florentino, who, it is thought, may also have painted the portrait of João I now at the Museu Nacional de Arte Antiga in Lisbon

By far the most brilliant contribution to painting during this period was the introduction of Flemish-influenced painted altarpieces called retables (*retábulos* in Portuguese). In 1428, the Flemish master Jan van Eyck was invited to the court of João I to paint a portrait of the Infanta Dona Isabel, future wife of Philip the Good (1396–1467), Duke of Burgundy. The Netherlands were, at the time, under the control of the dukes of Burgundy who were renowned for their excellent taste in art. When the Flemish artists turned from illumination to the painting of altarpieces, they added to their own love of realistic detail the Burgundian passion for gemlike decoration.

The polyptych of St Vincent

The most outstanding *retábulo* of the 15th-century Portuguese School is the polyptych of St Vincent attributed to Nuno Gonçalves, in Lisbon's Museu Nacional de Arte Antiga. The mystery that enshrouds this work has increased

LEFT: detail from Nuno Gonçalves' *The Adoration of St Vincent* polyptych, a 15th-century masterpiece.
RIGHT: detail from the same altarpiece *(retábulo)*, showing Henry the Navigator and the future João II.

its aura. The panels were lost for centuries, and there are conflicting accounts of their reappearance at the end of the 19th century. No sooner were they cleaned and hung publicly than an angry controversy arose as to the identity of their author as well as of the figures depicted. A touch of drama was added when one eminent scholar committed suicide after a dispute concerning two documents which radically altered the direction of the research. The documents were later proved false.

The theme of the polyptych has also given rise to dispute. Some see in it the veneration of the Infante Santo Fernando, the uncle of Afonso V, who died at the hands of the Moors. But nowadays it is generally thought to represent the adoration of St Vincent, the patron saint of the kingdom and of the city of Lisbon. The important point of departure was the identification of the Infante Henrique (Prince Henry the Navigator) to the left of the saint in the third panel from the left.

The panels, from left to right, are known as the Panel of the Monks (of the Cistercian Order), the Fishermen, the Infante, the Archbishop, the Calvary and finally, the Relic Panel.

The work's real genius and originality lie in the exquisiteness of the portraiture: its masterful attention to realistic detail as well as its psychological dimension. It appears to be the visual representation of King Afonso's dreams of conquest and of the magical world of Prince Henry's navigations, blessed by the patron saint of the kingdom

The Flemish influence

During the reign of João II (1481–95), when voyages of discovery occupied the energies of the nation, there was a lull in painting activity. However, with the discovery of the sea route to India and the consequent prosperity, painted *retábulos* again became a dominant form of expression. At the end of the 15th century, Portugal was one of the largest importers of Flemish paintings. Many of the altarpieces in Portuguese churches were Flemish, and some can still be seen today, such as the *Fons Vitae* at the Misericórdia church in Porto.

Nevertheless, Portuguese painting main-

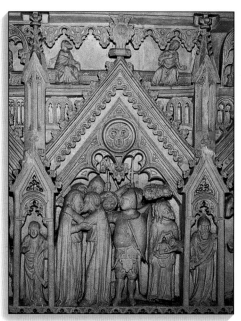

THE TOMBS OF PEDRO AND INES

While little surviving painting predates the 15th century, some lovely pieces of sculpture do. The crowning glory of 14th-century funerary sculpture are the tombs of King Pedro and his lover, Inês de Castro at Alcobaça *(see page 30 for the dramatic story of love, murder and revenge)*.

The sarcophogi do justice to the tale: the sculptor is unknown and the influences are hybrid, but the naturalistic detail and rich symbolism are unsurpassed. Inês, surrounded by angels, is crowned queen in death as she never was in life. Pedro's tomb, displays a magnificent rosette, believed to symbolise a wheel of fortune, representing life's vicissitudes.

tained local features, giving rise to the "Luso-Flemish" style. Manueline painting evolved during the reign of Manuel I (1495–1521), although the style is more closely associated with architecture (*see page 116*). It has been characterised by features such as monumentality, a fine sense of portraiture, brilliant gem-like colours, a growing interest in the naturalistic depiction of both architectural and landscape backgrounds, and an increasing preoccupation with expressive detail.

During this period painting was not the expression of an individual sensibility, but more often the collaborative effort of a master and his assistants. Attribution, then, is extremely difficult, and often paintings are known as the products of particular workshops. The two principal workshops were those of Jorge Afonso in Lisbon, and of Vasco Fernandes in Viseu. Afonso was appointed royal painter in 1508: documents identify various projects with which he and his workshop were involved, but none show his direct responsibility, although he is believed to have painted some of the panels in the rotunda of the Convento de Cristo in Tomar.

Grão Vasco

Vasco Fernandes, better known as Grão (the "Great") Vasco, is undoubtedly the most cele-

housed in the Museu Grão Vasco, Viseu) of a slightly earlier date. The stylistic differences between the two works confused scholars for some time, but it is now assumed that Flemish assistants at Lamego account for the differences. The panels for the chapels of the Viseu Cathedral (Museu also in the Grão Vasco), of which those of the Calvary and St Peter are the most renowned, are also attributed to him, but these date from his mature phase (1530–42).

Noteworthy for their emotional strength and drama, these works are also characterised by a denser application of paint than that used by the Flemish masters. Furthermore, the faces of

brated regional Manueline painter. For many years, the myth of Grão Vasco obscured his real work in a plethora of attributions – he was thought to be the author of Gothic and Renaissance paintings, although a single lifetime would not have sufficed for so large an output. But he was responsible for the altarpiece originally in the Lamego cathedral (now in the Museu Regional in that town), dated 1506–11, as well as the one for the Viseu Cathedral (now

FAR LEFT: detail from the sepulchre of Inês de Castro.
LEFT: Grão Vasco's depiction of Calvary.
ABOVE: a detail from *Calvário* by Gregório Lopes.
RIGHT: King Sebastian, by Cristovão de Morais.

the Portuguese works tend to be less stylised, more expressive, and, it would seem, often drawn from specific local models, just as the landscape backgrounds are drawn from the Beja region rather than being imaginary or purely symbolic.

The 16th and 17th centuries

As in architecture, the Renaissance, the "rebirth" of art based on classical models, was resisted by Portuguese artists and mainly represented by those from abroad. Mannerism employed many elements of Renaissance classicism but the sense of an ordered, harmonious whole gives way to an exaggeration of those defining elements. The most characteristic feature of this style is a certain elongation, together with unexpected highlighting of seemingly incidental sections of a work.

The 17th century saw the flourishing of portrait painting in Portugal as elsewhere in Europe. Perhaps the most celebrated portraitist of the period was Domingos Vieira (1600–78), known as "the Dark" to distinguish him from his contemporary Domingos Vieira Serrão. His nickname stemmed from his predilection, in works such as the portrait of Isabel de Moura (in the Museu Nacional de Arte Antiga in Lisbon), to make dramatic contrasts between the

deep, velvety backgrounds and the rich, creamy whites of ruffs and headgear.

Neo-classicism

During the 18th century, two outstanding painters emerged: Francisco Vieira, known as Vieira Portuense (1765–1805), and Domingos António Sequeira (1768–1837). The two met in Rome, which was the essential venue for any serious artist. Vieira Portuense also spent some time in London, where the classicising Roman influence was tempered by that of Sir Joshua Reynolds (1723–92).

The work of Sequeira is a study in the transition from neo-classicism to Romanticism, a

rare example of a single life encapsulating two eras. He was nominated court painter in 1802 by João VI, and was commissioned to provide paintings for the rebuilt Ajuda Palace. Political turbulence forced Sequeira to emigrate to France, and then to Italy, where he died.

His work can be divided into three stages: the first, largely academic and neo-classical in inspiration, corresponds to the first period he spent in Rome, and to his work as a court painter. The second stage (1807–23) which includes the *Alegoria de Junot* (in the Soares dos Reis Museum, Porto), is stylistically freer and more individualistic, with Goyaesque contrasts of dark and light, rapid brushstrokes and sudden bursts of luminous white.

The final phase of Sequeira's work corresponds to his visits to Paris and Rome. These late works show great painterliness and luminosity. The four cartoons for paintings in the Palmela collections, now in the Museu Nacional de Arte Antiga in Lisbon, are some of his most inspired, mystical works.

Romanticism and Naturalism

Romanticism was a form of escapism into medieval, oriental and mystical realms. Heroic, religious and ceremonial works gave way to more intimate and personal pieces. The mid-19th century also corresponded to the rise of the middle class. Courtly art had breathed its last. The liberal revolutions questioned the long upheld notion of history as the unfolding of a predetermined order, in favour of a relativism which heralded modern times. Similarly, the idea that art expresses timelessly valid principles gradually gave way to the subjectivist and individualist notions which continue to hold sway in art today.

Sequeira represented the mystical, religious side of early Romanticism. With his death, the movement in Portugal underwent a change: nature became the new religion. The humbling of man before the larger, inscrutable forces of nature was already a contemporaneous theme elsewhere. Tomás da Anunciação became the foremost romantic landscapist of his generation, along with Cristino da Silva.

Not surprisingly, portraiture not only became the art form of the bourgeoisie *par excellence*, but it also gave increasing emphasis to the sitter's inner life. In Miguel Luipi's *Sousa Martins' Mother*, now in the Museu Nacional de Arte Contemporânea, the illumination of the hands and face, the most expressive parts of the body, conveys a sense of pensive dignity.

At the end of the 19th century, Romanticism began to give way to Naturalism in both landscapes and portraits – although the difference between the two styles was largely one of emphasis. Silva Porto, José Malhoa, and Henrique Posão were the foremost Naturalist painters. But in stark contrast to their luminous outdoor scenes, Columbano Bordalo Pinheiro (1857–1929) continued in the tradition of studio painting. Columbano, as he is known, is considered the Grand Master of Portuguese 19th-century art. He studied under Miguel Lupi at the Academy of Fine Arts (founded in 1836), and then spent three years in Paris.

His brother, Rafael Bordalo Pinheiro, was perhaps even more popular in his day. A celebrated ceramicist, he was also known for his biting political caricatures.

Modernism

The artistic ferment that gripped Europe and America in the first decades of the 20th century arrived late, or in diluted form, in Portugal. The political turmoil that ended the monarchy in 1910 did not provide a propitious context for an artistic revolution, and there was then a window of only some 15 years before Salazar's authoritarian regime closed the door to external cultural influences.

But some ideas took root. In 1911, the Museu Nacional de Arte Contemporânea was founded in Lisbon, and the first Salon of Humorists represented a move away from conventional salon painting. One of the most daring and interesting of this generation of painters was the Cubist Amadeo Souza-Cardoso, whose premature death in 1918 was a great loss. Many of his works are now in the Centro de Arte Moderno at the Fundaçao Calouste Gulbenkian in Lisbon, and some can be seen in a museum in his home town of Amarante.

The military regime, initiated in 1926 and led by António de Oliveira Salazar from 1933–74, actively prevented contact with outside stimulus, so all the artistic and intellectual exchange

necessary to keep the arts alive had to be clandestine during these years. The return to democracy in 1974 breathed new energy into the arts and an outburst of fervent activity echoed the sense of exhilaration after long years of repression and censorship.

Portugal's artists now have free access to external ideas, and the age-old conflict between the imported and the indigenous still provokes lively debate. Among contemporary artists, Paula Rego is one of the brightest stars, although she no longer lives in her home country. A collection of her work can be seen at the Museu de Arte Contemporânea in Sintra. ❑

VOICE OF A GENERATION

One of the brightest lights among the generation represented in the 1911 Salon of Humorists was José Almada Negreiros (1893–1970), one of the most charismatic and energetic cultural figures in Portugal. His early cariactures drew the attention of the poet Fernando Pessoa who became his friend, and whose posthumously painted portrait now hangs in the poet's old home, with a replica in the Fundaçao Calouste Gulbenkian. One of Negreiros' most important commissions was for the frescoes at the port of Lisbon, in 1943–48 (*see page 84*). His last major project was the mural for the lobby of the Gulbenkian Foundation.

LEFT: René Lalique's art nouveau plaque in the Fundacão Calouste Gulbenkian, in Lisbon.
RIGHT: portrait of Fernando Pessoa by José Almada Negreiros, one of Portugal's 20th-century greats.

POUSADAS AND MANOR HOUSES

Pousadas and manor houses offer something different from ordinary hotels,
above all giving visitors a chance to experience local life and colour

Converted castles, palaces, monasteries, *quintas,* manor houses, water mills: there is no other country in Europe that offers good-quality accommodation in such variety. If taking a stroll around the castle walls before retiring to a grand bedroom once used by royalty, or waking to the tinkling sound of a stream

beneath a miller's cottage sounds appealing, Portugal could be just the right place.

Pousadas

Unlike some of the other accommodation available, *pousadas* have a clear identity. They are state-run establishments, usually historic buildings, national monuments or notable regional houses, and are found in both urban and rural areas throughout the country.

Architecturally and historically fascinating, *pousadas* have earned a reputation for quality and service. Lofty rooms and heavy stone walls do not always lend themselves to sumptuous luxury – in fact, some are extremely simple –

but the style of décor is always sympathetic to the character of the building. One constant concession to modernity is the provision of en-suite facilities, but some *pousadas* also provide air-conditioning and even a swimming pool. *Pousadas* pride themselves, too, on the high standard of their restaurants, which are also open to non-residents, and serve dishes based on local and regional recipes. A relaxed and distinctly Portuguese ambience is perhaps the one thing that they all have in common.

There is now a choice of over 40 *pousadas,* although many offer only a limited number of rooms, some as few as six.

For travellers in the lush green northwestern corner of Portugal, there is a good choice. To mention just a few: in the medieval town of Valença do Minho you will find the **Pousada de São Teotónio**. It sits on a high point inside the ancient walled city with a spectacular view of the Rio Minho across to Spain and the Galician mountains. It is also perfectly located for walks through the winding city streets.

Further to the east is the **Pousada de São Bento**, a chalet-style building on a hill just south of the Parque Nacional Peneda-Gerês. Its floor-to-ceiling windows overlook the Caniçada Dam and a forest. The *pousada* has its own swimming pool and tennis court.

Be the king of the castle

If castles hold a great fascination for you, the **Pousada do Castelo**, in the delightful old walled town of Obidos, north of Lisbon, is one which you might find most interesting. Built into a section of the 16th-century castle, the *pousada* is very small – with only nine rooms – and very popular. Advanced reservations are essential. **Palmela** is another castle *pousada* that is much in demand, and somewhat larger, with 26 rooms. Originally a fortress, it became a monastery in the 15th century and was severely damaged in the great earthquake of 1755. Now the old refectory has become the dining room and the cloisters are used on festive occasions for gala dinners.

Manor houses

The manor house scheme, to which numerous gracious old houses in Portugal belong, began in the north of the country. The scheme was created to conserve some of the country's most beautiful private manor houses and palaces. The owners of these magnificent homes can no longer afford the expensive maintenance and have opened them up to tourists, who are quite often treated as guests of the family.

The term "manor houses" has now broadened

THE NITTY GRITTY

For descriptions, addresses and telephone numbers, of *pousadas*, manor houses and other historic lodgings in Portugal, see pages 362–70* of *Travel Tips*.

according to the period and are sometimes stuffed with antiques and valuable works of art.

● *Quintas and Herdades*: both of these are agricultural farms but a *quinta* differs in being a walled estate. Although mostly located in rural settings, some are handily situated for towns.

● *Casas Rústicas*: these are usually located in the heart of rural villages or on farms, and often quite isolated, they offer more simple architecture but still maintain a good level of comfort and amenities. ❑

to encompass an extremely wide range of accommodation, which is available throughout the country. Privately-owned manor houses are also known as *solares*. Stately manor houses, elegant country homes, farm houses and rustic cottages are all included in this one general description. They are often listed under three categories:

● *Casas Antigas:* elegant manor houses or country estates mostly originating from the 17th and 18th centuries. They are furnished

LEFT: an elegant corridor in the Pousada dos Lóios, in Évora.
ABOVE: the Pousada do Castelo, in a prime spot in the walled town of Obidos.

WHERE TO BOOK

Although reservations can be made directly, there is a central agency in Lisbon which handles bookings for all *pousadas*. There is no minimum stay requirement. Contact ENATUR, Rua Santa Joana Princesa 10, 1700 Lisbon, tel: 21 844 2001, fax: 21 844 2085; www.pousadas.pt. Several agencies handle bookings for Manor Houses. The chief ones are PRIVATUR, Central de Reservas, Manor Houses of Portugal, Apartado 596, 4900 Viana do Castelo, tel: 258 741 400, fax: 258 741 493; *www. manorhouses.com; and TURIHAB, Praça da República, 4990 Ponte de Lima, tel: 258 741 672, fax: 258 741 444. Another useful website is www. solaresdeportugal.pt.

NATURAL PORTUGAL

This is a land where complex forces of nature have created
diverse environments and opportunities for different lifestyles

For a country no more than 565 km (350 miles) long and 220 km (137 miles) wide, at best, and edged by the Atlantic Ocean, Portugal enjoys a surprising diversity of topography, geography and climate. Half a day's journey in almost any direction leads through climatic zones, from wet to dry, hot to cool, through mountains to plains, from rich pastures to poor, from large estates to small farms, and from affluence to poverty. Adaptation, community by community and region by region, to the heterogeneous forces of nature has fashioned a country set apart from its neighbours and unique in Europe.

Climate

Portugal is the mixing pot of three powerful climatic regimes. It is attacked from the west by moist westerlies from the Atlantic, carrying rain deep into the country. These are arrested by a dry continental climate giving hot dry summers and cold dry winters in the interior. From the south a Mediterranean climate invades bringing hot dry summers and cooler, moist winters.

The high land mass of Serra da Estrela acts as a fulcrum point for all these climatic types. Descend from the mountain at any point and you will find a different country on the other side. The biggest contrast is from the wet northwest to the drier southeast.

Rain patterns vary from north to south, with the north receiving the highest rainfall, especially between November and March. Summer conditions are not too dissimilar, with all regions generally enjoying high temperatures tempered in coastal regions by Atlantic influences. Inland regions, particular in the port wine areas and Alentejo, suffer very high temperatures in summer.

One of the most useful indicators of a Mediterranean climate is the olive tree. This grows happily throughout most of Portugal with the exception of the mountainous regions and the most northerly part of Trás-os-Montes.

However, only Algarve enjoys anything approaching a truly Mediterranean-type climate and this has allowed its development as a year-round destination for holiday-makers. Even

Algarve is not immune from Atlantic westerlies which sometimes bring spells of wet weather in winter.

Mountain life

Rolling granite mountains, safe refuges in ancient times, dominate the north. Many settlements from those early days remain even today. Here residents eke out an existence in a harsh environment using tools (adapted for their own needs) which have hardly changed over the centuries.

Although most of the mountain areas are lightly populated, there is an area of near-wilderness tucked away on the northern border

PRECEDING PAGES: hillside vineyards in the Douro valley.
LEFT: an isolated dwelling in the Alentejo plains.
RIGHT: a gnarled old cork tree.

of the country. Recognised as a sanctuary of wildlife and valued for the traditional way of life which persists in the villages on the fringes, the Parque Nacional Peneda-Gerês area, covering 720 sq km (278 sq miles) was opened in 1971. It is the country's only *national* park although other areas of natural beauty have been designated *natural* parks and are protected, but by less stringent regulations.

Most of the highest peaks in the northern mountains lie within the park. Many of these exceed 1,300 metres (4,265ft) with Nervosa reaching a height of 1,545 metres (5,070ft). But although this region is the most mountainous in the country, it is not home to the highest peak of all. This distinction is reserved for the Serra da Estrela (Mountain of the Stars), an isolated, majestic mountain range in central Portugal which rises from the plains of Alentejo. Here, Torre, at 1,993 metres (6,539ft), marks the summit of Portugal. This area too enjoys protection but as a natural, not a national, park.

Geology

For its size, Portugal has remarkably diverse geology. Ancient crystalline rocks of granite and gneiss predominate in the mountainous regions, often presenting a landscape of grey

rounded hills and steep valleys. For many inhabitants, it is the only natural building material available and they have perfected the tools and ways to work this material to an art form. Granite is a hard material but it has just enough malleability to make it workable. The evidence is all around, especially in the north. Farms, churches, water mills and fencing posts for the vines are all solidly constructed from granite.

Limestone and marble are found in the central region, especially near Évora, where it is mined commercially, and near Coimbra. The Coimbra deposit is particularly valued by sculptors who have used it extensively. There is another significant limestone region, now pro-

THE STORY OF MAIZE

The introduction of maize in the 16th century proved a lifeline for the people of the hill villages, for here was a crop they could adapt to their own situation. Land around the villages was pressed into use for maize and animals were moved to still higher pastures for the summer. More changes were demanded to meet the problems of storing the crop and grinding the corn. This resulted in granite-built stores perched on mushroom-shaped legs, *espigueiros*, as seen at Soajo. Water provided the power for grinding the corn. Water mills, again built of granite, were erected in profusion, often with the water of a single stream powering a succession of mills.

tected as the Parque Natural das Serras de Aire e Candeeiros *(see page 245)*. This area is riddled with deep caves, and three of them are open to the public.

River communities

Many of the rivers arising in the mountainous interior on the western side of the Iberian Peninsula flow to the Atlantic through Portugal. In fact, only one river, the Mondego, is truly Portuguese, rising in the region of Serra da Estrela and flowing into the sea at Coimbra. Some of these rivers were navigable in the past allowing boats access deep into the country-

see in Portugal, where productive farming has been practised for centuries.

In modern times, the Rio Douro has played a significant role in the development of the port wine trade. Good roads now penetrate the area but at the height of the port trade, all the wine had to be shipped down this difficult and dangerous river.

Perhaps the largest remaining river community is Lisbon itself, on the shores of the Rio Tejo (Tagus). The mouth of the Tejo proved to be a natural harbour offering safe anchorage to early traders. The prosperity of Lisbon has barely faltered throughout the ages.

side. Early settlers were not slow to use the Rio Guadiana in this way to penetrate inland in search of metal ores. Mértola in Alentejo developed as a port under the Romans, to ship ores down the Guadiana from nearby São Domingos, and there are significant remains of the port area still to be seen.

The Romans were overwhelmed by the beauty of the Rio Lima in the north. This, for them, was the Lethe, the mythical River of Forgetfulness. This meandering river has created a fertile valley as beautiful as any you'll

LEFT: an ancient rock resembling a giant tortoise.
ABOVE: gathering shellfish on the Rio Gilao.

Coastal life

With 832 km (516 miles) of coastline, it is not surprising that the Portuguese are people of the sea. Fishing has sustained them over the centuries, providing an industry which has grown large on the one hand, especially through cod fishing, yet has also remained a small local activity. The coast is still littered with villages which rely heavily on reaping the harvest of the sea and especially on the sardine, which keeps many small fishermen in business.

Tuna fishing is another sector of this industry which grew to massive proportions. Shoals of tuna migrate along the southern shoreline towards spawning grounds in the Mediterranean. Floating traps were used to catch the fish and fishermen were on hand to complete the job. Regrettably, over-fishing led to a decline in numbers and the industry collapsed.

Fish, of which there is reckoned to be more than 200 species off these shores, is not the only commercial product. Algarve has produced salt from ancient times; the Romans salted fish here to export back to Rome, and there are still salt pans in operation. Seaweed for fertiliser is now less of an industry at Aveiro than it once was. Here, specially shaped boats, *moliceiros*, are used to collect seaweed from the extensive system of lagoons in the area *(see pages 86–7)*.

found almost exclusively in the far west of the country. They can coexist with Mediterranean cistus species. Algarve offers the best display of Mediterranean flora including a rich array of wild orchids, like the bumblebee orchid (*Ophrys bombyliflora*) and the yellow bee orchid (*Ophrys lutea*).

Narcissus is especially associated with the Iberian peninsula and many are endemic, although some are found throughout the Mediterranean region. Portugal has its fair share, from the diminutive jonquil, *Narcissus gaditanus*, to more popular garden species like *N. bulbocodium* and *N. triandrus*.

The magnificent beaches adorning much of the coastline have themselves become an important commodity for tourism in this modern world. A lifelong dependence on the sea has yielded now to dependence on a transient industry subject to whim and fashion.

Flora

With so many different habitats, climates and micro-climates in this hugely diverse country, the flora responds with equal diversity. Many species simply reflect the climatic influence of the region. Certain erica heaths, green lavender (*Lavendula viridis*), and ulex species (gorse) typify Western Atlantic species and are

Fauna

Wild boars are one of the largest mammals roaming Portugal. Their foraging marks can be seen in many parts of the country, from the golf courses of Algarve – much to the fury of the green keepers – to the inland forests. Hunting for boar is a form of tourism which Alentejo is keen to develop. Rabbits and foxes are extremely common, genet (Egyptian mongoose) less so, but the best wildlife sanctuary is the Parque National Peneda-Gerês, in the north *(see page 134)*. Brown bears have not been seen for centuries but there are still some wolves, and plenty of beech martens, deer, badgers and otters around.

Birdlife is particularly rich in some areas, especially around the old saltpans in Algarve, where some 300 species have been recorded. Around Lisbon, too, 200 sq km (77 sq miles) of the Tejo estuary are protected as one of the most important wetland areas in Europe. Apart from variety, the birds are often present in great numbers with, for example, as many as 10,000 avocet to be seen. The west coast estuaries and wetlands are situated on some of the major migratory routes, so spring and autumn can be particularly rewarding for ornithologists. Sadly, in some areas years of uncontrolled hunting have significantly reduced wildlife.

The Australian eucalyptus was introduced in 1856 for the paper industry, on account of its rapid growth, but its future is now in the balance. Environmentalists have thrown their weight behind farmers who oppose further plantations on the grounds of its destructive influence. Not only are eucalyptus rapacious in their demand for water, but they provide poor natural habitats and their litter is so slow to decompose that it further inhibits naturally occurring cycles within the soil.

The almond and the carob are indigenous to Algarve, the latter bearing long wizened beans which yield a fine variety of oil. ❑

Trees of life

Forestry in Portugal is big business with around one-third of the country, some 3 million hectares (7.5 million acres), under forest. Pine, said in Portugal to be of use from cradle to grave, is used to produce timber for furniture and construction as well as resin for pitch and turpentine. Pine accounts for around 40 percent of the country's wooded land. Pulp, used to manufacture paper and cardboard, is economically the most important woodland product.

FAR LEFT: the *Narcissus bulbocodium*.
LEFT: thousands of avocet visit the Tejo estuary.
ABOVE: at work in a Portalegre cork factory.

THE CORK INDUSTRY

About half the cork in the world, from stoppers in champagne bottles to the linings of spacecraft, comes from Alentejo. The cultivation of cork is not for the impatient: there's a wait of 25 years before the first crop is stripped from the trunk and a further decade before the next harvest. Cork is a labour-intensive industry, as machines cannot duplicate the expertise of the men who strip bark from the trees, although the punching out of corks and stoppers is increasingly mechanised. Although plastic corks are becoming popular for wine bottling, it will be a long time before such artificial products make any significant impact on the Portuguese cork industry.

PLACES

*A detailed guide to the entire country, with principal sites
clearly cross-referenced by number to the maps*

There isn't a wrong way to explore Portugal – except to make too many plans in advance. A car is the handiest way to travel because, although the trains are good and the buses adequate, they won't allow you the freedom to go just over the next hill… and the next, and the next. Portugal is wonderfully seductive.

Roads are good and a motorway links Lisbon with Porto in the north, two hours' drive away, and goes on to Galicia in Spain. The roads south from Lisbon cross the Tejo and head for Alentejo and Algarve. Away from the national highways, east–west expressways help you leap distances but north–south roads tend to be narrower, more winding.

Lisbon and its environs are the best starting point for a first taste of Portugal. From there, if the weather is fine, you may want simply to head south, to the glorious beaches of Algarve. After relaxing for a few days, you might start meandering back through the Portuguese countryside. Begin by exploring the expanse of Alentejo, spectacular plains with the entrancing ancient town of Évora in their midst.

Cutting back towards the Atlantic, still heading north, you could visit the old university town of Coimbra and the surrounding sights. Look in on some of the traditional fishing communities along the coast: to the north is Porto on the Rio Douro and the wine districts of Douro and Minho. Here, world-famous port, delicious *vinhos verdes* and other wines are produced.

The far interior north of Portugal is called Trás-os-Montes, a marvellous remote and hauntingly beautiful area. And below Trás-os-Montes, still ruggedly hilly, is the Beira Alta; below that, the plains of Alentejo creep up into the province of Beira Baixa. And if you have time to visit the islands of Madeira and the Azores, you'll discover a different world altogether.

Taste decides where you go, whether you prefer the north, rural and quiet, or the south, hot and crowded. You'll wander through towns with a rich and ancient architecture – and with discos and smart shops. Accommodation ranges from luxury hotels, *pousadas* and private manor houses to simple rooms above village restaurants. Portugal is small, but almost everywhere you may have the sensation of being lost in a magical landscape – yet knowing that Lisbon, or wherever you next want to go, is handily close.

Once upon a time, fleets of bold explorers sailed from these shores. You might think discovery an out-dated notion – until you discover for yourself the pleasures of Portugal. ❑

PRECEDING PAGES: rooftops of port bodegas in Vila Nova de Gaia, opposite Porto; a festival in Viana do Castelo; a shaggy traffic jam in the streets of Carviçais.
LEFT: proud prow of a painted boat.

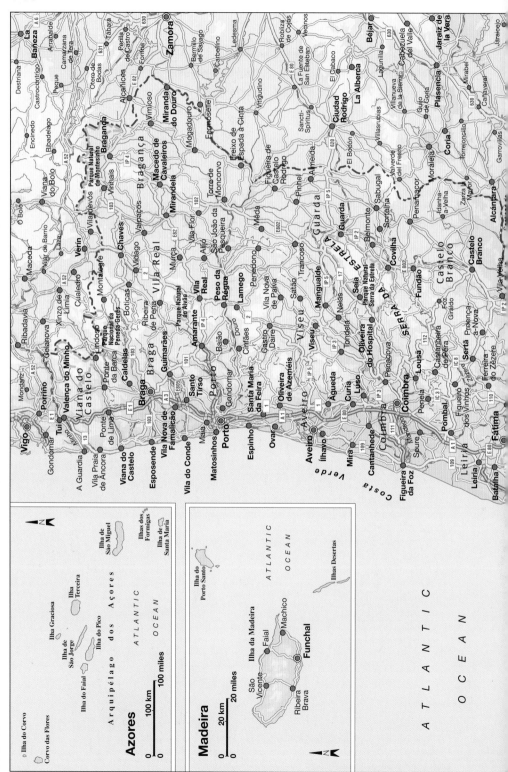

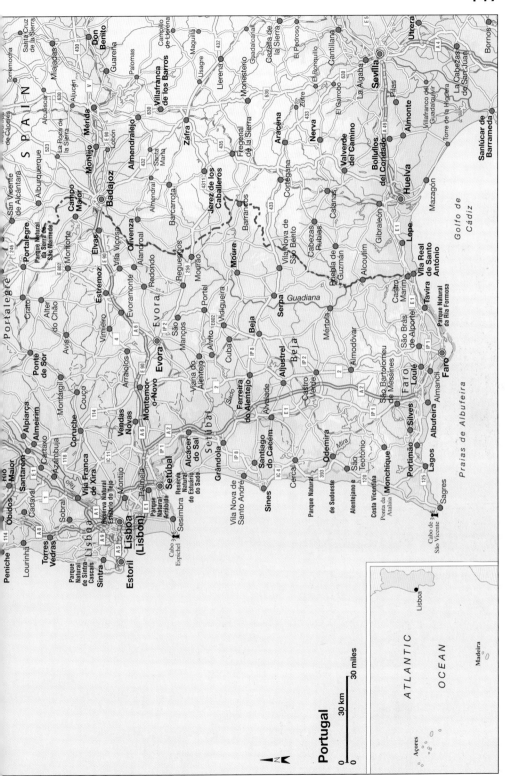

LISBON

With cafés, culture and a castle, Lisbon is a vibrant city, mixing old-world charm, local colour and modern amenities. A good local transport system will help you discover the best of it

Map on pages 164–5

L isbon (Lisboa) offers a wealth of delights to indulge all tastes, from cultural forays to endless shopping opportunities and an abundance of places in which to sample the local gastronomy. There is no shortage of pleasant leafy retreats, and *miradouros* (viewpoints) are liberally dotted around the city. By day, life centres around the cafés where delicious coffee and cakes will tempt even the most ardent dieter. The city really comes alive in the evening and can justifiably claim some of the best nightlife around, especially in the small wine bars and restaurants of Alfama and Bairro Alto. This is where you are most likely to chance upon impromptu *fado*, the soulful songs of lost loves and past glories.

A flavour of what Lisbon has to offer can be sampled in a crowded one-day visit, but that is barely enough to scratch the surface of the city's complexities, which include more than 30 museums. Three days allow time to absorb the atmosphere, and city lovers will probably find a week too short. Lisbon's climate of hot summers and mild winters makes it an ideal place to visit for most of the year, although spring and autumn are good times to enjoy the city at its best.

Many of the highlights of a visit to Lisbon are conveniently concentrated in two main areas, the heart of the city centred around the Baixa, and a significant cluster out along the riverside at Belém. Baixa is the hub of the city centre, watched over by Castelo São Jorge, below which cling the narrow streets and alleys of Alfama. To the west lies the hill of Bairro Alto, entered through the Chiado area. North, beyond Rossio, the main thoroughfare, Avenida da Liberdad, leads to Praça Marquês de Pombal and Parque Eduardo VII.

PRECEDING PAGES: a view of Castelo de São Jorge. **LEFT:** Monument of the Discoveries. **BELOW:** the Ponte 25 de Abril.

Building bridges

Most architecture in the city is post-1755, after the great earthquake, except for Alfama and Belém which escaped virtually unscathed. There has been an upsurge in the restoration of old buildings and many dilapidated palaces and mansions have been tastefully renovated. Many have become elegant restaurants, fashionable boutiques, art galleries and even discotheques. Crumbling houses in the old quarters are also being restored and in outlying neighbourhoods there are new hotels, vast and popular shopping malls, office complexes, cinemas and museums.

Visitors usually arrive by air and enter the city from the northeast but a spectacular entrance is over the Ponte 25 de Abril from the south. Completed in 1966, the Ponte de Salazar was renamed in 1974 when democracy was restored to Portugal. A second bridge, Ponte Vasco da Gama, further up the river, was built for Expo '98, which was sited on the riverfront nearby and has become the Parque das Nações.

A touch of history

The mythical founding of the city on seven hills is attributed to Ulysses (Odysseus) and his encounter with the nymph Calypso. Left behind when he departed, the heartbroken nymph turned herself into a snake whose coils became the seven hills. In reality, there has been a settlement on the site at least since pre-historic times. Its advantageous geographical position caught the attention of Phoenician traders in search of safe anchorage who developed a port, Alis Ubbo (Serene Port), around 1200 BC. The Greeks then the Carthaginians subsequently laid claim to the site. In 205 BC Olisipo (as it was then known) was incorporated into the Roman province of Lusitania. Julius Caesar elevated the status of the city to a *municipium* in 60 BC and renamed it Felicitas Julia. What little remains of the Roman occupation today is from this period of relative prosperity and growth. As the Roman Empire crumbled, the city was left unprotected and vulnerable to attacks by a succession of barbaric Germanic tribes.

After the arrival of the Moors in the 8th century, the city enjoyed 400 years of stability and increasing prosperity, which came to an end in 1147, when the first king of the newly formed nation of Portugal, Dom (King) Afonso Henriques, captured Lisbon. Around 1260 the Moors were finally vanquished and the capital moved here from Coimbra. A university was established in 1290 by Dom Dinis but transferred to Coimbra in 1308. A power struggle between the Church and the Crown over the next 200 years saw the university shunted between the two cities. In the end, Coimbra won that particular battle and Lisbon was left without a university until 1911.

The dawn of the "Age of Discoveries" at the end of the 15th century turned Lisbon into an important trading centre. Wealth from the opening up of the sea

BELOW: a 16th-century panorama of the city.

LISBONA

route to India by Vasco da Gama flowed into the country and the city entered a golden age that lasted for a century. A 60-year period of Spanish rule saw a decline in fortunes, and for a while after the Spanish were ousted Lisbon suffered economically as maritime trade declined. The discovery of gold in Brazil ensured a return to former prosperity but most of this fortune was squandered by Dom João V on lavish building projects that were destroyed in the massive earthquake of 1755. The Marquês de Pombal was on hand to oversee the rebuilding of the city.

Since then, Lisbon has witnessed the end of the monarchy, gunned down in its main square, and endured a period of dictatorship under Salazar, which kept the city free of modern development, perhaps the only thing we can thank him for.

Baixa and the city centre

Baixa (the lower quarter) covers the level area in between the hills of Alfama and Bairro Alto. It slopes gently to the banks of the Rio Tejo (Tagus) from Rossio and down through Pombal's famous grid system of streets. City life centres around the vast expanse of the **Praça do Comércio ❶** by the riverside. The earlier name of the square, Terreiro do Paço, is still used and dates back to the time before the earthquake when the 16th-century royal palace stood on the site. Behind the elegant Pombaline neo-classical arcades are municipal and judicial offices, and on the west side of the square is the city tourist office's **Welcome Centre**. Lisbon's Stock Exchange, or Bolsa, is to the east. In splendid isolation in the middle of the square stands a bronze statue of the ruler at the time of the earthquake, Dom José I, which gave rise to the English name of Black Horse Square. The riverside serves as a quay for ferry boats along the

Map on page 154

TIP

Walking is the best way to see the city, but there is a good transport system of trams (eléctricos), buses, taxis, lifts (elevadors) and Metro. One-, two- and three-day passes are a good investment for visitors.

BELOW: the Praça do Comércio.

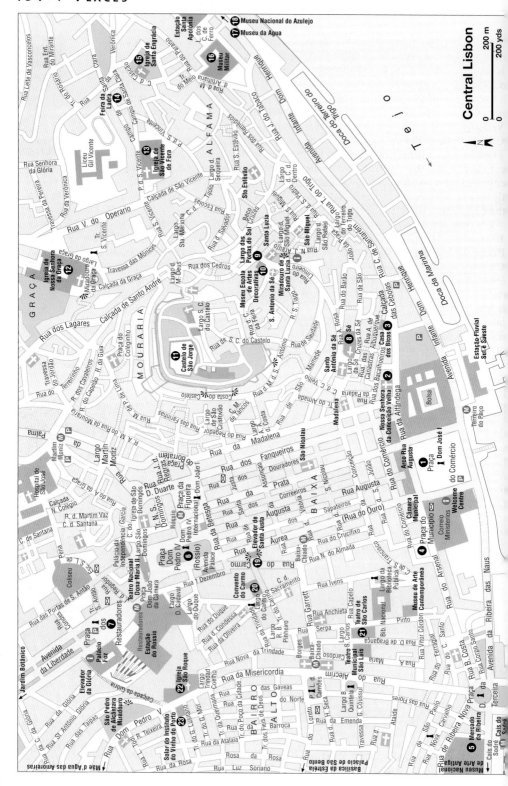

Central Lisbon

Tagus and across to the *Outra Banda*, the communities on the southern shore of the river. Completely overshadowing the delicacy of the arcaded buildings is the impressive triumphal **Arco Rua Augusta**. The arch is a late 19th-century addition to the square.

A short walk along the road, from the northeast corner of the square, is the notable Manueline doorway of the church of **Nossa Senhora da Conceição Velha ②**. Further along, the unusual pyramidal stone façade of the 16th-century **Casa dos Bicos ③** ("House of the Pointed Stones") seems almost modernistic. There is a clear distinction between the lower storeys, which survived the 1755 earthquake, and the top two storeys which were faithfully reproduced from old engravings during the 1980s. A short distance further along the road lies the little noticed 13th-century fountain **Chafariz d'el Rei**, once the major source of the city's water supply.

Leaving the square from the northwest corner you pass the spot where, in 1908, Carlos I and his heir, Luís Felipe, were assassinated. Close by is the **Praça do Municipio ④**, with an 18th-century *pelourinho* (pillory) and the **Câmara Municipal** (Town Hall), where Portugal was declared a republic in 1910. Further west, trains arrive from Estoril and Cascais at the Cais do Sodré railway station close to the city's main market, **Mercado da Ribeira ⑤**. This is a colourful place selling an amazing array of fresh produce, including fish landed at the nearby Ribeira dock, as well as regular first-floor crafts markets run by the Lisbon tourist office. There's a lively atmosphere here, with plenty of bars, bistros and restaurants.

Back in the Praça do Comércio, make a grand entrance through the Arco Rua Augusta into the neat grid of streets which form the main area of Baixa, the lower town. Pedestrianised Rua Augusta provides plenty of diversions along the way as it sweeps up towards Rossio. Shops are definitely the main attraction but, at busy times, street entertainers and balloon sellers lend a carnival atmosphere and pavement cafés bring a Parisian feel to the scene. At one time, the streets of the grid represented various crafts, hence names such as Rua da Prata (silver), Rua do Ouro (gold) and Rua dos Franqueiros (habadashers). Today, many of these streets are home to banks and offices as well as shops.

Rua Augusta opens into **Praça Dom Pedro IV ⑥**, better known by its common name of **Rossio**, and the focus of major city events for 500 years until the 18th century. This was where citizens gathered to enjoy carnivals and bullfights or to witness public executions, particularly the *autos-da-fé* of the Inquisition. Now, cafés, flower sellers, shops, kiosks and traffic create a swirl of activity and colour in a square much favoured by the locals, who spend the time of day at one of the many pavement cafés, such as **Café Nicola**.

At the northern end of the square, the **Teatro Nacional** (Dona Maria II Theatre), built in the 1840s, overlooks the two fountains brought from Paris in 1890 which flank the statue of Dom Pedro IV. They are rather more authentic than the statue, which is a cobbled version of a statue of Emperor Maximilian

Map on page 154

Lottery tickets, on sale everywhere.

BELOW: the neo-Manueline Rossio Station.

of Mexico. A ship carrying it from Marseilles to Mexico docked in Lisbon just as news came of the Emperor's assassination. Pressed for cash, the city council snapped it up as the bargain of the day and attempted some remodelling in the hope no one would notice. **Paço dos Condes de Almada** (Palace of the Counts of Almada), just to the east of the theatre, is where the "Restorers" (*Restauradores*) conspired in 1640 to wrest power back from the occupying Spaniards. The Igreja de São Domingos nearby oversaw the sentencing of victims of the Inquisition, who had been tried in the palace which once stood on the Teatro Nacional site. South of the church lies the quieter ambience of **Praça da Figueira** (Figtree Square) with its statue of João I.

To the northwest of Rossio is the **Estação do Rossio** (Rossio Station), with its lovely neo-Manueline façade. Trains from Sintra arrive on the fourth floor, at the level of Bairro Alto (the upper part of town), from where an escalator takes passengers down to Baixo level. They emerge not far from **Praça dos Restauradores ❼**, named in honour of the Restorers. In this square stands the 18th-century **Palácio Foz**, now used by *Turismo* as a tourist information centre. Until 1821, access to the square was closed off to keep out the rabble inhabiting Rossio Square and thereby create a peaceful haven for the gentry. It was then opened up to the general public and used for celebrations and dances.

East to Alfama

BELOW: flowers for sale in the Rossio.

Alfama is the oldest part of the city, and clings tenaciously around the feet of the Castelo de São Jorge. The steep narrow streets and alleys of this old Moorish quarter spill down to the riverside, and a succession of conquerors over the

millenniums have left vestiges of their occupation. A tapestry of life unfolds around every corner: drink it all in, but keep a tight hold on your valuables. The area really comes alive on 12 and 13 June for the feast of St Anthony of Padua (1195–1231), the unofficial patron saint of Lisbon who was born in the area (he acquired his title after a sojourn in Italy).

Head up from Baixa past the Igreja de Madalena, dating from the late 18th century but preserving a Manueline porch from an earlier church. On the left, as the Romanesque façade of the Sé comes into view, is the small church of **Santo António da Sé**, built on the alleged site of St Anthony's birthplace. The neighbouring **Museu Antóniano** is devoted to his life.

Seeing the Sé

Dom Afonso Henriques, the first king of Portugal, ordered the **Sé (Cathedral)** ❽ (open daily 9am–5pm) to be built soon after banishing the Moors from Lisbon. The first incumbent was an Englishman, Gilbert of Hastings, who fared rather better than the 14th-century Bishop Martinho Anes, who was flung from the north tower for harbouring Spanish sympathies. Today the cathedral's fortress-like façade stands testament to the turbulent times in which it was constructed. There has been much restoration over the centuries but the two original crenellated towers, softened by the large rose window in between, remain the most striking feature.

St Anthony is the unofficial patron saint of Lisbon.

Inside, the barrel-vaulted ceiling leads to a low lantern and to the left, on entry, is the baptismal font where St Anthony was christened in 1195. Further along, in the first chapel on the left, is a beautifully detailed *crèche* – nativity scene – by the sculptor Joaquim Machado de Castro. The chancel is 18th cen-

LEFT: a colourful façade in Alfama.
BELOW: old cinema in Rossio.

The knife-grinder is a familiar figure in the streets of Lisbon, as in any Portuguese town.

BELOW: the ruined cloisters of the Cathedral.

tury and the ambulatory was remodelled in the 14th century. In the third chapel from the south side of the ambulatory are the tombs of Lopo Fernandes Pacheco and his wife. He was a companion in arms to Afonso IV (1325–57), and responsible for much remodelling during those years.

The ruined cloisters are worth the modest entrance fee to view the excavations in what were once the gardens. Vestiges of Moorish buildings overlay Roman remains, and beneath those are evidence of an Iron Age settlement.

In the sacristy is the cathedral treasury where numerous sacred objects are on view. Of most importance is the casket containing the remains of St Vincent, the patron saint of Lisbon, which were brought here by the order of Afonso Henriques from Sagres in Algarve. Legend relates how ravens accompanied the boat that carried his remains from Spain and again on the journey from Algarve to Lisbon. To this day, the raven is a feature of Lisbon's coat of arms.

Still heading uphill, you will reach the **Miradouro de Santa Luzia** which is a good vantage point to look down over Alfama. The church of the same name is decorated externally with some interesting *azulejo* panels, one showing the heroic soldier Martim Moniz, who died keeping the city gate open – an act which enabled Afonso Henriques to capture Lisbon. A little further up is **Largo das Portas do Sol ❾** (Sun Gate), where one of the original city gates once stood. A statue of St Vincent looks out over the city from this popular viewpoint. Terrace cafés provide an excuse to linger, and the 17th-century palace of the counts of Azurara, now the **Museu Escola de Artes Decorativas (Museum of Decorative Art) ❿**, is certainly worth a visit (open Tues–Sun; entrance charge). The museum is a showcase for the work of Portugal's master craftsmen.

The Castelo de São Jorge

Perhaps the most beautiful view of the city is from the ramparts of **Castelo de São Jorge ⓫** (open daily; entrance free), which crowns the first hill east of the city centre. If you want to take the hard work out of the climb up to the castle, you could take a taxi or catch the Number 28 Graça tram to Portas do Sol, then visit the Sé and surrounding sites on the walk down. The castle can be seen from nearly anywhere in Lisbon, serving as an apt and romantic reminder of the capital's ancient roots. Many of the castle walls and towers are from the Moorish stronghold, although there were earlier fortifications on this site.

After the Portuguese drove out the Moors in 1147, the residence of the Moorish governor, Paço de Alcáçova, became the royal palace of Dom Dinis (1279–1325). It remained a royal residence until Dom Manuel (1495–1521) decided to build a more comfortable royal residence down by the river. Except for a short period, when Dom Sebastião preferred the military fortification of the castle to the graceful splendour of the palace, it served its time as a barracks and prison until 1939, when it was freed from any official duties. **Olisipónia** (open 10am–6.30pm, closed Wed) is a multimedia history of the castle and city in the heart of the complex.

All that is left now are walls, 10 towers and the remnants of the palace, but shaded gardens, fountains, cafés and a restaurant, presided over by a statue of Afonso Henriques, make it an ideal spot to escape the heat of summer. The *miradouro* (lookout spot) provides a marvellous panorama of the city, and from here it is possible to pick out many of the city's landmarks. Further good viewpoints lie to the north at the baroque **Igreja de Nossa Senhora da Graça ⓬** and beyond that, the even higher Senhora do Monte.

Map on page 154

The Spanish patron saint of Lisbon, St Vincent, has never enjoyed the same popularity as St Anthony of Padua, who was born in Alfama.

BELOW: moonrise over Castelo do São Jorge.

Outside the city walls

A short walk from the castle leads to the **Igreja de São Vicente de Fora**  (open daily; entrance free). *De fora* describes the church's position outside the city walls. It was built on the site of a 12th-century monastery dedicated to St Vincent to commemorate the battle fought by the crusaders to capture Lisbon. The white limestone building, with short twin towers, was designed by the Italian architect Filippo Terzi; construction began in 1582, and took more than 40 years.

Of more interest than the church interior are the cloisters (open daily; entrance charge), which are covered with 18th-century *azulejos* depicting La Fontaine's *Fables*. The former refectory, off the cloisters, has served as the Pantheon of the Royal House of Bragança since the mid-19th century. Portuguese kings, queens, princes and princesses, from João IV (who died in 1656), are entombed here.

A flea market, **Feira da Ladra** ⑭ – literally, the Thieves' Market – takes place on Tuesday and Sunday morning in the Campo de Santa Clara. You must cross this square to reach the baroque **Igreja de Santa Engrácia** ⑮, now the National Pantheon (**Panteão Nacional**; open daily; entrance charge) containing monuments to many of Portugal's non-royal heroes. Work on this church started in 1682 but was not completed until 1966, giving rise to the Portuguese idiom for a project never finished: *"obras [works] de Santa Engrácia"*. Although the building is in the compact, satisfying shape of a Greek cross, with a central dome, the stamp of Salazar on its eventual completion has left it a somewhat sterile monument.

Back down towards the riverside, opposite **Estação Santa Apolónia**, the railway station for international arrivals, is the **Museu Militar** ⑯ (open Tues–Sun; entrance charge). This museum charts Portugal's military history in paintings and extensive collections of armour and weapons in a building which was, until 1851, the national arsenal.

Head eastward, along the coastal route, paralleling the railway lines, then turn left up Calçada dos Barbadinhos to the **Museu da Agua da EPAL** ⑰ (Water Museum; open Mon–Sat, closed public holidays; entrance charge). Named after the engineer of the Aqueduto das Aguas Livres *(see page 162)*, it was the first steam pumping station of its kind in Portugal. The building, in a surprisingly tranquil oasis, records the history of Lisbon's water supply from Roman times and includes the story of the aqueduct.

Further east stands the tile museum, the **Museu Nacional do Azulejo** ⑱ (open Tues pm, Wed–Sun 10am–6pm; entrance charge). Again, the easiest route runs parallel to the railway track, but you may find it worth taking a taxi. The building was originally part of the Convento da Madre de Deus, founded in 1509 by the widow of João II, Dona Leonor of Lancaster. All that remains of the original exterior is the Manueline doorway, but the 18th-century interior of the main church provides the perfect foil for the national collection of *azulejos*, in a breathtaking combination of gilded woodwork, blue-and-white Dutch *azulejos* and superbly painted walls and ceilings. One of the most outstanding tile scenes is a 1730 panorama of Lisbon,

The exiled King Carol of Romania, who died in 1953, is buried, with his wife, in the church of São Vicente de Fora.

BELOW: the Aqueduto das Aguas Livres.

some 37 metres (120 ft) long. Besides tiles and architecture, there are paintings to admire, a bookshop to browse in, and a very pleasant café/restaurant.

Beside the Oriente metro station, 5 km (3 miles) upriver is the **Parque das Nacões**, the Expo '98 site, stretching along 2 km (1¼ miles) of waterfront. Its attractions include one of the largest sealife centres in Europe, the **Oceanário de Lisboa** (open daily, entrance charge), the huge Atlantic Pavilion, Camões Theatre, a waterside cable car ride and the **Vasco da Gama Tower** with a restaurant and viewing area (open 10am–6pm daily, entrance charge). The place is popular with families at weekends when many shops in the large mall stay open until midnight.

Through Bairro Alto

Bairro Alto (the upper quarter) rises to the west of Baixa. This area is renowned for its shops and restaurants. Shoppers can stroll up past the delights of the fashionable **Chiado** district, looking in at the popular French-owned Fnac department store, built after the 1988 Chiado fire, or take a great coffee in A Brasileira in Rua Garrett, favoured by generations of artists and politicians. The walkway into the Chiado from the top of Raoul Mesnier de Ponsard's **Elevador de Santa Justa** ⑲ has been closed for some time, but you can still take the lift to the top of the tower to the café and viewing platform (9am–6pm daily).

The walkway, alongside the roofless **Convento do Carmo** ⑳, used to connect the lift with the Largo do Carmo and entrance to the **Museu Arqueológico do Carmo** (open 10am–6pm Tues–Sun; entrance charge). This remarkable ruin is one of Lisbon's most poignant sights. It was built by Nuno Alvares Pereira, João I's young general at the Battle of Aljubarrota (1385), who spent the last

Map on page 154

The tram is the most pleasant way to get around in Lisbon – No. 28 from Chiado to the castle has the most scenic route.

BELOW: taking it easy in the Chiado.

eight years of his life here. Left unrestored after the 1755 earthquake, the remains of the nave give the most eloquent reminder of that tumultuous event. Gothic arches soar skywards over a grassy nave, a venue for occasional concerts, while the part which survived serves as an archaeological museum with some curious tombs and an eclectic mix of exhibits from South America to England.

From the convent, turn right on Rua Garrett, then left on Rua Serpa Pinto, to reach Lisbon's opera house, the **Teatro de São Carlos ㉑**. La Scala in Milan and the San Carlos theatre in Naples were the inspiration behind its construction in 1792, and the Italian influence is obvious.

A short walk to the northwest, along Rua Nova da Trindade, brings you to **Igreja São Roque** (St Rock Church) **㉒** (open daily 10am–5pm; entrance charge). Behind an unremarkable post-1755 façade lies an opulent interior. The ceiling has been painted to give a beautiful *trompe l'oeil* effect, and the eight chapels are all individual works of art. There are notable *azulejos* by Francisco de Matos and an excellent canvas, *Vision of St Rock,* painted by Gaspar Dias around 1584. The main draw is the **Capela de São João Baptista**, said to be the costliest chapel in the world and commissioned in 1742 by João V. Luigi Vanvitelli and Niccolo Salvi designed and built it in Rome, where it was blessed by the Pope, then dismantled and transported to Lisbon. Gold, silver and bronze decorate the extravagant confection of lapis lazuli, alabaster, marble and ivory, central to which is a mosaic of St John. Adjoining the church is the **Museu de Arte Sacra**, a small but impressive collection of vestments and ecclesiastical furnishings in rich baroque designs.

If you continue up Rua Dom Pedro V, you will reach the **Solar do Instituto do Vinho do Porto ㉓**, the Port Wine Institute. A vast selection of ports can be sampled in the cosy bar of this former 18th-century palace. Virtually opposite is the shady São Pedro de Alcântara *miradouro* (viewpoint) which offers a very admirable panorama of the city.

The Portuguese delight in gardens, so naturally Lisbon is laced with green spaces. Perhaps the finest of them all is the **Jardim Botânico ㉔**, to the right of the Praça do Príncipe Real, one of the richest such gardens in Europe. Created in 1873, it has a magnificent wall of 100-year-old palm trees, banana trees, bamboo and water lilies, and many tropical plants.

Northwest, up the Rua das Amoreiras beyond Largo do Rato, is a large, simple building, the **Mãe d'Agua das Amoreiras ㉕**, which once stored the city's water supply, brought in along the **Aqueduto das Aguas Livres** (enquire at the water museum about visits). Eager shoppers may be tempted to investigate the shops in the nearby **Centro Comercial Amoreiras**.

South from Amoreiras (head down Rua Ferreira Borges into Domingo Sequeira) are the attractive Jardim da Estréla and the splendid late 18th-century **Basílica da Estréla ㉖**, with its great dome and multi-hued marble interior. This neighbourhood is in some ways an Anglo-Saxon oasis. Close by is the British Hospital, the little English Church of St George, and the adjacent **Cemitério dos Ingleses** (English Cemetery) where Henry Fielding (1707–54), the author of *Tom Jones*, was buried, after a trip to the warmer

BELOW: the atmospheric ruins of the Convento do Carmo.

climes of Lisbon failed to cure his gout or asthma. Special permission is required to visit the nearby **Palácio de São Bento ㉗** (east along Calçada da Estréla), now the Portuguese Houses of Parliament. Originally built as a monastery, the palace was transformed into the parliament building at the end of the 19th century and was renovated in 1935.

From here, take the Avenida Dom Carlos I down to the river and turn right to reach the **Museu Nacional de Arte Antiga ㉘** (Museum of Ancient Art; open Tues 2–6pm, Wed–Sun 10am–12.45pm, 2–6pm; entrance charge). This, one of Lisbon's most important museums, is located in a fine 17th-century palace (property of the Counts of Alvor), with a tasteful modern extension. The term "ancient" may be misleading, as most of the exhibits are only a few centuries old, but there are fine displays of 16th-century porcelain, brought back by Portuguese sailors from India, Japan and Macau, and displays of furniture, sculpture and glass. Perhaps of most interest, the museum's galleries also hold a wide selection of paintings by Nuno Gonçalves and other artists of the 15th–16th-century Portuguese School *(see page 123)*, as well as works by Hieronymus Bosch, Brueghel the Younger, Hans Memling, Giambattista Tiepolo, José de Ribera and other great masters.

Belém

In a green spacious zone by the river, on the western side of town beyond the **Ponte 25 de Abril ㉙** and the restaurants and nightclubs around the renovated dock at **Alcântara**, a number of monumental buildings stand as testimony to Portugal's maritime past. Belém means Bethlehem, and reflects the country's involvement with the crusades. It is here that you will find Lisbon's most

Maps on 154 & 164–5

The landmark Amoreiras Shopping Centre is a very popular destination for shoppers in Lisbon. It has over 300 shops.

BELOW LEFT: the Centro Comercial Amoreiras.
BELOW: interior of the Basílica da Estréla.

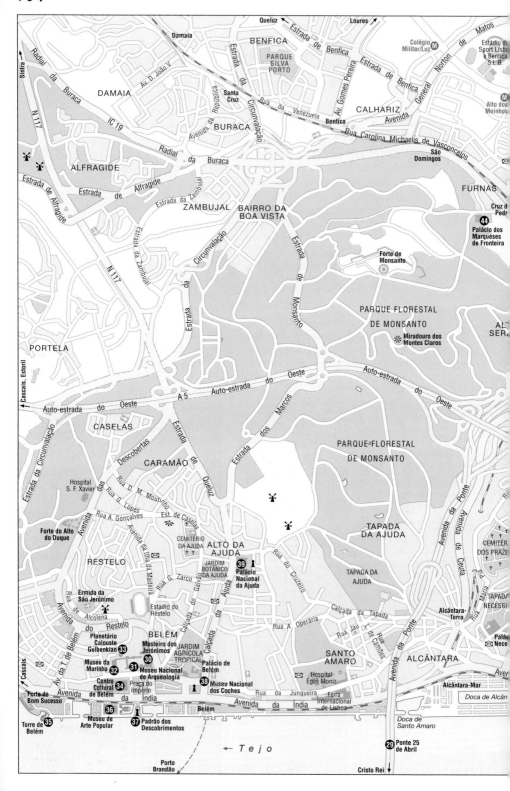

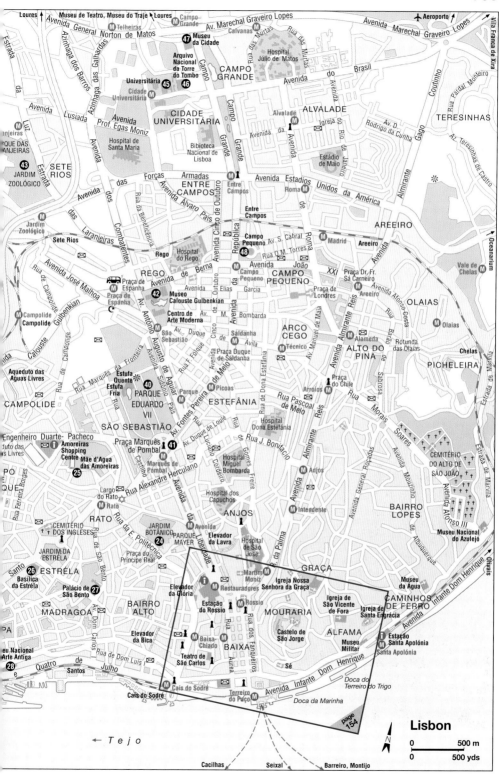

Lisbon

| 0 | 500 m |
| 0 | 500 yds |

glorious monument, the **Mosteiro dos Jerónimos** ❸⓿ (open Tues–Sun; closed holidays; entrance charge to cloisters), built to honour Vasco da Gama and his successful journey to India in 1498, and now a UNESCO World Heritage Site. This vast opulent limestone building, a masterpiece of Manueline (or late Gothic) architecture *(see page 117)*, took 70 years to complete. Entrance is through the west door into a low vaulted section, where effigies of Vasco da Gama and Luís de Camões lie. This contrasts sharply with the soaring elegance of the main body of the church. Ribbed vaulting, supported by polygonal columns, becomes an eye-catching star-shaped feature where the transepts cross, and elephant-supported tombs are a reminder of India. The delicacy of the sculpting make the double-storey cloisters well worth a visit.

A local speciality are sweet tarts, known as "Pastéis de Bélem". You can buy them from the Pastelaria Casa dos Pastéis de Bélem.

Built on the western side of the monastery, in the latter part of the 19th century, is a wing which houses the **Museu Nacional de Arqueologia** ❸❶ (National Museum of Archaeology), which has an interesting collection of folk art dating to the Stone and Bronze Ages (open Tues pm, Wed–Sun 10am–6pm; entrance charge). Part of the same wing, the **Museu da Marinha** ❸❷ (Maritime Museum) tells the story of Portugal's seafaring discoveries with redundant royal barges and fishing vessels on display in a separate building (open Tues–Sun; closed Mon and holidays; entrance charge). The **Planetário Calouste Gulbenkian** ❸❸ (Planetarium) behind gives regular presentations (Wed, Thurs, Sat and Sun; entrance charge).

Close by, the huge and highly controversial **Centro Cultural de Belém** ❸❹ opened in 1992 when Portugal assumed the EC (now EU) presidency, impinges on the glorious architecture of an earlier age and continues to affront the sensibilities of local people, but exhibitions and events here are worth looking out for.

BELOW: the splendid portal of the Mosteiro dos Jerónimos.

On the bank of the Rio Tejo, on the far side of the broad Avenida da India and a small park, stands the **Torre de Belém** ❸❺ (open Tues–Sun; entrance charge), on the site where Vasco da Gama and other navigators set out on their explorations. This exquisite little 16th-century fortress is another fine example of the Manueline style, with its richly carved niches, towers and shields bearing the Templar cross.

A short distance to the east is the **Museu de Arte Popular** ❸❻ (open Tues–Sun; closed 12.30–2pm; entrance charge), with regional displays of local folk art. On the waterfront close by, you can't miss the impressive **Padrão dos Descobrimentos** ❸❼, the Monument of the Discoveries (open Tues–Sun; closed holidays; entrance charge). Erected in 1960, the monument is a stylised caravel, with Prince Henry the Navigator at the fore gazing seawards and other leading figures of the age behind him.

East of the monument, on the Calçada da Ajuda, rises the ornate rose-coloured **Palácio de Belém**, which once served as a royal retreat but is now the official residence of the President of the Republic. Adjacent, in what was once the royal riding-school, is the **Museu Nacional dos Coches** ❸❽ (Coach Museum), which houses one of the finest collections of coaches in Europe (open Tues–Sun 10am–6pm; entrance charge). Up the hill to the side of the palace is the imposing **Palácio Nacional da Ajuda** ❸❾,

built after the earthquake as a royal palace but never completed. It is now used for exhibitions and concerts, and some rooms are open to the public (open Thur–Tues; entrance charge).

The northern hills

Travelling northeast and crossing the Avenida da Ponte again (all but the most hardy will do this by public transport or taxi), you will find that the **Parque Eduardo VII** ⑩ provides an immediate escape from the clamour of the city and offers magnificent views back down to the Tejo. The park was named to mark the state visit of King Edward VII of England in 1903, which was the first he made to a foreign country after his coronation. In the top left-hand corner of the park, but reached from Rua Castilho, are two greenhouses, the **Estufa Quente** (hot-house), originally built to house exotic orchids, and the better known **Estufa Fria** (cold-house).

At the southeast corner of the park is the **Praça Marquês de Pombal** ⑪, or the Rotunda, as it is more commonly known. From his lofty perch in the centre, a statue of the Marquês looks out over the city he rebuilt. From here, the **Avenida da Liberdade** sweeps southwards, linking the Rotunda with the Baixa area. The Avenida was developed as a dual carriageway in 1879 and became the epitome of style, with palm trees and water features lining the route. Cafés and old façades still lend pockets of shaded elegance, despite modern-day intrusions. The little **Parque Mayer**, about two-thirds of the way down, is an enclave of restaurants and theatres, the latter specialising in popular comedy known as *revistas*, satirical variety shows commenting on current political events.

Map on pages 164–5

TIP

The giant Centro Comercial Colombo is opposite the new Benfica Football Stadium and museum, site of the 2004 European World Cup Final. It opens daily 10am–9pm. Colegio Militar metro.

LEFT: the Torre de Belém. **BELOW:** tranquillity in the Parque Eduardo VII.

A colourful kiosk in the Avenida.

Gulbenkian's legacy

Instead of returning to Baixa, leave the Parque Eduardo VII by the northern exit and walk northeast for a short way to a large landscaped complex containing the **Museu Calouste Gulbenkian** ⓬ (open Tues pm, Wed–Sun 10am–6pm; entrance charge). The Calouste Gulbenkian Foundation was set up by the Turkish-Armenian oil magnate, who was born in Istanbul in 1869 and became very attached to Portugal after being harrassed and hounded by the Allies in World War II and seeking refuge in neutral Portugal. The Foundation is the most important funding source for the arts in the country, and there are Gulbenkian libraries and museums throughout the country. When Calouste Gulbenkian died in 1955 his collection, one of the richest private collections in the world, was bequeathed to the nation.

The museum's contents include displays of Middle Eastern and Islamic art, Chinese porcelain, Japanese prints and gold and silver Greek coins. Among magnificent exhibits from the West are paintings by 17th-century masters like Rubens and Rembrandt, and by Impressionists such as Renoir, Manet and Monet. There are also rich Italian tapestries; and a whole room dedicated to the Art Nouveau creations of René Lalique. A pleasant walk through the park-like complex leads to the **Centro de Arte Moderna**, which displays the work of 20th-century Portuguese artists (open Tues pm, Wed–Sun 10am–6pm; entrance charge).

For a rather different form of entertainment, you can take the metro one stop northwest to the zoo, or **Jardim Zoológico** ⓭ (open 10am daily; entrance charge), which is set in the Parque das Laranjeiras (Orange Tree Park). Just southwest of the zoo, on the edge of the Parque Florestal de Monsanto, you'll

find an unexpected gem in the form of the walled, pink-washed 17th-century **Palácio dos Marquéses de Fronteira** ❹ (guided tours daily: June–Sep; 10.30am, 11am, 11.30am, 12 noon; Oct–May; 11am, 12 noon; closed Sun; entrance charge). The house and garden are decorated with some unusual and captivating *azulejos*.

Map on pages 164–5

Campo Grande: north and south

On Campo Grande you'll find the group of pleasant modern buildings that make up the **Cidade Universitária** ❹ (University) although the nearby **Arquivo Nacional da Torre do Tombo** ❹, a fort-like building which holds the national archives, is architecturally more striking. In an 18th-century palace at the end of Campo Grande is the **Museu da Cidade** ❹ (City Museum; open Tues–Sun; closed 1–2pm; entrance charge), with an interesting collection of archaeological pieces and engravings. Opposite, the Campo Grande becomes a shady promenade with a small lake.

Sculpture in the park of the Gulbenkian complex.

Heading south along Avenida da República, the large 19th-century bull ring, **Campo Pequeno** , ❹ is hard to miss, and is not a bad place to witness one of Portugal's relatively animal-friendly bullfights. Across the street, the **Feira Popular** is a permanent, brightly-lit amusement park (open Mon–Fri 4.30pm–midnight, weekends and holidays 2pm–midnight).

If you head in the opposite direction, north from Campo Grande up Avenida Padre Cruz, you reach **Parque do Monteiro-Mór**. Located in old manor houses in these gardens are the Museu do Trajo (Costume Museum; open Tues–Sun 10am–6pm; entrance charge); and the Museu do Teatro (Theatre Museum; open Tues pm, Wed–Sun 10am–6pm; entrance charge). ❑

BELOW: Palácio dos Marqueses de Fronteira, famous for its *azulejos*.

AZULEJOS: HOW TILES BECAME AN ART FORM

Featuring in everything from cathedral cupolas to beer houses, azulejos *are an integral part of Portugal's architectural heritage*

The Portuguese have had a lasting love affair with *azulejos* – painted ceramic tiles – ever since they first set eyes on those imported from Seville in the 15th century. *Azulejos* are not unique to Portugal, but they have become almost a national emblem.

Local production of tiles began soon after the arrival of the geometric Sevillian prototypes. Early ones, used mostly in church interiors, were mainly in shades of blue, with patterns established during the course of firing by separating the colours, using rivulets of linseed oil or ridges of clay. Quality improved with the introduction of the Italian majolica technique, in which the tile was covered with white enamel onto which paint could be applied directly. This greater freedom permitted more artistic expression. Tapestry designs, based on Moorish patterns, began to appear, founded on a module of four tiles, in blue, yellow, green and white.

The next leap was the introduction of Delft blue from Holland. The Portuguese took to it immediately and it dominated tile production for a period, but by the mid-18th century there was a return to high-quality polychrome tiles. During the rebuilding of Lisbon after the great earthquake of 1755, the demand for tiles escalated. They were used for internal and external decoration in every aspect of architecture: churches, private homes, public buildings and even on park benches. New factories opened to supply the demand but, inevitably, artistic standards fell and many tiles had to be imported.

The best place to trace the development of the tiles is in the Museu Nacional do Azulejo, in Lisbon.

◁ **HISTORY IN THE PARK**
Azulejos can be instructive as well as decorative: here a park bench in Portimão depicts scenes from Portuguese history.

△ **EXUBERANT DESIGN**
The god Bacchus, depicted in a 17th-century tile pattern, is a flamboyant early example of the use of *azulejos* for secular, as well as sacred, design.

MASTERPIECES OF DECORATIVE ART

△ **CERVEJARIA, LISBON**
Using tiles for internal decoration, as in this beer house, offers great opportunities for artistic expression.

▽ **LISBON VERNACULAR**
Azulejos became popular in vernacular architecture, lending distinction to façades such as this.

Towards the end of the 17th century, tile painting became a recognised art form in Portugal. One of the earliest masters to find fame in this field was António de Oliveira Bernardes. Together with his son, Policarpo, he set up a school of painters in Lisbon which rapidly became influential. Many beautiful works produced by this school in the first half of the 18th century found their way into churches, monasteries and palaces.

The interior of the Capela de São Lourenço in Algarve *(illustrated above)* is covered with *azulejos* depicting the life of the saint, many believed to be the work of Policarpo. Art historians have also identified the works of António Bernardes in Nossa Senhora da Cabaça at Évora.

◁ **FLORAL PATTERNS**
A letter box set into a wall in Obidos is tiled with a floral motif. Once *azulejos* were no longer confined to churches and palaces, they cropped up everywhere.

▷ **RESTORER AT WORK**
Many of the earlier *azulejo* tiles are recognised as part of the country's heritage, and highly regarded. Restoring them is skilled and demanding work.

ESTORIL AND CASCAIS

*Close to Lisbon, these neighbouring resorts are well connected
to the city, convenient for exploring as far north as Sintra,
and also a delight for windsurfers and golfers*

Map
on page
176

Handily located for **Lisbon ❶**, south-facing Estoril and Cascais are the most significant coastal resorts outside Algarve, although neither is especially large. They grew to prominence as a playground for Lisboetas, but modern times have witnessed a role reversal: these resorts and their environs are dormitories for wealthy Lisbon commuters, and are preferred places to stay for many visitors whose main intent is to explore the capital.

The electric train offers the quickest and most convenient way of travelling the 29-km (18-mile) distance into Lisbon. It arrives in Cais do Sodré station on the west side of the city, close to the riverside, where the green (Verde) Metro line begins. Some of the mainline trains also stop at Belém which is convenient for visiting one of the capital's most interesting areas.

The *Marginal* (N6) route along the riverside out of Lisbon leads through Belém to the elegant hillside neighbourhood of Restelo, the location of many embassies and diplomatic residences. **Algés** is the first town outside the city limits, and it is here that taxi drivers turn off their meters and start calculating by kilometres.

A string of small riverside towns follow. **Dáfundo** has several splendid old mansions standing in rather sad contrast alongside dilapidated rent-controlled housing. It also has the **Aquário Vasco da Gama** (open daily 10am–6pm; entrance charge), a fascinating world of sea turtles, eels, barnacles and all kinds of fish, though rather eclipsed by the Oceanarium in the Parque das Nacões. **Cruz Quebrada** is the site of a stone-seated soccer stadium, while **Caxias** is known for its flowering villas, 18th-century gazebos and an infamous hillside prison-fort. In **Oeiras** you'll find a fine 18th-century baroque church, a lovely park, modern apartment blocks and an austere 16th-century fort and vintage car museum.

Just beyond lies the 17th-century fortress of **São Julião da Barra**, marking the point where the Tejo meets the Atlantic. **Carcavelos** has several moderate hotels and a broad sandy beach.

Elegant Estoril

And so to **Estoril ❷**, the first point of what has often been called the Golden Triangle, and includes Cascais and Sintra. A flowering, palm-lined, pastel-coloured resort, it first gained fame at the turn of the century for its therapeutic spring waters. During World War II, Estoril became known as the haunt of international spies. Later, this corner of the Atlantic, with its mild weather and gracious lifestyle, became a home-from-home for dispossessed European royalty and for refugees fleeing the political upheavals after the war. Among the Triangle's illustrious residents

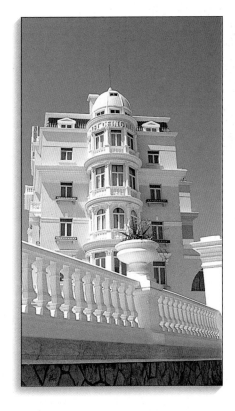

PRECEDING PAGES:
Cascais is well
geared to visitors.
LEFT: windsurfing at
Praia do Guincho.
BELOW: Costa do
Sol Hotel, Estoril.

TIP

The train service
between Lisbon and
Estoril and Cascais is
frequent, and the
journey only takes
about half an hour.

were former kings Simeon of Bulgaria and Umberto of Italy, and Bolivia's ex-leader, Antenor Patiño.

With changing times, local aristocrats are selling or renting their villas. More and more Portuguese and foreigners come to the Triangle to live, retire or keep summer homes. Estoril has now become a cosmopolitan playground with its celebrated casino, first-rate hotels, restaurants and a range of popular international tennis and golf tournaments. There is no brashness here: the sophisticated image remains untarnished by rashes of modernity like fast-food outlets, trading posts, kiss-me-quick hats and the like. It is not that sort of resort.

Estoril's fine sandy **Tamariz** beach is attractively set with a touch of the picturesque, added by a castellated private house surrounded by palms at the eastern end. Even this Atlantic location has suffered from water pollution in recent years, although the situation is improving, with continued investment in the infrastructure. Even so, beaches further west offer reliably safer waters.

The **Casino** in the heart of the town is a low, white modern building with

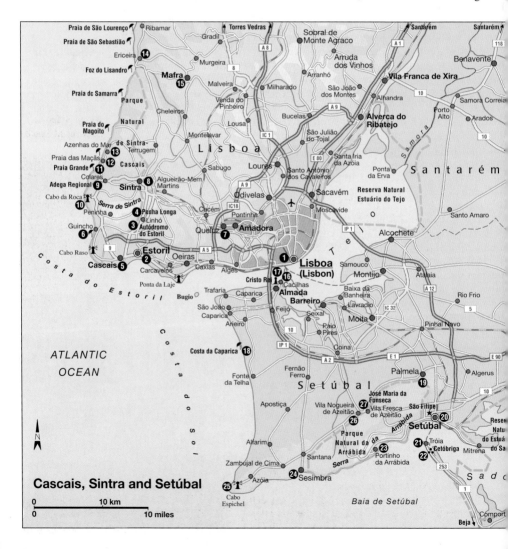

Cascais, Sintra and Setúbal

immaculately kept gardens. To gamble here, you need a passport, driver's licence or identity card to get in, and the minimum age limit is 18. Some people come to the Casino just to see the show, usually a colourful international extravaganza, but it's fun to keep an eye on the betting. As in all crowded venues, keep your valuables hidden. There is also an elegant dining room, an art gallery, a cinema and a bar.

Map on page 176

Festivals and rallies

The **Estoril Music Festival** takes place from mid-July to mid-August. Concerts and recitals are held in Estoril Cathedral, Cascais Cidadela (fort) and other impressive settings. The **Handicrafts Fair** has become a major production, lasting throughout the months of July and August. Located near the railway station, the fair features arts and crafts, food, wine and folk music from all over the country.

There is a lot to do in the way of sports in the Triangle. The **Autódromo do Estoril ❸**, the automobile race track located inland on the road to Sintra, used to draw large crowds for the Grand Prix Formula One races but the track fails to meet current safety requirements for Formula One racing and is now used for other events, such as the start and finish of the annual international Port Wine Rally. A huge shopping development nearby with car parking for 3,000 vehicles has attracted many international stores.

Mild winters and summers tempered by cool westerlies provide ideal weather conditions for golf all year around. There are nine courses on the north side of the Tejo and four within easy reach on the south. **Penha Longa ❹** *(see box below)* is one of the best.

BELOW: faded elegance at Estoril.

GOLF IN THE GOLDEN TRIANGLE

The Estoril Golf Club's course, on the outskirts of town, is one of the loveliest in Europe. It was laid out by McKenzie Ross on a hillside dotted with pine and eucalyptus groves. The smaller, 9-hole Estoril-Sol Golf Course is located in a pine wood at Linhó near Sintra. Overlooking the Atlantic coast just beyond Cascais is the Marinha Golf Club, with swimming pools, tennis and riding facilities and an 18-hole course designed by Robert Trent Jones. Quinta da Beloura, which was designed by William Roquemore and opened in 1993, lies beneath the hills of Serra de Sintra. Six lakes provide golfers with plenty of watery challenges.

Penha Longa, built with Japanese finance, is more than a golf course; it is a country club with a whole range of sporting activities, and includes a five-star hotel. The 18-hole and 9-hole courses designed by Robert Trent Jones II embrace natural woodland and rocky outcrops. This is located between Serra de Sintra and the Atlantic. Finally, there is Quinta da Marina, which lies just west of Cascais. Designed by Robert Trent Jones, this attractive course weaves through umbrella pines, water features and wind-blown sand dunes. *(See Travel Tips, page 377, for telephone numbers and other details.)*

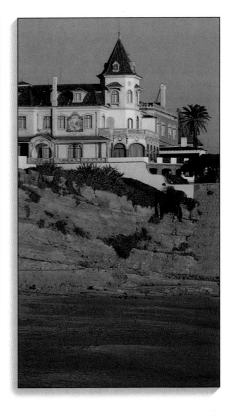

Cascais: resort of kings

Although it was once a royal resort, the attractive town of **Cascais** ❺ lacks the glamorous reputation of Estoril. In 1870, King Luís I established his summer residence in the 17th-century Citadel on the Bay of Cascais. Before that, it was known only as a fishing port. Locals claim that it was a fisherman from Cascais, Afonso Sanches, who actually discovered America in 1482, and Christopher Columbus merely repeated the trip 10 years later and got all the glory. In 1580, the Duke of Alba attacked Cascais when Spain was laying claim to Portugal. And in 1589 the English arrived here to retaliate for the Spanish Armada's 1588 foray. The fishing port still remains, with the comings and goings of the colourful fishing boats in the bay, the noisy nightly auction at the central fish market, and good shopping and restaurants.

Around the port has grown a resort with all the vibrancy that Estoril lacks, and yet it has managed to avoid spilling beyond its original boundaries. Pedestrianised streets are paved with traditional black-and-white *calçada* blocks, recreating dynamic wave patterns, which may make seamen feel at home but can make landlubbers a little queasy. They are colourful for all that, especially where the street cafés spill out and the street traders set up stalls. A Wednesday market where you can buy fresh fruit and vegetables as well as handicrafts is repeated on a smaller scale on Saturday morning.

There are several old churches and chapels in Cascais, including the 17th-century **Nossa Senhora da Assunção** with its plain façade, lovely tiles and marble nave. It contains several paintings by the 17th-century artist, Josefa de Obidos. On the outskirts of town, in an exotic garden, is the **Museu Condes de Castro Guimarães** (open Tues–Sun 10am–5pm; entrance charge). Housed in the for-

Estoril and Cascais are joined by a pedestrianised promenade which is a delight to walk. It passes by the beaches, and there are snack bars and restaurants along the way.

BELOW: The Museu Condes de Castro Guimarães.

Map on page 176

mer residence of the Conde de Castro Guimarães, this museum displays 17th-century Portuguese silver, tiles and furniture, and some good 19th-century paintings, as well as prehistoric finds. The **Museu do Mar Dom Carlos** is the best place to glimpse the community's past (open Tues–Sun 10am–5pm; entrance charge). It tells the lives of the fishermen and has many photographs of King Carlos, a keen oceanographer, who started the bathing season with his arrival here each September during the 1890s.

Cascais also has its own bullring, although few fights are scheduled: it's usually too windy. There are also opportunities for horse riding at the Escola de Equitação de Birre on the road to Sintra, and at the Centro Hípico da Marinha, inland from the beach at Guincho *(see below)*.

The main beaches lie between Cascais and Estoril; there is a small beach to the west, **Praia de Santa Marta**, but it's barely big enough for a game of volleyball. Take a short walk beyond, along the main road, and you will come to the **Boca do Inferno** ("Mouth of Hell"), a narrow inlet with arches and caverns. Waves crash into the inlet with some ferocity, especially when the Atlantic swell is running high. An informal flea market around the Boca do Inferno has been regularised with custom-built stalls selling colourful woven rugs, sheepskin carpets and craft work, which has taken over as the main attraction.

Beyond here lies the rocky Atlantic coast. Lisboetas flock here on weekends to enjoy seafood at several popular restaurants. Some also swim at the broad clean beach of **Praia do Guincho ❻**, where the waves can be wild and the undertow fierce. Windsurfers love it. Some people, however, simply like to take the road to Sintra, through the pines and along the open coast. ❑

Omnipresent Dom Pedro, immortalised in Cascais.

BELOW: the Boca do Inferno.

SINTRA

Known by the Romans as the Mountains of the Moon, the Serra da Sintra holds a delightful confection of palaces and monuments along with some splendid beaches

Map on page 176

With its lush forests and gentle surrounding plain, Sintra has long been a favourite summer resort for Portuguese and foreign visitors. People delight in the area because of its sheer natural beauty and it was declared a World Heritage Site by UNESCO in 1995. Lord Byron, who could find little good to say about the Portuguese, was enamoured of Sintra and likened it to "Elysium's gates". In *Childe Harold*, he wrote: "Lo! Cintra's glorious Eden intervenes in variegated maze of mount and glen".

Some 32 km (20 miles) to the northwest of Lisbon, Sintra is another world with its own special climate – a clash of warm southerlies and moist westerlies over the Serra da Sintra – and an almost bucolic way of life. The most practical way to go is by train from Rossio. If you drive, rush hour traffic should be avoided if at all possible. The road to Sintra from Lisbon starts at the Praça Marquês de Pombal and is well marked. Avenida Duarte Pacheco runs into the *auto-estrada* or super highway that leads out of town, past the Aqueduto das Aguas Livres, up the hill through Parque de Monsanto, turning right to join the highway to Sintra. Trains go regularly from Rossio station, taking 35 minutes and stopping at Queluz-Belas, for the palace, after 20 minutes.

LEFT: the Swan Ceiling in Sintra's Palácio Nacional.
BELOW: the splendid palace and gardens at Queluz.

Queluz Palace and Sintra Vila

A slight detour to visit **Queluz ❼** is well worthwhile. The town has become a rather drab Lisbon dormitory, but its rose-coloured palace is anything but drab. The **Pálacio** and gardens (open Wed–Mon; closed holidays; entrance charge) was built as a simple manor for King Pedro II in the mid-1600s and was enlarged when the court moved there. Most of the palace, including its magnificent façade, is baroque, but the courtyard and formal gardens were modelled after Versailles. In summer, concerts are sometimes held in the Music Room. At other times, the public may visit the lavishly decorated Throne Room with its fine painted wood ceiling, the Hall of Mirrors, the Ambassador's Room, and others. The great kitchen, with stone chimney and copperware, has been turned into a luxury restaurant called **Cozinha Velha**. Palace and gardens are a spectacular stage during August and September for **Noites de Queluz** (Nights at Queluz), enchanting musical recreations of 18th-century court life.

Back on the main road continue along rolling hills, past modest whitewashed villages and rich *quintas,* or manors, to arrive at the Serra de Sintra. At the base of the mountain lies the village of **São Pedro de Sintra**, where on the second and fourth Sunday of each month, a wonderful country fair takes place. São Pedro is also known for its popular tavernas,

Making use of the high winds.

BELOW: the Palácio Nacional at Sintra, with its distinctive chimney cones.

with spicy sausages, hearty codfish and heady wines. The road now climbs slightly and curves around the mountain to reach **Sintra Vila ❽**, the historic centre of Sintra. Here lies the *Turismo* office and, on the upper floor, the municipal art gallery, the **Museu Regional ❹** (open Mon–Fri; closed noon–2pm; weekends and holidays pm only; entrance charge).The road to the left, Rua Gil Vicente, leads down to **Museu Ferreira de Castro ❸**, which is dedicated to the works of the great Portuguese novelist, Ferreira de Castro (1898–1974). A little further on is the **Hotel Lawrence ❻**, formerly Estalagem dos Cavaleiros, where Lord Byron stayed in 1809, and now restored as an inn under its original name.

The centrepiece of Sintra is the royal palace, the Paço Real, now called the **Palácio Nacional de Sintra ❹**, parts of which date from the 14th century (open 10am–5pm; closed Wed and public holidays; entrance charge). Broad stairs lead up to the stately building with Gothic arches, Moorish windows and two extraordinary chimney cones above its enormous kitchens. Of special interest are: the Sala dos Brasões, with remarkable ceiling panels painted in 1515, which show the coat-of-arms of 71 Portuguese noble families (that of the Távoras was removed after the conspiracy against King José in 1758); the Sala dos Arabes, with marble fountain and 15th-century Moorish tiles; and the Sala dos Cisnes, an enormous reception hall with swans painted on the panelled ceiling; the Sala das Pegas, its ceiling covered with magpies brandishing banners reading "Por Bem". It is said that when Queen Philippa caught João I dallying with a lady-in-waiting he claimed it was an innocent kiss. "Por Bem", he said, which loosely translated means: "It's all for the best". Philippa's response is not recorded.

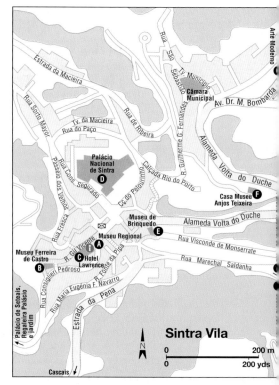

Sintra Vila

0 — 200 m
0 — 200 yds

The other Sintra

Estefânia, the third district of Sintra, is where you go to catch the train or a local bus to Lisbon. Walking in that direction from the historic centre, you pass the **Museu de Brinquedo** (Toy Museum; open Tues–Sun; entrance charge) and then the **Casa Museu Anjos Teixeira** ❻ (open Tues–Sun; closed 12–2pm; entrance charge), which houses an important collection of sculptures. Shortly after this, on the left and before the bus and railway stations, is Sintra's handsome Town Hall. It has a square castellated tower with a steeple in an exuberant Gothic style. Housed in a grand building, in Av. Heliodoro Salqado, is the **Museu de Arte Moderna** ❼ (open Tues–Sun; entrance charge) containing works by Hockney, Lichtenstein and other 20th-century artists.

Mountain retreats

Sintra's other palace-museum, the **Palácio Nacional da Pena** ❽ (open Tues– Sun; closed 1–2pm and holidays; entrance charge), dominates the town from the top of the mountain. The road winds up steep rocky slopes through thick woods to the castle, built on the site of a 16th-century monastery: you can walk up, drive or take a quaint bus. You enter through the **Parque da Pena** where there are lakes with black swans, a wide variety of flora, tangled forest and tiled fountains. Some think the palace is better viewed from afar. Close at hand, the castle is an architectural pot-pourri of various styles and influences: Arabic minarets, Gothic towers, Renaissance cupolas, Manueline windows. But its interior of cosy domesticity is greatly appealing, with rooms furnished as they would have been around the start of the 20th century. It was commissioned by Prince Ferdinand of Saxe-Coburg-Gotha, husband of Queen Maria II, and built

Maps:
Area 176
City 182

TIP

If there is a queue of people waiting for information at the tourist office in Sintra station, head towards the palace for the other, larger tourist office.

BELOW: architectural excess at the Palácio da Pena.

Tile detail on a wall outside at the Quinta de Monserrate.

by German architect Baron von Eschwege around 1840. At the entrance to the castle a tunnel leads to the ruins of the original monastery. The old chapel walls are decorated with fine 17th-century tiles and there is a splendid altar of alabaster and black marble by 16th-century French sculptor Nicolas Chanterène.

Across the way, reached by the bus to Palácio Nacional da Pena, are the ruins of another mountain-top castle, the **Castelo dos Mouros ⓘ**, dating from about the 11th century. The fortifications visible along the mountain ridge were restored in the middle of the 19th century. To the southwest rises the highest peak, **Cruz Alta**, at 540 metres (1,772 ft) and marked by a stone cross. The mountainside is a luxuriant mass of vegetation – subtropical plants, mossy boulders, giant ferns, walnut, chestnut and pine trees, and rhododendron bushes. One of the strangest sights on the mountain is the **Convento dos Capuchos**, a 16th-century monastery built entirely of rocks and cork. Some say the monks lined their cells with cork to obtain absolute silence, but there is little noise here other than bird sounds. More likely, the cork helped insulate the monks from the long bitter winters.

Palatial accommodation

On the outskirts of Sintra Vila (on the way to Colares) stands the **Palácio de Seteais**, an obscure name said to mean "the seven sighs". This was where the Convention of Sintra was signed in 1809, after the defeat of Napoleon by British and Portuguese forces. It is said that the terms of the treaty upset the Portuguese so much that the palace became known for their sighs of despair. Seteais was restored and turned into a luxury hotel and restaurant in 1955 and should be seen, if only for tea or a drink. The elegant rooms contain crystal chandeliers, wall-hangings, murals and antique furnishings. From the gardens you have a magnificent view of the surrounding countryside.

Almost opposite is the remarkable **Quinta da Regaleira** (open to visitors, tel: 219 106 650 to book a tour), built at the close of the 19th century as an assembly of Gothic, Manueline and Renaissance styles that would be out of place anywhere but Sintra.

Nearby is the **Quinta de Monserrate**, a strange Moorish-type villa built in the 19th century. The exotic garden and greenhouse are worth seeing for the trees and plants from all over the world: palms, bamboos, cedars, magnolias, cork-oaks, pines and giant ferns. Once part of the Monserrate gardens, the **Quinta de São Thiago** is a 16th-century manor with a fine chapel, splendid kitchen, cell-like bedrooms, gardens, and its own swimming pool. The owners found taxes and other expenses prohibitive and opened the *quinta* to paying guests. You can also stay in the nearby **Quinta da Capela**.

Coastal excursions

For a delightful excursion, the road to **Colares** leads through vineyards, whitewashed hamlets and stone walls to the sea. En route, it is possible to visit the **Adega Regional ⓾**, a traditional winery, on week days. Colares grapes grow in sandy soil in a humid maritime climate. The wines are dark ruby and very smooth.

BELOW:
Palácio de Seteais.

Cabo da Roca ⑩ is a wild desolate cape, the westernmost point of continental Europe, and visitors receive a certificate to mark their visit. Heading north, there are several beaches frequented mainly by the Portuguese: broad, sandy **Praia Grande** ⑪ and **Praia das Maçãs** ⑫. The attractive fishing village of **Azenhas do Mar** ⑬ has a natural rock seashore swimming pool.

Maps:
Area 176
City 182

Magnificent Mafra

Following the road north towards the coast from Sintra, you reach the beach resort and fishing village of **Ericeira** ⑭. From here it is an easy 10 km (6 miles) drive inland to **Mafra** ⑮, a name shared by both a modest village and a vast palace-convent (open Wed–Mon; closed holidays; entrance charge) nearby, which rises like a dark mirage across the plain. The complex of buildings almost as large as Spain's Escorial was erected by João V in fulfilment of a vow. Work began in 1717 and took 18 years, drawing so many artists from so many countries that João founded the School of Mafra, making these talented men masters to local apprentices. The most famous teacher was Joaquim Machado de Castro, who also worked on Lisbon's Basílica da Estrela *(see page 162)*.

The limestone façade is 220 metres (720 ft) long. At its centre is the church, with two tall towers and an Italianate portico. The interior is decorated with the finest Portuguese marble, while the 14 large statues of saints in the vestibule were carved from Carrara marble by Italian sculptors. The church also contains six organs. Most impressive is the library, full of baroque magnificence and light. Among its 35,000 volumes are first editions of *Os Lusíadas* by Camões and the earliest edition of Homer in Greek. Other areas open to the public include the hospital, pharmacy, audience room and the chapterhouse. ❏

Mafra is the site of the church of Santo André. Pedro Hispano was priest here before he was elected Pope John XXI in 1276 – the only Portuguese pope in the history of the Vatican.

FOLLOWING PAGES: looking out to sea. **BELOW:** the great library at Mafra.

SETÚBAL AND THE ARRÁBIDA PENINSULA

Map on page 176

A mixture of industrial sprawl, nature reserves, ancient sites and huge sandy beaches, the Arrábida Peninsula attracts few visitors but is the preferred place to live for many Lisboetas

L isboetas call it *Outra Banda*, the other shore, meaning the southern bank of the Tejo, long neglected because of the inconvenience of getting there. This changed after 1966 with the completion of what was then Europe's longest suspension bridge, the Ponte 25 de Abril, and an even longer bridge, the Vasco de Gama, in 1998. At present rail passengers must take a ferry across the Tejo to continue any journey south, but a rail link is under way.

The region between the Tejo and Sado rivers, known as the Arrábida Peninsula, has developed rapidly and not always wisely. Directly across the Tejo is the unassuming ferry-boat port of **Cacilhas** ⑯. Its main charm is a string of riverfront fish restaurants with a grand view of Lisbon. About 5 km (3 miles) west of Ponte 25 de Abril is **Trafaria**; the whole town was burned to the ground on the orders of Pombal in 1777 as punishment for resisting press gangs, but was later rebuilt. Most visitors tend to drive through the neighbouring industrial town of Almada without stopping, except those who want to examine the **Cristo Rei** ⑰ (Christ the King monument) at close hand. You can go to the top of the 82-metre (276-ft) pedestal – so high it seems to dwarf the 28-metre (91-ft) figure on top – by elevator and stairs, for a magnificent view of Lisbon.

Most people avoid the *Outra Banda* dormitory district by taking the A2 highway leading directly from the bridge. After a few kilometres, a turn-off leads to **Costa da Caparica** ⑱, a series of broad Atlantic beaches with moderately priced hotels and restaurants. This popular coast is cleaner than the Estoril/Cascais coast, and the currents are safer than those of the Atlantic north of the Tejo.

On to Palmela

Continuing south on the highway, you pass new factories. The road marked **Palmela** ⑲ leads to a small town with a great medieval castle. This has been restored and converted into a luxury *pousada (see page 364)* with a lounge in the cloisters and an elegant dining-room in the old refectory. The church is a beautiful Romanesque structure, its walls covered with 18th-century tiles.

Built by the Moors, the castle was reconstructed in 1147 as a monastery and the seat of the Knights of the Order of Saint James. In 1484, the bishop of Évora was imprisoned in the dungeon for his role in the conspiracy against João II. He died a few days later, probably poisoned. The castle was badly damaged by the 1755 earthquake, but was rebuilt and monks remained here until the abolition of religious orders in 1834.

Just outside Setúbal rises another great castle turned *pousada*, **São Filipe**, with a magnificent view of the

LEFT: the lighthouse at Cabo Espichel.
BELOW: the Cristo Rei monument.

Setúbal may be an industrial town, but it is certainly not devoid of aesthetic sights, ranging from this relatively modest fountain to the fine Igreja de Jesus.

BELOW: the remarkable Igreja de Jesus, Setúbal.

Sado estuary. Felipe II of Spain ordered its construction in 1590, to keep a watch over the area – Portugal was under Spanish rule at the time. The chapel is decorated with tiles that recount the life of the king's namesake, Saint Philip, signed by the master painter Policarpo de Oliveira Bernardes, and dated 1736.

Setúbal and the Tróia peninsula

According to local legend, **Setúbal** ⑳ was founded by Tubal, the son of Cain. It is said that Phoenicians and Greeks, finding the climate and soil of Arrábida similar to their Mediterranean homelands, started vineyards. Setúbal is known to have been an important fishing port since Roman times. Today it is an industrial town, a centre of ship-building, fish-canning, and the production of fertilisers, cement, salt and moscatel wine.

Setúbal's pride is the **Igreja de Jesus**, a spectacular monument dating back to 1491. The church was designed by Diogo Boytac, one of the founding fathers of the Manueline style of architecture. The narrow building has a high arched ceiling supported by six great stone pillars that look like coils of rope; its apse is etched with stone and lined with tiles. Arrábida marble was used, and the pebbled, multi-coloured stone gives it a distinct appearance. There are also lovely tiled panels along the walls. The cloister houses a museum, the **Museu de Setúbal** (open Tues–Sun; closed 12.30–2pm; entrance charge).

Nearby is the **Praça do Bocage**, with palm trees and a statue honouring one of Setúbal's illustrious sons, 18th-century sonneteer, Manuel Barbosa du Bocage. Off the square stands the church of **São Julião** with a handsome Manueline doorway, built in 1513. The inside walls are decorated with 18th-century tiles showing fishing scenes and the life of the saint. Also of interest is the

Museu de Arquelogia e Etnografia with models depicting the main industries: fishing, farming and textiles (open Tues–Sun; closed noon–2pm; entrance charge).

Setúbal's harbour is fascinating, especially in the morning when brightly painted trawlers arrive, loaded with fish. There's a continual show, as fishermen mend nets and work on their boats. Best of all is the lively fish auction.

Setúbal is the main point of departure for the peninsula of **Tróia** ㉑, a long narrow spit jutting out into the Sado estuary. Ferry-boats make the 20-minute crossing frequently in season. On the northern end of the peninsula, there is a rather unattractive modern beach resort. The Tróia Golf Club has an 18-hole course designed by Robert Trent Jones. On the southern end of the peninsula, however, there are still miles of pine forest and glorious empty beaches and dunes. Tróia is said to be the site of the Roman town of **Cetóbriga** ㉒, destroyed by a tidal wave in the 5th century. Substantial ruins have been found but little has been excavated except for a temple and some tombs. Underwater, you may see remains of the walls of Roman houses.

Serra da Arrábida

A delightful excursion from Setúbal goes west through the **Parque Natural da Arrábida**, along the ridge of the Serra da Arrábida which rises to 600 metres (2,000 ft). As you leave the city, the only sight that mars the natural beauty of the coast is the cement factory, usually spitting black smoke. A road descends to **Portinho da Arrábida** ㉓, a popular bathing beach with transparent waters, white sand and the splendid **Gruta da Santa Margarida**. Hans Christian Andersen, who visited the region in 1834, marvelled in his diaries at this cave with its imposing stalactites. Scuba diving is popular here. But it was the poet and historian of

Map on page 176

TIP

From Cetóbriga you could choose to return to Setúbal via Alcácar do Sal, a drive of some 120 km (75 miles), though of course it is much quicker to take the inexpensive car ferry from Tróia.

BELOW: the fine sandy beach of Tróia peninsula stretches as far as the eye can see.

The poet Robert Southey fell in love with Portugal, its climate, landscape, food and wine, and once wrote to a friend that he would "gladly live and die here".

the Peninsular War, Robert Southey (1774–1843), who consecrated Arrábida for English readers, calling it "a glorious spot". He tells of going swimming at the base of the mountain and writes: "I have no idea of sublimity exceeding it".

Regaining the ridge, continue along the skyline drive. The next turn-off leads to **Sesimbra** ㉔, a fine resort with a nearby port and a long fishing tradition. The castle above the village, although known as Moorish, has been entirely rebuilt since that time (open daily, free). Afonso Henriques captured it in 1165, but the Moors utterly razed the structure in 1191. King Dinis almost certainly helped with the rebuilding, and King João IV again enlarged added and repaired it in the 17th century. Inside the walls are ruins of a Romanesque church. João IV also ordered the fort of São Teodosio to be built, to protect the port from pirates. A newer fort, the Nova Fortaleza on the sea front, occupied by the police, is at the heart of the town. Small bars and restaurants fill the streets around it and they are always full of appreciative diners at weekends. Swordfish is the local speciality.

Going westward about 11 km (7 miles), the road ends at **Cabo Espichel** ㉕. This promontory, and the shrine of **Nossa Senhora do Cabo**, used to be an important pilgrimage site, as shown by the long rows of dilapidated pilgrims' quarters on either side of the church. There is still a fishermen's festival here each October. On the edge of the high cliff is the small fishermen's chapel of Senhor de Bomfim, with a breathtaking view; the cliffs are wonderful for walking.

Olive tree village

The road back to Lisbon goes through **Vila Nogueira de Azeitão** ㉖, sometimes simply called Azeitão, which means "large olive tree". In the centre of this charming village is the stately Palácio Távora, where the Duke of Aveiro and his

BELOW: freshly caught fish for sale. **BELOW RIGHT:** a local olive farmer.

friends are said to have plotted to overthrow King José. They were burned at the stake in Belém in 1759. Lovely baroque fountains border the town's main street. The Igreja São Lourenço has been restored and has beautiful 18th-century altars, paintings and tile panels.

Map
on page
176

The Azeitão fair, held in the central square on the first Sunday of the month, became so popular that it caused havoc and had to be moved to the outskirts of town. Less picturesque now, it is still a major attraction offering everything from shoes and pottery to furniture, plus a large section devoted to livestock.

In the village is the original **José Maria da Fonseca Winery ㉗**, founded in 1834. The old family residence, which now houses a small museum, stands nearby. The winery still produces one of Portugal's best red table wines, the soft rich Periquita, as well as Setúbal's popular moscatel wines. Visitors are welcome on weekdays to tour the factory and see its assembly-line production.

Not far from town stands one of the oldest inhabited manors in the country, the **Quinta da Bacalhoa**, built in 1480. It had fallen into ruins and was saved by an American woman from Connecticut, Mrs Herbert Scoville, who bought it in 1936. The gardens, open to the public, are admirable with their clipped boxwood in geometric design, orange and lemon groves, and pavilion with beautiful tile panels. One of these scenes, showing Susanna and the Elders, is dated 1565, and said to be the earliest known dated panel in Portugal.

Another attractive manor, the **Quinta das Torres**, stands just outside the neighbouring village of **Vila Fresca de Azeitão**. This 16th-century *quinta*, decorated with tile panels and set in a romantic garden, has been converted into a cosy inn and restaurant. In the village, there is yet another charming church, São Simão, with more ancient tile walls and polychrome panels. ❏

BELOW: Cabo Espichel sweeps into the Atlantic.

ALGARVE

Moorish arches drenched in sunshine and spectacular coves of golden sand: Algarve offers a touch of the exotic which attracts visitors by the million

Map on pages 198–9

I f one region of Portugal stands alone, it is Algarve. Its history under long Moorish control, its climate – more typically Mediterranean – and its abundance of fine sandy beaches endow Algarve with a character so different it could easily be taken as a separate country. In the minds of many visitors, it is.

Separated from the rest of Portugal by rolling hills, Algarve, the southernmost province, seduced the ancient Phoenicians with its abundance of sardines and tuna, which they salt-cured for export almost 3,000 years ago. Four centuries later, around 600 BC, the Carthaginians and Celts arrived, followed in turn by the Romans, who adopted the Phoenician practice of curing and exporting fish – the precursor of Portugal's large tinned sardine industry. They built roads, bridges and spas, such as that in Milreu.

But Algarve really blossomed under Moorish rule, which began in the early 8th century. The province's name comes from the Moorish *Al-Gharb* meaning "The West". The Moorish period was one of vivacious culture and great scientific advances. Moorish poets sang of the beauty of Silves, its principal city, while the more practical settlers introduced orange crops, and perfected the technique of extracting olive oil, which is still an important Portuguese product. The blossoming almond trees in February are one of the most beautiful sights of Algarve thanks, according to folklore, to the passion a Moorish king once felt for a northern princess.

Legend has it that the princess, pining for the snows of her homeland, slowly began to waste away. Distraught, the king ordered thousands of almond trees to be planted across the region, then one February morning carried her to the window where she saw swirling white "snow flakes" carpeting the ground – the white almond blossoms. She quickly recuperated, and the two lived happily ever after.

Moorish legacy

King Afonso Henriques led the Portuguese conquest southward in the 12th century, and later his son Sancho I, with the help of a band of crusaders, was to spearhead the siege of Silves and its estimated population of 20,000 people. It took 49 days before the Moors of Silves surrendered. But in 1192 they reconquered the city and remained there for another 47 years. It was Sancho II, supported by military-religious orders under Paio Peres Correia, who finally crushed them. The last major city to fall was Faro in January 1249.

But the Arabic influence is visible even today: in many town names, in words beginning with the "al" prefix, in the so-called "North African blue" used in trimming the whitewashed houses, in the roof terraces used for the drying of fruit, and the white-domed

PRECEDING PAGES: the rocky coast near Lagos. **LEFT:** a languid lady at the palace in Estoi. **BELOW:** a typical Algarve chimney.

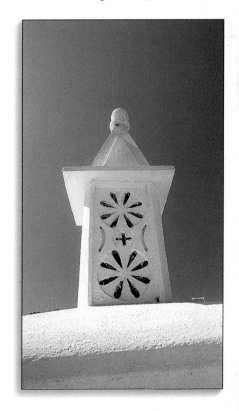

buildings still popular in many towns. Algarvian sweets made of figs, almonds, eggs and sugar called *morgados* or *Dom Rodrigos* are yet another reminder of the area's ancient heritage.

For centuries almond, fig, olive and carob trees represented a major part of Algarve's agriculture, as they are suited to dry inland areas. The carob, whose beans are now fed to cattle but which also produce a variety of oil, are said to have sustained the British troops in Portugal during the Peninsular War. Thanks to the gentle climate Algarve also produces pears, apples, quinces, loquats, damask plums, pomegranates, tomatoes, melons, strawberries, avocados and grapes.

Regional specialities

Wine critics regard all Algarve wines as undistinguished, and even in quite modest restaurants the house wine is usually from the better Alentejo range, or perhaps from even further to the north. But many local wines are quite palatable. You will find good beer, the preference of most young Algarvios, widely available. Older men passing the time in *tavernas* and *tascas* drink *medronho,* a clear firewater with the kick of a mule, distilled from the fruit of the strawberry tree, *Arbutus unedo.* Another individual drink in Algarve is *Brandymel,* a type of honey brandy.

The pleasant market town of Loulé *(see page 210),* with its central tree-shaded walkway, is the craft centre of Algarve, but local handicrafts are widely sold everywhere. Among them are rush or straw baskets, hats, mats and hampers, which are made by women who pick and dry the esparto in spring, then shred it into thin strips before they weave and plait it. You will see mats of grass, and of cotton and wool (some of them come from Alentejo). Cane basketry is almost

Fashion accessories for the beach.

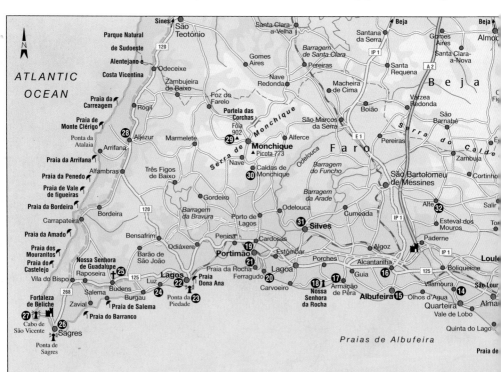

always the work of men in the eastern towns of Odeleite, Alcoutim and Castro Marim. Despite a modern prevalence of cardboard boxes, baskets are still used to carry eggs, to display golden smoked sardines, and as fish traps.

Lagos, Loulé and Tavira – as well as numerous stores along the main N125 highway – are good places to find pottery, from big pitchers, plant pots, hand-painted plates and tiles, to the distinctive, lace-like chimney tops that embellish Algarve's skyline. You'll find a considerable range of copper pots and bowls – one shop is on a street corner beside the market in Loulé. If you walk down the avenue you'll see – and hear – coppersmiths at work in tiny workshops.

Woodwork is also a regional craft, from spoons made in Aljezur to the brightly-coloured mule-drawn carts you'll still see on the roads. Hand-made lace is a skill that's being kept alive in such places as Azinhal. Up in the hills of Monchique (where a small craft shop has grown to an extensive display) you'll find wooden furniture and woollen weaves.

Key routes and places

The southern coastline, so richly endowed with golden sandy beaches in spectacular settings, is the region's prime asset. At the onset of mass tourism it attracted developers and much of the central region, around Albufeira, is now well developed. Those looking for smaller, quieter coastal resorts can still find them by travelling out to the west beyond Lagos and, to a lesser extent, east of Faro. Inland Algarve has its share of pretty villages and remains largely unspoilt countryside, although it is rapidly becoming the preferred dormitory for expatriate settlers.

Driving around Algarve is not difficult. The N125 travels the length of the

Map below

BELOW: a leisurely ride in the country.

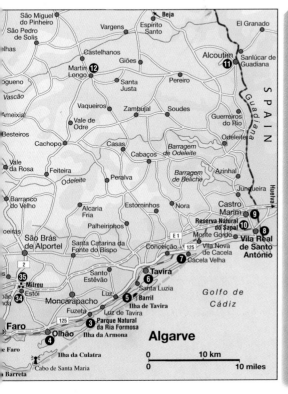

coast, while the toll-free motorway shadows it just inland. It is possible to drive from Spain in the east to Sagres in the west in a little over two hours.

Faro: the hub of Algarve

The roots of **Faro ❶**, the capital of Algarve, are ancient but not well documented. Certainly it was used by Greeks and Romans as a trading post before it became a flourishing Moorish town. Largely devastated by the 1755 earthquake, the city now has an architectural hodge-podge of styles and eras.

The centre of Faro is walkable, its character changing as you wander through streets of tiny houses, 19th-century mansions, modern villas and shops. It's a bustling capital and has considerable charm. The main pedestrianised street, Rua de Santo António, is in the middle of the Moorish quarter (Mouraria) which lies between the old city (Vila-Adentro) and the 19th-century Bairro Ribeirinho, all of which lead from the port.

On the south side of the little harbour, through the 18th-century Arco da Vila that penetrates the old city walls, lies a peaceful and historic inner town, the Vila-Adentro. At its centre is the Renaissance **Sé (Cathedral)** (open weekdays 10am–6pm; entrance charge) with its 13th-century tower. Eighteenth-century polychrome tiles are an impressive feature in its chapels as well as in the body of the church. The red chinoiserie organ is also 18th-century, and the choir stalls a notable trophy from Silves Cathedral when the seat of the diocese was moved to Faro in the 16th century.

In the square behind the cathedral a former convent with strikingly beautiful Renaissance cloisters is now the **Museu Municipal** (open Tues–Fri 9.30am–5.30pm, Mon and Sat pm only; entrance charge), with a selection of

BELOW:
Faro harbour.

Roman mosaics and stonework from Faro and the important Roman site at Milreu, 12 km (7 miles) to the north *(see page 210)*. The **Museu Regional do Algarve**, (open weekdays; closed 12.30–2pm; entrance charge), in the district assembly building in Praça Alexandre Herculano (at the top end of the main pedestrian street in Mouraria), has replicas of traditional Algarve homes, costumes and handicrafts.

Beside the harbour, in the Port Authority building in the Bairro Ribeirinho, the **Museu Marítimo** (Maritime Museum; open Mon–Fri pm; closed noon–2pm, public holidays; entrance charge) is worth a visit to see the broad range of Algarve fishing methods. Among the exhibits are model boats and a vivid depiction of the old way of trapping tuna in the bloody "bullfight of the sea".

Faro's most bizarre and macabre sight is a **Capela dos Ossos** (Chapel of Bones), reached through the baroque Igreja do Carmo with its impressive façade and twin towers. The little chapel was built in 1816, its walls entirely covered with bones and skulls (allegedly 1,245 of them) from the church cemetery. Some find this grim display of mortality less depressing than the high-rises that contrast with the church's fine façade.

Map on pages 198–9

Look out for the view of Faro as you fly into the airport. It's quite spectacular.

Lighthouse and lagoon

Faro is protected on the seaward side by a huge lagoon dotted with sand banks, with the airport on the western edge. Some of the sandbanks are huge, especially the outer barrier islands and the southern most point is marked by the Cabo de Santa Maria lighthouse (*faro* means "lighthouse" in Portuguese).

The sand spit which starts near the airport and extends out as a long crescent, Ilha de Faro, can be reached by car and is the location of **Praia de Faro ❷**, a sandy resort much loved by the locals. Ilha da Culatra is the only other inhabited sand spit and can only be reached by ferry from Olhão. The whole of this natural lagoon and the adjacent area, stretching some 50 km (30 miles) from Anção in the west to Cacela in the east, is protected as the **Parque Natural da Ria Formosa ❸**. This lagoon system provides 90 percent of Portugal's harvest of clams and oysters. It is also an important bird sanctuary, especially for waders such as egrets and oyster catchers, and some rare species, including the purple gallinule.

BELOW: the exterior of Faro's Igreja do Carmo.

East of Faro

Travelling eastwards out of Faro takes you to the busy 17th-century town of **Olhão ❹**, built in the Moorish style, with a large fishing port. On the seafront by the leisure boats' pontoons are the town's modern (1998) market halls. Arrive at the fish market early and be prepared to use your elbows to reach the slithery hills of fish which the women hawk at the tops of their voices, poking them to prove their freshness. The best buys are gilt-head bream *(dourada)*, bass *(robalo)* and sole *(linguado)*. The other halls sell fruit and vegetables.

If you are not catching the ferry out to Culatra, move on to **Fuzeta**, with a sandy beach and a boat which can take you out to uninhabited **Ilha da Armona** for a spot of sunbathing. Almost next door to Fuzeta is Pedras del Rei, the starting point for an

Glistening white bell-tower in the architectural gem that is Tavira.

BELOW: Tavira.

exciting little journey by train over to **Barril ❺** on the Tavira sandbank, the Ilha de Tavira. There is a footpath by the track, should the train be full.

A café or restaurant along the broad palm-lined promenade of **Santa Luzia,** a colourful fishing village overlooking the lagoon, is the place to sit and watch the fishermen stacking up encrusted octopus pots *(alcatruzes)* after removing their catch.

Tempting Tavira

One of the larger towns on the eastern side, **Tavira ❻** has avoided the excesses of development and lost none of its grace. It elegantly borders both sides of the Rio Sequa, which becomes the Gilão as it slides under the seven-arched Roman-style bridge, the Ponte Romana, towards the sea. With its estuary and outlying island, Tavira flourished in the 16th century. But trade dwindled as the fish disappeared, and this lovely town composed of narrow streets, pastel-coloured patricians' houses, miniature towers, domes, unusual four-sided roofs and minarets today leads a quieter life.

There are more than two dozen churches and chapels in Tavira, of which the most interesting are the **Igreja da Misericórdia** (with some lovely *azulejo* decorations) and the church of **Santa Maria**, rebuilt on the site of the town's old mosque. Many of the churches are closed, but information about access to the major ones, as well as maps of the area, are available from the tourist office, to be found up the steps from the town hall in the main square.

Atmospheric fortified hamlets where time appears to have stood still are not what you expect to find along the southern coast of Algarve, but there is one at **Cacela Velha ❼**. It has a miniature 18th-century fortress and a gleaming

white church. The whole village clings tightly to a perch looking over a lagoon.

The border with Spain is reached at the Rio Guadiana. Facing Spain is **Vila Real de Santo António** ❽, its grid of geometric streets bearing the stamp of the Marquês de Pombal – the man who was responsible for redesigning old Lisbon in the 18th century. Pombal intended this town to be a model administrative, industrial and fishing centre, and he founded the Royal Fisheries Company here, but he lost favour with the court, and his plans never really took off. All the same, fishing remains an important activity.

Just west of Vila Real is the largest touristic development this side of Faro, **Monte Gordo**. The clutch of high-rise buildings overlooking a vast flat beach as yet remains fairly compact.

Map on pages 198–9

The village church on the banks of the river in Sanlucar de Guadiana has interesting bas-relief carving on the baptismal font dating from the 16th century.

Moors, mines and marshlands

Further inland along the Guadiana is the architecturally appealing **Castro Marim** ❾. This little town is also one of the oldest and historically most important areas of Algarve. Once a major Phoenician settlement, it also played host to the Greeks and Carthaginians before the Moors and Romans invaded. Portugal's kings later used it as a natural point from which to fight the infidel to the east. The huge castle built by King Afonso III after he dispelled the Moors in 1249 is still standing, overlooking the surrounding valley. In 1319, it was the first headquarters of the Order of Christ. The fort on the hill opposite dates from 1641.

Surrounding the town is the Castro Marim fen or marsh, wetland home of many migratory birds including storks, cranes and flamingos, and a hundred different species of plant life. An area of 2,000 hectares (5,000 acres) is now protected as the **Reserva Natural do Sapal** ❿ and information is available at the office inside the castle.

Among the least travelled routes in Algarve is the peaceful road along the Rio Guadiana. It is a soothing meander through golden, furze-covered hills dotted with corks, olive and fig trees. (Road numbers are N122 and 1063 for the riverside drive.) **Alcoutim** ⓫ is the northernmost Algarve town, and here it often seems as if time has stood still. Sunning dogs in the only square in town have priority, so you'll have to park around them.

From the promenade that extends along the edge of the Guadiana river you can see the nearby Spanish town of **Sanlucar de Guadiana** reflected in the slow-moving water. Signs to the "castle" are a little misleading, as they lead to an empty shell of walls – but the view from here is worth the short walk.

An inland return route will take you through **Martim Longo** ⓬, where it is possible to make a diversion to the open-air copper mine at Vaqueiros, now transformed into the **Parque Cova dos Mouros**, with a Neolithic settlement and donkey rides (daily, depending on weather conditions; closed Jan–Feb; entrance charge). Continue through Cachopo to reach Faro.

BELOW: a bridge to Spain, near Castro Marim.

West of Faro

The coastal route out to the west heads towards the main area of tourist development and to some of the most picturesque beaches. First stop outside Faro is at

Lobster for lunch.

São Lourenço for the small 18th-century church of the same name. Inside it is tiled, from top to bottom, in beautiful blue *azulejos* (tiles) depicting the life and martyrdom of São Lourenço himself.

All the well-known golf courses, around two dozen of them, lie west of Faro, each one an exclusive development with luxury accommodation. Among them are Quinta do Lago, Vale do Lobo and Vila Sol at **Vilamoura** ⑭, which has a sixth hole right over the Atlantic. They take up a huge area on the edge of the Ria Formosa reserve, presenting a neat face of colourful flower beds and well-manicured lawns.

Just to the west of Vilamoura is the small resort and fishing village of **Olhos d'Agua**. The bonus here is that it is too small to attract the large tour operators, otherwise it would be a sell out. Tucked into a small cleft, the fishing village is as picturesque as any in Algarve, with sculptured rock stacks decorating the beach.

Albufeira: holiday heaven

Once a small fishing village favoured by the Romans and Moors, **Albufeira** ⑮ today is a populous and popular tourist spot with an active nightlife, scores of bars with a taste for rock music, plenty of restaurants ranging from La Pizza to more typical regional fare, and late-night discos. The steep streets descending into the old part of town are still very attractive, as are the rock-protected beaches where the fishermen keep their boats, traditionally painted with large eyes to ward off evil, as well as stars and animals. There is a bustling fish market near the fishermen's beach and a fruit, meat and vegetable market in the main square. Although development is fairly intense in this region, the coast westward is a delightful symphony of eroded cliffs,

BELOW: the beach at Albufeira.

tacks, gullies, grottoes and arches reaching a crescendo at Lagos. It is still possible to follow your nose and divert off to quiet beaches.

Whichever route you take towards the west, it is likely you will end up in **Alcantarilha** ⓰. It's worth a stop here if only to look in on the parish church, and especially the Capela da Ossos around the corner which is packed with a chilling array of skulls. Head south from here into **Armação de Pêra** ⓱. This Arab resort is rescued by an attractive promenade and beach, and it is a good place to eat fish.

All the might and cragginess returns to the coastline and it's a fair descent to reach the beach at **Rocha da Pena**. Sitting on a bluff between two sandy coves is the simple white church of **Nossa Senhora da Rocha** ⓲ dedicated to the fishermen. Inland from here is **Porches**, famous for its painted pottery.

At the next roundabout on the N125 is **Lagoa**, where people stop mainly for the lively morning market. This is also where farmers bring their grapes to the central cooperative wine cellar. A left turn at this roundabout leads down to Carvoeiro, a craggy coastline of isolated beaches, like that of Algar Seco. **Praia de Carvoeiro**, which is a lively tourist spot itself, has a pleasant little beach framed by villa-studded cliffs.

Portimão ⓳ (once a Roman harbour, Portus Magnus) lies west of Caroeiro. An important fishing port, it is also one of the best shopping towns on the coast. Built on the west bank of the Arade estuary, Portimâo is famous for its grilled sardines – have lunch beside the river – and its pastry shops. Facing it is the pretty fishing village of **Ferragudo** ⓴, with cobbled streets, sidewalk cafés and a good fish market. Close by is ocean-fronted **Praia da Rocha** ㉑, which has a superb, much-photographed beach characterised by

Map on pages 198–9

Algarve has many spectacular beaches but Praia da Marinha, south of Porches, is one of the most photogenic. For a huge expanse of sand backed by colourful cliffs, try Falésia just west of Quarteira.

BELOW LEFT: a dramatic rock formation at Praia da Rocha
BELOW: flourishing Algarve vegetation.

*A street corner
in Lagos.*

BELOW: the
fortifications at
Lagos look as
though they mean
serious business.

strange towering rock formations standing in the blue-green sea. The village itself, however, is a bit of a concrete jungle, although it does have all the facilities a tourist could ask for.

Lagos

Moving west you will come to **Lagos ㉒**, with a fine maritime tradition and a safe harbour beside a river estuary. Founded by the Carthaginians, it was taken by the Romans in the 5th century BC, when it was called *Lacobriga* (Fortified Lake). The Moors took it over in the 8th century and renamed it *Zawaia* (Lake). The city finally fell to the Portuguese during the reign of Afonso III. In 1434 Gil Eanes left from Lagos and became the first sea captain to round Cape Bojador off northwest Africa, south of the Canary Islands – then the limit of the known world. Most of Lagos was rebuilt in the 18th century, but some evidence of its darker past still stands in the columns and semicircular arches of Portugal's first slave market (now an art gallery) in the **Praça da República**; nearby stands a statue of Henry the Navigator who sent ships from here off into the unknown. Note, too, the modern monument by João Cutileiro recording King Sebastião's departure to the disastrous battle of Alcácer-Quibir in 1578.

A walk through the city's attractive streets will lead you to the **Igreja de Santo António**, on the outside a sober-looking church, but inside an extraordinarily beautiful example of gilded carving. The nave has an impressive painted wooden barrel-vault and baroque paintings on the walls. The church can only be visited through the **Museu Municipal**, which has a delightful collection of exhibits on local life in Algarve (open Tues–Sun; closed noon–2pm; entrance charge). Its eclectic collection of local finds, dating

Map on pages 198–9

rom the Bronze Age and Roman times, is layered over with fascinating glimpses of local life, and though the layout may at first seem old-fashioned, it is one of the finest museums in the country.

Lagos has several pretty coves and beaches, especially **Praia Dona Ana**. Don't miss the rock formations at **Ponta da Piedade ㉓**. From the cliffs you might also hire a boat from a local fisherman to explore the grottoes, with their cathedral-like natural skylights.

Beyond Lagos lie three relatively unspoilt fishing villages, each of a different character and each worth as visit. **Luz ㉔** is the first of these, and perhaps the most developed, and is followed by **Burgau** and **Salema**. The countryside changes drastically, particularly after Salema, to a rockier and more undulating landscape. The trees look smaller and squatter, permanently bent from the unrelenting wind. Improved roads make driving easier now in this area but the new road actually bypasses the Knights Templar church of **Nossa Senhora de Guadalupe ㉕**, where Henry the Navigator is said to have worshipped. It is easier to spot it when travelling west and visit it on the return.

Sagres

Sagres ㉖ is a small fishing town, with Baleeira Bay as its port. The attraction to visitors is **Fortalaza de Sagres**, the fortress at **Ponta de Sagres**, used by Henry the Navigator early in the 15th century. He invited the most renowned cartographers, astronomers and mariners of his day to work here, and thus formed a fund of knowledge unsurpassed at the time, although modern historians believe he did not found a formal School of Navigation. Nothing that Prince Henry built is left so it is hard to be sure. But you can see clues – notably a huge, 43-metre (140-ft) compass rose on the stone ground of the fortress. There is a modern exhibition hall and tourist facilities in the fort, and a 1-km (½-mile) walk along the top of the cliff.

All that remains now is to continue driving through this windswept terrain passing the small Fortaleza de Beliche, now a small *pousada* and restaurant, to reach **Cabo de São Vicente ㉗**, known to ancient mariners as *O Fim do Mundo*, the End of the World. From within the walls enclosing the lighthouse you can look down upon St Vincent's rocky throne.

Legend has it that in medieval times Christian followers of the martyred St Vincent defied the Moors and buried his body on the cape, with a shrine to honour him. Sacred ravens were said to have maintained vigil over the spot and over the ship that carried the bones of the saint to Lisbon. Here, even on a calm day, waves crash against the cliffs with spray-tossing violence. In spring, the smell of the sea competes with the scent of cistus, the rock-rose bush whose perfumed leaves were once supposedly used by the Egyptians for embalming.

The wild west coast

Algarve's west coast is virtually a continuous sand dune frequently pounded by a restless ocean and almost constantly under surf and spray. Although there are endless beaches, there are few towns of

It was to Sagres that seafarers returned in 1419 with the news that they had discovered an uninhabited island they called Porto Santo, which was later found to be part of the Madeiran archipelago.

BELOW: Sagres fortress by night.

significance. **Odeceixe**, the most northerly town on this stretch of Algarvia coastline, is a small Moorish-style, windmill-topped village. A road follow the river for 3 km (2 miles) to a beautiful sandy beach beneath towering clift at Praia de Odeceixe.

The most popular west coast circuit starts from Cabo de São Vincente an continues north through the vast, dune-backed Carrapateira to the attractive vil lage of **Aljezur** ㉘. The 10th-century castle was the last to be taken from th Moors. Directly to the west are the great sweeps of the **Monte Clérigo** and **Arr fana** beaches, the best on this coast. Heading inland from Aljezur toward Monchique leads back into the heart of Algarve.

Mountains and rural villages

Towering above rolling hills, the granite mountains of **Serra de Monchiqu** attract streams of visitors to enjoy the views from the summit. In spring Monchique is covered in flowering mimosa, and wild flowers bloom in the va leys between the Fóia and Picota peaks. **Fóia** ㉙ is the highest point of Algarv reaching 902 metres (2,960 ft) above sea level. It is easily accessible along winding road lined with cheerful restaurants selling roast chicken. The summ is heavily forested with aerials and the promised views are revealed only on clea days. Picota is a different challenge and can be reached only on foot.

The town of Monchique is rather disappointing if you merely drive throug but park the car and walk the steep streets to get a better feel for the place. No to be missed is **Caldas de Monchique** ㉚, off to the right heading south, hic den in a deep valley and surrounded by chestnut, cork, pine, orange and euca lyptus trees. The spa has been in use since Roman times and the waters ar

The eucalyptus trees which now grow in profusion in the Serra de Monchique smell lovely but are unpopular with environmentalists since they are bad for the soil and highly flammable.

BELOW: the Serra de Monchique.

believed to cure a number of ailments, from convulsions to rheumatism. The springs pour out an estimated 20 million litres (4 million gallons) of water a year.

Descending from the heights, but away from the coastal tourist zone, a more rural lifestyle is found in the towns and villages. Here, locals have managed to shrug off the effects of regular visitors and continue their traditional ways. One of the most interesting places is **Silves** , between Albufeira and Portimão. Silves was populated by the 4th century BC and reached its greatest splendour under the Moors, who made it capital of Algarve.

In its glory days Silves was the home of some of the greatest Arab poets. They recorded its ruin when the city fell to Portugal's King Sancho I in 1189: "Silves, my Silves, once you were a paradise. But tyrants turned you into the blaze of hell. They were wrong not to fear God's punishment. But Allah leaves no deed unheeded," wrote one. Two years later the Moors occupied Silves again before it was finally reconquered by the Portuguese.

Yemenite Arabs built the walled city, but the castle (atop a Roman citadel, itself built on Neolithic foundations) and the defensive towers were rebuilt in the later Almohad period (12th–13th centuries) and heavily restored in modern times. The Moorish castle and Christian Cathedral dominate the city, the dark-red sandstone contrasting with the soft pinks and faded blues of the older surrounding houses. A sense of history still permeates Silves and the castle – except in June when a beer festival considerably changes the atmosphere.

The Moorish cistern to the north once supplied the city's water, and is architecturally similar to 13th-century cisterns found in Palestine and in Cáceres, Spain. Built by both the Romans and the Moors, the advanced irrigation system transformed Algarve into the garden of Portugal.

Map on pages 198–9

BELOW:
Silves Cathedral, rebuilt after the earthquake of 1755.

Map
on pages
198–9

TIP

Estói market is the
biggest and the best in
Algarve. Try to be
there on the second
Sunday of the month.

RIGHT: Ponta de
Sagres.
BELOW: chickens
for sale at Loulé
market.

The **Sé** (**Cathedral**) is 13th-century Gothic, restored in the 14th century and almost destroyed by the earthquake of 1755. Its apse is decorated with square arches, pyramidal battlements and fanciful gargoyles. The inner chapel of João de Rego dates from the 1400s. Various tombs here are said to be those of crusaders who helped capture Silves from the Moors in 1244. Here, too, for four years lay the remains of João II, who died in nearby Alvor in 1495, aged 40 – from dropsy, according to some doctors, from poisoning according to others.

From Alte to Estói

Northeast of Albufeira on the N124 is **Alte** ㉜, an elegant village lying at the foot of hills and huddled around its parish church. Nossa Senhora da Assunção dates from the 16th century and has magnificent 18th-century tile panels. The tiles in the chapel of Nossa Senhora de Lurdes, among the best in Algarve, are of 16th-century Sevillian origin. Alte is a typical village of the province with its simple houses, delicate white laced chimneys, and timeless serenity.

A nearby stream has transformed the area into an oasis amid the region's arid landscape. It's a lush garden of oleanders, fig and loquat trees and rose bushes. The blue-and-white tile panels at Fonte Santa (Holy Fountain) are inscribed with verses by local poet, Cândido Guerreiro. This area is perfect for picnics, or a walk up the Pena hill where you can visit the **Buraco dos Mouros** (Moors' Cave). Further up the mountain is **Rocha dos Soidos**, a cave filled with stalactite and stalagmite formations.

Heading back towards Faro you reach **Loulé** ㉝, a small town whose old quarter – Almedina – is a maze of narrow streets, reminiscent of a North African *casbah*. The interior of the chapel of Nossa Senhora da Conceição (near the tourist office) is tiled with attractive 17th-century *azulejos*, and the Igreja da Misericordia has a fine Manueline doorway. One of Loulé's greatest attractions is the Saturday market, held in the onion-domed market halls, selling food of every kind, from home grown fruit to live chickens.

Take a very slight detour east before you reach Faro and you will come to **Estói** ㉞, a pleasant village with a fine parish church, but best known for its 18th-century **Palácio dos Condes de Carvalhal** (open Mon–Sat; closed 12.30–2pm; entrance charge). With 28 rooms under restoration, some of the palace may not be accessible, but the highly ornamental gardens of this "Queluz of the south", with their statues and rococo fountains, and a splendid tiled staircase, are well worth seeing.

The town has a huge market – more of a country fair, held on the second Sunday of the month. It is a lively affair where you can buy a horse, sell a few sheep, stock up with fruit and vegetables or just buy sugared cakes to eat as you mingle with the crowds taking in the atmosphere.

Close by is the **Vila Romana de Milreu** ㉟, a Roman site discovered in the late 1800s. There are some lovely mosaics, the remains of thermal baths, and a well-preserved villa dating from the 2nd century. The largest structure, a temple, was consecrated as a Visigothic basilica in the 3rd century. ❑

EVORA AND ALENTEJO

*The Romans left more than a few footprints here, and
there are historic towns and castles around almost every corner.
Alentejo is one of the country's best-kept secrets*

Map on page 216

A lentejo, literally "beyond the Tejo" (the River Tagus), has a distinctive character and beauty unlike that of any other Portuguese province. Its vast plains, coloured burnt ochre in summer, are freckled with cork oaks and olive trees which provide the only shade for the small flocks of sheep and herds of black pigs. Nicknamed *terra do pão* (land of bread) because of field upon field of wheat and oats, Alentejo supports acres of grapevines, tomatoes, sunflowers and other plantations.

The largest and flattest of the Portuguese provinces, about the size of Belgium, Alentejo occupies one-third of Portugal's total area yet has only six percent of its population. It stretches from the west coast east to the Spanish border and separates Ribatejo and Beira Baixa in the central regions from Algarve in the south. The open countryside is punctuated by picturesque whitewashed towns and villages, many built on the low hills which dot the horizon.

Alentejo is rich in handicrafts. Rustic pottery with naive, colourful designs can be found everywhere. In addition, certain towns specialise in particular crafts or products: hand-stitched rugs from Arraiolos, loom-woven carpets from Reguengos; cheese from Serpa; tapestries from Portalegre; sugar plums from Elvas. All can be purchased, of course, elsewhere in Alentejo, or in Lisbon or Porto, but for price, selection, freshness and adventure, isn't it more satisfying to go to the source?

PRECEDING PAGES:
a typically busy
scene in Monsaraz'
main street.
LEFT: looking at life.
BELOW: a local
handyman.

Getting familiar

Geographically the province is split into two regions, Upper *(Alto)* and Lower *(Baixo)* Alentejo. Évora is the capital of the former and Beja of the latter. To the east are two low mountain ranges, the Serras of São Mamede and Ossa. Some of the towns in these ranges, particularly Marvão, have breathtaking, even precipitous settings. Portugal's third longest river, the Guadiana, flows through the province and in places provides the border between Portugal and Spain. This is by no means the only waterway. The region is crisscrossed by a network of small rivers and dams.

Roads which connect the towns are excellent. Most of the traffic is local and slow moving. You will need to equip yourself with a reliable road map; signposting is limited, and without a map you could drive miles before discovering you've taken a wrong turn.

The Portuguese in general are not renowned for their tidiness but the Alentejanos are the exception. The towns are litter-free and there is always a *dona de casa* in view whitewashing her already pristine home. Cool and simple is the theme for Alentejo architecture; low, single-storey buildings are painted white to reflect the sun's glare, with a traditional blue or yellow skirting. Large domed chimneys indicate chilly

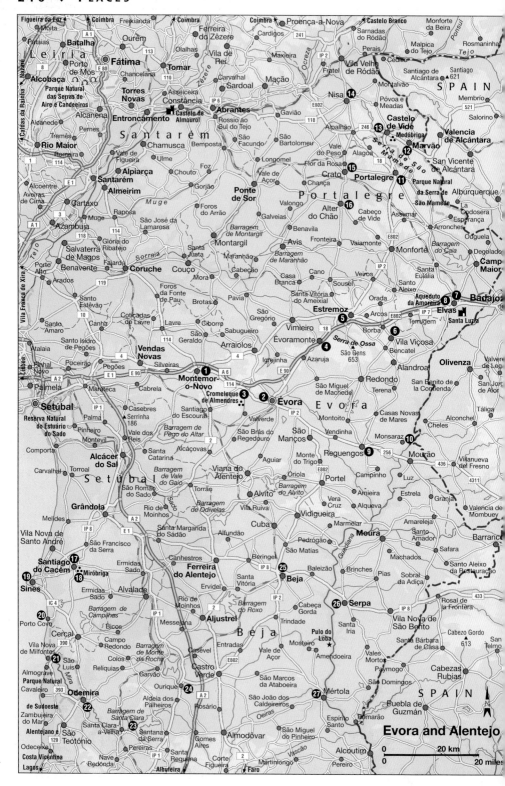

Evora and Alentejo

winters. This practical style is followed from the humblest cottage to the large hacienda-style homes of the wealthy landowners; ornate and impressive architecture is reserved for cathedrals and churches.

Inland, Alentejo's temperature in the summer can reach inferno level: what little wind there is blows hot and dry from the continental land mass – no cooling sea breezes here. Temperatures can drop dramatically in winter, resulting in bitterly cold nights.

Alentejo is steeped in history which goes back to the days of Roman colonisation. Later, it was the seat of the great landed estates *(latifundia)* of the Portuguese nobility and home to former kings. Even as late as 1828, Évora – the capital of the Alto Alentejo – was considered the second major Portuguese city, an honour which was first bestowed on it by King João I (1385–1433).

Estremoz, whose ancient castle has been converted into a comfortable *pousada*, was a nerve centre of medieval Portugal. Vila Viçosa was the seat of the dukes of Bragança, whose royal dynasty began in 1640 with the coronation of João IV and ended in 1910 with the fall of the monarchy.

Politics, pastimes and popular song

Modern Alentejo is a far cry from the days of aristocratic domination, although farming techniques in the smallholdings have changed little. The greatest change is political: after the restoration of democracy in 1974 Alentejo became the heartland of Portuguese communism. Many of the great estates – so vast that they included villages, schools and even small hospitals – were taken over by the farm workers during the revolution. Some of the landowning families were forcibly ejected, but the majority were absentee landlords anyway, living in properties nearer Lisbon or Porto. There is now a new landowning generation with a modern approach to agriculture and skilled at effective farm management.

You'll find evidence of Alentejo's long history all over the region. This ancient pottery is from the town of Mértola.

BELOW: walking the sheep.

Farming is the pulse of Alentejo, and the lives of its people revolve around the seasons. Aside from Évora the towns are small and the population is scattered in hamlets linked to farms. Secondary schools are restricted to the larger towns; in the more remote areas the general practice among young people is to leave school early to work in the fields, or head to the cities.

Throughout the year, but particularly at harvest time, you will see the field workers making their way to and from work on foot, by bicycle or crammed into open-topped trucks. Some rural Alentejanos still adopt the traditional dress: black wide-brimmed hats for both men and women, black trousers, waistcoats, jackets and white collarless shirts for men, black shawls and thick black skirts for women, or trousers for field work. Neckerchiefs for extra protection against sun and dust are loosely knotted around the men's necks, while women favour head-squares worn under their hats. The faces of the old people are extraordinary – leathery skins baked a deep brown, furrowed like tree bark and coloured like walnuts.

One of the traditional pastimes for the menfolk is a wild boar hunt near the Spanish border. During the season (October–February), you will often see men out with their shotguns, pouches and a pack of dogs.

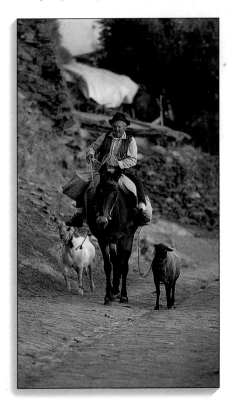

Singing and dancing are popular across the length and breadth of Portugal, and Alentejo does its share. Here, the folk songs are the domain of the men. The songs are slow, rather melancholic, but of a completely different style from the haunting *fado* that is heard elsewhere. A slow tempo is set by the stamping of the men's feet as they sing in chorus, swaying to the rhythm by the time they reach the end of the song. A performance is well worth listening to; ask at an Alentejo tourist office about where to hear the *ceifeiros*.

Évora, capital of the Alto Alentejo, is the largest and most important of all Alentejana towns. It is a superb city, full of fascinating sights, all of which are in a good state of preservation. They are likely to remain so as the entire city has been proclaimed a World Heritage Site by UNESCO.

It takes about two and a half hours to drive from Lisbon to Évora, and a tour could comfortably be managed as a day trip. But that would not leave time to see the lovely towns and villages along the way. To base yourself in Évora is easy; there are plenty of small guesthouses and hotels.

To find out about the Alentejo wine routes, visit the Alentejo Wine Route Support Office, at 20–20 Praça Joaquim Antônio de Aquiar in Évora.

The route from Lisbon

To reach Évora, leave Lisbon on the A2 via the Ponte 25 de Abril and head down past Setúbal to the A6 (IP7) turn-off to Montemor-o-Novo and Évora. You will not need a welcome billboard to tell you that you have just reached Alentejo; suddenly the road is broad and less pot-holed, and you will find yourself at the edge of the rolling plains. Look for the jumbles of twigs on top of the high walls and buildings – homes to the storks that flourish in the province. As you drive further inland you will also notice the waning breeze and the increase in temperature.

BELOW: the Temple of Diana, Évora.

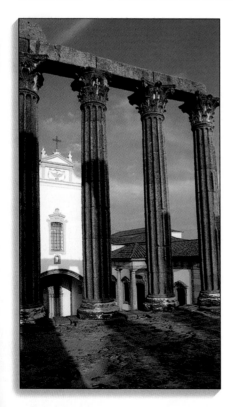

Pegões is the first small Alentejo town on the route. It's a rather dry, dusty and deserted town, by-passed by the highway. A little further along is **Vendas Novas**, also off the road. Shady, neat and with an air of affluence, it is typical of modest Alentejo towns.

Montemor-o-Novo ❶ can be seen from quite a distant approach, its ruined medieval castle crowning its low *monte* (hill). The castle ramparts are thought to date from Roman times. The town is divided into the upper old town and lower new town. As you might expect the old town is more interesting. It was here that St John of God (São João de Deus) was born in 1495. He was baptised in the ruined parish church, of which only the granite Manueline portal is still intact. In the square outside the church is a statue commemorating the saint, a Franciscan monk of great charity and humility. Although it does not have the population to support them, the town has five churches, three convents and two monasteries.

Évora: Alentejo's city

As you enter **Évora ❷** on the main Lisbon road, there is a small tourist office just before the Roman walls, where you can pick up a street map marked with suggested walks that take in the most important sights. The best place to park is outside the walls then walk to **Praça do Giraldo ❹** at the centre of the city where the main tourist office is located. This large square is arcaded on two sides and has a 16th-century church and fountain at the top. From here you can explore the inner city with ease.

The city's history can be traced back to the earliest civilisations on the Iberian peninsula. Évora derives its name from *Ebora Cerealis*, which dates from the Luso-Celtic colonisation. The Romans later fortified the city, renamed it *Liberalitas Julia*, and elevated it to the status of *municipium,* which gave it the right to mint its own currency. Its prosperity declined under the Visigoths, but was rekindled under Moorish rule (711–1165). Much of the architecture, with arched, twisting alleyways and tiled patios, reflects the Moorish presence. Évora was liberated from the Moors by a Christian knight, Geraldo Sem-Pavor ("the Fearless"), in 1165, in the name of Afonso Henriques I, Portugal's first king.

For the next 400 years Évora enjoyed great importance and wealth. It was the preferred residence of the kings of the Burgundy and Avis dynasties, and the courts attracted famous artists, dramatists, humanists and academics. Great churches, monasteries, houses and convents were also built. The splendour peaked in 1559, when Henrique, the last of the Avis kings (and also Archbishop of Évora), founded a Jesuit university. In 1580, following the annexation of Portugal by Spain, Évora's glory waned. The Castilians paid little attention to it, except as an agricultural and trading centre and even after Portuguese independence was restored in 1640, it did not regain its former brilliance.

Maps:
Area 216
City 219

Roman remains

The oldest sight in Évora is the **Temple of Diana (Templo Romano)** ❸, at the top of the lanes opposite the tourist office in Praça do Giraldo. It dates from the 2nd or 3rd century AD and is presumed to have been built as a place of

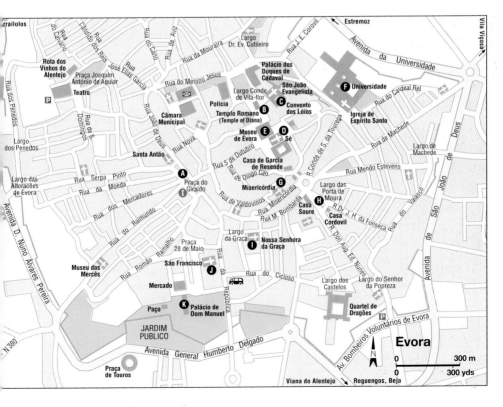

There's nothing austere about the pousada *in the old Convento dos Lóios.*

imperial worship. The Corinthian columns are granite, their bases and capitals hewn from local marble. The façade and mosaic floor have disappeared completely, but the six rear columns and the four at either side are still intact. The temple was converted into a fortress during the Middle Ages, then used as a slaughterhouse until 1870, an inelegant role which nevertheless saved the temple from being torn down.

From a good viewpoint in the shady garden just across from the rear of the temple, you can look down over the lower town and across the plains: the tiny village of Evoramonte is just visible to the northeast. To the right of the temple is the **Convento dos Lóios** and the adjacent church of **São João Evangelista**. The convent buildings have been converted into an elegant *pousada* but the church is open to the public. Founded in 1485, its style is Romano-Gothic, although all but the doorway in the façade was remodelled after the 1755 earthquake. The nave has an ornate vaulted ceiling and walls lined with beautiful tiles depicting the life of St Laurence Justinian, archbishop of Venice, dated 1771 and signed by António de Oliveira Bernardes. The sacristy and wax room behind the altar contain paintings and part of the Roman wall, and beneath the nave you can see an ossuary and Moorish cistern. The church is privately owned, as is the neighbouring palace of the Dukes of Cadaval, a wonderful building sometimes open for exhibitions.

The Cathedral

BELOW: 14th-century apostles at the entrance to the Cathedral in Évora.

The nearby **Sé (Cathedral)** is a rather austere building. Its granite, Romano-Gothic-style façade was built in the 12th century, while its main portal and the two grand conical towers – unusual in that they are asymmetric, with one tower

adorned with glittering blue tiles – were added in the 16th century. Before going inside, take a close look at the main entrance, which is decorated with magnificent 14th-century sculptures of the apostles. With three naves stretching for 70 metres (230 ft), the Cathedral has the most capacious interior in Portugal, and the vast broken barrel-vaulted ceiling is quite stunning.

Once you've seen the cathedral, it is worth paying the nominal sum to see the cloisters, choir stalls and **Museu de Arte Sacra** (open Tues–Sun 9am–5pm; closed 12.30–2pm and public holidays). The latter, in the treasury within one of the towers, contains a beautiful collection of ecclesiastical gold, silver and bejewelled plates, ornaments, chalices and crosses. The Renaissance-style choir stalls, tucked high in the gallery, are fashioned with a delightful series of wooden carvings with motifs both sacred and secular. From the choir stalls you get a good bird's-eye view of the Cathedral. The marble cloisters are 14th-century Gothic, large and imposing, more likely to inspire awe than meditative contemplation.

Next door to the cathedral is the **Museu de Évora ❺**, which is undergoing extensive renovation and expected to reopen in 2005.

Map on page 219

Particularly interesting carvings in the cathedral choir stalls are those of everyday life: wine pressing, wheat threshing, singing and feasting.

More Évora landmarks

At the old **Jesuit University ❻**, some elegant and graceful cloisters are visible. You have to follow a short road down to the east of the city to reach it. The marble of the broad cloisters seems to have aged not at all since the 16th century, and there is still the peaceful atmosphere of the serious academic.

The classroom entrances at the far end of the cloister gallery are decorated with *azulejos* representing each of the subjects taught. If you take a slow walk back up the hill and head for the Igreja São Francisco, you'll pass by another

BELOW: bones lying in wait in the Capela dos Ossos.

A MOTHER'S CURSE

The church of São Francisco *(see next page)* dating from the late 15th or early 16th century, has a remarkable chapel, the *Capela dos Ossos*. This bizarre and macabre room is entirely lined and decorated with the bones of some 5,000 people. It was created in the 16th century by a Franciscan monk. The skulls and bones have not merely been stored here in a random fashion; a lot of creative thought has gone into their placement. At the entrance you will see the inviting inscription: *Nós ossos qui estamos, pelos vossos esperamos* – "We bones lie here waiting for yours."

Hung at the far end of the chapel are the corpses of a man and a small child. These centuries-old bodies are said to be the victims of the curse of a dying wife and mother. Father and son were supposed to have made her life a misery and their ill treatment eventually killed her. On her death bed she cursed them, swearing that their flesh would never fall from their bones. The corpses are far from fleshy, but there is plenty of leathery substance attached to their bones.

Braids of human hair dating from the 19th century are hung at the entrance of the chapel – votive offerings placed there by young brides.

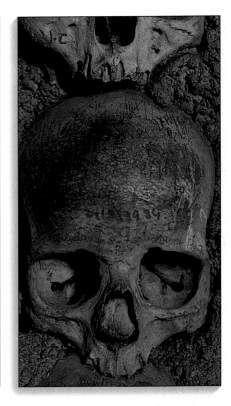

TIP

If you're visiting Évora during the summer and want to cool off, go to one of the local swimming pools on the edge of town. Although well patronised because they are inexpensive, they are spotlessly clean, with plenty of lawn on which to stretch out and dry off.

BELOW: the view over Évora is impressive.

church, the **Misericórdia** , noted for its 18th-century tiled panels and baroque relief work. Behind it is the Casa Soure, a 15th-century Manueline house formerly part of the Palace of the Infante Dom Luís.

As you walk, have a good look at the houses. Nearly all have attractive narrow wrought-iron balconies at the base of tall rectangular windows. An odd tradition in Évora, as elsewhere in Portugal, is that visiting dignitaries are welcomed by a display of brightly coloured bedspreads hung from the balconies.

When you reach the Misericórdia church, take a brief detour to **Largo das Portas de Moura** ❶. The gates mark the fortified northern entrance to the city, the limit of construction and safety as it was in medieval times. This picturesque square is dominated by a Renaissance fountain, built in 1556.

Heading west along the Rua Miguel Bombarda, keep an eye out for the church of **Nossa Senhora da Graça** ❶ (Our Lady of Grace), just off the Rua Miguel Bombarda. Built in granite, it is a far cry from the austerity of the cathedral. A later church (16th-century), its influence is strongly Italian Renaissance. Note the four huge figures supporting globes which represent the children of grace.

The most interesting thing about the **Igreja de São Francisco** ❶ is the Capela dos Ossos *(see previous page)*, but the chapterhouse that links the chapel to the church is worth seeing too. It is lined with *azulejos* depicting scenes from the Passion and contains an *altar dos promessas* (altar of promises) on which are laid wax effigies of various parts of the body given in thanks for cures. The church also has an interesting Manueline porch.

Évora's public gardens – the **Jardim Público** – near the church provide a very pleasant walk; if you're lucky you may catch the band playing on the park's old-fashioned wrought-iron bandstand. The delightful **Paláçio de Dom Manuel** ❶

(1495–1521), or what remains of it, stands in the park. It has paired windows in horseshoe arches, typical of the style which gained its name from Dom Manuel. Exhibitions are held in the long Ladies' Gallery.

If you're not intent on going inside Évora's monuments, a night stroll reveals its exterior architecture admirably. Nearly all the monuments are floodlit until midnight, and the winding narrow streets are very inviting on a balmy evening.

During the last week of June, Évora is filled with visitors who come to enjoy the annual **Feira de São João** (24–30 June). This huge fair fills the grounds opposite the public gardens. There's a local handicraft market, an agricultural hall, a display of local light industry, the general hotchpotch of open-air stalls, as well as folk singing and dancing, and restaurants serving typical cuisine.

Évoramonte and Estremoz

Alentejo has a number of megalithic monuments scattered across its plains, and some of the most important are just outside Évora. (*Turismo* will give you a map.) The best preserved and most significant stone circle, or cromlech, on the Iberian peninsula is 12 km (7 miles) west of the city. Close to the hill of Herdade dos Almendres, the **Cromeleque do Almendres ❸** has 95 standing stones.

Near to the Agricultural Department of the University of Évora in Valverde, just southwest of Évora, is the largest dolmen on the peninsula. The **Zambujeiro Dolmen** stands some 5 metres (17 ft) high with a 3-metre (10-ft) diameter and dates from about 3000 BC.

On the road from Évora to Estremoz lies **Évoramonte ❹**, a village at the foot of a 16th-century castle. It was here that the convention ending Portugal's civil war was signed on 26 May 1834. A plaque commemorating the event is placed

Maps:
Area 216
City 219

The ruins of Évora's Palácio de Dom Manuel, built by the creator of the "Manueline" style – of which the palace's arched windows are a fine example.

BELOW: the ancient standing stones at Almendres.

over the house where the historic event took place. **Évoramonte Castle** perches high on a hill and offers remarkable views: well worth the detour and the clamber up to the top. Built in Italian Renaissance style with added Manueline knots, it grew out of a Roman fort.

Estremoz: steeped in history

About 22 km (14 miles) northeast lies the lovely town of **Estremoz** ❺. Although much smaller than Évora, it has some fascinating monuments. The old part of town, crowned by a castle now converted into a *pousada*, was founded by King Afonso III in 1258, but is most often associated with King Dinis, whose residence it was in the 14th century. His wife, the saintly Queen Isabel of Aragon, is honoured by a statue in the main square, and a chapel dedicated to her can be seen in one of the castle towers (ask at the *pousada*).

Estremoz is famous for its pottery, which is on sale in shops all over town, and also at the Saturday market in Rossio, the main square of the lower town.

The chapel is at the top of a narrow staircase; small, and highly decorated, it is where Isabel is said to have died. Mind you, some also say that she died in the nearby King's Audience Chamber. The chapel walls are adorned with 18th-century *azulejos* and paintings depicting scenes from the queen's life. Behind the altar is a tiny plain room bearing a smaller altar on which the Estremoz faithful have placed their ex votos, or offerings.

BELOW: the rooftops of Estremoz.

The most impressive part of the castle is the wonderful 13th-century keep which is entered via the *pousada*. To get to the top you need to be fairly fit – or make a slow and steady ascent. The second floor has an octagonal room with trefoil windows. From the top platform there is a breathtaking view. The red rooftops contrast beautifully with the whitewashed houses and the green plains beyond, much of which are planted with rows of olive trees.

Across the square from the *pousada* is King Dinis's palace. It must have been a beautiful place, but all that remains standing after a gunpowder explosion in the palace arsenal in 1698 is the Gothic colonnade and star-vaulted **Audience Chamber**. It is used nowadays for exhibitions of work by local artists.

Having survived the narrow roads and hairpin bends on the drive up to the castle, the descent seems easy. The upper town is connected to the lower by 14th-century ramparts and fairly modern buildings: the wrought-iron balconies here are decorated with coloured tiles.

If you like Portuguese wines then you may be familiar with the name Borba, where a co-operative produces a good red wine. The ancient village of **Borba** (about 11 km/6 miles from Estremoz), which is said to date back to the Gauls and Celts, does not have much to show except for a splendid fountain, the Fonte das Bicas, built in 1781 from local white marble.

Vila Viçosa: Bragança's base

Down the road from Borba is **Vila Viçosa ❻**, the seat of the dukes of Bragança. It comes as quite a surprise after the Moorish-influenced towns perched on the hilltops. It is cool and shady, its large main square (Praça da República) is filled with orange trees, and elsewhere there are lemon trees and lots of flowers. Viçosa means lush, and its luxuriant boulevards are a pleasure to walk along.

A lovely, if rather overgrown, medieval castle overlooks the town square. It is very peaceful there, the only sound being the cooing of the white fan-tail doves which nest in the ramparts. The drawbridge is lowered across the (dry) moat and the first floor has become a modest archaeological museum.

Vila Viçosa is best known for the **Paço Ducal** (the Ducal Palace of the

Map on page 216

Old-fashioned street light in Estremoz.

BELOW:
a sleepy afternoon in Vila Viçosa.

Alentejo is full of unexpected buildings such as this Moorish-inspired oddity in Monsaráz.

Braganças), a three-storey building with a long façade, which is open to the public for guided tours. Its furniture, painting and tapestries are very fine, and definitely worth seeing. The palace also contains an excellent collection of 17th- to 19th-century coaches.

The palace overlooks a square in which stands a bronze statue of João IV, the first king of the Bragança dynasty. To the north of the square is a striking gateway, the Manueline **Porta do Nó** (Knot Gate), a stone archway which appears to be roped together, and is part of the 16th-century town walls.

From Elvas to Monsaraz

Heading east for about 28 km (17 miles) along the main road to the Spanish border from Estremoz, you will come to the strongly fortified town of **Elvas ❼**. Founded by the Romans, it was long occupied by the Moors and finally liberated from them in 1230 – about 100 years later than Lisbon. The town was of great strategic importance during the wars of independence in the mid-1600s. The fortress of **Santa Luzia**, south of town, was built by a German, Count Lippe, for the purpose of repelling the Spanish. The older castle above the town was originally a Roman fortress, rebuilt by the Moors and enlarged in the 15th century.

If you walk around the ramparts that once encircled the town you cannot fail to be impressed by the effective engineering. The town itself is very attractive, from the triangular "square" of Santa Clara, with its 16th-century marble pillory, to the main Praça da República, with its geometric mosaic paving.

Elvas has a country-house-style *pousada,* whose restaurant is particularly popular with Spanish visitors. One of its specialties is a *bacalhau dourado* – slivers of salted cod fried with potatoes, onions, olives and scrambled egg. (If you stay overnight, be sure to ask for a quiet room – the *pousada* is close to the main A6/E90 highway.)

The **Aqueduto da Amoreira ❽**, just outside the town, was designed by a great 15th-century architect, Francisco de Arruda. Its 8 km (5 miles) and 843 arches took nearly 200 years to complete. The cost was borne by the people of Elvas under a special tax named the *Real de Agua.*

Handwoven rugs used to be manufactured throughout Alentejo, but nowadays the small town of **Reguengos ❾** is the only place where they are still made, in a factory that has been using the same looms for the past 150 years. To reach it, return to Borba then travel south for about 60 km (38 miles). Reguengos is a nucleus of megalithic stones and dolmens, found at several sites near the town, and is known for its wine.

About 16 km (10 miles) northeast of Reguengos is the delightful walled town of **Monsaraz ❿**, so small it can easily be explored on foot – leave your car at the gate. It was fortified by the Knights Templar when the Moors were the enemy. Later, its proximity to the Spanish border together with its height made it of great strategic importance. Once the threat from Spain had passed, however, Reguengos became more influential and Monsaraz less so, which helped it become the relaxed and peaceful village it is today. Its main street, Rua Direita, is all 16th- and 17th-century architecture, yet the town maintains a medieval atmosphere.

BELOW: Vila Viçosa's Manueline Porta do Nó.

Portalegre

The lush countryside which surrounds **Portalegre ⓫** is rather different from that in the low-lying lands. This area is in the foothills of the **Serra de São Mamede**, and the cooler and slightly more humid climate makes it much greener. To get there, return to Estremoz and take the N18/E802 north.

Quite a large town by Alentejo standards, Portalegre is unusual in that it is not built on top of a hill, but on the site of an ancient ruined settlement called Amaya. In the mid-13th century, King Afonso III issued instructions that a new city was to be built. He called it Portus Alacer: Portus for the customs gate which was to process Spanish trade and Alacer (*álacre* means "merry") because of its pleasing setting. King Dinis ensured that the town was fortified in 1290 (although only a few of those ruins can be seen today) and João III gave it the status of a city in 1550.

The lofty 16th-century interior of the **Sé** (**Cathedral**) is late-Renaissance style. The side altars have fine wooden *retábulos* and 16th- and 17th-century paintings in the Italian style. The sacristy contains lovely blue-and-white *azulejo* panels from the 18th century depicting the life of the Virgin Mary and the Flight to Egypt. The cathedral's façade is 18th-century, and is dominated by marble columns, granite pilasters and wrought-iron balconies.

Portalegre's affluence began in the 16th century, when its tapestries were in great demand. Continued prosperity followed in the next century with the establishment of silk mills. One tapestry workshop remains, the **Fábrica Real de Tapeçarias**, in the former Jesuit Monastery in Rua Fernandes, where looms are still worked by hand. Examples of the town's handiwork can be seen in the **Museu do Guy Fino**, in an 18th-century mansion in Rua da Figueira.

Map on page 216

BELOW: plenty of time for reflection in Monsaraz.

Portalegre was home to one of Portugal's major writers: poet, dramatist and novelist José Régio (1901–69). His house has been opened as a museum. Of particular interest is his collection of regional folk and religious art. Also of note is the 17th-century Yellow Palace, where the 19th-century radical reformer Mouzinho da Silveira lived. The ornate ironwork is quite remarkable.

Spectacular Marvão

Marvão ⓬ is one of the most spectacular sights of Alentejo. About 25 km (15 miles) north of Portalegre, it is a medieval fortified town perched on one of the São Mamede peaks. Its altitude (862 metres/2,830 ft) affords it an uninterrupted view across the Spanish frontier. The precipitous drop on one side made it inaccessible to invaders and an ideal defensive barrier.

At this height the land is barren and craggy. The seemingly impenetrable castle was built in the 13th century from the local grey granite. Clinging to the foot of the castle is the tiny village, a few twisting alleyways flanked by red-roofed whitewashed houses. Close by the church of Espírito Santo, on the street of the same name, is a baroque granite fountain. On the same street is the sober-looking Governor's House, its only decoration two magnificent 17th-century wrought-iron balconies.

On the road to Castelo de Vide are the ruins of the Roman settlement of **Medóbriga**. Many artifacts from here are now in Lisbon.

BELOW: Marvão, bathed in early morning light.

Castelo de Vide: fort and spa

Completing the triangle of noteworthy upper Alentejo towns is **Castelo de Vide** ⓭, a delightful town built in the shadow of an elongated medieval castle

situated on the summit of a foothill on the northern *serra*. The town was originally a Roman settlement. Alongside it ran the major Roman road which traversed the Iberian peninsula. The settlement was sacked by the Vandals at the beginning of the 4th century, occupied by the Moors during their domination of the southern part of the peninsula, and eventually fortified by the victorious Portuguese in 1180.

Castelo de Vide is a spa town. You can drink its curative waters from plastic bottles, which are sold in the supermarkets, or sip from one of the numerous fountains located in and around the town. Perhaps its prettiest outlet is the quadrangled, covered fountain (Fonte da Vila), set in the small square below the Jewish Quarter. The baroque fountain has a pyramid roof supported by six marble columns. The central urn is carved with figures of boys and the water spills from four spouts.

As in nearly all fortified Alentejo towns, Castelo de Vide has two very distinct faces. The first is the older one, situated next to the castle, and the most interesting and picturesque part of it is the medieval **Judiaria** (Jewish Quarter). This host of back alleys, cobbled streets and whitewashed houses is splashed with green, as potted plants sprout their tendrils from every available niche, windowsill and step. Notice the doors: this section of Castelo de Vide has the best-preserved stone Gothic doorways in Portugal. It also has the oldest synagogue, dating from the 13th century. The majority of the inhabitants of the neighbourhood appear to be elderly people who sit in the doorways of their homes calmly watching the world go by.

Further down the hill is the newer part of town: essentially 17th- and 18th-century buildings with wider, less steep streets, more space, more order and

Map on page 216

Carrying greenery in the Jewish Quarter of Castelo de Vide.

BELOW: Igreja Santa Maria, Castelo de Vide.

more elegance. On the main square, **Praça Dom Pedro V**, stand the grandiose 18th-century parish church and the old town hall, **Paços de Concelho**, remarkable for its huge 18th-century wrought-iron gate securing the main entrance.

Near Castelo de Vide you will find still more megalithic stones: these *pedras talhas* seem to be everywhere, standing in fields, in open scrubland or in local villages, inscrutable and ageless.

Flor de Rosa used to be a thriving pottery centre. The trade has dwindled in recent years, but pots are still made in the traditional way.

Portalegre's western neighbours

Nisa  is a small, rather rambling town northwest of Castelo de Vide. It has the mandatory medieval castle, walls and an unusual squat, round-towered chapel. Homemade cheese is Nisa's speciality.

Some 24 km (15 miles) south of Nisa on the road back to Estremoz is **Flôr da Rosa**, where you may be able to buy local pots. But the most interesting place to see is the Convento de Flôr da Rosa, dating from 1356 and founded by the Order of Knights Hospitallers of St John. An eclectic building, with a solid Gothic cloister, it was in use as a monastery until the end of the 19th century.

Two royal marriages took place in **Crato**, a couple of kilometres down the road. The first was that of Manuel I, who married Leonor of Spain in 1518 (his third marriage); the second was seven years later when King João III married Catarina of Spain. The main square is dominated by a splendid 15th-century stone veranda, the **Varanda do Grão-Prior**, which is all that survives of the former priors' residence.

BELOW: the picturesque Jewish Quarter in Castelo de Vide.

Some 13 km (8 miles) further south, in countryside filled with olive groves, is **Alter do Chão**, a medieval town with equine traditions. It is from here that the Alter Real horse, one of several Lusitano breeds, takes its name. The state-owned Alter stud farm *(coudelaria)* was founded in 1748 by José I (as he became two years later). Based on Andalusian stock, the animals thrived until the Napoleonic Wars when the best animals were stolen and the royal stables abolished. Happily, the breed, which excels in dressage, has been revived to a highly respected standard. There are guided tours of the stud farm.

Unspoiled beaches

If you like unspoiled cliffs and beaches, quiet roads and villages, then you will delight in the Alentejo coast, although more and more tourists are discovering it. It borders on the open Atlantic and the ocean is therefore much rougher than on the south coast. There are plenty of sheltered bays for swimming, although the water is chilly.

Alentejo's coast is not renowned for its nightlife. Bars, discos and fancy restaurants hardly exist; nor do large hotels, except at Vila Nova de Milfontes. There are campsites, however, and all the villages have at least one *pensão*. You'd better bring along your phrase book. Where tourists are relatively rare, so are natives who speak English.

Most people approach the coast from Lisbon, from where access is easy thanks to the extended motorway network. Heading south, the IP8 branches southwest just before Grândola to **Santiago do Cacém**, crowned by a castle built by the Knights Templar, which gives good views over the town and coast. Anyone interested in things Roman should consider a trip to nearby **Miróbriga** ⑱ (open Tues–Sun; entrance charge). This Iron-Age/Roman site is quite extensive and has been well excavated. There's also an interesting little Museu Regional nearby, concentrating mainly on the local cork industry.

Now it's just a short hop to Alentejo's largest coastal town, **Sines** ⑲, which is famous for being the birthplace of Vasco da Gama in 1460. It's not what you would call a beauty spot. The old part is still picturesque, but the nearby oil refinery and power station is hard to ignore.

Leaving Sines in a hurry, you can clear your lungs at the village of **Porto Covo** ⑳. Though development has begun at the back of the village, it remains an intimate place, with cobbled streets swept scrupulously clean. The main square, grandly named Largo Marquês de Pombal, is very small, bordered by houses and the tiny parish church. A few small trees and plentiful benches surround the square. Down by the sea you can find shops, cafés and restaurants. Nearby secluded coves are easy to walk to. Just off the coast of Porto Corvo is the fortified **Ilha do Pessegeiro** (Peach Tree Island), which in bygone days provided protection from raids by Dutch and Algerian pirates.

Returning to the main road, some 15 km (9 miles) south of Porto Corvo is the small town of Cercal, beyond which you reach **Vila Nova de Milfontes** ㉑, the busiest of the coast's resorts – and very pleasing it is, too. The only time it gets really busy is in high summer when many Alentejanos and Lisboetas come for their annual holiday at the large campsite. Again, there is little nightlife but there are a few more seafood restaurants and a range of accommodation that includes the pricy Castelo de Milfontes, converted from an ivy-clad fortress –

Map on page 216

BELOW: some things look better with age.

drawbridge and all – which overlooks the estuary of the River Mira. The river estuary provides long golden beaches and a calm sea. Park out at the headland overlooking the ocean, and you can turn back to see the town to your left, the winding river and the hills beyond – all very idyllic. If you are planning a day or two on this coast, then this is the place to stay.

Almograve and Zambujeira do Mar offer more stunning, deserted beaches and some fine clifftop viewpoints across the basalt cliffs to the sea. Of the two very small villages, Almograve is by far the nicer. Between these two beaches is another, Cabo do Girão, but it is naval property and access is prohibited.

Southern Alentejo

You may well choose to start an exploration of the Lower Alentejo from a base in Lisbon, but you can start from here by going inland to the pretty town of **Odemira ㉒**, set on the banks of the Rio Mira, after which it's named. It is full of flowers and trees, so green that you are apt to forget that it is in Alentejo at all. Nearby is **Barragem de Santa Clara ㉓**, a huge dam on the Mira, where water sports are popular.

Ourique ㉔ is an agricultural town north of the dam. In its surrounding fields (Campo do Ourique), fruit, olives and cork trees grow. These fields, however, have seen far more than mere farming in their time. In the nearby hamlet of **Atalaia**, archaeologists have excavated an extraordinary Bronze-Age burial mound. And it was on the site of a battle called Ourique in 1139 (which may or may not have taken place) that a fateful encounter was fought between the Portuguese and the Moors. Afonso Henriques had just become the first king of Portugal, and the victory on this battlefield strengthened his

BELOW: cork trees dot the Alentejo plain.

determination to dispel the Moors from all Portuguese soil, and gave a tremendous boost to the flagging morale of his battle-weary forces.

Map on page 216

Beja: a hot place

The capital of Lower Alentejo, **Beja** ㉕, is the hottest town in Portugal during the height of summer. It is a three-hour drive from Lisbon and an hour or so from Évora, or, if you are following the route from Ourique, it's about 60 km (38 miles) on the E802. A town existed on the present-day site as early as 48 BC, and when Julius Caesar made peace with the Lusitanians the settlement was named after this event, Pax Julia. During the 400-year Moorish occupation the name was adulterated to Baju, then Baja, until it finally became Beja.

It is now a fairly prosperous town, its income derived from olive oil and wheat. A long-time German Air Force base has been turned over to the Portuguese. Beja is not a beautiful town, but it does have some interesting sights.

The 15th-century **Convento da Conceição** is a fine example of the transition between Gothic and Manueline architecture. The baroque chapel is lined with carved, gilded woodwork. The chapterhouse, which leads to the cloisters, is tiled with superb Hispano-Arabic *azulejos* dating back to the 1500s. Their quality is rivalled only by those to be found in the Royal Palace at Sintra. The convent also houses the **Museu Regional** (Tues–Sun; closed 12.30–2pm; entrance charge).

Storks on a stalk, in Serpa.

The small and modest **Santo Amaro** is the oldest church in Beja. It is thought to date back to the 7th century and is a rare example of Visigothic architecture. The **Misericórdia** church in the Praça da República is also worth a look. Beja's 13th-century **castle** still stands, and its castellated walls run around the town perimeter. The tall keep contains a military museum, and a narrow balcony

BELOW: dressed for the fiesta in Beja.

on each side from which you can enjoy a remarkable view across the plains.

Driving in to **Serpa** ㉖ (about 30 km/18 miles east of Beja) is – as with so many small Alentejo towns – like driving into a time warp. The castle and fortified walls were built at the command of King Dinis. A difference here from other 13th-century walls is that these have an aqueduct built into them.

A well-preserved gateway is the **Portas de Beja**; the gates along with the rest of the walls, were almost sold by the town council in the latter half of the 19th century. Cooler heads prevailed and the walls were saved, though a great part of them had been destroyed in 1707 when the Duke of Ossuna and his army occupied the town during the War of the Spanish Succession.

There are several churches worth seeing (notably the 13th-century Santa Maria), as well as the delightfully cool and elegant palace belonging to the Counts of Ficalho, the **Paço dos Condes de Ficalho**. It was built in the 16th century and has a majestic staircase and lovely tiles. The present Marquise, incidentally, is the granddaughter of José Maria Eça de Queiroz (1845–1900), one of Portugal's great 19th-century novelists.

The Rio Guadiana is considered the most peaceful of Portugal's three big rivers (the others being the Tagus and Douro), but an exception is at **Pulo do Lobo** (Wolf's Leap) between Serpa and Mértola. This is a stretch of high and wild rapids, which can be reached by road and is worth a visit if you're in the area – you'll probably find you are the only tourist there.

Mértola

The ancient fortified town of **Mértola** ㉗, set in the confluence between the Guadiana and the Oeiras rivers, is one of Alentejo's hidden gems. To get here

José Maria Eça de Queiroz, a diplomat and a graduate of Coimbra University, wrote passionate, biting novels which attacked the upper-class mores of his day.

BELOW: The Igreja Matriz at Mértola.

from Serpa you can either take a secondary road to the south, or return to Beja, then take the main road south and turn off to the left. Whichever way you approach, the sight of the town's strongly built walls crowned by a **castelo** (open daily 9am–5pm; entrance charge to climb the tower) is as impressive as it is unexpected.

Map on page 216

Mértola has a long history reaching back to Roman times. For five centuries under the Romans it was an important port on the then navigable Guadiana for exporting mineral ores from the nearby Minas de São Domingos, near the Spanish border. Its importance continued under the Visigoths, whose handiwork can be seen in the castle tower, and later the Moors. Twice in the 11th and 12th centuries it was capital of a kingdom which included Beja. With the growth of agricultural produce in the region Mértola was active in exporting grain to North Africa. When the river eventually silted up the town slipped quietly into oblivion.

Leave plenty of time to explore the astonishing remains of the Roman port, the parish church, the castle and museums (a single ticket covers all sites), as well as the **Igreja Matriz**. Outwardly a Christian church, this pristine white building was originally a mosque and one of the few in Portugal to have survived virtually intact.

Alentejo produces some fine wines. Its reds are full-bodied and mature well in the bottle.

The exhibition of Islamic pottery in the **Museu Islâmico** (Museum of Islamic Art) is not enormous, but it is the finest in Portugal, and the **Museu Romano** (Roman Museum), born from a twist of fate, is very sophisticated. The town hall here burned down some years ago, and during the clearing operation the remains of a Roman villa were discovered. After finishing a thorough excavation, the town hall was rebuilt and the Roman villa tuned into an elegant basement museum. ❑

BELOW: Moorish influence in Mértola.

FOOD AND DRINK

Alentejo's culinary specialities should not be missed. Try *sopa Alentejana* – a filling soup of bread, with lots of coriander (a herb used a great deal in Alentejo cooking), garlic and poached eggs. One of the classic meat dishes is *carne de porco à Alentejana* – chunks of pork seasoned in wine, coriander and onions and served with clams. Two much heavier but delicious stewed dishes are *ensopada de cabrito* – kid boiled with potatoes and bread until the meat is just about falling off the bone, and *favada de caça*, a game stew of hare, rabbit, partridge or pigeon with broad beans. The best Alentejo cheese comes from Serpa. Made from sheep's and goat's milk it has a creamy texture and a strong, slightly piquant flavour. Évora has its own goat cheese which is hard, salty and slightly acid. It is preserved in jars filled with olive oil.

Alentejo is a *região demarcada* – a demarcated wine region. Most towns have their own co-operative winery from which you can buy stocks at rock-bottom prices, and most restaurants have a low-priced co-operative house wine. In Lisbon, Alentejo reds are often drunk with *bacalhau*, instead of the more usual white. Try the reds from the Reguengos co-operative or those from Borba *(see page 225)* and white wines from the Vidigueira co-operative.

THE FIGHT TO PRESERVE ARTS AND CRAFTS

Local customs form a thread of continuity in rural Portugal, and none are stronger than the craft skills which are found throughout the country

Portugal is a land rich in tradition, and in rural areas the skills and artistry of local craftspeople have been passed from generation to generation. Most skills are specific to one locality: pottery is perhaps the only national craft – although with important variations in design and decoration. Craft work is a significant cottage industry, but there is a danger of skills dying out, especially in regions with few visitors. To prevent this, EU funding has been channelled towards promoting the work of artisans to save skills, create employment, and retain life in dying villages.

There are plenty of craft shops in the large towns, but the real joy is to stop in tiny villages and discover the spinning and weaving co-operatives formed by women, as in Mértola, see bobbin lace work, watch ceramics in the making, buy jute dolls, and marvel at the basket creations made from leaves of the dwarf fan palm.

The products of some regions have gained national importance. Arraiolos in Alentejo has a centuries-old tradition of rug and carpet-making which has grown into a major industry; and the hand-embroidered bedspreads of Castelo Branco, which have been made since the 17th century, are also popular throughout Portugal, and now in demand by tourists.

◁ **MERTOLA BLANKETS**
The women of Mértola specialise in making traditional brown and white blankets and other woollen goods.

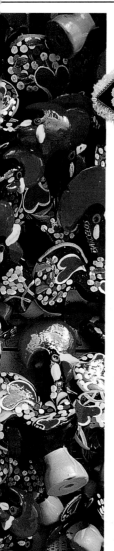

◁ **TAPESTRY WORK**
Home-grown flax is often used for tapestry work. The fibre must be soaked, combed, spun and whitened before use.

▽ **MOORISH LAMPS**
Decorative white lamp shades, an Algarvian speciality seen in many homes, retain a marked Moorish influence.

THE *GALO DE BARCELOS*

There is no escape from the Barcelos rooster. Its fame arises from a legend (as colourful as the little figure itself), which has been embroidered and enlarged with every telling. The central theme relates the story of a murder committed in the northern town of Barcelos many centuries ago. A certain Galician pilgrim came under suspicion as the perpetrator, and no matter how strong his protest, his pleas of innocence fell on deaf ears, and he was sentenced to death.

Before his execution he was granted a last wish: to make a final plea before the judge, who, in the midst of entertaining guests to dinner, agreed to see him. In desperation, the condemned man pointed to the roast fowl on the dinner table and cried, "As surely as I stand innocent, so will that cock crow." Miraculously, the rooster obliged. The judge forfeited his dinner, but the pilgrim gained his life.

Ceramic figures of the Barcelos cock are on sale everywhere. The symbol now also adorns everything from T-shirts to tea towels, and finds a place in most visitors' luggage.

A LOAD OF COCKERELS
profusion of cockerels can e found in shops and stalls l over Portugal, but owhere more so than in arcelos, where the legend iginated *(see side panel)*.

LOCAL INDUSTRY
stremoz is renowned for its ay pots and figurines. You ll find the best displays at e Saturday market in the wn square.

△ **VILA REAL POTTERY**
This distinctive black pottery is made by a simple but effective method: covering pots with soil and ashes to exclude oxygen and burning brushwood above them.

▷ **BASKETWARE**
Sweet chestnut, willow, the leaves of the dwarf fan palm and the giant reed are favoured materials in basketware *(matosinhos)*.

ESTREMADURA AND RIBATEJO

Map on page 242

Although ribboned with silver sand, the coast is not the major attraction in this region. It is inland that you'll find some of the country's finest and best loved monuments

The region north of Lisbon's environs reaching up towards Coimbra has not managed to establish itself as a tourist destination with a clear brand image in spite of its many attractions. Bordered by an endless ribbon of silver sand, the Costa de Prata – the Silver Coast – seemed a promising promotional aid, except that the coast, Nazaré apart, has only small resorts. Most of the region's attractions, the famous monasteries at Alcobaça, Batalha and Tomar, the religious sanctuary at Fátima and the spectacular deep caves in the limestone *serras* are all inland.

With its points of interest fairly widespread, it is an area tailor-made for touring. Allow around three days to take in most of the major sites and longer if you are intent on savouring everything the region offers. The circular tour described here follows an anti-clockwise route from Lisbon up to Batalha and back.

PRECEDING PAGES: a proud owner. **LEFT:** Obidos. **BELOW:** hard-working donkey.

North from Lisbon

The quickest ways to escape Lisbon are either by the A1 or the A8 heading north. The alternative for a slower but more interesting journey is to cross the Rio Tejo on the Ponte Vasco da Gama and take the road on the eastern side of the river.

Santarém ❶ is the central town of Ribatejo. It was named after Santa Iria, a young nun who was accused of being unchaste, and martyred in 653 near Tomar. Her body, thrown into the river, washed ashore here. A riverbank shrine has a statue whose feet act as a sacred gauge to the water level – if they are touched by floods, even Lisbon is in danger.

Among several fine churches, the Romanesque-Gothic church of **São João de Alporão** contains a fine archaeological museum (open Tues–Sun; closed 12.30–2pm; entrance charge), as well as the beautifully carved tomb of Duarte, a son of Pedro I who died in the Battle of Alcácer-Quibir in 1458. It contains just one of Duarte's teeth, the sole relic which was delivered to his wife.

In northeastern Santarém is the church of **Santa Clara**, originally part of a 13th-century convent, containing the elaborate tomb of Dona Leonor, daughter of Afonso III. The church of **Nossa Senhora da Graça**, a bold Gothic structure with a beautiful nave, holds several tombs, among them that of Pedro Álvares Cabral, discoverer of Brazil.

In **Alpiarça**, across the river, look for the 19th-century architectural gem of the Casa dos Patudos, today a wonderfully eclectic museum.

A diversion to **Abrantes ❷** is worthwhile, if only

to see the nearby Castelo de Almourol, romantically located on an island in the middle of the Tejo. The road on the east of the river offers the most interesting route. Abrantes itself is well sited above the Tejo but it has little to offer visitors except perhaps for the castle of **Santa Maria do Castelo**.

Turn back along the north bank just before Tancos and look for the sign to **Castelo de Almourol ❸**. It crowns a rocky island in the river and the ferryman (Sr. João; tel: 914 506 562), who normally operates between 9am and 5pm, will row visitors across for 75 cents. If you want a trip around the island it will cost more. The Romans recognised the importance of the site on this key communication route and built a castle, although there may well have been an earlier settlement. Later, the castle experienced a succession of tenants, the Visigoths, the Moors and finally the Christians. Afonso Henriques entrusted it to the Knights Templar in 1147 for their help in fighting the Moors. The Grand Master Gualdim Pais rebuilt the castle leaving an inscription over the door, and it remained garrisoned for a time. When the Moors were finally expelled from Portugal the strategic importance of the castle declined and it eventually fell into disuse. It takes only a few minutes to wander around the walls of this irregular-shaped fortress (entrance free).

Foreign visitors often prefer Portuguese bullfights (touradas) to those in Spain since Portuguese bullfighters do not kill their bulls – at least not in public.

Tomar: the haunt of knights

From the castle it is a fairly short run north to **Tomar ❹**, a delightful town with a host of good points: a setting on the banks of the Rio Nabão; the splendid Convento do Cristo, which is a UNESCO World Heritage Site; and medieval streets paved with stone and fancifully patterned with exuberant flowers. With its pleasing ambience and rich culture, its ancient legends and appealing daily life, Tomar is a town in which to linger and explore for a couple of days.

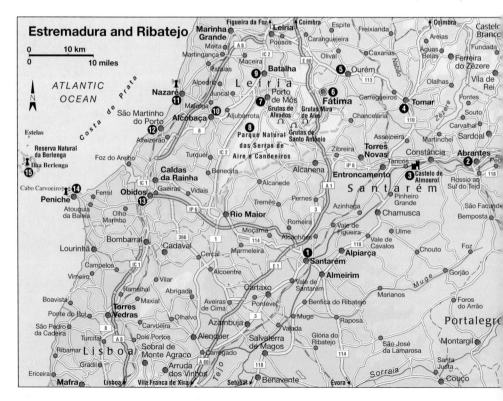

Tomar was the headquarters of the Knights Templar in Portugal, an order which was formed in 1119, during the crusades. The order spread quickly throughout Europe, gaining extraordinary wealth. It also made powerful enemies, and in the early 1300s, amid accusations of heresy and foul practices, and finally the suppression of the order altogether, the Knights took refuge in Tomar, where Grand Master Gualdim Pais had built a castle back in 1162. They re-emerged in 1320, reincarnated as the Order of Christ, whose proud symbol, the Cross of Christ, became the banner of the Age of Discoveries. In Tomar they left behind the marvellous ruins of the old castle and, within its walls, the still-intact church and cloisters. The castle is set on a hill above the city, a 10-minute walk away, and commands a view over the rooftops of the old town.

Map on page 242

The monastery and other Tomar sights

The **Convento do Cristo** (open daily; summer, 9am–6pm; winter, 9am–5pm; entrance charge) is a maze of staircases, passages, and nooks and crannies. The seven cloisters (just four are open to the public) have been added at irregular angles and over several centuries, and even the beautiful main entrance is oddly tucked into a corner. The original Templar church is on the right, just inside the entrance . Begun in 1162, the octagonal temple was modelled on Jerusalem's Church of the Holy Sepulchre. Here, the knights would hear services while seated on their horses, and pray for victory in battle.

The chapterhouse and Coro Alto, added much later, provide a sharp contrast to the original temple, as does the adjoining 16th-century cloister with 17th-century tiles where some of the tombs of the knights are found. From here there is access to the upper level and then into the other cloisters. From the terrace of the small Claustro de Santa Bárbara, there is a view of the amazing, ornate Manueline window, structured around two deep relief carvings of ships' masts, knots, cork, coral and seaweed. The whole is topped by a shield, crown and cross, symbol of the union of church and king.

From the opposite side of the building there is a view of the surrounding forest and the castle yard where the knights trained their horses and spent their off-duty hours. Also on this side lies an unfinished chapel: bad luck during construction persuaded the superstitious knights to abandon it.

Tomar's Synagogue in Rua Joaquim Jacinto is now the **Museu Luso-Herbraico de Abraão Zacuto** (open 10am–5.45pm; free entrance). Although a high percentage of Portuguese people have Jewish ancestry, and Tomar was once the home of a thriving Jewish community, there are very few Jews left. When King Manuel I married Isabella of Castile in 1497, a condition of the marriage contract was the expulsion of the Jews. They were allowed to remain if they converted, although laws governing fair treatment were not closely monitored. Later, the Inquisition legitimised brutal discrimination against them. The synagogue/ museum is simple and moving, decorated with gifts from all over the world.

The church of **São João Baptista** has a dark wood ceiling and a rather sombre atmosphere. Sixteenth-century wood panel paintings on the walls depict

BELOW: a stairway in Tomar's Convento do Cristo.

scenes such as the Last Supper and Salome with the head of John the Baptist. On the left is a delicately carved pulpit.

Standing alone on the edge of town, **Santa Maria dos Olivais** is a simple church dating from the 12th century and containing many Templar tombs. The town's tourist office is located on Avenida Dr Cândido Madureira, near the road to the castle, and there is a regional tourist office at 1 Rua Serpa Pinto.

En route from Tomar to Fátima, it is well worth a stop at **Ourém** ❺, or more particularly at Ourém Velha, the fortified site on top of an easily defended hill. The history of the castle is known only from the time it was recovered from the Moors in 1148 by King Afonso Henriques. Little was attempted in the way of restoration until King Dinis (1279–1325) arrived on the scene. He rebuilt this as he did many other castles in Portugal.

The Lourdes of Portugal

Fátima ❻, some 12 km (8 miles) from Ourém, is not a place for non-believers, and there is even a notice to advise you of this. It is a place for pilgrims – of which there are up to 2 million a year. On 13 May 1917, three shepherd children had a vision of the Virgin here. Thereafter, she appeared before the children and, on one occasion, as a shining light to the townspeople who gathered with them on the 13th of the subsequent months *(see page 77)*. The two younger children died shortly after the apparitions, but one, Lucia de Jesus Santos, lived well into her eighties in a convent near Coimbra. The processions that take place on the anniversaries of the visions – 13 May and 13 October – draw thousands of people from around the world.

Surrounded by acres of car parks is the vast white basilica, consecrated in

In June 2000 the Vatican revealed the third "secret" of Fátima, which prophesied the assassination attempt on Pope John Paul II on 13 May 1981.

BELOW: Fátima, one of the best-known shrines in the world.

1953, built in recognition of the importance of this site to pilgrims. In front of it is a huge esplanade large enough hold to 100,000 worshippers, and the **Chapel of Apparitions**, which Our Lady of the Rosaries ordered to be built in her sixth and final appearance on this spot. Inside the basilica lie the tombs of the two visionary children who died, Jacinta and Francisco Marto.

Map on page 242

Castles and caves

West of Fátima, along scenic well-paved roads, lies the pleasant town of **Porto de Mós ❼**, worth a brief stop even if only to look at the castle, capped with green cones and standing on a hill. The castle has a fairly long pedigree and still contains some original Roman stonework. As with Ourém castle, King Afonso Henriques recovered it from the Moors in 1148. After several restorations, it remained in military use at least until the Battle of Aljubarrota in 1383 when João I is said to have rested his troops here before the fight. Afterwards the king rewarded his captain, Nuno Alvares Pereira, with the gift of this fortress for leading his troops so bravely. It was his grandson, Afonso, a cultured and much travelled man, who endeavoured to convert the castle into a palace and disguise the strong military lines.

As a change from monuments, a diversion into the **Parque Natural das Serras de Aire e Candeeiros ❽** offers fine limestone scenery and a chance to visit Portugal's largest caves. Take the N243 towards Torres Novas to find **Grutas Mira de Aire**, **Grutas de Santo António** and **Grutas de Alavdos**. The latter two lie on a spur off the main road. All three are open to the public and are different enough to be worth visiting. If only one is possible then perhaps Grutas Mira de Aire (open daily 9.30am–5.30pm, 8.30pm in July and Aug; entrance

BELOW: the great monastery at Batalha.

A characteristically graceful vaulted dome inside the monastery at Batalha.

fee) is the best choice. The caves are reached down more than 600 steps through well-illuminated caverns with imaginative and descriptive names, to the underground river. At least the return is by elevator.

Batalha: an essential stop

Batalha ❾ is one of Portugal's most beautiful monuments, and another UNESCO World Heritage Site. The origins of **Mosteiro de Santa Maria da Vitória**, to use its full name, lie in Portugal's struggle for independence from Castile. One of the decisive battles for independence was fought at Aljubarrota, not far from Batalha. The Castilian king, Juan, who based his claim to the throne on his marriage to a Portuguese princess, invaded Portugal in 1385. The 20-year-old Dom João, Master of the Order of Avis and illegitimate son of Pedro I, promised to raise a monastery to the Virgin Mary if the Portuguese won. With his young general, Nuno Alvares Pereira, João defeated the Castilian, and became João I. The monastery was constructed between 1388 and 1533.

Enter the large front portal. Inside, the arches sweep upward to a sculpture representing the hierarchy in the heavenly court, as it was perceived in the Middle Ages. In the centre is Christ surrounded by the four gospel writers. Though the outside of the monastery is ornate, the interior is endowed with a simple Gothic elegance and dignity. Vaulted ceilings arch above a slender nave which is illuminated through stained-glass windows. To the right is the **Capela do Fundador** (Founder's Chapel), built around 1426 by João I, and here are the tombs of João and his English queen, Philippa, effigies eloquently holding hands. Tombs of their children, including that of Prince Henry the Navigator, are set into the walls under regal arches. The room is topped by a dome supported by star-shaped ribbing.

BELOW: exquisite carving at Batalha.

On the other side of the building you may enter the **Claustro Real** (Royal Cloister). Arches filled with Manueline ornamentation surround a pretty courtyard and are patterned with intricate designs. The chapterhouse is the first room off the cloister. It has an unusual and beautiful ceiling and its window is filled with a stained-glass Christ on the Cross, remarkably rich in colour. This chamber holds the tombs of two unknown soldiers, whose remains were returned to Portugal from France and Africa after World War I. The sculpture of "Christ of the Trenches" was given by the French government, and a photograph of its extraordinary discovery on the battlefields of Flanders can be seen in the refectory opposite, where there is a shop and small museum of the Great War, which claimed 8,145 Portuguese soldiers' lives.

To reach the **Capelas Imperfeitas** (Unfinished Chapels), go outside the monastery. This octagonal structure is attached to the outside wall and its abrupt rooflessness is a shock. Ordered by King Duarte I to house the tombs of himself and his family, the chapel was begun in the 1430s but construction was never finished. No one is quite certain why. The shell contains simple chapels in each of seven walls. The chapel opposite the door holds the tomb of the king and Leonor, his wife. The eighth wall is a massive door of limestone, with endless layers of beautifully detailed ornamentation in carved Manueline style.

Alcobaça

Twelve km (8 miles) south of Batalha is the town of **Alcobaça** , named after two rivers, the Alcoa and the Baça. At its heart is the magnificent **Cistercian Abbey** (open daily from 9am), yet another UNESCO World Heritage Site. The first king of Portugal, Afonso Henriques, founded it to commemorate the capture of Santarém from the Moors. He laid the foundation stone himself in 1148.

The abbey's Cistercian monks were energetically productive. Numbering, it is said, 999 ("one less than a thousand"), they diligently tilled the land around the abbey, planting vegetables and fruit. In Sebastião I's reign, the exceedingly wealthy and powerful Santa Maria Abbey, as it is also known, was declared by the Pope the seat of the entire Cistercian order. The monks here were particularly known for their lively spirits and lavish hospitality. They ran a school, perhaps the first public school in Portugal, and a sanctuary and hospice as well. In 1810, however, the abbey was sacked by French troops. In the Liberal Revolution of 1834, when all religious orders were expelled from Portugal, the abbey was again pillaged.

The long baroque façade, added in the 18th century, has twin towers in the centre, below which are a Gothic doorway and rose window surviving from the original façade. Directly inside the serene and austere church, the largest in Portugal, three tall aisles and plain walls emphasise the clean lines. In the transepts are the two well-known and richly carved tombs of Pedro I and Inês de Castro *(see page 30)*. Off the south transept are several other royal tombs, including those of Afonso II and Afonso III, and a sadly mutilated 17th-century terracotta of the Death of St Bernard. To the east of the ambulatory there are two fine Manueline doorways that were designed by João de Castilho.

Map
on page
242

There is little else to see in Batalha other than the monastery. Nearby Leiera makes a good base for exploring the area.

LEFT: Alcobaça's Cistercian abbey from without…
BELOW: …and from within.

Mending nets, a task that doesn't change.

An entrance in the north wall of the church leads to the 14th-century **Claustro de Silencio** (Cloister of Silence). Several rooms branch off the cloister, including the chapterhouse and a dormitory. There is a kitchen, with an enormous central chimney and a remarkable basin through which a rivulet runs: it supposedly provided the monks with a constant supply of fresh fish. Next door is the refectory, with steps built into one wall leading to a pulpit. To the left of the entrance is the **Sala dos Reis**, with statues of many of the kings of Portugal probably carved by monks themselves. The panel in the same room, which tells the history of Alcobaça Abbey, is a rare example of a manuscript *azulejo* panel.

Alcobaça today is the centre of a porcelain and pottery industry. There are many shops around the central square, and some factories welcome visitors. There is also a wine museum, the **Museu Nacional do Vinho**, in the town.

The Silver Coast

From Alcobaça, it is a relatively short drive out to the coast to reach **Nazaré** a fishing port which nestles along a sweeping bay. In summer, thousands of holidaymakers pack the beach in rows of peaked, brightly-striped canvas tents that create a striking image.

The abundance of tourists vitiates some of Nazaré's charm, but it also assures that all the visitor's desires will be catered to. Pleasant seafood restaurants and small hotels line the sandy bay; esplanade cafés, bars and souvenir shops abound. But the life of the hardy fishermen goes on.

Because they had no natural harbour, the fishermen used to launch their boats from the beach. They managed this by pushing their craft down log rollers into the sea then clambering aboard and rowing furiously till they overrode the

BELOW:
looking down on a boatyard at Nazaré.

incoming breakers. When they arrived home again, the boats were winched ashore by oxen and later by tractors. The building of a modern anchorage to the south of the beach has relieved the Nazaré fishermen of this arduous task.

Map on page 242

The Nazaré fisherfolk's traditional dress is today seen more in souvenir shops than on the street. Some women still wear coloured petticoats under a wide black or coloured skirt and cover their heads with a black scarf; the men still favour woollen shirts in traditional plaids, but few wear the distinctive black stocking bonnets.

Nazaré, named after a statue of the Virgin that a 4th-century monk brought to the town from Nazareth, lives literally on two levels. In the lower part of town, small, white-walled fishermen's cottages line the narrow alleyways. High above on the cliff that towers 109 metres (360 ft) above the old town is the quarter known as **Sítio**. Reached by a funicular that climbs the tallest cliffside in Portugal, Sítio is dominated by a large square, and on its edge a tiny chapel, built to commemorate a miracle in 1182, when the Virgin saved the local lord by stopping his horse plunging off the cliff as he pursued a deer. The 17th-century **Nossa Senhora da Nazaré** on the other side of the square is the focus of festivities during the second week of September that include processions and bullfights in the Sítio bullring. The steep, narrow pathway and steps from the lighthouse west of the church afford stirring views of Atlantic breakers.

Calm waters and a walled town

The road south out of Nazaré leads first past the new fishing harbour and then down the coast to **São Martinho do Porto ⓬**. Here a huge encircling sand bank creates a virtual lagoon, although there is a small opening to the sea. These

BELOW: the Romaria of Nossa Senhora da Nazaré.

Map
on page
242

*Between Obidos and
Peniche some
delightful coastal
scenery and excellent
restaurants make it
worth taking a short
detour to Baleal. For
golfers, the Praia
d'el Rei course offers
a splendid challenge.*

RIGHT:
Nazaré fishing
fleet at dawn.
BELOW:
a gilded statue in
Obidos church.

calm, shallow waters are readily warmed by the sun but, with only a limited exchange of water, the risk of pollution in the bay is high. Moving south again, the road sweeps grandly by the university town of **Caldas de Rainha** (Queen's Spa), where there's a regular morning fruit market, and on to Obidos.

A picture-postcard view of town walls crowned by a castle announces **Obidos ⑬**. The old walled town, its streets tumbling with bougainvillea, presents a well-groomed appearance to the steady influx of day trippers. At least the town retains some authenticity, as there has been no new building, and only existing structures within the walls are used as tea houses, residences and gift shops. Everything in the narrow jumbled streets is painted white, with blue or yellow trimmings and some colourful window boxes.

The town has a long history: it was occupied by the Moors before falling into Christian hands. The indefatigable castle-builder King Dinis tidied it up and restored the **castelo** early in the 14th century. Damaged in the great earthquake of 1755, the castle was subsequently restored and today is used as a *pousada*. It is the place where everyone wants to stay, and gets booked up well in advance. Apart from wandering around unprotected town walls and enjoying the ambience of the town, there is little to see in the way of monuments. The 17th-century **Igreja de Santa Maria** dominating the market square attracts the most attention, chiefly for the religious paintings by Josefa de Obidos (1634–84).

Back to the coast

Like many of Portugal's coastal towns, **Peniche ⑭** has no natural harbour, only a bay sheltered by the rocky promontory of **Cabo Carvoeiro**, the second most westerly point in Europe. A sea wall has been built to protect the bay. Peniche is an uncompromising town of around 18,000 people. Here, the spare white houses cling to the slopes for shelter from the sweeping northwesterly winds. Too stark and exposed for tourism to have taken hold, the town typifies life in Portuguese fishing communities.

The **Fortaleza** physically dominates the town. The veteran leader of Portugal's Communist Party, Alvaro Cunhal, escaped from this notorious prison in 1960 by climbing down the cliffs to a waiting boat that reportedly took him to a Soviet-bloc submarine. Today, the building serves as a local museum.

You can get a sense of the Atlantic swell that is the fisherman's constant companion by taking the ferry from Peniche to **Ilha Berlenga ⑮**, 7 km (4 miles) offshore. The ferry takes an hour and runs from June to September. Once out of the shelter of the peninsula, the powerful current rocks the boat with unexpected force, but it's worth the discomfort. A 17th-century fortress, now converted to an inn, a lighthouse and a few fishermen's cottages are the only buildings. The entire island has been designated a national bird sanctuary, and seagulls and eider are everywhere. Officials patrol the makeshift paths to ensure that visitors don't disturb the birds. The greatest excitement lies in taking a trip around the reefs, caves and smaller islands, past a breathtaking sea tunnel called the **Furado Grande**.

The return to Lisbon is best made via the new highway from Obidos, entering Lisbon via the A8. ❑

COIMBRA

Maps:
Area 266
City 256

Coimbra grows old but never grows up. University freshers arrive each year to revitalise traditions and pour their souls into fado. *For visitors it's a great mix of history and youthful exuberance*

Perched on a hill overlooking the Rio Mondego, **Coimbra ❶** is surrounded by breathtakingly beautiful countryside. The city itself is a mixture of ancient and new, rural and urban. The tourist office in the centre of the lower town, in Largo de Portagem, will provide you with a good map of the city.

The university is the most stalwart guardian of Coimbra's colourful past. Students clad in black capes, the traditional academic dress, resemble oversized bats as they flit around town. The hems of the capes are often ripped, a declaration – at times – of romantic conquest. But these capes have only recently come back into style, since for a time they were associated with Salazar's New State, and therefore not worn in the years after the 1974 revolution.

In May each year, the university celebrates the *Queima das Fitas*, the "burning of the ribbons", when graduating students burn the ribbons they have been wearing, the colour of which signify their faculty – yellow for medicine, and so on. The celebrations last a week, and their grand finale is a long drunken parade.

Another Coimbra tradition is *fado*, a more serious cousin of the Lisbon variety. The sombre Coimbra *fado* theoretically requires you to clear your throat in approval after a rendition, and not applaud. It is performed only by men, often cloak-wrapped graduates of the university.

The country's third-largest city, Coimbra lies at the centre of an agricultural region and has a large market. The students are not the only ones in black: it is the traditional dress of many of the rural women who come to town as well. Coimbra also has a considerable manufacturing industry.

Roman roots

Coimbra traces its roots to the Roman municipality of *Aeminium*. It gained in importance when the city of Conímbriga *(see page 265)*, a few kilometres south, proved vulnerable to invasion. Convulsions in the empire and various invasions brought an end to Roman rule in the city. The Moors took over in 711, ushering in 300 years of Islamic rule, with a few interruptions. One such occurred in 878 when Afonso III of Asturias and León captured the city. But Coimbra was not permanently retaken by Christian forces until 1064. It then became a base for the reconquest and it was at this time that the city was walled. From 1139 to 1385 Coimbra was the capital of Portugal.

The 12th century was an age of considerable progress for Coimbra – including the construction, which began in 1131, of the city's most important monastery, Santa Cruz, still standing today. The city was a lively commercial centre and included both Jewish and Moorish quarters. Division was not only by religion, but by class as well. Nobles and clergy lived

PRECEDING PAGES: playing cards is a serious business. **LEFT:** a university student. **BELOW:** a fraction of Coimbra's library.

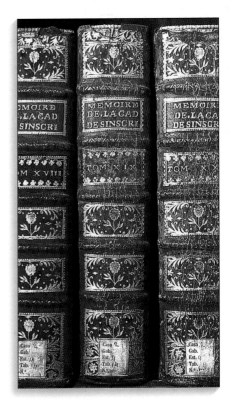

inside the walls in the upper town, while merchants and craft workers lived outside in what is today known as the Baixa, the "lower area", down by the river, and heart of the modern town.

The university founded in 1290 in Lisbon moved to Coimbra in 1308, only to return to Lisbon in 1377. These shifts were the result of continual political conflict between the monarchy and the academic hierarchy. It was not until 1537 that the university settled permanently in Coimbra. A few years later, it moved to its present site at the top of the hill.

Most areas of interest are easily reached on foot – that is, if you're willing to do some uphill walking. Don't try to drive within the city. The old city and the university crown Coimbra's central hill, and the Baixa, which is the main shopping and dining district, lies at the foot of the hill along the Rio Mondego. Santa Clara lies across the river, while the tourist office, *Turismo*, is handily located at the northern end of the bridge.

Decorative doorway in Coimbra.

The old city and university

Once enclosed within walls, the old city is a tangle of narrow streets and alleys, lined by ancient buildings and filled with squares and patios. The university buildings are a compelling mix of styles, from the odd baroque **Torre**, a clock-tower known to the students as *a cabra* (the goat), to bleakly Salazarist faculty blocks. The passage of centuries is evident. The modern centre of the university is the statue of King Dinis, its founder, on the site of an earlier castle in **Praça Dinis ❹**. Nearby are the buildings that house the Faculties of Science and Technology, Medicine and Letters and the New Library.

Of more historical interest than these stolidly functional buildings is the Pátio

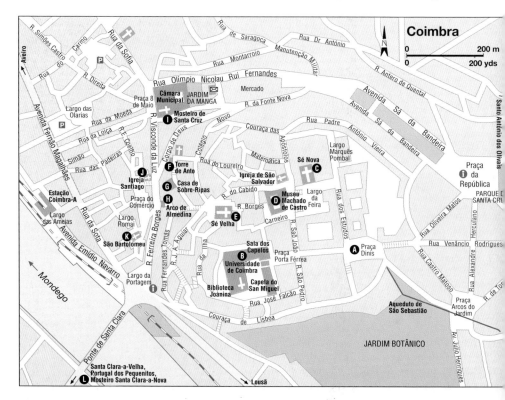

Map on page 256

das Escolas (Patio of the Schools), within the **Universidade Velha ⓑ**, the Old University. To enter the patio, pass through the 17th-century Porta Férrea, a large portal decorated in the Mannerist style, to a large, dusty courtyard, which is used for parking. Here are some of the oldest and stateliest buildings of the university. The figure of João III, who installed the university in Coimbra, still reigns from the centre of the patio. Behind him, there is a magnificent view of the river.

The building in the farthest corner from the Porta Férrea is the **Biblioteca Joanina** (open daily; closed for lunch noon–2pm; entrance charge), among the world's most resplendent baroque libraries. The three sumptuous 18th-century rooms were built during the reign of João V, whose portrait hangs at the far end. Bookcases, decorated in gilded wood and oriental motifs, reach gracefully to an upper galleried level; even the ladders are intricately decorated. Note the frescoes on the ceilings. More than 300,000 books fill the cases and are still consulted by scholars.

Next door is the **Capela do San Miguel** (St Michael's Chapel), begun in 1517, and remodelled in the 17th and 18th centuries. The chapel is notable for its carpet-style tiles, the painted ceilings, the altar and the baroque organ. Beside the chapel is a museum of sacred art.

The arcaded building to the right of the Porta Férrea on the Via Latina houses the **Sala Grande dos Actos**, where degrees are conferred and academic ceremonies take place. Portraits of the kings of Portugal hang from its walls. Other rooms that you may enter are the Rectory and, right by the bell tower, the **Sala do Exame Privado**, the Private Exam Room. Some of the university faculties have small museums, such as the **Museu de Fisica** (Physics Museum, open Mon–Fri 2.30–5.30pm) in Largo Marquês de Pombal.

Trains from Lisbon take 2–3 hours and stop at Coimbra B station 3 km (2 miles) north of the centre, where passengers take a linking train to Coimbra A, the delightful little station in the middle of town.

BELOW: the Old University is a dominant feature in Coimbra.

Old and New Cathedral

A short walk down from the university grounds takes you to the **Sé Nova** (**New Cathedral**) , whose sand-coloured façade presides over a rather uninteresting square. Built for the Jesuits in 1554, it became a cathedral in 1772. Inside, the altar and much else is of lavish gilded wood. Many of the paintings around the altar are copies of Italian masters.

The **Museu Machado de Castro** (closed for refurbishment until 2006) is housed in the old episcopal palace and the neighbouring 12th-century church of São João de Almedina. Constructed over the city's Roman forum and *cryptoporticus* (underground galleries), the palace was the residence of Coimbra's early bishops. The museum is named after Portugal's greatest sculptor Joaquim Machado de Castro (1732–1822), who was born in Coimbra. It holds an excellent collection, both extensive and varied, of medieval sculpture, as well as later work.

The **Sé Velha** (**Old Cathedral**) (open Mon–Sat 10am–6pm) renovated in the 20th century, was built between 1162 and 1184. It served as a cathedral until 1772, when the episcopal see was moved to the Sé Nova. The fortress-like exterior is relieved by an arched door with an arched window directly above. The intricate Gothic altar within is of gilded wood, created by two Flemish masters in the 15th and 16th centuries. Sancho I was crowned king here in 1185, and João I in 1385. There are several tombs in the cathedral, including those of the 13th-century Bishop Dom Egas Fa'es (to the left of the altar) and Dona Vetaça, a Byzantine princess who was a governess in the Coimbra court in the 14th century, attending to the mobility of the aristocracy in the late Middle Ages. The cloister is early Gothic and its construction began in 1218.

Work on the **Colégio de Santo Agostinho**, on Rua Colégio Novo, was started in 1593. The ecclesiastical scholars and monks who first occupied it would probably be astonished by its present-day purpose, for this pleasant building, lined with pretty *azulejos*, is now home to the university's Psychology Department.

Nearby, on Rua Sobre-Ripas (confusingly, also called Sub-Ripas), the medieval **Torre de Anto** (Anthony's Tower) was once part of the 12th-century walls of the city. Much later it was the home of poet António Nobre (1867–1900) during his undergraduate days.

The **Casa de Sobre-Ripas** , on the same street, is an aristocratic 16th-century mansion. Note the archetypal Manueline door and window, but don't bother knocking: it is the Faculty of Archaeology, and not open to the public. Here, according to tradition, Maria Teles was murdered by her husband João (eldest son of the tragic Inês de Castro) who had been convinced by the jealous Queen Leonor Teles that his wife – the queen's sister – was unfaithful to him.

Arco de Almedina , an entrance to the old city just off Rua Ferreira Borges (the main street – *see below*), was also part of the Coimbra walls that encircle the old town hill.

Baixa Coimbra

The Baixa is the busy shopping district. Rua Ferreira Borges, with many fashionable shops, is the busy, prin-

cipal street. Although this district lay outside the walls of the old city, it dates back to nearly the same time.

The **Mosteiro de Santa Cruz** ❶ in Praça 8 de Maio (a continuation of Rua Ferreira Borges) was founded in 1131 by the St Augustine Fathers. In the 14th century a grim scene was enacted when Dom Pedro had the body of his murdered lover exhumed, crowned and propped on a throne here, forcing his courtiers to pay homage to her corpse and kiss her decomposing hand. The façade and portal of the church date from the 16th century. Inside, although the church is small, it is light and spacious. Eighteenth-century *azulejos* adorn the walls: the right side depicts the life of Saint Augustine of Hippo; on the left, scenes relate to the Holy Cross.

Another striking work by a major 16th-century artist is the exquisite pulpit on the left-hand wall, by sculptor Nicolau Chanterène. The **sacristy** (open daily, Sun 4–6pm; closed noon–2pm; entrance charge) contains several interesting paintings including *The Pentecost* by the 16th-century painter Grão Vasco, a silverwork collection, and some clerical vestments. You can see the tombs of the first two kings of Portugal, Afonso Henriques and Sancho I, who are ensconced in regal monuments. The chapterhouse and the lovely Cloister of Silence may also be visited.

Behind the church of Santa Cruz lies the **Jardim da Manga** (Garden of the Sleeve), so named because Dom João III reputedly drew this oddity of a garden on his sleeve – although the design has also been attributed to João de Ruão, a French sculptor working in Portugal in the 16th-century. Curiously modernistic, this monumental garden was completed in 1535, and intended as a representation of the fountain of life. Beside the church is an atmospheric café in an ecclesiastic setting that was clearly part of the church.

Coimbra's greatest contribution to traditional folk music is the soulful and expressive fado. *This style of singing is an instinctive expression which springs from the soul in the form of a lament about love or life.*

BELOW: Coimbra students take part in the annual ritual of "the burning of the ribbons".

Map on page 256

TIP

To find the boisterous student nightlife, head for the restaurants around Rua la Sota, one street back from the river in Baixa Coimbra. And try the *chanfana* – goat stewed in wine.

BELOW:
a statue in Santa Clara-a-Nova.
RIGHT: part of the Jardim Botânico.

If you wander down the Rua da Sofia, which turns off 16th-century Praça 8 de Maio, you may be struck by the fact that it is extraordinarily wide for a street of that period. It was the original base for several colleges of the university before they were moved to new homes.

Praça do Comércio, off Rua Ferreira Borges, is an oddly-shaped square lined with 17th- and 18th-century buildings. At the north end stands the sturdy **Igreja Santiago ❶**, a church dating from the end of the 12th century. The capitals are decorated with animal and bird motifs. At the square's south end is the **Igreja de São Bartolomeu ❶**, built in the 18th century.

Santa Clara

The Santa Clara section of town lies across the river. **Mosteiro Santa Clara-a-Nova ❶** (New Santa Clara Monastery) is worth a visit if only for the view back across the bridge to Coimbra. Inside is the tomb of the saint Queen Isabel, who was canonised in 1625 and became the city's patron saint. Closer to the river, too close for its own comfort in fact, is **Santa Clara-a-Velha**, the old Santa Clara Monastery. This 12th-century edifice is simpler and lovelier than its replacement, for which it was abandoned in 1677. Waterlogged for centuries, its value has now been realised and money found for its restoration.

Quinta das Lágrimas, where Inês de Castro is believed to have been murdered *(see page 30)*, lies not far from Santa Clara-a-Velha. The family home has been restored into a tasteful small hotel and the grounds contain the **Fonte das Lágrimas**, the spring which is said to have risen on the spot where the luckless Inês cried for the last time and met her violent end.

Nearby, **Portugal dos Pequenitos** is an outdoor museum displaying small-scale reproductions of traditional Portuguese houses and monuments, popular with children and with those who like miniatures. To the east of the city, the **Mosteiro Celas** is notable for its cloister, and the pretty church of **Santo António dos Olivais** was once an old Franciscan convent.

Shops, parks and canoes

The lanes of the Baixa have some delightfully old-fashioned shops. The covered market on **Rua Olimpio Nicolau**, not far from Baixa, is open every morning but is best on Saturday.

Coimbra's numerous parks are agreeable resting places. The **Jardim Botânico** (Botanical Garden, open daily), on Alameda Dr Júlio Henriques, next to the 16th-century Aqueduto de São Sebastião, is a lovely garden, which was laid out in the 18th century. Unfortunately, not all of its grounds are open to the public, but there's much to see including a small museum (closed Sat, Sun).

Other parks are **Santa Cruz**, off the Praça da República, and **Choupal**, west of the city – a larger park which is good for walks and bike rides. The tiny **Penedo da Saudade** has a nice view.

If you want some physical exercise, and a complete change from historical monuments, you could rent a canoe from the municipal boat club near the Ponte Santa Clara, on the far side of the river. ❑

SIDE TRIPS FROM COIMBRA

Within easy reach of Coimbra you will find gleaming lagoons, colourful fishing villages, exotic forests, and the most extensive Roman ruins in the country

Map on page 266

Coimbra ❶ might be the main focus of interest in this vicinity, but there are plenty of opportunities for short excursions to other noteworthy places. The countryside towards the coast is especially bucolic and an old rural way of life can still be seen. The coast also offers plenty to see, especially Aveiro with its canals and lagoons. Castles and palaces feature too, not to mention Roman ruins.

Conímbriga: the Romans were here

Portugal's largest excavated Roman ruins are at **Conímbriga ❷**, 15 km (9 miles) south of Coimbra, near the town of Condeixa; the drive is easy, and there is also a bus service. The site (open daily 9am–8pm, 6pm in winter; entrance charge) is complemented by the **Museu Monográfico de Conímbriga**, one of the country's finest museums (open 10am; closed Mon). Only part of the estimated 13-hectare (32-acre) site has been excavated. Archaeologists believe remains may be found as far away as the main highway and even under the homes of people in the nearby village of Condeixa-a-Velha.

Conímbriga was probably settled as early as the Iron Age (800–500 BC), and it was not until the latter part of the 2nd century BC that the Romans arrived. Conímbriga profited from its location by the Roman road between Olisipo (Lisbon) and Bracara Augusta (now Braga). Some time around AD 70, the Roman Empire designated Conímbriga a *municipium*.

Conímbriga's prosperity was not to last. Crises in the empire and Barbarian incursions into Iberia prompted the construction of the defensive wall which is still prominent today. To take advantage of the natural defensive position of the area, the inhabited area of Conímbriga had to be reduced. Despite the new wall, in 464 the Suevi successfully attacked the city. Conímbriga continued to be inhabited, but it lost its status as an important centre to its neighbour, the more easily defensible *Aeminium* (Coimbra).

As you enter the site, you are walking down the road that gave Conímbriga its original importance: the highway from *Olisipo* to *Bracara Augusta*. In front of you is an enormous wall. Passing through the main entrance and continuing along the path to the right, you'll come to the arch of the aqueduct (rebuilt), parts of the aqueduct itself, and the remains of several buildings which may have been small shops.

The building known as Cantaber's House stretches to the south (on the left if you have your back to the entrance). The house is full of ornamental pools, but perhaps the most interesting part are the baths, which are at the extreme south end. They are easily recognisable by their hexagonal and round shapes, and by

PRECEDING PAGES: Mira beach, where little changes. **LEFT:** the remains of Conímbriga. **BELOW:** a Roman mosaic, Conímbriga.

the piped heating system (that great Roman innovation), which is visible through the stone grid covering the floors. Around the other side of the wall you can see more baths: public ones. For Romans, bathing was an important daily ritual, and the bathroom was also a place to discuss politics. Beyond the baths is an area of marvellously-patterned mosaics. The colours were once much brighter than the pleasing pastels to which they have mellowed today.

The museum is small but carefully designed. A long case displays ceramics, jewellery, and artifacts relating to weaving, agriculture, lighting, writing, hygiene and so on. There are also statues and a model of the forum and temple.

After taking a bath, the Romans would cover themselves with olive oil and then scrape their skins clean with a curved blade.

Serra do Buçaco

Northeast of Coimbra lies the **Serra do Buçaco** ❸ (Buçaco Forest), a darkly haunting area which for centuries has been protected, enabling 700 varieties of native and exotic trees to flourish. Benedictine monks established a hermitage here in the 6th century. The Carmelites, who built a monastery in 1628, began

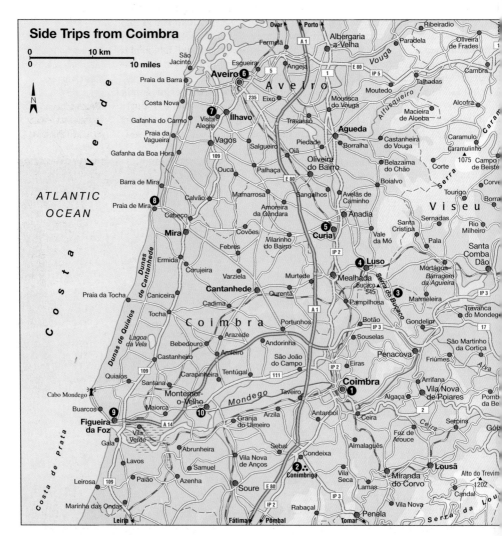

Side Trips from Coimbra

cultivation of the forest, planting species brought back from the Portuguese voyages, including Himalayan pines, monkey-puzzles, Japanese camphor trees, huge Lebanese cedars, and ginkgoes. In 1643 the Pope threatened to excommunicate anyone harming the trees.

A royal hunting lodge was built in neo-Manueline style at the end of the 19th century next to what remained of the convent. The Italian architect, Luigi Manini, somehow managed to inject his own interpretation of Romantic Revivalism into the construction and the intended modest hunting lodge turned into a sumptuous palace. After the fall of the monarchy in 1910, it became the spectacular and luxurious **Palace Hotel do Buçaco** (where you may still, at a price, lodge in the suite of the last king, Manuel II.) A small church, the cloister, and several monks' cells remain from the monastery. In one of these cells the Duke of Wellington spent the night before the Battle of Buçaco on 27 September 1810. His victory in this battle was the first serious setback suffered by Napoleon's army, as the French attempted for the third time to conquer Portugal. The victory is still celebrated annually on the anniversary, with a re-enactment of the battle, in full period costume. A military museum is among a host of sights.

Flowers seem to drip from every wall in Buçaco.

A wine of incredibly good quality is produced on the estate and is available in the restaurant. If you are keen to try it, book yourself in for lunch at the hotel and enjoy a real treat (tel: 231 937 970).

Downhill from Buçaco is the village of **Luso ❹**, renowned as a spa for the water which flows freely from fountains and which is available bottled throughout Portugal. A common sight here is locals overburdened with an assortment of plastic water bottles jostling to fill them at Fonte São João (St John's Fountain).

BELOW: the sumptuous Palace Hotel do Buçaco.

Visitors will find it hard to forget that Luso is a spa town.

Taking the N1 north towards Aveiro leads through the heart of the Barraid; wine country. A slight diversion into **Curia** ❺ allows the opportunity of pick ing up a special map of the region from *Turismo*. Armed with the map you ca; find your way to one of the three wineries, Caves Borlido, Caves Aliança an; Caves Império, which offer free wine tasting without prior appointment.

To the coast and Aveiro

Aveiro ❻ has been described as "the Venice of Portugal", but in truth it i; nothing like the Italian city. The comparison stems from the canals that travers; the city and the boats that ply them. The canal system is modest, however: ther; is only one main canal, with two smaller ones along the edges of town. Bu; they are linked with the Ria, the lagoon that extends 47 km (29 miles) jus; inland of the Atlantic Ocean and is fringed by dunes and long sandy beaches; Known to the Romans as Talabriga, Aveiro once lay directly on the ocean; However, over the centuries a strip of sediment has built up, creating the Ria bu; blocking ships and trade.

The lagoon plays a significant part in Aveiro's economic importance as a; expanding port for fishing fleets and industrial cargoes. Other important loca; industries include wood, cork, and ceramics from nearby Vista Alegre. Next t; the canals are large saltpans, another local resource. Particularly conspicuous ar; the brightly painted *moliceiros*, the boats with large graceful prows that wer; once widely used to gather *moliço* (seaweed) for fertiliser *(see page 86)*, an; which can still occasionally be spotted today.

Aveiro was a small settlement during the Middle Ages. It was designated; town in the 1200s, and in 1418 was encircled by fortified walls, at the suggestio;

BELOW: a graceful bridge over the canal in Aveiro.

of Infante Prince Pedro after whom the city park is named. Shortly after this, Aveiro was granted the concession of a town fair, and the March Fair still goes on to this day with local produce on display.

The 16th century was a time of growth and expansion for the town. With dredged access to the sea and to the interior, Aveiro became a trade centre from which products of the entire Beira region were exported. In 1575, a violent storm shifted the sandbanks in the lagoon, blocking the canal from the sea. The inevitable decline in Aveiro's importance encouraged emigration, which caused a dramatic decrease in population (to about one-third). In 1808, another storm reopened the sea passage, but it was not until the last half of the 19th century that Aveiro's fortunes picked up.

Map on page 266

Exploring Aveiro

Aveiro makes a good base for a trip on the Ria or to nearby beaches, but there are things worth seeing in the city as well. Aveiro is divided into two parts by the principal canal. The southern part is where the aristocracy once lived; the northern half is the old fishermen's section.

The southern half centres around the **Praça da República**. In the simple square, the nicest building is the solid and rather prim town hall. On the east side of the square, the 16th- and 17th-century **Misericórdia** church has a lovely Renaissance portal and 19th-century tiles on its façade. In a square further south the 17th-century **Carmelite Convent** once housed the barefoot Carmelite order who embraced a simpler way of life focusing on solitude. Note the paintings on the ceiling which depict the life of Saint Teresa of Avila.

Aveiro's **Museu de Aveiro** (open Tues–Sun 10am–5.30pm; entrance charge) is housed in the 15th-century **Convento de Jesus**. Although the labelling of exhibits in the museum is poor, guides will take you through and can answer questions. The convent has some fine 17th-century paintings and its church is effusively gilded. Arching over the choir are lovely hand-painted ceilings, and off the choir is a chapel with beautiful tiles. Just outside is the tomb of Santa Joana Princesa, daughter of Afonso V and patron of the city, who lived in the convent for 14 years until her death in 1489. Intricately carved in coloured marble and delicate inlays, with statues supporting and crowning it, the tomb took 2 years to construct.

The **São Domingos Cathedral** is near the museum. Its baroque façade has twisted columns and sculpted figures of Faith, Hope and Charity. Inside, an enormous skylight over the altar lends the church an airiness that many baroque churches lack. The huge blue altar rises strikingly in the all-white interior. The tomb of Catarina de Atalide is here, a woman honoured, under the name Natércia, by the poet Luis Camões in his sonnets. The church was founded in 1423 and remodelled during the 16th and 17th centuries.

Several blocks away is the refreshing **Parque Dom Infante Pedro**, in the grounds of the old Franciscan monastery. Colourful flowers, lush trees, fountains, and a small lake where you can rent paddle boats make this a nice spot for a break.

The best way to get around Aveiro is to pick up a free bicycle from a "Buga" park, under a local scheme to encourage cycling in the town.

BELOW: Aveiro's waterfront.

Map on page 266

TIP

The tourist office, in an Art Nouveau building at Rua João Mendonça 8, runs a boat tour to the Ria area daily during the summer. Trips last one hour. Minimum five people.

RIGHT: a day's sardine catch.
BELOW: collecting weed in the Ria.

The old quarter

North of the canal lies the fishermen's section, where narrow houses suppor façades that sometimes rise beyond roof levels. The arches and curves on th tops of these false fronts are reminiscent of the fishing boats and their curve prows. The fish market, where the catch is sold each morning, is in this area There is also the bright white, oddly shaped chapel of **São Gonçalinho** and th church of **São Gonçalo**. Inside this 17th- and 18th-century building gleam a gi altar and newly placed tiles.

The beautiful Ria is a prime reason for coming to Aveiro. You can tour it length by boat, car or bus, although boat is by far the most rewarding. Th lagoon and its subsidiary canals extend as far south as Mira and as far north a Ovar. There is a fair range of hotels in the area and many campsites. You wi see traditional colourful *moliceiros,* shorelines dotted with saltpans, forests a villages, glorious sea birds plummeting into the water, and the sandbar whic blocks the city's access to the sea. A road bridge takes you over the mouth of th estuary to **Costa Nova**, where there are brightly coloured traditional house and excellent fish restaurants. Whether you take a boat or drive, you will se why this region also bears the name of **Rota da Luz**, the Route of Light.

Castles and candy stripes

From Aveiro a good road leads south to Figueira da Foz and back to Coimbr along the riverside. Things to grab your attention along the way include a famou pottery factory, candy-striped houses and a castle. Fairly soon after leaving Aveir past Ilhavo, divert right to **Vista Alegre ❼** for its porcelain factory. Famou throughout Portugal, it started production in 1842 and is still run by the same fam ily. There is a shop and small museum (open Tues–F 9am–6pm, Sat and Sun 9.30am–12.30pm, 2–5pm).

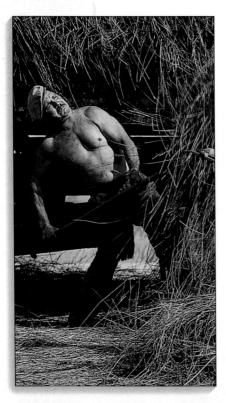

Mira lies close to the road a little further sout Keep going through the town and head for **Praia d Mira ❽** on the coast. This is the most southerly poir of the lagoon and canal system which surround Aveiro. Candy-striped beach huts add a jaunty air t the resort but the main attraction is the inland lagoo where there is safe boating and where picnicker enjoy shade from the surrounding pine trees.

Although industrialised around the mouth of th Mondego, **Figueira da Foz ❾** has become an impo tant holiday resort favoured by both Portuguese an Spanish visitors. To find the attractions, turn a blir eye to the high rise blocks and look at the broa expanse of beach and the gaily coloured beach hut again in delightful candy stripes.

There is a fast road along the north side of the riv to **Montemor-o-Velho ❿** dominated by a castle on prominent mound. Like many in Portugal, it was hel by the Moors before being taken by the Christians i the 11th century. Within the walls are some well-ma icured gardens, the ruins of a 16th-century Manue line palace and the restored **Igreja de Santa Mari da Alcáçova**, which was built around the time th castle was restored. To enjoy a rural atmosphere o the return to Coimbra, take the road from here alon the south side of the river.

PORTO

Maps on page 276

Once a river community, Porto is now a great commercial city, but life still centres on and around the Rio Douro. The north bank offers culture, and the south port wine

Porto ❶ is the commercial centre of northern Portugal and the hub of the lucrative port wine trade. Like Lisbon, Porto is clustered on hills overlooking a river, but unlike Lisbon, with its pastel walls and soft light, Porto is a northern European city with granite church towers, stolid dark buildings, narrow streets and hidden baroque treasures. There is keen rivalry between the two cities. Lisbon's hosting of Expo '98 and the resulting investment in infrastructure was keenly felt. This was compensated for by Porto's selection as European Cultural Capital in 2001. Money from the EU is helping to bring the city into the 21st century, and an entire new metro system will go a long way to improving communications.

Posed majestically on the rocky cliffs overlooking the Rio Douro, Porto is linked by six bridges to Vila Nova de Gaia, an industrial area where most of the port wine lodges are located, with their *barcos rabelos* moored in front of them. These days large ships often dock at the seaport of Leixões because of frequent silting of the Douro estuary, but coal barges, fishing trawlers and other small vessels still sail up the river, and a river trip is a good way to see the city. The climate in town is temperate and the Portuenses, as the inhabitants are called, are traditionally industrious. The population of Greater Porto is about 1.2 million.

PRECEDING PAGES: Cais da Ribeira houses in Porto. **LEFT:** life on the banks of the Douro. **BELOW:** a cooper making port barrels.

In Roman times, the twin cities at the mouth of the Douro were known as Portus on the right bank and Cale on the left. During the Moorish occupation, the entire region between the Minho and Douro rivers was called Portucale. When Afonso Henriques founded the new kingdom in 1143, he took the name of his home province and called it Portucalia.

Porto prospered from the seafaring exploits of the golden epoch of discoveries. Its shipyards, adapting Douro river *caravelas*, produced caravels that sailed around the world. Prince Henry, who initiated and inspired exploration, was born here.

The wine trade

In the 17th and 18th centuries, the wines of the Upper Douro were robust table reds. Then, in 1820, a "climatic accident" occurred, with warm weather producing unusually sweet grapes, and a wine appreciated by the British. In the following years the wine companies added *aguardente*, or brandy, to stop the fermentation and fix the sugar content. This was the beginning of the sweet fortified nectar as it is known today. England's long connection with the city they call Oporto had been developing with the wine trade *(see Wines of Portugal, pages 103–9)*. The Methuen Treaty of 1703 opened English markets to Portuguese wines, and the British shippers of Porto became increasingly rich and powerful. In 1727 they established a Shippers' Asso-

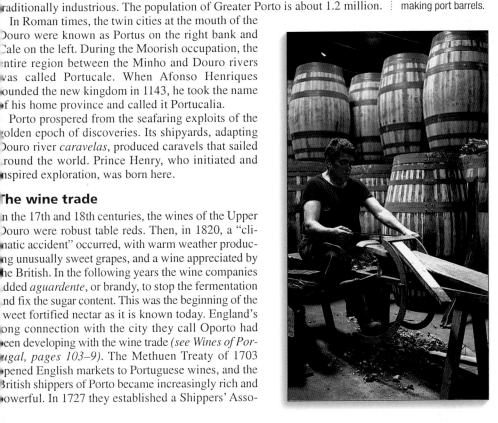

*Flower sellers add
colour to the streets
of Porto.*

ciation, which regulated the trade and controlled prices paid to Portuguese growers. Thirty years later, to combat the English monopoly, the Marquês de Pombal founded the Alto Douro Wine Company, and today the business is organised and controlled by the Port Wine Institute (www.ivp.pt).

Porto is an energetic and lively commercial city with an individual taste in food and drink. Regional specialities include roast pork, fresh salmon, lamprey, trout and tripe (Portuenses are sometimes referred to as *tripeiros*). Generally, it is a sober city. The most exciting bars and restaurants are by the river around Cais (quays) de Ribeira and in Vila Nova de Gaia opposite. You may hear *fado* in a few restaurants, such as Mal Cozinhado in Rua Outerinho 13, while young people in search of nightlife are likely to head for Foz de Duoro 4 km (3 miles) downstream by the sea. For any visitor to the city, a port aperitif at the excellent Solar do Vinho *(see below)* is always recommended.

The old city

The heart of the city is the **Praça da Liberdade Ⓐ**, with an equestrian statue of Pedro IV in the centre. On the north side of the square is the broad Avenida dos Aliados, its bright flower-beds dug up to build the city's new metro. The avenue leads uphill to the **Câmara Municipal Ⓑ** (Town Hall) and the modern statue of Almeida Garrett (1799–1854), liberal poet and novelist, and native son of Porto.

To the southeast of Praça da Liberdade lies the Praça da Almeida Garrett, where the railway station, the **Estação São Bento Ⓒ**, has a fine entrance hall decorated with traditional *azulejos* depicting historical scenes. From here you can catch a train for a journey along the Rio Douro to Pocinho.

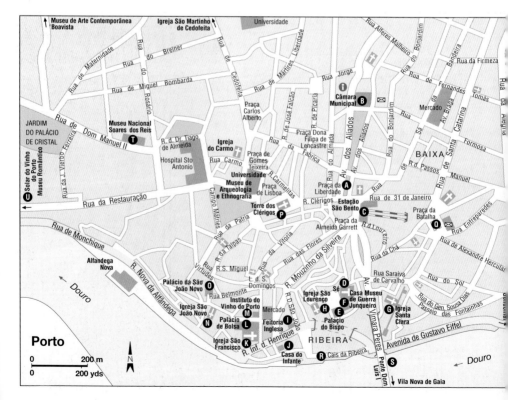

Porto

0 ___ 200 m
0 ___ 200 yds

Heading south, you arrive at the **Sé (Cathedral)** **D**, dating from the 12th century (open Mon–Sat, Sun pm; closed 12.15–2.30pm). It was here that King João I married the English Philippa of Lancaster in 1387, the year after the Treaty of Windsor was signed with England. The Gothic cloister is decorated with fine tiles. Outside the cathedral are good views down over the city rooftops and the river. Just below, in the Medieval Tower, is a tourist office offering tours of the city and river, as well as helicopter tours (tel: 351 222 000 073; www.portotours.com).

Nearby, on Pena Ventosa, the site of an ancient citadel, stands the impressive 18th-century **Palácio do Bispo** **E**, the Bishop's Palace. Just beyond is the **Casa Museu de Guerra Junqueiro** **F** (open Tues–Sat, Sun pm; closed noon–2pm; entrance charge), in the house of the highly-regarded poet of that name, who died in 1923. His memorabilia and furnishings are on display.

Across the avenue stands the 15th-century church of **Igreja Santa Clara** **G**, next to one of the best preserved sections of the old city wall. Santa Clara has been rebuilt several times but is noted for its splendid gilded wood choir stalls and altars. Sacheverell Sitwell wrote: "After it, every other building in Porto, even São Francisco, is drab and dull".

To the west, the **Igreja São Lourenço** **H**, better known as Igreja dos Grilos (after the crickets that lodge there), was built in 1570 and is one of the earliest examples of Portuguese baroque.

The western side

At the end of Rua Infante Dom Henrique stands the bastion of English life, the **Feitoria Inglesa (English Factory House)** **I**. Here, the old British port wine

Map on page 276

BELOW: View across the Douro from Vila Nova de Gaia.

shippers do their business, play billiards or cards, read English newspapers and enjoy English cuisine, as they have for the past 200 years. Outsiders must obtain special authorisation from the British Port Wine Shippers' Association to visit.

Around the corner, on Rua da Alfândega, stands the much restored **Casa do Infante** ⓙ, where Prince Henry the Navigator was born in 1394. For a time it served as the customs house; it is now a museum (open Mon–Fri 8.30am–5pm; entrance charge).

Going by the Praça do Infante Dom Henrique, you reach the **Igreja São Francisco** ⓚ, founded by King Sancho II in 1233 and rebuilt in the 14th century (open daily). The interior glitters in baroque splendour with gilded columns, arches and statues. On the site of a convent, which burnt down in 1832, is the **Palácio de Bolsa** ⓛ or Stock Exchange, noted for its opulent neo-Moorish reception hall (open daily 9am–5.30pm; 30-minute guided tours). Up the hill is the **Instituto do Vinho do Porto (Port Wine Institute)** ⓜ, the government agency established in 1932 to control the quality of port.

Following the Rua Belmonte past old homes with balconies and tiled walls, you arrive at the church of **São João Novo** ⓝ, built in 1592. Across the way stands the 18th-century **Palácio de São João Novo** ⓞ, a whitewashed granite building that houses the Museu de Etnografia e História (temporarily closed for renovation). The collection includes archaeological finds, wine presses and wine boats, fishing equipment, ceramics, costumes, jewellery and folk art, as well as a pharmacy.

The road leads to the singular 18th-century **Torre dos Clérigos** ⓟ (open daily), the tallest granite tower in Portugal. This was designed, along with its church, by Nicolau Nasoni, who was also architect of the fine baroque Solar de

The well-known Sandeman silhouette is hard to avoid in Porto.

BELOW: celebrating the Dia de São João on 24 June.

Mateus near Vila Real. Unless you really have no head for heights it's worth climbing the 225 or so steps for the view over the city. Just north of the tower lies the main **university** building, a handsome granite structure built in 1807 as the Polytechnical Academy.

East of São Bento railway station lies the busy **Praça da Batalha Q**, with a statue of Pedro V in the middle, and the imposing 18th-century church of São Idelfonso with a façade of bright blue-and-white tiles. The main shopping street is **Rua Santa Catarina**, where bargains may be found in a variety of goods, from shoes to pottery. Rua das Flores has the best gold and silver shops.

Cais da Ribeira

Taking the steep roads down to the river, you will soon find yourself drawn to the **Cais da Ribeira R**, one of the liveliest parts of the city and a UNESCO World Heritage Site. Many small shops and restaurants are built right into what remains of the old city wall, some showing watermarks around two metres (six feet) from the floor where the river has flooded. During the day you can take a river trip from here, and in the evening its restaurants brim with locals and visitors.

Ten minutes' walk downriver brings you to the *electrico* stop, a tram that goes out to Castelo de Quejo on the coast, and the Alfendega (Customs House), now a gallery space. Just beyond is a site that is destined for a new, much needed **Port Wine Museum**.

The splendid steel arch farther up-river is a railway bridge, **Ponte de Dona Maria Pia**, built in 1876 to a plan by Alexandre Gustave Eiffel and only recently put out of use by the new Ponte São João. In the centre of Porto is the handsome **Ponte Dom Luís I S**, built in 1886, which provides splendid views. This two-

Map on page 276

BELOW: *azulejos* adorn a church wall in Porto.

Map
on page
276

On the Dia de São João (24 June), festivities take place near the Ponte Dom Luís I. There is a regatta of the port wine boats, people sing and dance around bonfires and feast on roast kid and grilled sardines.

RIGHT: beneath the Torre dos Clérigos
BELOW: catching up on the news, Rua de Santa Catarina.

storey iron bridge has two decks, the upper of which will carry the new metro line, and leads directly to port cellars in Vila Nova de Gaia *(see below)*.

Outside the old town

On the western side of the city, in the old royal Palácio dos Carrancas, is the **Museu Nacional Soares dos Reis**  named after a 19th-century sculptor (open Tues pm, Wed–Sun 10am–6pm; entrance charge). It has a fine collection of archaeological artifacts, religious art, regional costumes, ceramics and contemporary paintings, as well as sculpture. Paintings by Grão Vasco are on display, among them pictures of St Catherine and St Lucy.

On the western side of the Jardim do Palácio de Cristal is the **Solar do Vinho do Porto** (entered from Rua Entre Quintas). This is the best place to go in Porto to taste a wide variety of port wines (open Mon–Sat 2pm–midnight; closed holidays). It is located in the old wine cellar and stable of the Quinta da Macieirinha, where King Charles Albert died in 1849, after abdicating the throne of Sardinia. Now an intriguing **Museu de Romântico** (open Tues–Sat 10am–12.30pm, 2–5.30pm, Sun 2–5.30pm; entrance charge), the mansion is set in a rose garden and contains most of its original furnishings.

To the northwest, in Boavista, is the art deco **Museu Serralves** (open Tues, Wed, Fri 10am–7pm, Thurs 10am–10pm, Sat, Sun, holidays Oct–Mar 10am–7pm, Apr–Sept 10am–8pm), set in an attractive 18-hectare (44-acre) estate. The mansion holds temporary exhibitions of modern art. In the grounds is the **Museu de Arte Contemprânea**, designed by Oporto architect Alvaro Siza Vieira and opened in 1988, which has both permanent and temporary exhibitions. As well as a large exhibition space, the building comprises an auditorium, a restaurant and a library.

Port wine lodges

Vila Nova de Gaia, across the Ponte Dom Luís I, is an industrial zone with ceramic, glass, soap and other factories. But above all, Gaia is the true seat of the port wine industry, where most warehouses or lodges are to be found.

There are about 80 port wine lodges: many of the larger ones welcome weekday visitors to tour the installations and taste their wines. Most prominent is **Sandeman** (Mon–Fri 9am–1pm, 2–5pm), whose distinctive silhouette, designed in 1928, rises on the skyline. They line the waterfront with and fly their flags from *barcos rabelos* moored alongside.

In spring, the new wine is brought down from the Upper Duoro by truck, and is then left to mature in 530-litre (140-gallon) oak casks, or pipes. Here the blending takes place, with wines from different vineyards and years blended to produce a distinctive aroma, taste and colour before the wine is bottled and again is left to mature.

In the evenings, many people cross the bridge to eat and enjoy a great view of the city opposite. Apart from traditional restaurants, at the far end of the quay there is a wide choice of places to eat and drink in the modern riverside Cais de Gaia complex, with terraces and river views. ❏

THE DOURO VALLEY

*Renowned worldwide for the wine it produces, the Douro valley
is graced by its centuries-old vineyards growing
on steeply terraced hillsides*

Map
on pages
286–7

The romantic history of port wine has endowed the Douro region with unrivalled respect. Douro means "of gold" and the river, on certain glowing days, does resemble a twisting golden chain as it winds through the narrow valley between the steep hills and terraced vineyards. The countryside is exceptionally beautiful, particularly in spring and autumn, and is enhanced by the neat rows of vines which grace the hillsides.

Although the Douro stretches from Spain to the Atlantic at Porto, only the inland part of the valley, the Alto Douro, is recognised for growing the grapes used for port wine. The demarcated region starts some 100 km (60 miles) upstream from Porto at Barqueiros, just before Régua and follows the river all the way to Spain. Some of the tributaries of the Douro, the Corgo, Torto, Pinhão and Tua, are included in the area. It was Portugal's authoritarian Marquês de Pombal who staked out the Douro in 1756, making it the first officially designated wine-producing region in the world. Subsequent legislation designated the Upper Douro as the port wine region.

Characteristically, the schistose soils are stony and impoverished and the climate extreme. Summers are very hot and dry, and made hotter by the direct rays of the sun reflected on the crystalline rock; winters are cold and wet. The large lumps of surface schist act as storage heaters, absorbing the sun's heat in the day and releasing it throughout the night. The slopes nearest to the river grow the finest grapes and this land is highly prized.

PRECEDING PAGES:
the sleepy Rio
Tâmega.
LEFT: vineyards high
in the Douro Valley.
BELOW: Amarante's
historic bridge.

Choosing a base

Peso da Régua *(see page 288)* is the capital of the Douro Valley, with an office of the Port Wine Institute; it is also the headquarters of the port growers' association, which grades and certifies the wine travelling to Porto. The much smaller town of Pinhão 25 km (15 miles) further upstream is regarded as the centre of the wine industry, and this is where all the famous names have their farms. It is a handy place to stay although it is hardly bristling with hotels. Taylors have restored and extended a *quinta* on the banks of the Douro and in 1998 it opened as the Vintage House Hotel, providing quality accommodation. The area does have a number of restored houses and farms which are part of the Manor House system *(see page 129)*, some of them in very fine locations.

Casa de Casal de Loivos, above Pinhão, has a fine overview of the Douro or, if you prefer to bury yourself in the country, Casa da Lavada, a restored 14th-century fortified manor house provides modern comforts. It is high in the mountains of the Serra do Marão in a village where visitors are still a curiosity. Traditional hotels are found in the surrounding towns

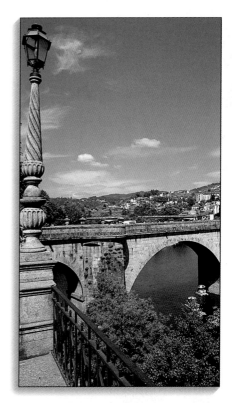

Balconies overhang the Rio Tâmega in Amarante.

of Amarante, Vila Real or Lamego. If your intention is to go on brief excursions into the area, then **Porto ❶** is a good base for organised trips. Coach trips are well advertised but it is easy enough to catch a train from São Bento station on the Douro line. The end of the line is Pocinho, not too far from the Spanish border. There are branch lines to Amarante, Vila Real and Mirandela. The river is now navigable for much of its length and boat trips up the river are a regular feature and a pleasant way to see the countryside. One option is to go by boat as far as Pinhão and return by train.

Upriver from Porto

There is little to detain the motorist between Porto and Amarante so the fast A4 is the best way to travel. It speeds an otherwise very slow journey through *vinho verde* growing countryside. The main area for *vinho verde* lies to the north in Costa Verde and Minho.

Amarante ❷, on the banks of the Rio Tâmega, is delightful, at least in the old part of town. Geese paddle contentedly among punts and trailing willow trees on the river while afternoon tea-takers look on from overhanging wooden balconies. Dominant in the town is the three-arched **Ponte de São Gonçalo** built in 1790. It became a battle ground in the Peninsular War in 1809 when General Silveira, supported by Beresford's troops, successfully fought off the French. The bridge leads to the **Convento de São Gonçalo**, named after the local patron saint, protector of marriages.

Amarante's association with fertility rites reaches back into the mists of time and some claim the town's name is derived from *amar*, meaning "to love". These ancient beliefs have empowered São Gonçalo, beatified in 1561, to assist

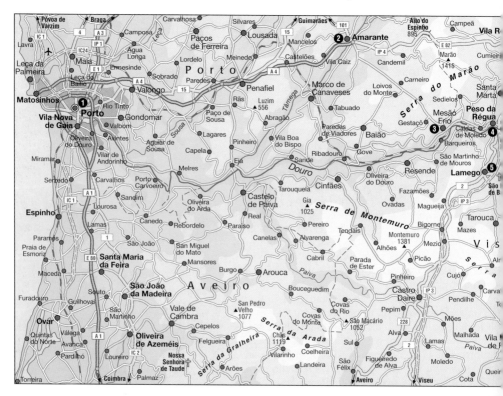

believers in everything pertaining to love and marriage. He is honoured every June by a festival which, as you may imagine, is a particularly raucous occasion, with the local men out in the streets offering distinctly phallic cakes to any women prepared to accept them.

The convent, however, is much more sombre. It was begun in 1540 but not completed until 1620. Inside is the tomb of São Gonçalo, who died about 1260, and some lush gilded carved woodwork. Anyone aspiring to love and marriage need only touch the effigy of the saint to be blessed within the year. Sadly, the limestone effigy is now quite worn in places.

Above the rear cloister is the **Museu Municipal Amadeo de Souza-Cardosa** (open Tues–Sun; closed 12.30–2pm; entrance charge), which has some interesting modern Portuguese paintings – Souza-Cardosa was a Cubist artist who came from Amarante.

Nearby is the **Quinta da Aveleda**, seat of one of Portugal's main wine empires and a leading exporter of the country's special *vinho verde*. The *quinta* is included on some wine-tasting tours (open Mon–Fri 9am–noon, 2–5pm; entrance charge). A tour of the 200-hectare (500-acre) Aveleda estate includes a visit to the family chapel, which was built in 1671. The luxuriant gardens contain a ruined window said to be from the palace of Prince Henry the Navigator in Porto. You can also observe contemporary *vinho verde* production: mile upon mile of grapes; climbing poles, trelliss and crosses; and mechanical crushers, modern concrete storage vats and mechanised bottling and labelling. At the wine lodge you can taste different types of *vinho verde* and buy a bottle or a case from the old distillery, which has now been converted to a store; if you want to lunch here, book in advance (tel: 255 718 200).

Boat trips on the river are privately run and therefore not promoted through tourist offices. Trips last from a few hours to a few days, and most hotels and quintas will tell you what's on offer.

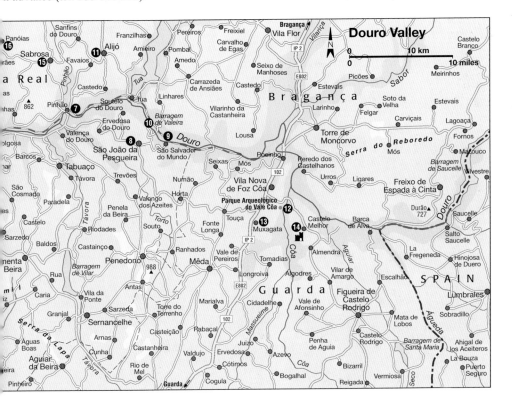

Ready to pour.

Beyond Amarante the road turns abruptly south to twist and climb through the Serra do Marão. *Vinho verde* vines climb the trees here and huge granite tors stand in the summit region. Beyond is a descent to the small village of **Mesão Frio ❸**, and a sweeping view of the Upper Douro winding peacefully through the gorges of the port wine country. The road follows the river's north bank, passing through the small spa town of **Caldas de Moledo** before reaching **Régua ❹** (its full name is Peso da Régua), a busy river port and the headquarters of the **Casa do Douro**, an organisation which has a great deal of power in the regulation of port wine production. In this area lie some of the oldest British and Portuguese estates, and information can be had from both the Casa do Douro and the tourist office near the market. Here the road crosses the Douro and runs along the picturesque southern bank.

South of the river

BELOW: pilgrims' stairway at the Nossa Senhora dos Remédios church in Lamego.
BELOW RIGHT: fountain at the same church.

Before following along the south bank towards Pinhão, there is a worthwhile diversion to **Lamego ❺**, which is a city of historical importance. The Lusitanians arose in revolt against the occupying Romans, refusing to pay the heavy taxation, so the Romans burned the town to the ground. Fernando of León and Castile took the city, aided by the legendary El Cid, and allowed the Muslim *wali* to continue to govern Lamego, as long as he converted and paid tribute to the king. But the city's most significant moment in Portugal's history was in 1143, when the *cortes* met for the very first time. At this meeting, the nobles declared Afonso Henriques to be Afonso I, first king of Portugal.

Lamego's 12th-century castle, on one of the city's two hills, preserves a fine 13th-century keep, with windows that were added later, and a very old and

unusual vaulted cistern, possibly Moorish, with monograms of master masons.

Atop Lamego's other hill is its most visually striking building, the pilgrimage church of **Nossa Senhora dos Remédios** crowning a vast stairway reminiscent of Braga's Bom Jesus. The first chapel of the sanctuary was founded by the Bishop of Lamego in 1361, and dedicated to St Stephen. In 1564, it was pulled down, and a new one built. From that time, there has been a steady stream of the faithful seeking cures. The first week in September is the time of the major pilgrimage, and there's a very jolly accompanying festival which seems to have little to do with healing or piety. The present sanctuary was started in 1750, and was consecrated 11 years later – but the magnificent baroque-style staircase leading up to it, begun in the 19th century, was completed only in the 1960s. Fountains, statues and pavilions decorate each level of the 600 or so steps.

The **Sé (Cathedral)**, a Gothic structure, was built by Afonso Henriques in 1129. Only the Romanesque tower is left from the original building. The city museum, housed in the 18th-century Bishop's Palace, has a collection which includes 16th-century Flemish tapestries and works by Grão Vasco.

Just outside Lamego (start on the Tarouca road), in the valley of the Rio Balsemão, is the tiny **São Pedro de Balsemão ❻**, a Visigothic church believed to be the oldest in Portugal.

Following the south bank of the Douro towards Pinhão is a rewarding drive; you can enjoy the flowing lines of vineyards patterning the hillsides and broken only by signs displaying such well-known names as Sandeman, Barros and Quinta Dona Matilde.

Pinhão ❼, on the north side of the river, seems an unlikely town to lie at the heart of the port wine region. There is little to visit but it is worth a stop at the

Map on pages 286–7

TIP

The best time to visit the Douro Valley is during the *vindima*, in late September and early October, when the grapes are being collected.

BELOW: ageing the wine at the Sandeman *quinta*.

Backbreaking work in the vineyards.

BELOW: a port wine *quinta* in an idyllic spot on the Douro river.

railway station to see the *azulejo* panels depicting scenes of the Rio Douro or to taste some wine in the barrel-shaped café by the river. The tourist office next to the railway station has information about the wine estates in the region.

A scenic circular tour

A tasty sampler of typical Douro scenery and traditional villages can be enjoyed on a short circular tour from Pinhão, taking around half a day. It starts on the south side of the river, along the road climbing the hillside to **São João da Pasqueira** ❽. This village has some fine 18th-century houses mixed with surprisingly modern property. Follow left turns signposted Barragem de Valeira to drive through dilapidated, overgrown vineyards ravaged by the Phylloxera scourge many years ago and never replanted. Watch out on the descent towards the *barragem* (reservoir), for the pointed hill, **São Salvador do Mundo** ❾, littered with churches and chapels.

The **Barragem de Valeira** ❿ is where Baron Forrester, the 19th-century English pioneer, lost his life in 1861: in those days the river here tumbled over dangerous rapids. Born in Hull in 1809, Joseph James Forrester came out to Portugal as a young man to work for his uncle in Porto. He was fascinated by the wine industry and spent many years boating up and down the river making a detailed map. His widely acclaimed work won him his title in 1855, the first foreigner to earn such an honour. It was the river that eventually claimed his life at the age of 51. He was out boating with Antónia Adelaide Ferreira and others when they ran into trouble at the Cachão de Valeira rapids. The boat capsized and Baron Forrester drowned, dragged down, it is said, by the weight of his money belt. Antónia Adelaide Ferreira survived, helped by the buoyancy of her crinoline dress.

Cross the *barragem* to regain the north shore and zigzag up the hillside towards Linhares. Vineyards make the patterns and create the scenery for much of the way towards Tua and Alijó. **Alijó ⓫** is one of the bigger towns in the area and is the location of a *pousada* named after Baron Forrester. The route back heads through Favaios to Pinhão.

Rock art

Winding eastwards from Pinhão through **São João da Pasqueira** and along the hill contours, past quaint churches and villages, you will come to Vila Nova de Foz Côa and the valley of the Rio Côa. Work in the 1990s to build a dam in this remote region uncovered a remarkable collection of rock paintings. In 1996 the Portuguese government declared the Côa Valley protected as the **Parque Arqueológico do Vale Côa ⓬** (open daily; closed 12.30–2pm; visits must be reserved, tel: 279 768 260). In 1998, the park, which has the largest area of paleolithic engravings in Europe, was declared a UNESCO World Heritage Site.

At present, only three rock art sites, at Penascosa, Ribeira de Piscos and Canada do Inferno, can be visited, not by individuals, but on a guided tour with a vehicle. Tours last around 90 minutes. Tours to Canada do Inferno start from the Park Office in Vila Nova de Foz Côa; tours to Ribeira de Piscos start from the Visitor Centre at **Muxagata ⓭**, while tours to Penascosa leave from the Visitor Centre in **Castelo Melhor ⓮**.

North to Vila Real

Going from Pinhão to the north leads to **Sabrosa ⓯**, the birthplace of Fernão de Magalhães, known in English as Ferdinand Magellan, the man who led the first

Pressure to stop the flooding of the Côa Valley included a rap song recorded by high school students from Vila Nova de Foz Côa, with the line "Petroglyphs can't swim".

BELOW: the tiled railway station at Pinhão.

ESTAÇÃO VITI-VINÍCOLA
DO DOURO RIO TORTO

Map on pages 286–7

circumnavigation of the world between 1519 and 1522, under the Spanish flag. Just before Constantim, look out on the right for a diversion to the sanctuary of **Panóias** ⓰. All there is to see is a field with a series of enormous carved stones, believed to have been used as altars for human sacrifice. Inscriptions in Latin invoke the ancient god Serapis, known to both Greek and Egyptian mythology.

Beyond Constantim but before Vila Real is the village of **Mateus** ⓱, with its celebrated palace and gardens. It was built by Nicolau Nasoni in 1739–43 for António José Botelho Mourão. Today, an illustration of the palace graces the distinctive label of the less-than-distinctive rosé wine from this area. Created in 1942 by the grandfather of the current owner, Mateus Rosé is still Portugal's best-selling wine export, with distribution in more than 150 countries. The exquisite building with its striking baroque façade, double stairway and huge coat of arms is open daily for visits, and frequently hosts musical events.

Vila Real

An ancient settlement in the Terra de Panóias, **Vila Real** ⓲ was founded and renamed by Dom Dinis in 1289. Its name, literally "royal town", is appropriate, as Vila Real once had more noble families than any city other than the capital. Ignoring the modern city and walking through ancient streets, you will see many residences marked, often above the main entrance, with the original owners' coats-of-arms. As likely as not, descendants of the family will still be living there.

The 19th-century writer Camilo Castelo Branco lived in Vila Real and wrote many of his most enduring works using the town as a backdrop. "In what century are we on this mountain?" asks one of his characters. "In what century?" comes the reply. "Why, it is the same 18th century here as it is in Lisbon." "Oh!" says the first. "I thought time here had stopped in the 12th century."

FOLLOWING PAGES: bringing home the vegetables. **RIGHT:** setting off for the local fair. **BELOW:** strange things happen in the countryside.

Vila Real became a city proper only in 1925, but the importance of the region dates from 1768, when the vineyards were developed commercially: the area has good red and white wines, but it is the rosé that is best known – especially Mateus. Now a lively bustling industrial centre, Vila Real is one of the largest towns in the region.

The **Sé** (**Cathedral**) was originally the church of a Dominican convent. Although much of the present building dates from the 14th century, Romanesque columns still remain from an earlier structure.

Vila Real's oldest church is the ancient **Capela de São Nicolau**, on a promontory of high land behind the municipal hall, overlooking the valley of the Rio Corgo. Another church of note is **São Pedro**, whose baroque touches were completed by Nicolau Nasoni (1691–1773), the Tuscan-born architect who designed the manor house in Mateus.

Among fine houses dating from the 15th to 18th centuries is the **Casa de Diogo Cão**, an Italian Renaissance-style building that was the birthplace of Cão, the navigator who discovered the mouth of the River Congo in 1482.

As far as local crafts are concerned, the Vila Real region is particularly noted for the black pottery of Bisalhães and the woollen goods of Caldas do Alvão and Marão. ❑

PORT WINE – TREASURE FROM STONY SOIL

The story of port wine is one of triumph over adversity. From bare, inhospitable terrain came a wine that some prize above all others

Upstream from Porto lies the Cinderella of harsh regions, which, at the pop of a wine cork, was transformed into a beautiful princess.

Dry and stony, with barely a covering of dusty soil, and with excessively high summer temperatures combined with months of drought, the Upper Douro seems an unlikely area to enjoy a fairy-tale transformation into a global producer of a unique wine – port.

The source of encouragement that provided the life force for this industry's growth was the high-quality wine already being produced by the locals. Exploiting the region to produce wine in commercial quantities was beset by huge problems, but it seemed that every disadvantage, every deterrent, contributed to its success. The soil, or rather the lack of it, was just one. Vines planted into the schist (rock) sent their roots searching deep down through the cracks and crevices to find water. The vast root system which developed allowed the plants to survive burning summers without irrigation, so yielding grapes high in sugar.

The Rio Douro, steep banked and virtually unnavigable, was another apparent drawback which proved essential to the region's success, for without it there would have been no means of exporting the wine. Grapes harvested at the steep higher levels were transported to the split-level factories below, and the resulting wine was then lowered to the river for transportation on the distinctive flat-bottomed *barcos rabelos*.

▷ **INFINITE VARIETY**
More than 80 varieties of grape have been used in port wine but modern plantings are limited to about six varieties.

△ **MATURING PROCESS**
The length of time port spends in wood is one factor which determines its variety. Vintage port does most of its ageing in glass.

▽ *BARCOS RABELOS*
The flat-bottomed *rabelos*, designed to suit the shallow waters of the Douro, carrie the port barrels down-rive Accidents were common.

◁ **GRAPE PICKING**
Teams of women spread along the rows and sweep systematically across the vineyard, leaving men to carry away the baskets.

△ **TREADING GRAPES**
Once all grape juice for port wine was extracted by the old treading process, but nowadays most of this work is done mechanically.

△ **VINTAGE PORT**
Vintage port on display at Sandeman's Wine Lodge in Vila Nova de Gaia, where most of the prestigious lodges are now found.

◁ **QUINTA DO CRASTO**
The close-packed vineyards create geometric green patterns on the hillsides transforming the dusty landscapes of this region.

BRINGING IN THE HARVEST

The Upper Douro is a pleasure to visit at any point during the summer, but harvest time is the most rewarding. The harvest *(vindima)* usually starts towards the end of September – the exact date being dictated by the conditions of any particular year – and by this time temperatures have cooled to a pleasant heat.

In spite of recent mechanisation, grape picking is still largely done by hand. Extended families of itinerant workers from surrounding villages often return year after year to the same farms to bring in the harvest. Traditionally, men and women adopt different roles in the field, but they all come together at meal times. Lunch is almost party time: the estate owners provide a fulsome meal and the pickers relax and enjoy it.

When the mood is right, and with a contented team of workers, the sound of singing can be heard emanating from the vine terraces. It is a time of great celebration, of relief that the crop has survived the vagaries of the weather and of thanksgiving for a harvest, even in years when it is not at its most bountiful.

COSTA VERDE AND THE MINHO

Map on page 300

Verdant and lush, this is a land of vineyards, tranquil riverside towns, busy markets, and Europe's last great wilderness, the Peneda-Gerês National Park

The Minho region north of Porto is often described as Costa Verde, or the Green Coast, a reference to the vineyards and lush green of its well-watered landscape. In reality it is a much bigger area than just the coast. It extends northwards to the Rio Minho, the boundary with Spain, eastwards to include the Parque Nacional da Peneda-Gerês and south to encompass Braga and Guimarães. It is a region of great natural beauty, especially the verdant Lima Valley and the wild and mountainous Peneda-Gerês, where farming techniques and lifestyles pass from generation to generation without perceptible change.

Grapes are grown everywhere. They hang from trees, pergolas and porches, and climb along slopes and terraces. They grow in poor rocky soil where little else flourishes. To get the most out of the land, the Minhotos train their vines to grow upwards, on trees, houses and hedges, leaving ground space for cabbages, onions and potatoes. This free-wheeling system has made it difficult to modernise grape production, but in recent years the larger farms have begun to use a system of wire-supporting crosses called *cruzetas*.

The *vindima,* or grape harvest, is still done by hand and is a wonderful sight to behold. Harvesting takes place in September and October and lasts until early November. It is often a hazardous task, requiring towering 30-rung ladders to get at the elusive treetop grapes, though most vines now are trained at lower levels. In the hilly country, men still carry huge baskets of grapes weighing as much as 50 kg (110 lb) on their backs. On some back roads, squeaky oxcarts transport the grapes to wine-presses. In these modern times, however, the fruit is generally transported in trucks.

While harvest is a festive occasion, it is no longer quite the unbridled merry-making of yore. In the old days, workers used to perform a kind of bacchanal dance, their arms linked, stamping on the grapes with their bare feet. It was said that this was the only way to crush the fruit without smashing the pips and spoiling the flavour of the wine. This was often accompanied by music and clapping, glasses of spirits and a good deal of sweat. Nowadays, mechanical extractors often remove the pips and presses are generally used to crush the grapes, although treading still takes place in some vineyards.

LEFT: the unusual grain stores of Soajo.
BELOW: Vila do Conde.

North from Porto

A good way to visit the Minho is to drive up the coast from Porto and return by an inland route. The Atlantic beaches are generally broad with fine sand, but the sea is cold and rough. A fishing town and resort, **Vila do**

The Associação Para O Desenvolvimento da Rota dos Vinhos Verdes in Oporto publishes a booklet with suggested vinho verde wine routes and estates to visit (tel: 226 077 300.)

Conde ❶, is the site of the vast Convento de Santa Clara, which was founded in 1318, the 16th-century parish church of São João Baptista and a lovely 17th-century fortress. Travellers are welcome to watch how fishing boats are made and to visit the lace-making school and museum (Museu de Rendas). Nearby, **Póvoa de Varzim ❷** is another popular fishing port-resort, with an 18th-century fort and a parish church. There's also a casino and a modern luxury hotel, the Vermar, with heated pools and tennis courts. Further north, **Ofir ❸** is a delightful seaside resort amid pine forests. Just across the Rio Cávado lies the town of **Esposende ❹** with the remains of an 18th-century fortress. There are many new, often garishly-painted houses in towns and villages along the way which have often been built by emigrants returned from France, Germany and elsewhere.

A lively fishing and ship-building port at the mouth of the Rio Lima, **Viana do Castelo ❺** was called Diana by the Romans. This was the centre of Portugal's wine trade until the port declined in the 18th century and Porto became pre-eminent. There is a good deal to see in Viana, starting with the 18th-century

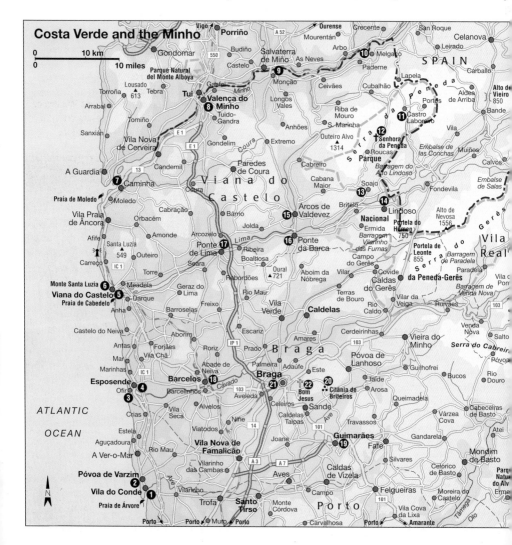

Costa Verde and the Minho

Palácio dos Távoras, now the main tourist office. In the central Praça da República there's a beautiful 16th-century fountain and the remarkable Misercórdia hospital, with a three-tiered façade supported by caryatids. Nearby stands the handsome 15th-century parish church with a Gothic portal and Romanesque towers. The town is dominated by **Monte Santa Luzia** ⑥, with a large and inappropriate modern basilica. To the west of the town, the baroque Nossa Senhora da Agonia church is the site of a popular pilgrimage each August. Dancers, musicians and other celebrants, wearing vivid embroidered traditional costumes, come from all over the Minho to take part in the three-day *festa*, which is among Portugal's most spectacular.

Along the Rio Minho

Continuing north, the road leads to **Caminha** ⑦ on the banks of the Rio Minho, an attractive town with echoes of its past as a busy trading port. The church, dating from the 15th century, has a beautiful carved-wood ceiling. There are several lovely 15th- and 16th-century buildings near the main square.

At the estuary of the Minho, the road turns inland and follows the river, which forms the border with Spain. **Valença do Minho** ⑧ is a bustling border town with shops and markets. Spaniards come here regularly to purchase items that include table linen and crystal chandeliers. The Portuguese, on the other hand, cross the border to Tui or Vigo to buy canned goods such as asparagus and artichokes, and ready-made clothing. The old town of Valença is still fairly intact with cobbled streets and stone houses with iron balconies, surrounded by 17th-century granite ramparts. The ancient convent, with a splendid view of the Minho and of Spain, is now a *pousada*.

From **Monção** ⑨, a fortified town known for its spring water and classy *vinho verde*, you can either take the road south through the heart of the Minho, or continue along the riverside and cross over the mountains of Serra da Peneda and sense the isolation. Either way the routes meet at Ponte da Barca.

Grapes grow everywhere, even on telegraph wires.

BELOW: Valença do Minho's cheerful town square.

The mountain route

Follow the river as far as **Melgaço** ⑩, another fortified town, and turn inland for **Castro Laboreiro** ⑪, an ancient settlement with an 11th-century castle, but more famous for a large breed of dog which was introduced to protect the villagers from marauding wolves. Take the road to **Senhora da Peneda** ⑫ to find an amazing "Bom Jesus" style church *(see page 307)* in the middle of nowhere. A long flight of steps ascending to the church is adorned with 14 chapels, each containing a tableau depicting a major event in the history of Christ.

Dramatic mountain scenery opens up as you pass through a number of villages, including Rouças and Adrão, to meet the road outside the village of **Soajo** ⑬, where there is a colourful market on the first Sunday of the month. Of particular interest are the communal *spigueiros*, granite grain stores built on mushroom-shaped legs, grouped around a threshing floor.

The road onward leads to **Lindoso** ⑭ (from *lindo* meaning beautiful) and a finely situated border castle

Feeding the hens.

keeping watch for invaders from Spain. Below the castle ramparts lies another cluster of *espigueiros*. Return from Lindoso on the road to Ponte da Barca. You'll see lush countryside, crisscrossed by rivers with medieval stone bridges, simple white churches with elaborate granite doorways and windows; and, of course, unending vineyards. Due to the high population density, the land has been divided and sub-divided for generations, so the average property now consists of just an acre or two.

The road passes **Arcos de Valdevez** 15, a charming hillside town built on the banks of the Rio Vez, with a magnificent view of the valley. Just to the south, **Ponte da Barca** 16, on the south bank of the Rio Lima, has a lovely 15th-century parish church and an old town square, but the principal attraction is the fine arched bridge, built in 1543 and often restored. This is a possible starting point for a tour of the nearby **Peneda-Gerês National Park** *(see below)*.

The Lima Valley and the south

Here you might turn westward, along the beautiful valley of the Lima river, which the Romans believed to be the *Lethe*, the mythical River of Forgetfulness. The area has numerous great estates or *solares,* which stand as a tangible reminder of the glories of the old empire. Some are now guesthouses, and arrangements to visit or stay in these manors should be made beforehand, if possible *(see page 128).*

BELOW: waterfall in Peneda-Gerês.

Ponte de Lima 17 is one of the loveliest towns in Portugal, mainly because of its location on the south bank of the Lima; its market, held every other Monday, is a splendidly colourful "tent city" on the riverbank. The town faces

A TOUR OF THE PARQUE NACIONAL DA PENEDA-GERÊS

It is easy to make a round trip of the Peneda-Gerês National Park by car, taking in some of the most spectacular scenery on both sides of the border. From Ponte da Barca take the road east towards Lindoso, past the hydro scheme to the border at Madaleina. Cross into Spain – there are no formalities – and continue alongside the reservoir until you come to a right turn signposted Lobios and Portela do Homen. Take this turn and you eventually cross back into Portugal.

On the Portuguese side you have a choice: continue straight down the "main" road to the old spa town of Caldas do Gerês then towards Braga, or, shortly after crossing back into Portugal, take the right turn down a dirt track which follows the Vilarinho reservoir to Campo do Gerês. Campo do Gerês has an excellent visitor centre portraying traditional life in Vilarinho das Furnas, the village submerged by the reservoir. Then drive towards Covide, passing a well-stocked craft shop, then west to Vila Verde. Of the two options, the latter is the more interesting. Note that roads can get very busy at weekends in summer and at peak times the park authority may impose traffic restrictions.

a magnificent Roman bridge with low arches, and remains of the old city wall still stand. A 15th-century palace with crenellated façade is now the town hall. Across the river, the 15th-century **Convento de Santo António** has beautiful woodwork, including two baroque shrines.

Continuing towards Viana do Castelo, you pass more manor houses, such as the Solar de Cortegaça, with its great 15th-century stone tower. This is a working manor, with wine cellars, flour mill and stable. Guests are welcome to take part in the farm life (tel: 258 971 639).

Barcelos: cock and bull

Heading south from Ponte de Lima, you reach the charming market town of **Barcelos** ⑱, on the north bank of the Rio Cávado. Barcelos has 15th-century fortifications, a 13th-century church and a 16th-century palace, but more than that, it has one of the best craft markets in the country. Every Thursday, traders and artisans display their folk art and other goods in the centre of town.

It was here that the late Rosa Ramalho, the most famous folk art sculptress in Portugal, created her world of fanciful ceramic animals and people – a style that has been continued by her grand-daughter. There is a crafts exhibition and shop in the medieval keep alongside the tourist office in the **Largo da Porta Nova**. It displays copperware, hand-made rugs, wooden toys, bright cotton tableware, and, of course, the *galo de Barcelos* – the ubiquitous Barcelos cockerel. A monument, the so-called Senhor do Galo cross, is the most apt reminder of the extraordinary legend that lies behind the rooster's elevation to Portugal's unofficial national emblem *(see page 237)*. There is a small pottery museum, the Museu de Olaria, in the town.

There's no escaping the Barcelos cockerel.

BELOW: lovely Ponte de Lima.

Guimarães: birthplace of a nation

A busy manufacturing town noted mainly for textiles, shoes and cutlery Guimarães still possesses many reminders of its past glory as birthplace of the Portuguese nation. Around the year 1128, an 18-year-old boy named Afonso Henriques proclaimed independence for the region of Portucale from the kingdom of León and Castile. In the field of São Mamede, near Guimarães, the young Afonso Henriques defeated his mother's army, which was battling on behalf of Alfonso VII, king of León and Castile.

Guimarães has long been the centre of the Portuguese linen industry. It still produces high quality, coarse linen from home-grown flax naturally bleached by the sun. The region is also known for its hand embroidery.

A good place to begin a tour is at the 10th-century **Castelo** (open Tues–Sun June–Sept 9.30am–7pm; Oct–May 9.30am–5pm; entrance charge), on the northern side of town. It is believed that Afonso Henriques was born here in 1110, the son of Henri of Burgundy, Count of Portucale, and his wife Teresa. The castle is a large mass of walls and towers on a rocky hill with a magnificent view of the mountains. The dungeon and fortifications were restored many times. Early in the 19th century, the castle was used as a debtors' prison; it was restored again in 1940. At the entrance stands the small Romanesque chapel of **São Miguel de Castelo** with the font where Afonso Henriques was baptised in 1111.

Heading into town, you pass the 15th-century Gothic **Paço dos Duques de Bragança** (open daily 9am–7pm, 5pm in winter; entrance charge), now occasionally used as an official residence by the President of the Republic. This massive granite construction consists of four buildings around a courtyard and has been completely restored. Outside is a fine statue of Afonso Henriques by Soares dos Reis. Visitors may also view the splendid chestnut ceiling of the Banquet Hall, the Persian carpets, French tapestries, ancient portraits and documents.

The Rua de Santa Maria, with its cobblestones and 14th- and 15th-century houses with wrought-iron balconies, leads to the centre of town. On the left lies the **Convento de Santa Clara**, built in the 1600s and now used as the town hall.

The church of **Nossa Senhora de Oliveira**, dating from the 10th century, was rebuilt by Count Henri in the 12th century and has undergone several restorations. Still visible are the 16th-century watchtower and 14th-century western portal and window. The church takes its name from a 7th-century legend of an old Visigoth warrior named Wamba who was tilling his field nearby when a delegation came to tell him he had been elected king. Refusing the office, he drove his staff into the ground, declaring that not until it bore leaves would he become king. It turned into an olive tree and the church was later built on the spot.

Adjacent to the church of Oliveira, the convent has been converted into the **Museu de Alberto Sampaio** (open Tues–Sun; closed 12.30–2pm; entrance charge) displaying the church's rich treasury of 12th-century silver chalices and Gothic and Renaissance silver crucifixes, as well as 15th- and 16th-century statues, paintings and ceramics.

Guimarães' Festival of Saint Walter, the Festas Gualterianas, dates from the middle of the 15th century. This three-day celebration, on the first weekend in August, includes a torchlight procession, a fair with traditional dances, and a medieval parade.

BELOW: the cross of the Senhor do Galo, Barcelos.

The busiest square in Guimarães is the Largo do Toural. Just beyond, the **Igreja São Domingos** was built in the 14th century and still has the original transept, rose window and lovely Gothic cloister. The latter houses the Museu Martins Sarmento (open Tues–Sun; closed 12.30–2pm; entrance charge), with objects from Briteiros *(see below)* and other *citânias* (ancient Iberian fortified villages) of northern Portugal, as well as Roman inscriptions, ceramics and coins.

Continuing along the broad garden called the Alameda da Resistência ao Fascismo, you reach the **Igreja São Francisco**, founded in the 13th century. There is little left of the original Gothic structure, but the sacristy has impressive 17th-century gilt woodwork and ceiling.

High on the outskirts of the city stands **Santa Marinha da Costa**, founded as a monastery in the 12th century and rebuilt in the 18th century. The church functions regularly and may be visited. The cells of the monastery, which were badly damaged by fire in 1951, have recently been restored and turned into a luxury *pousada*. Visible in the cloisters are a 10th-century Mozarabic arch and vestiges of a 7th-century Visigothic structure. The veranda is decorated with magnificent 18th-century tile scenes and a fountain.

Citânia de Briteiros

After the Briteiros exhibit at the Martins Sarmento museum, you could visit the original site, 11 km (7 miles) north of Guimarães. At first, the **Citânia de Briteiros** ⓴ appears to be nothing more than piles of stones on a hillside, but it is in fact one of Portugal's most important archaeological sites. Here are the remains of a prehistoric fortified village said to have been inhabited by Celts. It was discovered in 1874 by archaeologist Francisco Martins Sarmento.

Map
on page
300

A knight rides into battle.

BELOW: the Pousada de Santa Marinha da Costa in Guimarães.

Splendid wooden doorway of Braga Cathedral.

Near the summit, two round houses have been reconstructed. Also visible are the remains of defensive walls, ancient flagstones and the foundation walls of over 150 houses. The houses were circular with stone benches running around the walls. A large rock in the centre supported a pole which would have held up a thatched roof. Several of the houses are larger, with two or more rectangular rooms, presumably the homes of prominent members of society. The town evidently had an efficient water system: spring water flowed downhill through gutters carved in the paving stones to a cistern and a public fountain.

Braga

Some people still refer to **Braga** ㉑, somewhat wistfully, as "the Portuguese Rome". In Roman times, as Bracara Augusta, it was the centre of communications in north Lusitania. In the 6th century two synods were held here. Under Moorish occupation, Braga was sacked and the cathedral badly damaged. But in the 11th century, the city was largely restored to its former eminence by Bishop Dom Pedro and Archbishop São Geraldo. The Archbishop claimed authority over all the churches of the Iberian peninsula, and his successors retained the title of Primate of the Spains for six centuries.

Like a Renaissance prince, one of his successors, Archbishop Dom Diogo de Sousa, encouraged the construction of many handsome Italian-style churches, fountains and palaces in the 16th century. Zealous prelates restored many of these works in the subsequent two centuries, but often with unfortunate results. Braga lost its title as ecclesiastical capital in 1716, when the Patriarchate went to Lisbon. But it is still an important religious centre, and the site of Portugal's most elaborate Holy Week procession.

BELOW: the grand stairway of Bom Jesus.

A visit to Braga usually begins at the **Sé**, the cathedral built in the 11th century on the site of an earlier structure destroyed by the Moors. Of the original Romanesque building there remains only the southern portal and the sculpted cornice of the transept. Although it has been greatly modified by various restorations, the cathedral is still imposing. The interior contains some fine tombs, including those of the founders, Count Henri and his wife Teresa, a granite sculpture of the Virgin, an 18th-century choir loft and organ case, and richly decorated chapels and cloister. Of particular interest the **Tesouro da Catedral** (Cathedral Treasury; open daily 8.30am–6.30pm, 5.30pm in winter; entrance charge), with a fine collection of 15th-century vestments and silver chalices and crucifixes dating from the 10th and 12th centuries.

Nearby, with plain west walls set off by an 18th-century fountain, is the **Palácio de Arzobispo** (Archbishop's Palace), built in the 14th century. It, too, has been reconstructed several times. The palace now houses the Public Library, with city archives dating back to the 9th century, 300,000 volumes and 10,000 manuscripts. On the western side of Praça Agrolongo stands one of Braga's Rome-inspired churches, **Nossa Senhora do Pópulo**, built in the 17th century and remodelled at the end of the 18th. It is decorated with *azulejos* depicting scenes from the life of St Augustine.

The **Palácio dos Biscainhos** (open Tues–Sun, closed 12.15–2pm; entrance charge), across the way, is a 17th-century mansion with lovely garden, and fountains. It is now a museum, and the collection includes 18th-century tiles, ceramics, jewellery and furniture. Part of the museum has been set aside for artifacts from recent excavations on the site of a protected zone established in 1977, after some damage from modern construction. The University of Minho is directing the excavations, which have uncovered Roman baths, a sanctuary called Fonte do Idolo and the remains of a house called Domus de Santiago.

On the northern side of the city, the church of **São João de Souto** was completely rebuilt in the late 18th century. But here is the superb **Capela do Conceição**, built in 1525, with crenellated walls, lovely windows and splendid statues of St Anthony and St Paul.

Bom Jesus

There are many other churches and chapels of interest in the religious centre, but the best known is **Bom Jesus ㉒**, which is conspicuously set on the wooded Monte Espinho, about 5 km (3 miles) outside Braga. This popular pilgrimage centre is remarkable for its grandiose stairway and the view from its terrace of the Rio Cávado valley and the mountains in the distance. The double flight of stairs is flanked by chapels, fountains and often startlingly bizarre figures at each level, representing the Stations of the Cross.

If you don't wish to climb the steps, there's a funicular and a winding road to the top. There, among oak trees, eucalyptus, camelias and mimosa, stands the 16th-century church, rebuilt in the 18th century. In its **Capela dos Milagres** (Chapel of Miracles) are votive offerings and pictures left by past pilgrims. Several hotels, souvenir shops and restaurants are also located in the vicinity of the sanctuary.   ❑

Map on page 300

BELOW: the Café Brasileira in Braga.

TRAS-OS-MONTES

Map on page 312

Isolated by distance and mountains, Trás-os-Montes has developed an individuality which distinguishes it from the rest of Portugal

To most Portuguese, the remote northeastern province of Trás-os-Montes ("behind the mountains") could be on the other side of the moon. Lisboetas are inclined to look at it as from a vast distance – albeit with fierce affection. The word *"trás"* – "back" or "behind" – fits the region like a glove. Before Portugal joined the EU, this region was backward in almost every aspect: cut off from the rest of the country by mountains, poor road and rail systems, and grinding poverty which drove the workforce of almost every village to migrate to urban areas, or emigrate to the more advanced economies of northern Europe, or overseas. Now, improved roads, better communications and farming subsidies have led to rapid improvements in living standards, although pockets of poverty still exist.

Regional differences

There has been higher emigration from the north of Portugal than from the south, and one of the principal reasons is the division of land. The south is an area of *latifúndios* – large landholdings – while the north has *minifúndios* – smallholdings. A farmer's land in the north is often insufficient to provide him and his family with a living. The northern people are conservative, and resist such cooperative farming as operates in the southern province of Alentejo. Another reason for *minifúndios* is the terrain – high mountains and steep-sided valleys make it difficult to organise large-scale farming.

A more subtle factor affecting Portugal's conservative north is the Church. While all Portugal is Roman Catholic, the sheer remoteness of the northeast corner has meant that national government has little impact, while tradition and religion predominate. This has affected education, particularly; until recently, often the only educated man in a village was the priest, whose wisdom and opinion would be sought on every matter ranging from the spiritual to crop harvesting.

Geographically, Trás-os-Montes covers the extreme northeast corner of the country, from Bragança in the north to the Rio Douro in the south and, as far as this chapter is concerned, west to Chaves and Montelegre. Climatically, the region is different, too. Cut off from the influence of the Atlantic, it is hotter and drier in summer and colder in winter, especially in the far northeastern *Terra Fria*, the cold lands. In contrast, the southern part is called *Terra Quente*, the warm lands. Vines on a commercial scale are not viable in the *Terra Fria* so their place is taken by grain crops, which changes the landscape appreciably. Trás-os-Montes remains one of the most interesting areas of the country, for its towns, its countryside and its historical connections.

PRECEDING PAGES: passing the time. **LEFT:** *al fresco* spinning in Barroso. **BELOW:** proud of his wooden-wheeled cart.

Who will buy?

Entering the region

You can enter the region, which includes the Alto Douro, from a number of directions. Northern border crossings from Spain are at Vila Verde da Raia, on the road leading south to Chaves (this is a historical invasion route – employed by the armies of Napoleon in the early 1800s); at Portelo, in the Parque Natural de Montesinho; from the east at Quintanilha, east of Bragança; and at Miranda do Douro and Bemposta, where the Douro forms the frontier. From inside Portugal, the main routes into the region are from Porto or Lamego via Vila Real; or from Guarda via either Torre de Moncorvo or Freixo de Espada à Cinta.

This itinerary enters the region at Vila Real and follows a meandering route to absorb the sights and atmosphere of the area without ignoring the major points of interest.

Serra de Alvão

Two scenic routes lead north out of Vila Real, one on each side of the high Serra da Padrela – to Chaves in the north, and Bragança in the northeast. But the adventurous traveller may strike northwest into the rugged Serra de Alvão, and be treated to one of the most lavish vistas the country has to offer. The road leads through a small natural park and across the Rio Olo to **Mondim de Basto ❶** on the banks of the Rio Tâmega. There it forms the border between Trás-os-Montes and the Minho.

Granite gives way to slate – many of the houses are roofed by it – and in the high passes you can hear the rushing of mountain waters, the tinkle of goat bells, or the calling of a herder to his dogs. In the winter there is snow here, but at other times of the year you are likely to encounter a profusion of wild flowers

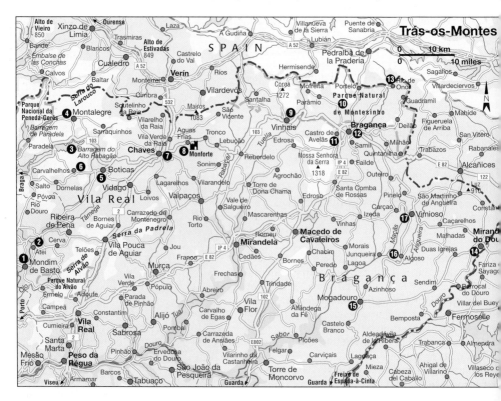

and pine forests. Pine resin, which is used in the manufacture of paints and turpentine, is a major product of this area.

A side trip of some 12 km (8 miles) from Mondim de Basto will take you to **Atei ②**, a delightful little village containing numerous archaeological remnants of Roman occupation. From here a curious subterranean passage of either Roman or Arab construction leads down to Furaco on the banks of the Tâmega.

Leaving Mondim de Basto, the road winds northwards to **Cabeceiras de Basto**, which is actually in the Minho province, at the head of a small "peninsula" that juts up into Trás-os-Montes. Stop at the imposing baroque **Mosteiro Refóis** before heading into the high Serra de Cabreira and back into Trás-os-Montes at Póvoa.

Barroso district

You soon join the main Braga–Chaves road that runs beside **Barragem do Alto Rabagão ③**, a gigantic expanse of lake formed behind a dam, but here again another side trip could take you north – to Montalegre, the towering Serra do Larouco, and the primitive villages of the Barroso district.

As the largest town in the area, **Montalegre ④** might be considered the capital of Barroso. Given a charter in 1273 by King Afonso III, and restored and expanded in turn by King Dinis and King Manuel I, Montalegre (*monte* meaning hill, *alegre* meaning happy or cheerful) is thought to have enjoyed its status from a much earlier time, for the pillory in the centre of town carries the coat-of-arms of King Sancho I, who reigned from 1185 to 1211.

The hill on which the town stands commands a view over an extensive area, so it's hardly surprising that this has been a military centre for centuries. Montalegre is rich in archaeological finds. Lusitanians, Romans, Suevi and Visigoths were all here, and the magnificent four-towered castle was much used during the many wars that Portugal fought against Spain.

North of the region rises the **Serra do Larouco**, the second highest range of mountains in the country (after the Serra da Estrela), with a number of passes leading into Spanish Galicia.

The district of Barroso stretches from the foothills of the Serra do Larouco southeast towards the city of Chaves. There is no absolute boundary, but it would include such villages as Meixido, Padornelos and Tourém. If you can shut out the "emigrant architecture" – uncontrolled modern housing that is built with money saved by the Portuguese who work abroad – you will find in these settlements a sense of history utterly remote in time.

The ancient houses are built of enormous granite or slate blocks. Doors, windows and balconies are of weathered antique wood. Until recently, many houses were thatched. Once common, dirt streets are rapidly becoming paved, and electricity has only recently been installed. Almost every church is Romanesque, with the typical façade rising to a twin-columned peak to house the church bell.

For centuries the people of Barroso lived out their lives cut off from the outside world. They developed

BELOW: storks' nest near Bragança.

Map on page 312

their own customs, songs, festivals and habits. In many corners of the world under similar circumstances, local people may treat outsiders with suspicion or alarm. This is certainly not the case in Barroso. It is hard to imagine a more warm-hearted, hospitable people, willing to share the peculiarities of their daily lives with those who come to visit them.

Communal bulls

One of the region's most colourful festivals is the annual **Chega dos Toiros**, an inter-village competition which means "The Arrival of the Bulls". Each village takes enormous pride in its own bull, a communally-owned animal bred especially for the purpose of covering the various cows owned by the individual farmers. This bull, by both tradition and breeding, is the biggest and fiercest animal imaginable, intended as much to gain the honours at the annual competition as it is for stock purposes.

Held in June, July and August, the Chega is essentially a bullfight, where the bull of one village is pitted against another in a fierce battle. Each animal is decorated and fêted by his villagers, and paraded to the accompaniment of noisy bands and crowds. The fight itself is in deadly earnest, with the champions of each bull goading their animal into combat. The fight continues until one animal is injured, or turns and runs. The victor is led away by his villagers with much celebration.

At the end of the season there will be a regional champion, and this is the lucky animal who'll be put out to pasture with the region's cows. He is a source of great pride to the residents of the village from which he comes, even if he doesn't know what all the fuss is about. He's just doing what comes naturally.

BELOW: an example of Barroso's archaic building methods.

Wine of the dead

Boticas **❺** is the place to drink *vinhos mortos*, "wine of the dead". In order to protect their wine stocks from the French during the Peninsular War in the early 1800s, the villagers buried it in the ground. When it was later retrieved, the wine was found to be much improved. The practice is still followed, with good results. For another regional drink, divert a short way west to the spa village of **Carvalhelhos ❻**. The spring water here is particularly sweet and is sold all over the country. Most refreshing is *com gas*, the sparkling version.

Chaves

Chaves **❼**, just a few kilometres down the road from Barroso, seems a world away. An ancient city, the fortified Lusitanian village of the present site was captured by the Romans in AD 78. The Emperor Flavius founded the city of *Aqua Flaviae* there, inaugurating the still popular hot springs and baths. Chaves is now a bustling town with a population of about 15,000. An agricultural and textile centre, it is famous for its *presunto*, or smoked ham; you could taste it, with a glass of wine, at Faustino's, which claims to be the largest taverna, or *tasca,* in Portugal.

   Situated on the Rio Tâmega, Chaves commands a strategic position in a wide valley that extends from the Spanish frontier into the heart of Trás-os-Montes. Just about every invader who set his heart on Portugal, or chunks of it, routed his armies through this channel. Here the Romans built one of the largest of their bridges in the Iberian peninsula. Completed in AD 104, it has 20 arches, is 140 metres (150 yards) in length, and is still very much in daily use. In the middle of the bridge are two inscribed Roman milestones. *Chaves* means "keys" in

Map
on page
312

Dom Afonso, standing proud in the centre of Chaves.

BELOW: a novelty store in Chaves.

Portuguese, but the ancient *Aqua Flaviae* was later shortened to *Flavias*, and local mispronunciation may have produced the current name.

Sights include the parish church, rebuilt in the 16th century; and the former Bragança ducal palace, now the **Museu Região Flaviense** (open Tues–Fri 9am–5.30pm, Sat–Sun 2–5.30pm; entrance charge), in the Praça de Camões. Prior to the formation of Portugal, the fortified city was a part of the original County of Portucale. Various of Portugal's early kings added significantly to its castle, one of the most important in the land.

A second castle, in its day also an integral part of the defences of this strategic valley, still stands at **Monforte ❽**, about 12 km (8 miles) northeast.

East from Chaves

Heading eastwards towards Bragança you will pass the old town of **Vinhais ❾**. Its castle is barely more than a ruin, though there was a significant population here. The town is set high in the Serra de Montesinho, on the south flank of the **Parque Natural de Montesinho ❿**, a wildly rugged park, the habitat of wolves, boars and foxes. The area survives on agriculture, particularly vines, woodwork, weaving and basket-making. To explore the region, first stop at the tourist office in Bragança and ask for a book about the park, which contains a detailed map of the area. Not all of the roads are paved. Whichever direction you take, you will have a journey through spectacular country.

A mountain, **Cidadela**, rises behind Vinhais. Over it passed the Roman road that led from Braga to Astorga; today this ancient route is rich in archaeological discoveries. In the 11th and 12th centuries there was a general movement by the population of this area towards the more fertile farm lands of the south. To

BELOW: On the road to Bragança.

prevent this, various monasteries were founded and encouraged by the early rulers of the region to develop their own agriculture and cottage industries. One of the most important of these was the **Mosteiro de Castro de Avelãs ⓫**, a few kilometres west of Bragança. Parts of the church of the Benedictine abbey have been incorporated into the present-day parish church.

Map on page 312

Bragança: a fascinating city

With a population of some 30,000, **Bragança ⓬** is the administrative capital, a university town, and also an agricultural trade centre (livestock, vineyards, olive oil, grains). It has a thriving textile industry, and has been famous for its ceramics since prehistoric times (in a nearby cave at Dine, archaeologists have found pottery dating from the Paleolithic period). In 2003 this apparently remote town hit the headlines when *Time* magazine published a story about 300 *meninas brasileiras*, Brazilian prostitutes, who were operating in the town in more than half a dozen strip clubs and numerous brothels. One of the strip clubs even sponsored a local football team. Wives got up petitions but to no avail and an uneasy truce resulted.

Known as *Brigantine* to the Celts and *Juliobriga* to the Romans, Bragança received its first *foral* (royal charter) from King Sancho I in 1187 – when the family from which the dukes of Bragança are descended started building their feudal castle there. The Braganças – still pretenders to the throne of Portugal – provided the land's kings and queens consistently from 1640 until the formation of the Republic in 1910, and the emperors of Brazil from 1822 to 1889. In 1662, Catherine of Bragança, daughter of the first Bragança king João IV, became Queen to Charles II of England, thus renewing the long alliance between the two nations. Since the fall of the monarchy, a foundation, the

BELOW: Bragança's medieval skyline.

Fundação da Casa de Bragança, has managed all royal properties including the family's 16th-century ducal palace in Vila Viçosa.

Bragança's ancient castle still stands – with a Princess's Tower full of tragic ghosts. The keep of the castle houses a military museum. You can also see an unusual medieval *pelourinho* (or pillory), its shaft piercing a granite boar. Nearby, still within the castle walls, you will find the 12th-century five-sided **Domus Municipalis**, the oldest municipal hall in the land. The town walls with their 18 watchtowers are still largely intact, and the city has a fine cathedral and fascinating museum of archaeology, furniture and ethnography, the **Museu do Abade de Baçal** (open Tues–Fri, 10am–5pm, Sat and Sun 10am–6pm; entrance charge) in what used to be the Bishop's Palace.

Excursions north

Basing yourself in this historic city, it is relatively easy to make short day trips out into the surrounding region.

First, to the north, in the farthest corner of Portugal, there is **Rio de Onor** , a tiny village that straddles the border with Spain. Only recently, after a rare presidential visit, did the village acquire its first bus service. The people of Rio de Onor developed their own dialect and intricate communal social system. In their music and folk dances a common instrument is the *gaita-de-foles* – a bag-pipe, with Celtic associations similar to those of Scotland and Ireland.

A good time to visit the villages that extend in an arc from Vinhais, across Bragança, and down as far as Miranda do Douro and Freixo de Espada-à-Cinta, is between Christmas Day and Epiphany (6 January), when the local population celebrates a number of feasts connected with the Christian calendar – but incor-

You will see people in the fields working with traditional agricultural tools, beasts of burden and wooden-wheeled carts – things that are rarely seen in the rest of Europe.

BELOW: a woman carries a traditional farm implement.

porating ferocious masks and unearthly costumes. These celebrations date back to the dawn of time, when the agrarian people of these pastoral regions practised fertility rites and paid more than passing attention to magic. Carnival, in February, is another good time to visit. Forty days before Easter the masks come out again, and you cannot be sure if it is the Christian spirit or the bogeyman that dominates the season. As in so many places, the Catholic Church incorporated pagan elements in order to appease the local people, and the rites became entangled.

Map on page 312

Excursions south

South of Bragança you may head towards the Spanish frontier at **Miranda do Douro ⑭**. This fortified town sits above a craggy gorge overlooking the Douro. Like many of the country's border towns, it has suffered a turbulent history in its attempts to keep out the Spanish. These days invaders from across the river are welcomed with open arms – provided they bring a supply of euros.

Fifteenth-century houses with granite doorways, a 16th-century cathedral with a sequence of gilded wood altarpieces, an excellent folk museum, the **Museu da Terra de Miranda** (open Tues–Sun; closed 12.30–2pm; entrance charge), and the medieval Rua da Costanilha make it a worthwhile stop.

It is possible to make a circular tour by following the road on to sleepy **Mogadouro ⑮**, which slumbers in the shadow of a 12th-century castle built by King Dinis on earlier Roman foundations.

If you like castles, don't miss the impressive ruins at **Algoso ⑯**, on the way back to **Vimioso ⑰**. Since the 12th century, this fortress has guarded the area surrounding its lofty perch – a hill called Cabeça da Penenciada – while 500 metres (1,650 ft) below, the Rio Angueira flows westwards to the Rio Maçãs. ❑

FOLLOWING PAGES:
the hill village of Monsanto in Beira Baixa.
BELOW: the church at Miranda do Douro.

BEIRA ALTA AND BEIRA BAIXA

Map on page 324

This is a region of extreme contrasts, incorporating the Serra da Estrela (the highest mountain range in Portugal), an area of cattle-raising plains and a line of defensive castles

The provinces of Beira Alta and Beira Baixa, the Upper and Lower Beiras, constitute a large rural section of eastern Portugal – a modest and hardy geographical region in a country that is among the poorest in Western Europe. But it is rich historically, marked over centuries by the invasion routes of both the Spanish and Moors, in defensive castles and remnants of fortresses. The area has its natural attractions as well: the dramatic mountains of the Serra da Estrela and the stark plains and plateaux of the Baixa are some of the most beautiful natural landmarks in Portugal. The region is bounded by the Spanish frontier to the east, the Rio Douro to the north, and the Tejo (Tagus) to the south. The western boundary is a ragged line 60 km (38 miles) east of Oporto.

Beira Alta

Guarda ❶ is the principal city and administrative capital of the Beira Alta's eastern district. The charter of Guarda was granted by Sancho I, Portugal's second king, in 1199, although the city had been established by 80 BC, when it had a role in the attempted secession from Rome. Roman ruins can be found just outside town, near the Romanesque chapel of Póvoa de Mileu, notable itself for a small rose window and nicely carved capitals. Three town gates from the 12th- and 13th-century castle and town walls still stand: the Torre de Ferreiros (Blacksmiths' Tower), the Porta da Estrela (Star Gate), and the Porta do Rei (King's Gate), along with the castle keep. From the top there is a magnificent view of the mountains, and the broad plains to the north.

The **Sé (Cathedral)** was built of granite cut from the surrounding area. An earlier cathedral, close to the city's original walls, was destroyed before this one was begun, because it was believed to be in an unsafe position. Work started in 1390 and was not completed until 1540, so that there were many Renaissance and baroque elements added to the original Gothic architecture. Diogo Boytac (1494–1520) worked on the cathedral, which bears some resemblance to Batalha. The exterior has flying buttresses and fanciful gargoyles. Inside, the 16th-century stone *retábulo*, later highlighted with gilt, represents scenes in the life of Christ; the stone carving is the work of João de Ruão, also known as Jean de Rouen (1530–70). A beautiful Renaissance doorway, off the north aisle, leads to the Capela dos Pinas which contains the late Gothic tomb of a bishop.

The town museum in a 17th-century seminary has archaeological finds and a range of paintings.

LEFT: in the Serra da Estrela.
BELOW: a local sanctuary.

Guarda has been dubbed the city of four Fs – *fria, farta, forte e feia*, which means: cold, plentiful, strong and ugly. The predominance of heavy grey granite may be ugly to some, but the old parts of the city are pleasant. Strong alludes to Guarda's history as a defence point against the Moors and Castile. Plentiful refers, no doubt, to the rich land surrounding the town, noted particularly for its sheep farming. Cold it certainly is, in winter: situated some 1,066 metres (3,500 ft) above sea level, Guarda is Portugal's highest city – high enough for frost and snow during winter months.

Around Guarda

South of Guarda lie two handsome castle-towns: on the main road to Castelo Branco is **Belmonte ❷**, birthplace of Alvares Cabral, who discovered Brazil, and on the narrower N233 is **Sabugal**. About half-way between the two is the oddly enchanting **Sortelha ❸**, a tiny village with a castle surrounded by rocky crags, within a "magic ring" of stone. Ancient civilisations may have shaped

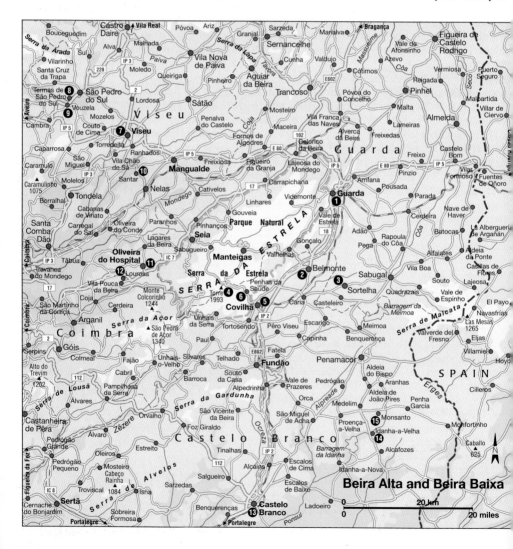

Beira Alta and Beira Baixa

some of the rocks, and they certainly mined in the area – there are entrances to mines that have been closed for centuries.

Map
on page
324

Stretching southwest is the **Serra da Estréla**, the highest mountains in the country and the source of Portugal's most highly-rated cheese. The highest point is the over-commercialised **Torre ❹**, at nearly 2,000 metres (6,500 ft). Nearby is a pilgrimage site, a statue of the Virgin carved into the rock, to which the faithful journey on the second Sunday of August.

The Serra offers skiing in winter and pleasant walking (or driving) with grand views in all directions. The prime winter resort is **Covilhã ❺**, southeast of Torre. It is too low to receive much snow itself, but it is a short drive to the ski area at **Penhas da Saúde ❻**.

Viseu: hub of Beira Alta

The western district of Beira Alta is governed by the city of **Viseu ❼**, about halfway between Guarda and Aveiro. In the 2nd century BC the Romans built a fortified settlement here, and some of their road system can still be seen, along with a number of Latin-inscribed stones.

The information offices for the Parque Natural de Estrela in Guarda and other towns around the park have details of hiking routes with places to stay.

A thorn in the side of the colonisers was a rebel Lusitanian named Viriathus, who harassed Roman legions until he was finally betrayed and killed. A monument to him lies at the edge of a park – the Cova do Viriato – on the site of a Lusitanian and Roman military encampment. Here, you can still see the old earthworks once used by the Romans. Viseu was made a bishopric during the 6th century AD, the time of the Suevian-Visigothic kingdom, and a record still exists: a signature of the Bishop of Viseu, dated AD 569.

The city suffered alternating invasions of Moors and Christians from the 8th to the 11th century. Fernando the Great of Castile and León captured it for the Christians in 1057. Teresa, mother of the first king of Portugal, granted the city its first charter in 1123. From the 14th to the 16th century, building in Viseu seems to have been concentrated in the upper part of town. About this time an active Jewish colony evolved here. In 1411 the Infante Dom Henrique (Prince Henry the Navigator) became Duke of Viseu, and towards the end of that century the town walls were completed. But the surrounding area was becoming a centre of vigorous agricultural activity, and by the 16th century the walled area was becoming depleted.

BELOW:
a woman with
her faithful friend.

Perhaps this was fortunate, because over the next two centuries much of this space was filled with a lavish assortment of baroque churches, chapels, mansions and fountains. Today the architectural richness lends a dignified air to the enclosed city.

Pure baroque

You should not miss the 13th-century **Sé (Cathedral)**. The ribbed vaulting is beautifully carved to look like knotted cables, and the ceiling of the sacristy is extravagantly painted with animals and plants. The twin-towered **Igreja da Misericórdia** across the square is whitewashed granite and pure baroque. You should also save some time for the **Museu Grão Vasco** (open Tues–Sun; closed 12.30–2pm; entrance charge), in the

old Bishop's Palace in the same square. Many of the works represent the fine school of Portuguese Primitive painting that flourished here in the 16th century, and of which Grão Vasco Fernandes *(see page 125)* was the acknowledged master.

The **Feira de São Mateus**, a fair held annually in August and September, is a major event in Viseu, and St John the Baptist is celebrated on 24 June. A Tuesday market is held all year round, with plenty of fresh produce, cloth, pots and pans, and crafts. Viseu is well-known for its lace, carpets and black pottery.

Around Viseu

Successive members of Portugal's royal family used to visit the spa at São Pedro do Sul, but whether it cured what ailed them is not known.

Northwest of Viseu is the small town of São Pedro do Sul and, some 4 km (2½ miles) southwest, the **Termas de São Pedro do Sul** ❽ – possibly the oldest, the best known and most frequented hot springs in the country. Sinus problems, rheumatism, hangovers or a foul temper – the springs are said to cure all ailments. There are other delightful villages in the area, too. Just south of São Pedro do Sul is **Vouzela** ❾, with a lovely 13th-century church, and close by is the village of **Cambra**, clustered around the remnants of its castle.

South of Viseu, just off the secondary road to Nelas, **Santar** ❿ is a little gem of a place, once known as "the Court of the Beiras". Due south is **Oliveira do Hospital** ⓫, a small town that once belonged to the Hospitallers. As a mark of this, tombs of the Ferreiros in the parish church (the Igreja Matriz) are crowned by a carving of an equestrian knight on the wall above.

To the southwest (continue down the main road in the direction of Coimbra), in the village of **Lourosa** ⓬, is the ancient church of São Pedro. King Ordoño II ordered its construction in 911; it has a central nave, horseshoe arches, Moorish windows and Visigothic decoration.

BELOW: a wall of *azulejos* in Viseu.

Beira Baixa

Travelling south now toward the Beira Baixa, you come to the Rio Zêzere, which roughly divides Beira Alta from Beira Baixa. The river flows most swiftly from early April to late June. A good place for water sports is the **Barragem de Castelo do Bode**, a long, many-armed lake that runs south into the province of Ribatejo. (The most direct route is to take the IC3/N110, then turn left about 8 km/5 miles south of Tomar.) Both the river and the lake have fine fishing, with canoeing in places.

The Rio Tejo marks the southern limit of Beira Baixa. Upstream the Tejo crosses into Spain. On both sides of the border is desolate scrub country. The gorge formed by the river is steep-sided and virtually inaccessible for vehicles other than four-wheel-drives. Along much of the Portuguese side of the river runs an ancient Roman road. Originally it was the route from Vila Velha de Rodão to the Spanish town of Santiago de Alcántara. Water now conceals large chunks of the work, but where the road rises above the surface, you will see that instead of building the road with flat stones, the entire way is paved with local slate stood on edge, its upper surfaces rutted by centuries of cart traffic.

Castelo Branco: ancient capital

The capital of Beira Baixa is **Castelo Branco** ⓲ (32,000 inhabitants), which stands at the junction of the IP2/E802 and the N112. It is an ancient city whose origins, like those of so many communities in Portugal, are lost in time. Its "modern" history dates back to 1182, when it and the surrounding area were given as a gift to the Knights Templar by Dom Fernão Sanches. It received a charter in 1213 and became a city in 1771, in the reign of José I.

The battlements of the Templar castle – the "white castle" which gave the city its name – provide a fine view, though the castle itself is not noteworthy. The old town is delightful, with narrow winding streets. Points of interest include two churches, São Miguel and Misericórdia Velha, the latter a 16th-century structure with a notable doorway; and the **Praça Velha**, also known as the Praça de Camões – a fine medieval square near the ancient municipal library.

The most important thing to see in Castelo Branco is the splendid **Palácio Episcopal**, built on the orders of the Bishop of Guarda, in 1596. It served as the winter residence of the bishops of the diocese. It now houses the **Museu Francisco Tavares Proença Júnior** (open Tues–Sun; closed 12.30–2pm; entrance charge), which displays archaeological and regional items, but is most interesting for its large collection of *colchas*, the beautiful hand-embroidered bedspreads for which the town is famous; you can see women at work in the museum's Embroidery School.

In 1725, Bishop João de Mendonça commissioned a garden to be laid out at the side of the palace. Athough it is not very large – you can walk around it in a matter of minutes – it is considered one of Portugal's finest formal gardens, and it is an extraordinary sight, with a multitude of statues, fountains and pools. These statues are all named, and have been placed in homage to just about everybody and everything the

Map on page 324

BELOW: there are numerous pretty villages in the region, including Monsanto.

bishops thought important: the kings of Portugal, of course (the two hated Spanish rulers of Portugal, Felipe I and II, are represented, but by smaller figures); the saints, apostles and evangelists, along with the virtues; and the seasons of the year, the signs of the zodiac and the elements of the firmament. There once were even more statues, but the invading French armies of 1807 carted off the best. The plinths have been left standing in their places, in many cases with the name of the missing item clearly engraved.

If you have been impressed by the bedspreads you saw in the museum, you might be inspired to buy a modern version to take home with you. Since the 17th century it has been the custom for brides-to-be to hand-embroider their wedding bedspreads. From this practice and skill, a cottage industry was born. Traditionally the spreads were white, but in recent years, they have become available in interwoven colours. Earlier patterns were geometric, echoing Persian carpets, but other decorative themes have become popular as well.

Monsanto: the typical village

From Castelo Branco it is easy to get to **Idanha-a-Velha** ⑭, northeast of the city. This was an episcopal see until 1199, when the see was moved to Guarda. There remains a strange, ancient basilica with dozens of Roman inscriptions inside. It is said that Wamba, the king of the Visigoths, was born here. A Roman bridge in the village is still in use, and various coins, pottery and bones have been found.

BELOW: the garden of Castelo Branco's Palácio Episcopal.

Nearby is the granite village of **Monsanto** ⑮, once declared "the most typical Portuguese village", with many of its houses tucked between giant boulders. Built around and atop a steep rocky mass in a broad valley some 50 km (30 miles)

northeast of Castelo Branco, Monsanto is located in the middle of a major invasion route. Its intriguing castle commands a superlative view in every direction. It is thought that this *monte* has been fortified since neolithic times, and the castle is so well integrated into the natural rock it looks as if it grew here.

Some say it was during the Roman invasion in the 2nd century BC, others claim it was some 1,400 years later during a Moorish invasion, that the people of Monsanto, under a long siege and nearly out of food, fooled their attackers by killing a calf, filling its belly with rice, and hurling it off the ramparts to the soldiers below. The attackers were so impressed with the evidence of ample supplies that they packed up and left. Today one of the biggest feast days is on 3 May, when young villagers toss down pitchers filled with flowers from the battlements, symbolically re-enacting the event.

Much of the castle was destroyed at the beginning of the 19th century. One Christmas Eve there was a tremendous thunderstorm, and a bolt of lightning hit the gunpowder magazine. The gunpowder exploded, and the irons flew from the hearth and struck dead the governor, an unpopular figure who that year had forbidden the traditional burning of a tree trunk in front of the parish church. Divine retribution, the people of the village believed.

The folk music of the Monsanto area is charming if strange. Half chanted, half sung, there is nothing quite like it elsewhere in the country. Its rhythm is beaten out with the assistance of a square tambourine known as an *adufe*.

The great Idanha plain stretches south from here, beyond Castelo Branco, where there are large areas of pine and eucalyptus. It's a vast area of cattle-raising country: bitterly cold in winter, scorching hot in the summer months, it is not a region that is much visited by tourists. ❑

Map on page 324

The Termes de Monfortinho, 20 km (12 miles) east of Monsanto, were visited almost exclusively by Spaniards until a road was built in the 1930s.

BELOW: ruins of the fortifications at Monsanto.

MADEIRA

Map on page 334

The archipelago has an individuality that marks it off from the rest of Portugal. Its beauty is varied, from the flowery elegance of Funchal to the remote inland craters

The discovery of the Madeiran archipelago, 608 km (378 miles) west of Morocco, was an early triumph for the ambitious seafaring inspired by Prince Henry the Navigator. In 1418, while sailing south to explore the West African coast, the caravels of João Gonçalves Zarco and Tristão Vaz Teixeira found shelter on a low-lying island they called, in gratitude, Porto Santo (Holy Port). Two years later they returned, to discover a large mountainous island 37 km (23 miles) to the southwest which they named Ilha da Madeira – the Island of Wood. Madeira Island and Porto Santo remain the only two inhabited islands in the archipelago.

Modern explorers will find Madeira is still a wild and idyllic place to visit. Its great forests may have gone – burnt down by the first settlers with fires that got out of control and are said to have raged for years – but man has contributed his own wonders to an Atlantic island whose natural splendour has earned it such titles as "God's Botanical Gardens" and "The Floating Flower-pot".

PRECEDING PAGES: fertile islands in the Atlantic.
LEFT: seafront at Funchal, with Reid's Palace Hotel at the far end.
BELOW: face beaten by the Atlantic sun.

The city of Funchal

A statue of Zarco now stands as a central landmark in **Funchal ❶**, the capital of Madeira and home to a third of the 280,000 islanders. The city squats in the centre of a wide bay on the sunnier south side of the island, its name inspired by the wild fennel *(funcho)* that the discoverers found growing on the surrounding plain. Behind it rises an amphitheatre of terraced hills and mountains that provide shelter from the northeasterly winds that frequently blow over the island – rain, storms and consolatory rainbows are the price you pay for Madeira's splendid verdancy.

For many, Madeira is a winter destination and New Year's Eve is the best time to appreciate Funchal's panoramic setting. The climax in a busy calendar of island festivities, the bay is crowded with brightly-illuminated cruise liners and pleasure boats, and the city is adorned with Christmas decorations and a haze of 300,000 coloured lights. At midnight Funchal erupts – as if sending some hedonistic signal to outer space – in a cacophony of fog-horns, sirens, fireworks and flashing lights. Up on hotel rooftops sunseeking Finns embrace overwintering English aristocrats, while in the streets below families celebrate the annual return of the emigrants from Venezuela or South Africa with dancing, wine and specially-made editions of the islanders' rich molasses-based cake, *bolo de mel*.

If you can't get to this party, there are plenty of other memorable ways to appreciate the island capital. Cruise ship passengers and tourists with limited time usually settle for the two essential Madeiran experiences, the Monte toboggan ride and tea at Reid's

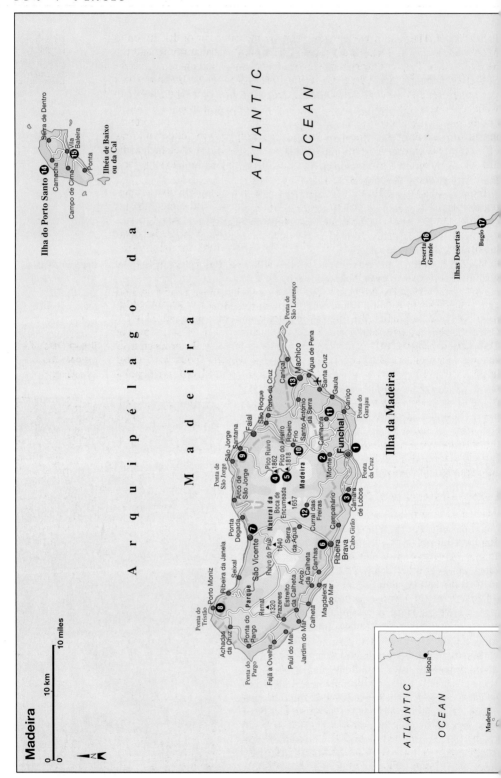

Madeira

10 km
10 miles

N

ATLANTIC OCEAN

Arquipélago da Madeira

Ilha do Porto Santo **14**

Serra de Dentro
Camacha
Campo de Cima
Vila
15 Baleira
Ponta
Ilhéu de Baixo
ou da Cal

Ilha da Madeira

ATLANTIC OCEAN

Ponta de São Lourenço
Caniçal
Porto da Cruz
São Roque
Faial **13** Machico
Santana
9 São Jorge
Ponta de São Jorge
Arco de São Jorge
Pico Ruivo ▲1862
4 Pico do Arieiro
5 ▲1818 Ribeiro
Frio
Boca de Encumeada
1657
12 Curral das Freiras
Santo António da Serra
Água de Pena
★ Santa Cruz
Gaula
Caniço
Ponta do Garajau
Ponta da Cruz
Câmara de Lobos
Madeira
Camacha **11**
Monte
Santo António **10**
Funchal **1**
2
3
Cabo Girão
Campanário
Ribeira Brava
6
Serra da Água
▲1640
Rio do Paúl
Parque Natural da Madeira
7
Ponta Degada
Seixal
Ribeira da Janela
Porto Moniz **8**
Ponta do Tristão
Achadas da Cruz
Ponta do Pargo
Fajã a Ovelha
Paúl do Mar
Jardim do Mar
Arco da Calheta
Calheta
Magdalena do Mar
Estreito da Calheta
Prazeres
Remat
▲1320
São Vicente

Deserta Grande **16**
Ilhas Desertas
Bugio **17**

ATLANTIC OCEAN

Lisboa

Madeira

Map on page 334

Palace Hotel. The first of these involves taking the cable car or driving up to **Monte ②**, a cool and leafy hilltop resort with *quintas*, sanatoriums and the **Monte Palace Tropical Gardens**. The nearby twin-towered church of Nossa Senhora de Monte contains the tomb of Emperor Charles I of Austria. From here you can descend to Funchal by *carro de cesto*, a kind of wicker sofa attached to wooden runners that is guided 2 km (1½ miles) down the steep lanes by a pair of drivers wearing boaters and white flannels. This unique form of transport was invented by an English resident looking for a speedy way to get down to his office from his *quinta* (don't ask if he had been at the Madeira when he had the idea); it's similar to the toboggan runs once used around the island to slide farm produce grown on the terraces to the harbours below.

Tea at **Reid's Palace Hotel** is far less strenuous, and simply involves climbing into a wicker armchair, ordering a pot of Earl Grey tea and some crustless cucumber sandwiches, then falling asleep with a copy of yesterday's *Times* over your face. A world-famous five-star hotel with a prestigious site overlooking Funchal harbour, Reid's was opened in 1891 to cater for the growing number of well-to-do visitors to the island – particularly the British who liked to stop over en route to and from their colonies.

Their presence on the island has proved influential in many ways – besides endorsing Madeira's reputation as a refined holiday destination acclaimed for its civility and hospitality, the English taste for cane furniture, acquired in the Orient, stimulated the island's wicker industry centred on the eastern town of Camacha *(see page 339)*. Another important cottage industry, the production of an intricate and understandably expensive kind of embroidery *(bordados)*, is also indebted to an Englishwoman, Elizabeth Phelps, who introduced it to supplement local incomes after disease devastated the island's vines, with disastrous effects on the islanders' living standards, in the 1850s. Rua dos Murcas is the best place to buy, and you can see more examples in the **Instituto do Bordado, Tapeçeria e Artesano** in Rua do Anadia 44 (open Mon–Fri; closed 12.30–2.30pm; entrance charge).

Lomquats and scabbard fish

Funchal's true pleasures are woven into the everyday life of the city. A visit to its cornucopious **Mercado dos Lavradores** (Workers' Market) costs nothing – unless, of course, you are tempted to buy some lomquats, tomarillos, pittangas or any of the many other exotic fruits and vegetables grown on the island.

Venture into the Mercado's inner halls and you can gaze in safety upon the gloriously ugly *espada* (scabbard fish) that frequently features on Madeiran menus (not to be confused with the equally common traditional dish called *espetada* – beef cooked on a skewer over a wood fire scented with laurel twigs). Despite its vicious teeth and eel-like appearance, *espada* tastes good and is something of a rarity as it is only caught here and off the coast of Japan. The most important catch in the archipelago, the fish lives at a depth of up to 760 metres (2,500 ft) and is hunted year-round by fishermen from **Câmara de Lobos ③**, just west of Funchal. They use lines with baited hooks

BELOW: Funchal's Mercado dos Lavradores.

You'll find flowers for sale in many corners of Funchal.

and flies spaced at regular intervals that can be over 1.6 km (1 mile) in length.

For a rewarding insight into Madeira's past, there are two places which are worth a visit: one is the **Museu de Fotografia Vicentes** in Rua da Carreira (open Mon–Fri 10am–5pm; entrance charge), which houses a collection of old photographs of life on the island as recorded since 1865 by the Vicente family. The second is the **Quinta das Cruzes** (Calada do Pico 1), the former residence of João Gonçalves Zarco, who discovered Madeira and became its first governor, and is now packed with art treasures. The *quinta's* attractive gardens stay open throughout the lunch break and are one of several exotic oases around the city, which include the **Boa Vista Orchids** and, the largest, **Jardim Botânico** (Botanical Gardens), on Caminho do Meio. Two other museums worth mentioning are **A Cidade do Açúcar** ("Sugar City") in Casa do Columbus, Praça Columbus, which shows Funchal in the 15th–16th centuries, and the **Municipal do Funchal (História Natural) e Aquário** at Rua Mouraria 31, in a beautiful 17th-century palace, which explains the fauna and flora of the island.

Most of Madeira's hotels are located on the west side of the capital – only a short bus or taxi ride away from Funchal's main square, **Praça do Município.** Decorously paved with black and white stones, this is bordered by imposing buildings with whitewashed façades and dark basalt outlines that remind visitors how church and state have lorded it over this Portuguese outpost. A Jesuit church and college, founded in 1569, fills its north side, while the 18th-century **Câmara Municipal** (Town Hall) to the east was once the palace of the Conde de Carvalhal. The Count's country residence was at **Quinta do Palheiro Ferreiro**, 8 km (5 miles) east of Funchal, which is now a 320-hectare (800-acre) estate owned by the Blandy family, with magnificent gardens open to the public.

BELOW: have some Madeira, "m'dear".

On the south side of Praça do Município, the former Bishop's Palace houses Madeira's principal art museum, the **Museu de Arte Sacra** (Museum of Sacred Art). Among its exhibits is a fine collection of 15th- and 16th-century Flemish paintings acquired during the island's profitable trade in sugar with Flanders. "White gold" was the spur that provoked Madeira's rapid colonisation – by the 1450s merchants from Lisbon had established lucrative plantations on the island, worked by slaves brought over from Africa and the nearby Canary Islands, 416 km (258 miles) to the south. By the 17th century, most of Madeira's terraces had been given over to producing its eponymous fortified wine, originally derived from Cretan vines introduced to the island by Henry the Navigator. Among these was the sweet *malvoisie* grape, which gave rise to the malvasia or malmsey wines that so besotted Europe in the 16th century. In Shakespeare's *Henry IV*, Falstaff is accused of selling his soul for "a cup of Madeira and a cold capon's leg".

Map on page 334

Wine routes

Madeira's fortunes have long been entwined with those of its famous sherry-like drink, and the names of English, Scottish and Irish immigrant families such as Leacock, Cossart, Gordon and Blandy have become synonymous with its history. In the 18th century it was discovered that long sea voyages through the heat of the tropics, far from spoiling the wine, improved its quality. This lengthy process of maturation has now been replaced by the *estufagem* system, where young wine is stored in hot-houses *(estufas)* for several months. Four main types of Madeira are produced today: a dry *Sercial* and medium-dry *Verdelho*, both ideal as aperitifs, and the richer *Bual* and dark, sweet *Malmsey*, both often served with desserts. Madeira wine travels well and keeps well, and few visitors leave for home

BELOW: into the mountains.

without a bottle or two. Funchal has many invitingly fusty wine lodges and tasting bars where you can indulge in some serious research. **D'Oliveiras** and **Henriques & Henriques**, both in Rua dos Ferreiros, are two worth seeking out, though the best initiation into the history and production of Madeira wine is provided by the Madeira Wine Company in the **Adegas de São Francisco**, Avenida Arriaga 28 (open Mon–Sat, guided visits at 10.30am and 3.30pm, Sat 11am; entrance charge).

Take any road out of Funchal, and the arduous work required to produce the island's wines, fruit and other crops soon becomes apparent. The true heroes of Madeiran history are its farm labourers and their enslaved predecessors, who over the centuries have toiled to win cultivable land from the island's steep and irregular terrain. Unaided by beasts of burden, who cannot keep a steady foothold on the sheer cliffs and valley walls, workers have resolutely sculpted the island with staircases of tiny stone-walled fields – sometimes built by suspending men on ropes from above, with baskets of soil carried up from the river beds far below. These *poios*, or terraces, are fed by a phenomenal network of irrigation channels, known as *levadas*, that today run for thousands of kilometres (*see left*), including 40 km (25 miles) through tunnels.

The maintenance paths running along-side the irrigation channels, or levadas, *that water the terraces provide 3,200 km (2,000 miles) of long, level walks into the silent heart of Madeira, with the stream of water serving as a faithful companion.*

Peaks, cliffs and villages

Even without the terracing that has transformed the island's landscape into a precipitous work of art, Madeira would be staggeringly attractive. A range of volcanic mountains runs east–west across the island, rising to a central conference of peaks of which the highest is **Pico Ruivo ❹** at 1,800 metres (6,000 ft). The nearby summit of **Pico do Arieiro ❺**, which can be comfortably reached by

BELOW:
traditional lifestyles prevail in Santana.

car, provides a physical and spiritual high point. From here, providing you have prayed away the clouds, you can follow an exhilarating on-top-of-the-world path across the peaks to **Achada do Teixeira**.

From all sides of these central mountains, deep ravines run seawards to boulder-strewn beaches where small villages have grown up – most spectacularly at **Ribeira Brava ⑥** and **São Vicente ⑦**, directly opposite each other on the south and north coasts respectively. The ridges above them invariably culminate in sheer cliffs that are among the highest in the world. If you have the head for it, a viewing platform at **Cabo Girão** enables visitors to contemplate a vertical drop of 580 metres (1,900 ft).

Along Madeira's wild north coast, narrow roads have been stitched into the cliffsides, threading through tunnels, round hairpin bends and under waterfalls that provide a free and unexpected car wash. **Porto Moniz ⑧**, a weatherbeaten town on the island's northwestern tip with several small hotels, fish restaurants and volcanic rock sea pools, provides a welcome goal for adventurous motorists searching for the raw side of Madeira.

Other popular points of call are the village of **Santana ⑨**, on the northern coast, where the islanders' traditional A-shaped thatched cottages have been colourfully restored; the forest resort of **Ribeiro Frio ⑩** on a winding road which traverses the island between Funchal and Santana; and, closer to the capital, the wicker-making centre of **Camacha ⑪** towards the east of the island.

For all this natural drama, Madeira is a fundamentally benign and relaxing island. Blessed with fertile soil, abundant water and an equable subtropical climate, the countryside is graced with a profusion of native plants and flowers that have been supplemented by exotic imports. The island is a heaven for walkers and the botanically-inclined, with the mountain pass at **Boca da Encumeada** and the **Parque das Queimadas** popular starting points for hikers.

Two-thirds of the island is a protected area, and the **Laurisilva forset**, which occupies one-fifth of the land between 330 metres (1,000 ft) and 1,300 metres (4,250 ft), is a UNESCO World Heritage Site.

Off the beaten track

Like all good islands, Madeira has plenty of secrets. An easy and worthwhile trip from Funchal is up to **Curral das Freiras ⑫** (Corral of the Nuns), a secluded crater-like valley that until the late 1950s could only be reached by the narrow mountain paths that still snake down its sides. It gets its name from the nuns of Funchal's Santa Clara convent, who fled here in 1566 when French pirates sacked the capital. Another pleasant surprise lies to the west of Ribeira Brava – a plateau of austere and often misty moorland known as the **Paúl da Serra**, where a tiny white statue, Nossa Senhora da Serra, supervises the grazing sheep and cows.

The east side of Madeira is less mountainous and is consequently the most developed part of the island. Here you can find the airport, two golf courses, stretches of intensive farmland and **Machico ⑬**, which can claim to be Madeira's second city even though it only has 13,000 inhabitants, one high-rise hotel and a seafront commandeered by a sandy football pitch.

Basket-making is a traditional industry in Camacha.

BELOW: a classic A-shaped cottage in Santana.

Map on page 334

Map
on page
334

São Lourenco
fortress in Funchal.

RIGHT: a willow-
worker in Curral
das Freiras.
BELOW: splashes of
vivid bougainvillea.

In the northeastern corner of the island the mood changes again as the land narrows to a low-lying, sandy peninsula called **Ponta de São Lourenço**, reached through a tunnel to the north of Machico. Here Caniçal was, until 1981, the island's principal whaling station.

Continue to the end of the headland, which offers good views and blustery walks, and you will often meet old men selling souvenirs carved from redundant stocks of whalebone.

Porto Santo and other islands

The arid landscape of Ponta de São Lourenço provides a foretaste of that found on Madeira's neighbouring island, **Porto Santo** ⓮. The sleepy world of Porto Santo is a relatively accessible one, connected daily by ferry (two hours) and aeroplane. The island is a complete contrast to Madeira: while the former has a surplus of mountains, water and vegetation but no beaches to speak of, Porto Santo has just a few parched volcanic hills and a south coast that is one long, 7-km (4½-mile) stretch of unspoilt sand. It is as if God was planning to add beaches to Madeira but, like a builder who leaves a pile of sand outside your front door then disappears, He somehow forgot.

This divine oversight is a blessing both for beach-lovers and for connoisseurs of small-island life, as well as wind-surfers who hold competitions here. Plagued by rabbits and erosion, and vulnerable to attack by pirates, Porto Santo has always been ignored in favour of its lush and fertile neighbour, but it is nevertheless well worth a visit. The capital, **Vila Baleira** ⓯, makes a virtue out of such inertia, and has only recently made efforts to cash in on its most famous resident, Christopher Columbus. The explorer was among the many sugar buyers who came to the islands in the 1470s, and later married the daughter of Porto Santo's first governor, Bartolomeu Perestrello.

During the summer, holidaymakers from Funchal and mainland Portugal flock to Porto Santo, giving it the semblance of a seaside resort. But even at the height of the season there is space enough to wander along its magnificent beach.

Porto Santo is linked underwater to another separate group of islands, the barren **Ilhas Desertas**. Only 16 km (10 miles) southeast of Madeira, they rise as high as 480 metres (1,570 ft) and can easily be seen from the main island's southern shores. Despite repeated attempts over the centuries, settlement of the two islands – **Deserta Grande** ⓰ and **Bugio** ⓱ – has proved impossible. They are now a nature reserve where seabirds, wild goats, poisonous black spiders and a colony of monk seals live in curious harmony. The Ilhas Desertas can sometimes be visited by boat trips from Funchal, and if you are interested in wildlife and wilderness regions it is worth enquiring at the tourist office.

Another set of islands also belong to the Madeiran archipelago and are even more inhospitable than the Ilhas Desertas. Known as the **Ilhas Selvagens**, these lie 215 km (135 miles) to the south of Madeira. Despite being closer to the Spanish Canaries, they remain under Portuguese jurisdiction.

THE AZORES

*Time seems to have stood still in the beautiful Azores islands.
Way out in the Atlantic Ocean, they have a character of their own,
yet are redolent of Portugal's maritime history*

Map
on page
346

The nine islands of the Azores floating in the Atlantic ocean are gratifyingly rich in romantic history, cryptic legend and stunning natural beauty. You cannot ignore their volcanic origins – deep craters or *caldeiras* are their most outstanding feature. But greenery and trim, patchwork fields impose order and a surprising gentleness. With their tall cliffs and farm-quilted countryside, their tiny homesteads sprinkling the lush landscape, the islands are a magical presence in a volatile ocean.

To Portuguese explorers, who first mapped them in the 15th century, the Azores (Açores in Portuguese) became vital stepping stones in an expanding empire. Christopher Columbus, returning from his momentous 1492 voyage to the New World, took on water at the eastern island of Santa Maria. For centuries the Azores have offered a safe haven and restful stopover to other mariners. This remote island group has an extra dimension if you share the view that the 650-km (400-mile) long archipelago's two tiny, westernmost islands, Flores and Corvo, more than a third of the way across the Atlantic, mark the true outermost limit of Europe. The Azores' capital, Ponta Delgada, is on São Miguel, the largest island in the group. The islands are meteorologically important to weather forecasters – an Azores High (high-pressure area) extending to the east means fine weather for western Europe.

Origins

The name Açores was bestowed on the archipelago by Gonçalo Velho Cabral who, with Diogo de Silves, landed at Santa Maria in 1427. These daring seafarers mistook the many buzzards there for hawks, which are called *açores* in Portuguese. But from myth, fable and fanciful charts, another legend persists. Here, some believe, is the lost Atlantis, from Plato's account of a sunken empire lying beyond the Pillars of Hercules. Yet chroniclers wrote that all the islands were uninhabited when the Portuguese arrived.

In 1439, settlement officially began on the seven then-known islands (Flores and Corvo were not discovered until 1452), through the efforts of Prince Henry the Navigator. His colonisation policy was so zealous that he offered land to Flemish farmers (the connection was through his sister, Isabel, who was married to the Duke of Burgundy and ruler of Flanders). Prince Henry not only foresaw the role of the islands in his larger purpose of African discovery but, in his businesslike way, realised they could be productive and profitable, and organised the planting of wheat and sugar cane.

Throughout Portuguese history, the islanders have held themselves apart from Lisbon, and have often chosen an opposing path. In the 19th-century War of

PRECEDING PAGES:
fishing boats and
houses on São
Miguel, the largest
island.
LEFT: patchwork
fields on the coast.
BELOW: a windmill
on Faial.

the Two Brothers – the Miguelist Wars – between two sons of King João VI, islanders supported the liberal Dom Pedro IV against his absolutist brother, Dom Miguel, who had the support of most of Portugal.

Hardy islanders today still live by farming and fishing. There's a significant dairy industry. You'll see cows milked on steep hillsides, their milk occasionally still carried in churns by farmers on horseback. But there are more cerebral pursuits, too, and from the Azores have emerged many of the finest poets, novelists and philosophers in Portuguese culture. One of several daily newspapers, *O Açoriano* is the third oldest in Europe. The islands' identity was established long ago; autonomous government came in 1976, two years after the coup which toppled Salazar's dictatorship *(see page 61)*.

Island attractions

In recent years, the Azores have become a modestly expanding tourist destination. Great for walking holidays, they are full of pleasant surprises, and invite the visitor to explore. In other words, a dream world for anyone seeking unspoilt nature, tranquillity and the chance to "get back to basics". What they are not, though, are bland resorts for sophisticates or sun-worshippers. There are relatively few sandy beaches, and these are mostly volcanic black – which some find oppressive. The weather is mild (the winter averages 14°C/57°F, summer 23°C/74°F) but except for June to September, it is often wet and windy.

Island pleasures are unpretentious and relaxed. You will discover awe-inspiring scenery of stunning beauty, a luxurious vegetation with exotic plants (50 of 850 species are endemic), enchanting lakes amidst extinct craters, tranquil hill country with rolling fields and lush meadows, magnificent coasts lined by

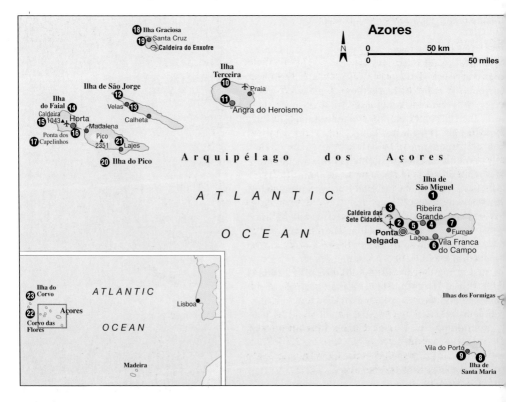

picturesque villages and historical towns, and spectacular hydrangea hedges criss-crossing the landscape. There is also much to see in the daily working life, which still has a rather traditional aspect. Entertainment is generally limited to discos and bars. Custom and religion are served by frequent *festas*, and the striking baroque churches carved from basalt.

On the island of Terceira, gaudy chapels *(impérios)* reflect the islanders' ardour for the Espírito Santo cult, which originated in medieval Germany and was promulgated in Portugal through the teachings of the 17th-century Jesuit priest, António Vieira. On Whit Sunday, the day of the Holy Spirit, there are processions in towns and villages throughout the island, and many villages have regular Sunday celebrations. Local people believe that worship of the Holy Spirit – whose insignia, a crown, sceptre and a white dove are kept in the *impérios* – will protect their communities from volcanic eruptions, earthquakes, and damage from storms.

You can see the relics of a long tradition of whaling, and will encounter the sons and grandsons of whaling men – and, in summer, numerous emigrant families on annual trips home. The Azores are worth a visit even if you only have time to see São Miguel. The Government Tourist Office *(Turismo)* is very friendly and helpful, and the Portuguese Tourist Board in London will provide plenty of information *(see page 356)*.

The islands are ideal for walking. The more ambitious can climb Pico (Peak) on Pico island: at over 2,300 metres (7,550 ft), this is Portugal's highest mountain, but there are numerous less demanding hikes. Additionally, an expanding number of sports facilities range from deep-sea fishing, whale-watching and diving to golf and tennis.

The islands divide naturally into three groups: São Miguel and Santa Maria in the east; Terceira, São Jorge, Graciosa, Faial and Pico in the centre; and Flores and Corvo to the west.

São Miguel

São Miguel ❶ is perhaps the most varied of the islands. It is also the largest, measuring 65 km by 16 km (40 miles by 10 miles), and the most populated, with nearly half the archipelago's population of 250,000.

On the south coast, the capital of **Ponta Delgada ❷** sprawls behind the waterfront – the Avenida Infante Dom Henrique – with its arcades and 18th-century city gates. The town is dramatically set off against numerous small volcanic cones rising on the distant hills. City sights include several fine baroque churches, among them the 16th-century parish church, Igreja Matriz de São Sebastião. Also of architectural interest are the Palácio da Conceição which houses the government; and the curious baroque Casa de Carlos Bicudo with its mermaid façade.

For a view that overlooks the city, head for the **Reduto da Mãe de Deus**, where in 1944 an ill-informed anti-aircraft battery shot at an aircraft carrying General Eisenhower on his way home. There's a good museum, the **Museu Carlos Machado** (open Tues–Fri, Sat and Sun pm; closed 12.30–2pm; entrance charge), installed in the Convento de Santo André, with exhibits on the island's natural history and ethnography.

Map on page 346

TIP

The main tourist office in the Azores is on Avenida Infante Dom Henrique, in Ponta Delgada, São Miguel island, tel: 296 285 743.

BELOW: a market vendor in Ponta Delgada.

In the west of the island are the enchanting twin lakes within the **Caldeira das Sete Cidades ❸**. This "Cauldron of the Seven Cities" is best viewed from Vista do Rei (The King's View), but you will be able to spot only one sleepy village in the crater. In sunlight, one lake is blue, the other green – stemming, legend has it, from the tears of a princess forced to part from her shepherd lover. A half-day circuit of the island might take you past pineapple plantations (visitors welcome) just north of the capital, on to Sete Cidades and the promontory of **Ponta dos Mosteiros**, eastwards to Capelas and its tobacco fields, and finally to the historical town of **Ribeira Grande ❹**. Further east are the Caldeiras da Ribeira Grande, a small spa in picturesque surroundings, and the tea plantations of Gorreana (open to the public).

Eastwards from Ponta Delgada, past sandy beaches, are the potteries of **Lagoa ❺** and the underwater diving centre at Caloura, and, beyond, the attractive town of **Vila Franca do Campo ❻** with three ornate baroque churches. The municipal museum has a good collection of musical instruments and pottery. Above Vila Franca, the pilgrimage chapel of **Senhora da Paz** affords a splendid view over the south coast. Just offshore, accessible from the pretty harbour, is the tiny crater island of **Ilheu**, with a natural seawater swimming pool.

Northeast and inland, past the crater lake of Lagoa das Furnas, is the village of **Furnas ❼**, with hot springs and boiling mud cauldrons that give off the rich stink of sulphur. But here, too, is a famous botanical park, a volcanically heated lake you can swim in, and a pleasant hotel and restaurant, the **Terra Nostra**. The dish of the house is *cozido à Furnas* – meats and vegetables steamed in underground ovens. For a picnic, you can boil your own eggs in the hot springs beside the crater lake.

BELOW: Ponta Delgada's city gates.

Santa Maria and Terceira

Map on page 346

The island of **Santa Maria** ❽, only 17 km by 9 km (10 miles by 5 miles), has peaceful fields and red-roofed whitewashed houses in a southern Portuguese style (initially settlers came from Algarve and Alentejo). Apart from the underlying volcanic massif, there is also sedimentary rock, and the beaches therefore are a shining gold, in bright contrast to the more usual volcanic black. Santa Maria is the driest, sunniest island, often called the "Algarve of the Azores". Just north of the airport in Anjos is the reconstructed church, where Christopher Columbus once knelt in prayer. The main town is **Vila do Porto** ❾.

In the central group, **Terceira** ❿ (29 km by 17 km/18 miles by 10 miles) derives its name from the fact that it was the third island in the archipelago to be discovered. All the settlements on Terceira stretch along the coastline, while the unpopulated interior of the island – a wild and rugged landscape partly covered with native brushwood of tree heather, juniper and mosses – is often enveloped in clouds.

At Ponta do Raminho on Terceira Island there is an old whalers' lookout post.

Terceira is distinguished by its capital **Angra do Heroismo** ⓫, which is, deservedly, on UNESCO's World Heritage list as it is undoubtedly the most beautiful town in the archipelago. Once the capital of the Azores, it was granted its heroic title by Queen Maria II, the daughter of Dom Pedro IV, whose regency the island stoutly supported. Severely damaged by an earthquake in 1980, Angra is gradually recovering. Its cathedral, several churches, castles and palaces are of considerable interest. A circuit of the island encompasses stunning views of green patchwork fields subdivided by stone walls. Terceira's most boisterous *festas* are around 24 June, the day of São João (St John the Baptist), and include *touradas à corda,* the running of rope-restrained bulls.

BELOW: Furnas, where the ground is hot enough to cook a meal.

From São Jorge to Corvo

Beautiful **São Jorge** 🄬, 56 km (35 miles) long by only 8 km (5 miles) wide, rises abruptly from the sea and culminates in a mountain ridge that is often shrouded in mist. Besides its glorious natural setting, São Jorge affords magnificent views of all the central islands. Almost all the villages are set on small coastal plains *(fajãs)* at the foot of tall cliffs; some hamlets can only be reached via narrow footpaths. **Velas** 🄭, with stunning views across to Pico, is the main town and a good base to explore the island.

Faial 🄮 rises almost symmetrically on all sides to the central **Caldeira** 🄯, an eerie crater with a depth of some 300 metres (1,000 ft). Faial's epithet, "Blue Island", was inspired by its hydrangea hedgerows running like blue ribbons over the countryside – a stunning sight for people used to seeing these bushes only in neat parks and gardens.

The lively capital of **Horta** 🄰 is extremely pleasant, with some interesting museums and churches. Its harbour is a port of call for transatlantic sailors, with each crew commemorating their journey by painting a picture on the *mole* (breakwater). **Ponta dos Capelinhos** 🄱 is a dramatic contrast to the lively town and flowery countryside: here, in 1957–58, an undersea volcanic eruption rumbled and grumbled and left vast, grim dunes of dark cinder.

Graciosa 🄲 is as gracious as its name suggests, with soft sloping hills and peaceful villages scattered over the island. Yet it also has a volcanic heritage: in Caldeira do Enxofre you may descend 182 stone steps to a huge cavern *(furna)* with a sulphurous subterranean lake. In the small, tidy capital of **Santa Cruz** 🄳 it becomes obvious why Graciosa was known as the "White Island": all its houses are traditionally whitewashed.

BELOW:
typical white-
washed houses
on Santa Maria.

The towering peak which gives the island its name is the main reason to visit **Ilha do Pico** ⑳, but a look round the island reveals fertile countryside in the east and bizarre rocky regions (called *mistérios*) in the west which have been flooded by lava comparatively recently. In the sheltered enclosures between dry-stone walls, grapevines are grown to produce the local wines.

In **Lajes** ㉑, a small whaling museum, the **Museu dos Baleeiros** (open Tues–Fri; closed 12.30–2pm, Sat–Sun pm; entrance charge) recalls the all-too-recent past, when men went out hunting the giant creatures: Herman Melville's *Moby Dick* is set in these waters. Rising to over 2,350 metres (7,700 ft), majestic Pico is the highest mountain not only in the Azores but in the whole of Portugal. To climb the main peak (this is best done in summer), you will need proper gear and a reliable route-finder.

Ilha das Flores ㉒ (17 km by 12 km/10 miles by 7 miles) does not abound in flowers, as its names suggests. But it is the most humid island of the Azores, its wet climate accounting for the lush evergreen vegetation. Flores offers some wild landscapes which are quite different from those of the other islands: basalt predominates, in the form of high-lying, boggy plateaux where waterfalls plummet down over steep rock faces.

From Flores, a boat runs daily, weather permitting, to **Ilha do Corvo** ㉓ (*corvo* is "cormorant" in Portuguese), which measures only 6 km by 3 km (4 miles by 2 miles). It is the smallest and quietest island in the archipelago, with its 300 inhabitants all living in **Vila Nova**, which is the only village. Corvo's prime sight is a tranquil lake embedded in an isolated crater, whose swampy islets reputedly resemble a map of the Azores. The voracious birds after which the island was named can still be seen around the shores. ❑

Map on page 346

TIP

Between May and September, daily whale-watching trips are organised by Espaço Talassa in Lajes, on Ilha do Pico (tel: 292 672 010; www.espacotalassa. com).

BELOW: island delivery service.

INSIGHT GUIDES
Travel Tips

✵ INSIGHT GUIDES Phonecard

One global card to keep travellers in touch. Easy. Convenient. Saves you time and money.

It's a global phonecard

Save up to 70%* on international calls from over 55 countries

Free 24 hour global customer service

Recharge your card at any time via customer service or online

It's a message service

Family and friends can send you voice messages for free.

Listen to these messages using the phone* or online

Free email service - you can even listen to your email over the phone*

It's a travel assistance service

24 hour emergency travel assistance – if and when you need it.

Store important travel documents online in your own secure vault

For more information, call rates, and all Access Numbers in over 55 countries, (check your destination is covered) go to **www.insightguides.ekit.com** or call Customer Service.

JOIN now and receive US$ 5 bonus when you join for US$ 20 or more.

Join today at

www.insightguides.ekit.com

When requested use ref code: **INSAD010**

OR SIMPLY FREE CALL 24 HOUR CUSTOMER SERVICE

UK	0800 376 1705
USA	1800 706 1333
Canada	1800 808 5773
Australia	1800 11 44 78
South Africa	0800 997 285

THEN PRESS ⓪

For all other countries please go to "Access Numbers" at **www.insightguides.ekit.com**

* Retrieval rates apply for listening to messages. Savings base on using a hotel or payphone and calling to a landline. Corre at time of printing 01.03

(INS001)

powered by **ekit**

"The easiest way to make calls and receive messages around the world"

CONTENTS

Getting Acquainted

The Place

Area: 92,072 sq km (33,549 sq miles) including Madeira and the Azores.
Capital: Lisbon
Principal rivers: Douro, Guadiana, Lima, Minho, Mondego and Tejo (Tagus).
Population: 10.3 million
Language: Portuguese
Religion: Roman Catholic
Time Zone: GMT (summer time March–October GMT +1); the Azores are 1 hour behind continental Portugal.
Currency: The euro (€)
Weights and measures: metric
Electricity: 220 volts, two pin plug.
International dialling code: outgoing 00; incoming 351

Climate

Spring and summer are definitely the best times of year to visit Portugal. Winter brings a distinct north–south divide in the weather. Southernmost Algarve enjoys mild winters with many fine sunny days. Sheltered, south-facing beaches provide ideal sun traps which allow sun-bathing throughout the year. Evenings might have a chill in the air but the weather is kind enough to attract a significant number of tourists, and Algarve is especially popular for long-stay holidays.

Around Lisbon, winters are mild with an unpredictable mixture of sunny and showery days. The weather is just about good enough on balance to attract some tourism along the Estoril coast.

In the northern and central regions winters are rainy, and while not freezing, are surprisingly chilly.

Spells of fine, clear weather between rainy periods provide excellent walking conditions but there is no reliability. In the mountains it's even colder, and variable snow falls on the Serra da Estrela and mountains to the north and east between November and February (sometimes enough for ski enthusiasts, although conditions are far from ideal). Winters are short, beginning in November or December and ending in February or March, averaging 12°C/53°F.

Generally, the weather starts getting warm in May and June throughout the country, and usually stays warm to very hot until September. Weather patterns are changeable and difficult to predict from year to year: winters can be considerably shorter or longer; the rainy season heavy or light.

Apart from Algarve, nights can be cool even in summer, especially along the Cascais/Estoril coast of Lisbon. Along the western coast, the Atlantic tends to be cool (22°C/72°F) until July. It warms up earlier along the southern coast.

Summers are generally hot throughout the country with endless days of sunshine. The north enjoys the same high temperatures as the rest of the country, although there is always the risk of more rainy days. Some inland areas experience extremely high temperatures – Alentejo in the south and the Upper Douro in the north often top 40°C/104°F for long periods. Algarve is moderately hot in summer (31°C/88°F) enjoying the benefit of cooling westerlies.

Geography

Continental Portugal is roughly rectangular in shape, bordered on the east and north by Spain and the west and south by the Atlantic. It measures about 560 km (360 miles) north–south and 220 km (130 miles) east–west. A 840-km (520-mile) coastline borders the country.

The mountainous northern half of the country is more populated. The intense greens of the northern valleys, with their winding riverbeds

UNESCO Heritage Sites

- Angra do Heroismo (Azores)
- Belém tower and Jerónimos monastery (Lisbon)
- Alcobaça Monastery
- Batalha Monastery
- Convento do Cristo (Tomar)
- Douro Valley (vineyards)
- Évora (historic centre)
- Guimarães (historical centre)
- Laurisilva forest, Madeira
- Porto (historic centre)
- Sintra
- Vila Nova de Foz Côa

and mountain peaks (the highest of which is the Serra da Estrela, at 2,000 metres/6,500 ft), make central and northern Portugal extraordinarily beautiful. But it's a matter of taste: there are those who prefer the great open spaces of the south.

Portugal is divided into eight principal regions: in the north and northwest are the rich wine lands of the Minho and the Douro valley; in the northeast the distant Trás-os-Montes, ("Behind the Mountains"). The Beiras – the litoral, Alta and Baixa ("upper" and "lower") – reach across north-central Portugal. In the middle, Estremadura and the Ribatejo encompass the areas just above Lisbon. In the southern part of the country the dry, flat and under-populated Alentejo (administratively divided into Alto and Baixo) occupies a third of Portugal. The far south, Algarve, is hilly, and has long stretches of beautiful beaches, most of which have been discovered by visitors.

The Azores have a temperate climate and Madeira has subtropical weather throughout the year.

The Government

Portugal is a democratic republic, with an executive president elected for a five-year term. The 230-member assembly is directly elected for four years. Appointed by the president, the prime minister commands a majority in the assembly. A council

Public Holidays

1 January New Year's Day
February Shrove Tuesday
March/April Good Friday
25 April Anniversary of the Revolution (1974)
1 May Labour Day
10 June Portugal and Camões Day
early June Corpus Christi
15 August Day of the Assumption
5 October Republic Day
1 November All Saints' Day
1 December Restoration of Independence
8 December Day of the Immaculate Conception
25 December Christmas Day

Local municipal holidays are as follows:
Aveiro – 12 May
Beja – 8 May
Braga – 24 June
Bragança – 22 August
Castelo Branco – 1 April
Coimbra – 4 July
Évora – 29 June
Faro – 7 September
Guarda – 26 November
Leiria – 22 May
Lisbon – 18 June
Porto – 24 June
Porto Alegre – 23 May
Santarém – 19 March
Setúbal – 15 September
Viana do Castelo – 20 August
Vila Real – 13 June
Viseu – 21 September

of ministers (cabinet) is responsible to the assembly. Portugal has 18 districts and two autonomous regions (the Azores and Madeira).

The Economy

About 15 percent of the labour force works in agriculture, but there is little real investment in farming. Major crops are wheat and maize, along with tomatoes, potatoes, cork and forestry products. Grapes are cultivated for wines – table wine as well as port and Madeira.

Away from the land, the main exports are textiles and clothing. Other products include footwear, processed food and, increasingly, electrical appliances and petro-chemicals.

Tourism and foreign exchange, primarily from Portuguese working abroad, are major foreign-currency earners. Portugal remains among Western Europe's poorer countries, despite significant advances since joining the European Union in 1986.

Etiquette

The Portuguese are usually courteous and hospitable. Taking a short while to learn the language basics, and liberal use of these thereafter, will serve you well. (*Turn to the Language section on pages 379–382 for some useful words and phrases.*)

Here are a few helpful hints:
• If you are invited to someone's house, it is polite to bring flowers for the hostess or a small toy or sweets if there are young children.
• There are always orderly queues at bus stops. Be certain to respect them.
• For some reason, stretching in public (on the street or at the table) is considered rude. Otherwise, use common sense and a smile and you shouldn't go far wrong.

Planning the Trip

Visas & Passports

European Union nationals may enter Portugal with a national identity card. Citizens of Great Britain and Australia need nothing more than a valid passport for a three-month stay. The same applies to Americans and Canadians staying for 60 days or less.

All other non-EU visitors must show a valid passport to enter Portugal. On arrival, your passport will be stamped with a 60-day tourist visa. No one with a tourist visa is permitted to work.

Bureaucracy is a serious problem, so you should apply for an extension at least one week before your time runs out.

Visas or extended stay visas can be obtained at any Portuguese consulate abroad, or contact the Serviço de Estrangeiros (Foreigners' Service) at Rua Conselheiro José Silvestre, 22, Lisbon, tel: 21 711 5000.

The British office which deals with extensions to visas is at 62 Brompton Road, London SW3 1BY, tel: (020) 7581 8722.

Money Matters

Currency

The escudo was superceded by the euro in January 2002. The euro is divided in 100 cêntimos which is the basic unit of currency. The smallest coin is the 1 cêntimo piece; and the largest is the 2 euro coin. Notes go from 5–500 euros. The symbol for the euro is € and is written before the number of euros, e.g. €7.50 is 7 euros 50 cêntimos.

Exchange

While you may want to buy a small amount of euros before you leave home, you'll get a better exchange rate if you wait until you are in Portugal. Once you have bought euros, however, it may be costly to re-exchange them for foreign currency. The best policy is to change money as you require it.

Money is best changed at banks, rather than at hotels or travel agencies. Outside normal banking hours, ATMs (Automatic Teller Machines), usually called *Multibanco*, are widely available and there are currency exchanges at Lisbon's Santa Apolónia railway station as well as at the airports. Major credit cards are acceptable. ATMs taking all the major cards, including debit cards, are widespread throughout the country.

Exchanging money at a bank or cashpoint works out far cheaper than paying the higher rate of commission on travellers' cheques.

Travellers' Cheques and Credit Cards

Travellers' cheques are accepted in all banks, although, as already mentioned, the commission charge is higher than for changing cash. It is best not to use them in stores, where, if they are accepted at all, you can be certain you are being charged at a disadvantageous rate. Major credit cards can be used in most hotels, restaurants and shops, but check in advance to avoid embarrassment. Country restaurants and *pensãos* may only accept cash.

What to Bring

You should bring your own film and photographic equipment, which will almost certainly be cheaper outside Portugal.

Toiletries and personal effects are all available locally, and are often much cheaper than in other countries. Most common methods of contraception are available, but some might be difficult to obtain in remote areas.

Health & Insurance

Portugal enjoys a healthy climate and no vaccinations are necessary. Bring enough prescription medication to last through your stay, if only to avoid confusion with brand names and/or language. Although the Portuguese health service has reciprocal emergency treatment arrangements with other EU countries (take your E111 form, available from main post offices, with you) it is advisable to have additional health insurance as well as insurance against loss, theft, etc.

All narcotics and illegal drugs are banned. Be warned: customs keep a close watch.

Portugese Tourist Offices Abroad

Canada
60 Bloor Street West Suite 1005,
Toronto, Ontario M4W 3B8
Tel: +1-416-921 73 76
Fax: +1-416-921 13 53

Ireland
Portuguese Trade & Tourism Board,
54 Dawson Street, Dublin 2
Tel: +353-1-670 91 33/34
Fax: +353-1-670 91 41

Spain
Paseo de la Castellana 141,
28013 Madrid
Tel: +34-91 761 72 30
Fax: +34-91 570 22 70

United Kingdom
22–25A Sackville Street,
London, W1S 3DW
Tel: 020-7494 5720
Fax: 020-7494 1868

United States
590 Fifth Avenue, 4th Floor,
New York, NY 10036 - 4785
Tel: +1-212-719 39 85
Fax: + 1-212-764 61 37

Useful Websites

www.discover-portugal.co.uk
www.portugal.org
www.portugalinsite.com

Getting There

BY AIR

Scheduled Flights

TAP **Air Portugal** (www.tap.pt) is Portugal's national airline and it has wide international links. Flights, particularly from Paris, can get very heavily booked in the summer (July/August) and around Christmas and Easter.

Many major airlines make non-stop direct flights to Lisbon from capital cities in Europe and other continents. There are several flights a week from New York, and from Boston.

You may also, from some countries, fly directly to Porto in the north, Faro in the south and to Madeira and the Azores. Links with London are particularly good, and the privately owned PGA – **Portugália Airlines** (www.pga.pt) – offers flights from Manchester to Porto and Lisbon with onward flights to Faro. Portugália also has a growing network of routes to regional airports in Spain, France and Germany; their service is of a consistently high standard. Budget airlines also operate between the UK and Lisbon.

Between regular airlines and charter companies the choice is considerable – and ticket prices vary a great deal.

Charter flights

Because Portugal is a popular tourist destination, charter flights from Britain and continental Europe to Lisbon and Faro are frequent in summer, less so in winter. There are similar flights from the United States. Although primarily intended for holidaymakers buying a complete package, including accommodation, spare capacity is sold off as seat only, and often at a discounted rate.

Airports

In Lisbon and Porto the international airports are on the outskirts of the city. Taxis will take you to the city centre. All have meters and lists of charges for out-of-town journeys. In Lisbon, taxis cost around €8 and drivers are entitled to charge an excess for luggage over 30 kg (66 lb). The Aerobus runs from the yellow bus stop outside the airport every 20 minutes and takes about 20 minutes to the centre of town, and can be quicker than a taxi when traffic is heavy. Tickets allow you a free day's travel on the city's transport system. Porto and Faro also have bus services to their city centres and good air links with each other.

Aeroporto de Lisboa,
Tel: 218 413 500
Aeroporto Dr Francisco Sá Carneiro (Porto)
Tel: 229 432 400
Aeroporto de Faro
Tel: 289 800 800
Aeroporto da Santa María (Azores)
Tel: 296 820 020
Aeroporto des Horta (Madeira)
Tel: 292 943 511

BY RAIL

Nowhere in Portugal is yet linked to the superfast TGV system, but there's a busy international (and national) train service run by the national railway company, **CP (Caminhos de Ferro Portugueses)**. A daily train, the Sud-Express, makes the Paris–Lisbon run (around 24 hours; about 2 hours less if you take the TGV to Irun); and the Paris–Porto route (from Paris to the Spanish border it's the same journey as above). The Madrid to Lisbon/Porto service (usually twice a day) is a sleeper and takes around 10 hours.

Rail Information

The main categories of train in Portugal are:
Regional – slow
Inter-Regional – fast
Intercidades – very fast
Alfa – express

For more information on train services, call CP: 808 208 208.

There are also routes from northern Spain (Galicia) or southern Spain (Seville) into Portugal. These last services tend to be slow and time-consuming. Once in Portugal, you have a good, fast north–south route (Porto–Lisbon–Faro) as well as slow, scenic rides, if you care for them, especially in the north.

Special Tickets

A variety of tickets and discount cards are available, including group tickets, Senior Citizens' cards, Inter-rail cards, Rail-Europe Senior tickets, and International Youth tickets. There are also Tourist tickets for periods of 7, 14 and 21 days and a Family card which allows a minimum of three people to travel and is valid for single journeys over 150 km (95 miles).

BY ROAD

By Car

Good roads link Portugal with its Spanish neighbour at numerous border points. Main east–west routes to Lisbon are from Seville via Beja; from Badajoz via Elvas; from Salamanca via Viseu (via the notoriously dangerous IP5 highway).

If driving from England, using the channel ferries, or the *Shuttle* through the Channel Tunnel, allow three days; or, via Plymouth–Santander or Portsmouth–Bilbao, two. There are drivers who boast of doing the journey faster, but don't try it. Road accident figures are appallingly high.

By Bus

From the UK: the National Express bus company runs Eurolines to Lisbon several times a week from London Victoria Coach Station, tel: 020 7730 8235. Although cheap, it may not be as cheap as a charter flight. The journey takes about 36 hours. Tickets tend to be open, so make sure you book a seat for the return journey. In Lisbon you can buy tickets at Inter Centro, Serviço Internacional at the Central Rodoviária, Av. Duque Ávila, Arco Cego.

Practical Tips

Business Hours

Most **stores** open for business Monday–Friday 9am–1pm, and from about 3–7pm. Stores are open on Saturday from 9am–1pm, and are closed Sunday and holidays. Some malls and supermarkets are open on Sundays and all day during the week.

Major **banks** are open Monday–Friday 8.30am–3pm and are closed Saturday, Sunday and holidays.

Museums usually open from 10am–12.30 and 2–5pm, and are closed on Mondays.

Tipping

A tip of 10 percent is sufficient in restaurants and for taxi drivers. Barbers and hairdressers expect to receive the same.

Media

NEWSPAPERS & MAGAZINES

Portugal has many daily newspapers, two of which are dedicated solely to football!

The principal general newspapers are now published in both Lisbon and Porto and tend to have a regional bias, as indicated: *Diário de Notícias* (Lisbon), *Jornal de Notícias* (Porto), *Público* (Lisbon and Porto), and *Diário Económico* (Lisbon and Porto).

Weeklies include the *Expresso* and the *Independente* (both up to *Sunday Times/Observer* standard).

There is a weekly English language newspaper – the *Anglo-Portuguese News*.

TELEVISION

RTP, the state-owned corporation, operates two national television channels (RTP 1 and RTP 2), two regional stations and one international (RTP Madeira, RTP Azores, RTP International). There are also two commercial stations (**Sic** and TVI).

Films are transmitted in the language of origin, with subtitles, as are many serials and documentaries. There is a high content of soap operas (many Brazilian) and quiz shows.

Most hotels have satellite/cable TV, which will include Sky News, Eurosport, CNN and CNBC.

RADIO

There are four national and five regional RDP (state-owned) radio stations as well as more than 300 local radio stations. Among them are Antenna I, which broadcasts popular music and news, and Antenna 2, which is a classical music station. There are also commercial radio stations, TSF and **RR**, which offer a similar mix of news and popular music.

Postal Services

Postal services, both international and domestic, are generally reliable and efficient. Allow five days for delivery within Europe. For next day delivery within Portugal, use Correio Azul, an internal express service.

Post Offices

These open Monday–Friday 9am–6pm; smaller branches close for lunch from 12.30–2.30pm. In district capitals, the main branch is usually open on Saturday morning. Mail is delivered Monday to Friday.

To buy stamps, stand in any queue marked *Selos* (Stamps). To mail or receive packages, you need to go to the queue marked *Encomendas*.

Be certain to write Via Aérea on all airmail items. To send large parcels home, if speed is not important,

consider the less expensive alternative of surface mail.

The Post Office also provides services such as express mail (*Expresso* and *Correio Azul* – see above), postal money orders *(vales)*, general delivery *(poste restante)*, registered mail *(registos)*, insurance on packages *(seguro)*, and telegraph, telephone and fax services.

Communications

All **phones** are equipped for international calls and accept coins, Telecom cards or credit cards, the latter being by far the easiest way to make an international call.

A Telecom phone card can be bought at kiosks and many shops. Instructions for using the phone are written in English and other major languages. You can also make calls (international and local) from post offices. Go to the window for a cabin assignment and pay when the call is finished. **PT Comunicacãos** is the national communication company. In Lisbon they have an office with phone booths and computers for using the **web** at 68 Restauradores, open 8am–11pm. In Porto there is one at 61 Praça da Liberdade.

In Lisbon there is also a phone office in the Rossio railway station, open daily from 9am–11pm; in Porto, there is one in Praça da Liberdade (same hours).

Many village stores and bars in Portugal have metered telephones. Phone first, pay later, but be prepared to pay more than the rate

Useful Numbers

To reach an English-speaking international operator, dial **171**. To call direct to the US or Canada, dial **00 1**, plus the area code and phone number. For the UK, dial **00 44** plus the number (minus the first zero of the code).

Note: Area codes do not exist; callers dial all 9 digits even for local numbers. For enquiries ring **118**.

for call box or post office calls. As elsewhere, calls made from hotels are higher still.

For US phone credit card holders, the major access numbers are:
• AT&T: tel: 800 800 128.
• MCI: tel: 800 800 123.
• Sprint: tel: 800 800 187.

Mobile Phones

Mobile phones with reciprocal GSM network arrangements will function throughout most of the country. Alternatively, the three national cellular networks (Telecel, TSM and Optimus) have short-term rental facilities at the main airports.

Telegrams

You may place telegrams by phone (tel: **1582**) or from a post office, but the rates are high.

Tourist Offices

The national tourist office (ICEP) has offices in Lisbon, Porto and at Faro airports. Most towns have *(turismo)* tourist offices, which are generous with maps and information. Some of the smaller ones close at weekends off season. Regional capitals have separate city and regional offices. Portugal's official website is www.portugalinsite.com.

Aveiro
Rua João Mendonça, 8
Tel: 234 420 760
Fax: 234 428 326
Azores
Rua Ernesto Rebelo, 14
Horta, Faial
Tel: 292 200 500
Fax: 292 200 502
Beja
Rua Capitão João Francisco Sousa, 25
Tel/Fax: 284 311 913
Braga
Avenida da Liberdade, 1
Tel: 253 262 550
Fax: 253 613 387
Bragança
Edificio do Principal, Largo do Principal
Tel: 273 331 078
Fax: 273 331 913

Castelo Branco
Alameda da Liberdade
Tel: 272 330 339
Fax: 272 330 350
Coimbra
Largo da Portagem
Tel: 239 855 930
Fax: 239 825 576
Estoril
Arcadas do Parque
Tel: 214 664 414
Fax: 214 681 697
Évora
Praça do Giraldo 73
Tel: 266 702 601
Fax: 266 730 039
Faro
City
Rua de Misericórdia, 8
Tel: 289 803 604
Algarve region
Avenida 5 de Outubro
Tel: 289 800 400
Fax: 289 800 489
Guimarães
Largo Conego José Maria Gomes
Tel: 253 518 394
Fax: 253 515 123
Lagos
Rua Vasco Da Gama
Tel: 282 763 031
Lisbon
Lisboa Welcome Centre
Praço do Comercio
Tel: 210 312 810
City and national (ICEP)
Palacio Foz
Praça dos Restauradores
Tel: 213 466 307
Fax: 213 468 772
Madeira
Avenida Arriaga, Funchal 18
Tel: 291 211 900
Fax: 291 232 151
Porto
City
Rua Clube Fenianos, 25
Tel: 223 393 472
Fax: 223 393 303
Rua Infante D. Henrique, 63
Tel: 222 009 770
National (ICEP)
Praça D. João 1
Tel: 222 057 514
Fax: 222 053 212
Setúbal
Travessa Frei Gaspar, 10
Tel: 265 539 120
Fax: 265 539 127

Tomar
Rua Serpa Pinto, 1
Tel: 249 329 000
Fax: 249 324 322
Viana do Castelo
Rua do Hospital Velho
Tel: 258 822 620
Fax: 258 827 873

Security and Crime

Portugal has a well deserved reputation for non-violence. It remains one of the few developed countries where you can both feel and be safe when walking almost anywhere at any time of day or night. This is changing in one or two of the larger cities, though, and petty theft is becoming a problem in some of the more run-down areas of Lisbon and Porto, and close to some of the larger shopping centres. Foreign registered cars or cars obviously rented may be targets for thieves if left unattended in out of the way locations.

However, with common sense and the usual degree of attention you should be able to take a fairly relaxed attitude towards security.

Stolen property

In the event of theft, report it to the police within 24 hours to reclaim insurance. In Lisbon the main Policia de Segurança Pública (PSP) station dealing with foreigners who have been robbed is at the Palacio Foz, in the Praça Restauradores.

Lost property

All lost property given to the Lisbon police ends up being dealt with at Olivais police station, Praça Cidade Salazar. You will need to wait 24 hours before trying to reclaim lost property, tel: 21 853 5403.

Medical Matters

There are no special health precautions necessary for visitors to Portugal. Beware of sunburn, especially on misty days when the combination of a cool

Embassies/Consulates

Australia
Avenida da Liberdade 200, 2º, Lisbon
Tel: 213 101 500

Canada
Edificio Vitória, Avenida da Liberdade 196, 3º, Lisbon
Tel: 213 164 600

Great Britain
Lisbon: Rua São Bernardo 33
Tel: 213 924 000
Porto: Avenida da Boavista 3072
Tel: 226 184 789
Portimão: Largo Francisco A. Maurício 7
Tel: 282 417 800
Funchal (Madeira):
Avenida Zarco
Tel: 291 221 221

Ireland
Rua da Imprensá Estrela 1, 4º, Lisbon
Tel: 213 929 440

United States
Lisbon: Avenida Forças Armadas, Sete Rios
Tel: 217 273 300
Porto: Avenida Da Boavista, 3523, 5º
Tel: 226 186 607

breeze and filtered sunshine can cause serious burning. Take sunscreen with you, or buy it when you get there, and wear a hat if the sun is fierce.

Tap water is generally potable but sometimes not very palatable, so it is best to use bottled water (*água mineral*).

Insect bites (usually by mosquitos) can be a problem in the summer so bring repellents. Out in the countryside, snakes are not uncommon but they are rarely a problem: apart from one species of viper in the north, the other venomous snakes have fangs at the back of their mouths, so even if you encounter one, and even if it were to strike, it is unlikely to poison you. There is no rabies in Portugal.

Useful Numbers

Ambulance (Portuguese Red Cross)
Tel: 219 421 111
Poisons unit
Tel: 217 950 143
Linha Vida (for information on drug use and abuse)
Tel: 1414
Linha Sida (AIDS help line)
Tel: 800 266 666

CHEMISTS

When closed, all chemists (*Farmácias)* have a list on their doors highlighting the nearest one that is open. Newspapers also publish a list of chemists open late.

HOSPITALS

Every town has a **Centro de Saúde** (Health Centre), some with 24-hour emergency service.

Lisbon

There are half a dozen large hospitals in Lisbon. The following have accident and emergency departments:
Hospital Cruz Vermelha, Rua Duarte Galvão 54 (situated behind the zoo), tel: 217 783 177 or 217 741 720.
Hospital de Santa Maria, Avenida Prof Egas Moniz (in the Cidade Universitária area not far from Sete Rios), tel: 217 805 000 for general enquiries or 217 805 111 for emergencies.
Hospital A. Serrano São Jose, tel: 218 822 339.
The British Hospital, Rua Saraiva de Carvalho 49 (overlooking the British cemetery near the Jardim de Estrela), tel: 213 955 067, has no casualty department, but

Help!

Police, fire and ambulance
Tel: 112 (toll free)
Credit card theft/sos
Tel: 213 132 900.

Conversions

1 metre	=	1.09 yards
1 yard	=	0.92 metre
1 km	=	about ⅝ mile
1 mile	=	1.6 km
1 kg	=	2.2 pounds
1 pound	=	about 0.46 kg
1 litre	=	1.76 pints
1 pint	=	about 0.57 litre
1 cm	=	about 0.3 inch
1 inch	=	2.56 cm
10°C	=	50°F
20°C	=	70°F
30°C	=	85°F
40°C	=	105°F

takes outpatients and may be able to help since all staff speak English.

Porto

Hospital Santo António, Largo Prof. Abel Salazar, tel: 222 077 500.

PRIVATE CLINICS

Lisbon

Clinica de Santo António, Avenida Hospitais Civis Lisboa 8, Reboleira, 2720 Amadora, tel: 214 952 541.

Porto

Hospital da Ordem Trindade, Rua Da Trindade, tel: 222 008 482.

Weights and Measures

Portugal uses the metric system of weights and measures. Listed below is a conversion table which may be useful.

Getting Around

By Air

TAP Air Portugal is the national airline. There is daily service between Lisbon, Porto, Faro, Madeira and the Azores.
The airline **Portugália** also operates a growing domestic and international service, and has a good reputation. The offices are located at Avenida Almirante Gajo Coutinho 88-1700 Lisbon, tel: 218 425 500.

By Train

Trains in Portugal range from the comfortable and speedy ALFA *rápidos* to the painfully slow *regionais*. Generally, the most efficient routes are the Lisbon–Coimbra–Porto and the Lisbon–Algarve lines. Algarve trains depart from the south side of the Tejo, *(see below)*. A rail link across the Tejo is due to open soon, allowing trains to continue south from Santa Apolónia station.
Rápidos (ALFA), which run only on the two routes mentioned above, are fast and punctual and cost more. Some *rápidos* have first-class carriages only; others have a very comfortable second-class as well. Next in line are the *directos intercidades*, which make more stops and travel more slowly. These have both first- and second-class compartments; second-class here is likely to be less comfortable than in the *rápidos*.
Finally, the *semi-directos* and especially the *regionais*, seem to stop every few metres and take longer than you could have believed possible. On *directos*,

semi-directos and *regionais*, second-class seats are not assigned, and the train company, **Caminhos de Ferro Portugueses (CP)**, has no qualms about issuing more tickets than seats if the need arises. If you want to be certain of a seat, board early. On rural routes, trains are almost always regional.

Furthermore, to reach more remote – or even not-so-remote – destinations, it may be necessary to change trains, and schedules are seldom coordinated. Unless you are catching *rápidos* (and *intercidades*), which are punctual, leave yourself plenty of time between transfers.
See also Getting There By Rail page 357.

Stations in Lisbon
There are four railway stations in Lisbon. Cais do Sodré and Rossio are commuter stations. International and long-distance trains to the north and east leave from Santa Apolónia, just to the east of Praça do Comercio. For trains to Alentejo and Algarve, take a ferry boat at the Terreiro do Paço station (the popular name of the Praça do Comércio).

The price of the boat is included in the train ticket, which you can buy at the boat station. Just be certain to buy the right one; there are two boat stations next to each other. For the train link-up, use the eastern station, i.e. the one to the left as you face the river.

A new metro link, connecting Cais de Sodre with Santa Apolónia, and a new bridge are proposed to link Santa Apolónia with the rail network in the south.

Stations in Porto and Coimbra
Porto and Coimbra each have two railway stations. Porto's São Bento and Coimbra A are located in the respective town centres. Most long-distance trains, however, arrive and leave from Porto's Campanhã station and Coimbra B station, outside the cities, and there are shuttle services between the central and outlying stations.

By Bus
Bus networks are privately-run but many companies have adapted their name from the former Rodoviária Nacional so that, for example, the main bus company in the far north is now **Rodoviária Entre Douro e Minho.** Only the Algarve bus company dropped the word Rodoviária, calling itself **Eva Transportes**. Except for routes between major cities, the bus is often faster than the train, and the system is certainly more extensive. This is particularly true in the north and between the smaller towns in Algarve and Alentejo.

There are quite a few private bus lines which specialise in particular areas of the country. Often they have more direct routes to smaller towns. Many travel agencies can book tickets on a private line, or may even run their own.

Driving
Traffic can be heavy, especially in rush hour, and towns can be difficult to negotiate. The best plan is to find a car park and walk. Take care on country roads. Drive on the right, giving priority to traffic on your left. Do not park within 18 metres (60 ft) of a road junction, 15 metres (50 ft) of a bus stop or within 3 metres (10 ft) of a tram or bus stop. Park facing the same direction as the moving traffic on your side of the road. Seatbelts are compulsory in both front and rear seats and children under 12 must travel in the back. Offences for this and other regulations are subject to heavy on-the-spot cash fines. Watch out for compulsory dipped headlight signs on motorways in the north.

The alcohol limit is 0.5g/litre and a blood/alcohol reading of more than 0.12 percent will result in imprisonment.

There are four categories of highway:
AE are motorways on which tolls are levied (120kph/75mph speed limit)
IP are Itinerários Principais (main trunk roads, 100kph/62mph)

IC are Itinerários Complementares (complementary trunk roads, 100 kph/62mph)
AN are Estradas Nacionais (main roads, 90kph/53mph)
The speed limit in urban areas is 50kph (30mph)

Car Hire
If you're determined to drive, the Yellow Pages are full of car rental firms. The big three – Hertz, Avis, and Europcar – have offices in Portugal, along with many other smaller (and often cheaper) companies. You can book a car before leaving home, which is often much less expensive. Transhire in London, tel: 020-7978 1922, is one of the most competitive.

It's advisable to shop around, as costs vary and many agencies offer special packages from time to time. There are various options to choose from, including having a driver. For more information look up car rentals in the local Yellow Pages under *Automóveis Aluguer com e sem Condutor* (which means cars to rent, with or without driver).

To rent a car in Portugal, most agencies require you to be at least 21 years old and to have had a valid drivers' licence for a minimum of one year. An international licence is not necessary.

Boat trips
Boat trips are offered in a variety of vessels, traditional and modern, on the country's three main rivers, the Tejo, Douro and Minho. Many are privately run, so tourist offices do not necessarily have all the information. Hotels, particularly in the Douro region, should be able to tell you all the options.
Rio Tejo Lisboa Vista do Tejo is a state-run lunch and dinner cruise from Alcântara docks (tel: 969 852 550; www.lvt.pt).
Rio Duoro Boats depart from the Cais de Ribeira in Porto. Trips range from an hour to several days, visiting *quintas* and stopping en route. The largest operating company is Douro Azul in Porto (tel: 223 402 500; www.douroazul.com).

Tourist Cards

The **Lisboa Card** and **Porto Pass**, on sale at tourist offices and elsewhere, give free travel and free or discounted museum entrance fees for 1–3 days.

The French shipping company Croise Europe has three boats (www.croisiereeurope.fr). Portowellcome in Vila Nova de Guia also organises trips (tel: 223 747 320; www.portowellcome.com). The government-backed PortoTours, in the Torre Medieval just below Porto's cathedral, organises boat and other tours (tel: 222 000 073; www.portotours.com).

Transport in Lisbon

Trains
Commuter trains to Cascais (stopping in Carcavelos, Estoril and other towns along the western coast) depart from Cais do Sodré station, west of the Praça do Comércio. Trains depart roughly every 15 to 20 minutes; the journey to Cascais (the end of the line) takes 35–40 minutes.

Trains to the northwestern suburbs, including Sintra, leave from the Rossio station at 15-minute intervals. The trip to Sintra takes about 45 minutes. This station houses an information centre for national services.

Buses and Trams
The city bus company, CARRIS, runs an extensive system of buses, trams (eléctricos) and funiculars. Bus stops are clearly marked by signposts or shelters. All stops display a diagrammatical map of the bus route; many have a map of the entire city system.

Pre-World War I trams ply the smaller, steeper streets where buses are unable to navigate. Some of them are quite beautiful, inside and out; they are slower and cheaper than the buses and are a good way to see the city. The tram is also supplemented with some larger, more modern vehicles

operating along the riverside.

CARRIS also runs two funiculars and an elevator. The Santa Justa Elevator is near the Rossio. One funicular climbs the steep Calçada da Glória from Praça dos Restauradores, the other is in São Bento. You pay after you've boarded.

Tickets and Passes
It is worth considering buying a 3-day or 7-day tourist pass, which gives unlimited access (see also Tourist Cards, left). If you have no pass, you pay a flat rate when you board, which works out more expensive. Less expensive are the pre-paid modulos that you can buy in packs of 20 from the kiosks. Don't board the bus without paying, as ticket inspectors appear from time to time and the fine is steep.

The CARRIS information kiosks scattered all over the city provide information and sell tickets and passes. Two of the most convenient kiosks are in Praça da Figueira, near the Rossio, and near Eduardo VII Park.

Metro
The metro is useful for travel in the central zone of the city. The system is easy to use and very cheap.

A tourist pass valid for 4 or 7 days can be used on the metro and buses. Metro passes valid for periods of 1, 7 and 30 days are available. You can also buy singles or books of 10 tickets, and validate your ticket at the machines next to the ticket booths.

Taxis

In all Portugal's cities, taxis are plentiful and cheap. The great majority of them are cream, while older ones are black with green roofs. In the city, they charge a standard meter fare, with no additions for extra passengers. (They carry up to four people.) Outside city limits, the driver may use the meter or charge a flat rate per kilometre, and is entitled to charge for the return fare (even if you don't take it). You should tip taxi drivers about 10 percent.

Where to Stay

Choosing a Hotel

Accommodation ranges from luxury hotels to basic private rooms. The middle range of reasonably priced accommodation has been considerably expanded thanks to an increase in the number of both Portuguese- and foreign-owned hotels. The French Ibis chain, for example, has opened hotels in several popular locations.

Pousadas and Manor Houses
Pousadas are state-run inns, which provide stylish and comfortable accommodation. They are to be found in most parts of the country, some in historic castles, and the majority serve excellent regional food (see Pousadas and Manor Houses, page 128–9). For reservations, contact the pousadas directly or call the central number (tel: 218 442 001; www.pousadas.pt).

Solares de Portugal
These offer a pleasant alternative to hotels, pensãos or pousadas. They are private properties or ones that have been adapted or totally converted for use by guests. They are in three groups:
Casas Antigas are manor houses and stately houses usually dating from the 17th and 18th centuries.
Quintas e Herdades are country states and farms. These include the wine estates of the north, with a rural setting and atmosphere.
Casas Rústicas are cottages and rustic houses in typical regional style, usually in tranquil spots. (www.solaresdeportugal.pt)

Guest Houses: TER
Bed and breakfasts in private homes are designated by an official

TER symbol on a metal plaque and the logo of the State Tourist Office (*Direcção-Geral do Turismo)*; there are three categories:

TH *Turismo de Habitação*: in houses of architectural merit.

TR *Turismo Rural*: characteristic rural houses.

AT *Agroturismo*: houses forming part of a farming estate.

Complaints

All accommodation has an official Complaints Book, which you can ask to write in. Observations and complaints may also be made to the Direcção-Geral do Turismo at Avenida António Augusto de Aguiar, 86, 1004 Lisbon and at Praça Dom João I, 4000 Porto.

Hotels

Hotels in Portugal come in several guises:

Hotels offer amenities such as restaurants and room service. All rooms have bathrooms. They are rated from 1–5-stars:

5-stars: a luxury hotel.

4-stars: not luxury but close.

3-stars: good value but sometimes slightly run-down.

1- and 2-stars: basic and often depressing places to stay.

Albergarias are essentially hotels offering 4-star comfort and meals.

Estalagems are very similar but may be 4- or 5-star.

Residencials have star gradings and are like small hotels but generally do bed and breakfast only. They usually have an "R" on a sign outside.

Pensãos are more basic, and again do bed and breakfast only. You can find 4-star *pensãos*, but the majority are less comfortable than that.

Hotel Listings

The list below includes a small sample of the wide variety of hotels in Portugal. Remember that you will probably have difficulty finding a decent room in July and August if you haven't made an advance reservation.

The following hotels are listed by area, beginning with Lisbon and the immediate area, and then running from north to south. In each place, they are listed in order of comfort, beginning with the most luxurious.

Note that *pousadas* and manor houses are with hotel listings.

Price Categories

Price categories are based on the cost of a double room for one night in high season. Out of season, prices can be less than half this rate.

€€€€ = above €200
€€€ = €120–€200
€€ = €60–€120
€ = up to €60

LISBON

Hotel Avenida Palace
Rua 1º de Dezembro
Tel: 213 460 151
Fax: 213 422 884
A grand 19th-century building, smack in the old town centre, between the Rossio and Praça dos Restauradores. €€€€

Lapa Palace
Rua do Pau de Bandeira, 4
Tel: 213 949 494
Fax: 213 950 665
Glamorously restored 19th-century mansion in the best residential quarter. €€€€

Meridien Park Atlantic Hotel
Rua Castilho, 149
Tel: 213 818 700
Fax: 213 890 500
Elegant. Overlooking the park. €€€€

Hotel Tivoli Lisboa
Avenida da Liberdade, 185
Tel: 213 198 900
Fax: 213 198 950
Big, handsome and handy for all parts of town. Friendly. €€€€

Pálacio Belmonte,
Páteo Dom Fradique
Tel 218 862 582
Fax: 218 862 592
A place for a special treat: beautiful bedrooms and enormous suites have been created in this 15th-century palace beneath the castle. The black marble pool is divine. €€€€

Pensão York House
Rua Janelas Verdes, 32

Tel: 213 962 435
Fax: 213 972 793
In a class by itself: comfort and charm combined. The great favourite of, among others, Graham Greene. In an interesting neighbourhood, about 15 minutes by bus from the Rossio. Reserve well in advance. The annex is down the street at number 47. €€€€

Albergaria Senhora do Monte
Calçada do Monte, 39
Tel: 218 866 002
Fax: 218 877 783
Beautiful views overlooking São Jorge castle, Alfama and down to the Tejo River. €€€

As Janelas Verdes
Rua de las Janales Verdes, 37
Tel: 233 968 143
Fax: 213 968 144
Next to the Museum of Ancient Art, this noble mansion belonged to an 18th-century writer. Beautifully furnished, some rooms with river views. €€€

Best Western Hotel Eduardo VII
Avenida Fontes Pereira de Melo, 5
Tel: 213 568 800
Fax: 213 568 833
Near the park with a beautiful view from the restaurant. Small and intimate, rather like a club. €€€

Hotel Britânia
Rua Rodrigues Sapaio, 17
Tel: 213 155 016
Fax: 213 315 5021
Small, comfortable hotel, recently refurbished, on a quiet street parallel to the Avenida da Liberdade. €€€

Hotel Diplomático
Rua Castilho, 74
Tel: 213 839 020
Fax: 213 862 155
Centrally located. €€€

Hotel Tivoli Jardim
Rua Julio C. Machado, 9
Tel: 213 539 971
Fax: 213 556 566
Run by the same company as the friendly 5-star Tivoli. €€€

Hotel Botânico
Rue da Mãe d'Agua, 16–20
Tel: 213 420 392
Fax: 213 420 125
Between the Bairro Alto and the Avenida da Liberdade; pleasant and comfortable. €€€

Hotel Flamingo
Rua Castilho, 151
Tel: 213 841 200
Fax: 213 841 208
Near the Praça Marquês de Pombal, but on a quieter street. €€€

Hotel Miraparque
Avenida Sidónio Pais, 12
Tel: 213 524 286
Fax: 213 578 920
Decent rooms; a good location on a quiet street overlooking the park. €€€

Hotel Regency Chiado
Rua Nova Do Almada 114
Tel: 952 868 771
Fax: 952 857 995
A modern hotel that rose from the ashes of the 1996 Chiado fire. Get a room with a balcony for great views over the city to the castle. €€€

Spina Classic Rex Hotel
Rua Castilho, 169
Tel: 213 882 161
Fax: 213 887 581
For those who can't afford the Ritz or the Meridian, the Rex is a nice hotel next door. €€€

Solar do Castelo
Rua das Cozinhas, 2, Castelo
Tel: 218 870 909
Fax: 218 870 907
In an 18th-century mansion inside the castle walls, with a contemporary makeover, this is a romantic place to stay. €€€

VIP **Eden Aparthotel**
Praça dos Restauradores, 24
Tel: 213 216 600
Fax: 213 216 666
The central Art Deco Eden Theatre has been beautifully converted into a hotel with one-bedroom and studio apartments. A wonderful rooftop pool with views over the city. €€€

Fluorescente Residencial
Rua das Portas de Santo Antão, 99
Tel: 213 426 609
Fax: 213 427 733
Tiled hallways and bright, clean rooms, some with full length baths. Very centrally located in a street of restaurants, near Praça dos Restauradores. €€

Residencial Alegria
Praça da Alegria, 12
Tel: 213 220 670
Fax: 213 478 070

A small family-run hotel just off the Avenida do Liberdade. €€

Residencial Dom João
Rua José Estêvão, 43
Tel: 213 144 171
Fax: 213 524 569
In a quiet residential neighbourhood, slightly off the beaten track, but only a 15-minute walk to the Praça Marquês de Pombal. €€

Roma Residencial
Travessa da Glória 22-A
Tel/Fax: 213 524 569
Has many of the amenities of a hotel, including private bath and TV in every room. In the heart of Baixa. €

Pensão São Jão de Praça
Rua de São Jão de Praça, 97
Tel 218 862 591
Fax: 218 881 378
In Alfama right below the cathedral. Some rooms without showers. Clean and friendly. €

AROUND LISBON

Cascais
Farodesignhotel
Avenida Rei Humberto II de Italia, 7
214 823 490
214 841 447
Next to the lighthouse above the sea, a stylish boutique hotel with a salt-water pool. €€€

Estoril
Estoril Sol
Parque Palmela
Tel: 214 390 000
Fax: 214 832 280
Big old-fashioned seaside hotel with wonderful sea views. €€

Setúbal
Pousada de Palmela
Palmela
Tel: 212 351 226
Fax: 212 330 440
Near Setúbal. Spectacularly set, inside castle walls. €€€€

Pousada São Filipe
Setúbal
Tel: 265 523 844
Fax: 265 532 538
In an old fortress, with lovely views overlooking the harbour. €€€€

Pousada Vale do Gaio
Barragem Tito Morais, Torrão
Tel: 265 669 610
Southeast of Setúbal. Small *pousada* beside a lake. €€€

Sintra
Lawrence's Hotel
Rua Consiglieri Perdosa, 38–40
Tel: 219 105 500
Fax: 219 105 505
Byron stayed in this five-star hotel, the oldest in Portugal, founded in 1764. Just 11 rooms and an excellent restaurant. Delicious breakfasts. €€€€

Hotel Central
Praça da Republica
Tel: 219 230 963
This comfortable old town hotel, bang opposite the palace, has been host to visitors for more than a century. €€

Pensão Residencial Sintra
Quinta Visconde de Trojal, Travessa dos Avelares 12
Tel: 219 230 738
Fax: 219 230 738
On the road to Cascais, this grand family guesthouse has a lovely garden and pool.

ALGARVE

Albufeira
Hotel Rocamar
Largo Jacinto D'Ayet, 7
Tel: 289 540 280
Fax: 289 540 281
High over the beach and ocean, sea-view rooms in 1950s style have picture windows and balconies. €€

Residencial Limas
Rua de la Liberdade, 25–27
Tel: 289 514 025
Fax: 289 585 802
Cheerful small hotel in the thumping heart of the resort. €

Faro
Hotel Dom Bernardo
Rua General Teófilo da Trindade, 20
Tel: 289 806 806
Fax: 289 806 771
Modern hotel near centre. €€€

Hotel Eva
Avenida da Républica, 1
Tel: 289 803 354
Fax: 289 802 304
Central, comfortable hotel with
rooftop pool. Make sure your room
overlooks the harbour. €€€

Estalagem Aeromar
Av. Nascente, 1, Praia de Faro
Tel: 289 817 189
Fax: 289 817 512
On the beach in the direction of
the airport. €€

Pensão Samé
Rua do Bocage, 66
Tel: 289 824 375
Fax: 289 804 166
One of a dozen pensions in town,
centrally located. €

Lagos

Hotel Belavista da Luz
Praia da Luz
Tel: 282 788 655
Fax: 282 788 656
Fine modern hotel with good sports
and entertainment facilities. €€€

Hotel de Lagos
Rua Nova da Aldeia, 83
Tel: 282 769 967
Fax: 282 769 920
Short walk from town centre; pool,
beach club, tennis courts. €€€

Hotel Golfinho
Praia Dona Ana
Tel: 282 769 900
Fax: 282 769 999
Well established and set among
coves and beaches. €€€

Hotel de Meia Praia
Meia Praia
Tel: 282 762 001
Fax: 282 762 008
Overlooking Meia Praia beach
near Lagos. €€€

Quinta das Achadas
Estrada da Barragem Odiáxere
Tel: 282 798 425
Fax: 282 799 162
Bedrooms in converted stables
surrounded by luxuriant
gardens. €€

Loulé

Hotel Loulé Jardim
Praça Manuel Arriaga
Tel: 289 413 095
Fax: 289 463 177
Handsome early 20th-century

Price Categories

Price categories are based on
the cost of a double room for
one night in high season.
€€€€ = above €200
€€€ = €120–€200
€€ = €60–€120
€ = up to €60

building near the centre; no
restaurant. €€

Portimão

Pestana Delfim Hotel
Praia dos Três Irmãos, Alvor
Tel: 282 400 800
Fax: 282 400 899
Set high above the sea; modern,
with good sports facilities. €€€

D. João II Pestana Hotel
Praia do Alvor
Tel: 282 400 700
Fax: 282 400 799
Modern; good sports and
recreational facilities. €€€

Pensão Alcaide
Praia do Vau, Portimão
Tel: 282 401 462
Fax: 282 401 695.
A comfortable 18-room hotel. €

Praia da Rocha

Hotel Algarve – Casino
Avenida Tomás Cabreira
Tel: 282 415 001
Fax: 282 415 999
Grand hotel, casino and cabaret
on gorgeous beach. €€€€

Hotel Bela Vista
Avenida Tomás Cabreira
Tel: 282 450 480
Fax: 282 415 369
Small and comfortable; no
restaurant. €€€

Sagres

Pousada do Infante
Tel: 282 624 222
Fax: 282 624 225
Near Cape St Vincent in the
village of Sagres, with sea views.
€€€

Hotel de Baleeira
Baleeira, Sagres
Vila do Bispo
Tel: 282 624 212
Fax: 282 624 425

Ocean views, with a seawater
pool and tennis court. €€

Navigator
Rua Infante Don Henrique
Tel: 282 624 354
Fax: 282 624 360
An apartment hotel with pool
and other facilities. Next to the
pousada with equally wonderful
ocean views. €€

São Brás de Alportel

Pousada de São Brás
Tel: 289 842 305
Fax: 289 841 726
Twenty minutes from Faro
airport; comfortable, with
good views. €€€

Tavira

Convento de Santo Antonio
Atalaia, 56
Tel: 281 321 573
Fax: 281 325 632
A lovely old Franciscan convent
virtually in the centre of the
village. €€€

Residencial Imperial
Rua José Pires Padinha, 24
Tel/Fax: 261 322 234
Small family-run hotel among
the restaurants on the west
bank of the river. €

Vilamoura

Hotel Atlantis Vilamoura
Tel: 289 389 977
Fax: 289 389 962
Very comfortable; comprehensive
sports facilities and ideal for
active children. €€€€

Hotel Dom Pedro Marina
Av. Tivoli
Tel: 289 381 000
Fax: 289 381 001
Modern; near the waterfront and
marina. €€€€

UPPER ALENTEJO

Alendroal

Casa de Terena
Rua Direita, 45
Tel: 268 459 132
Fax: 268 459 155
Restored 200-year-old house in
centre of Terena, 10 km (6 miles)
from Alendroal. €€

Herdade Dom Pedro
Tel: 268 459 137
Period house in a peaceful
country location. €€

Elvas
Pousada de Santa Luzia
Avenida de Badajoz
Tel: 268 637 470
Fax: 268 622 127
Close to the main road with the
usual high standard of *pousada*
food. €€€

Estremoz
Pousada da Rainha Santa Isabel
Largo Dom Dinis
Tel: 268 332 075
Fax: 268 332 079
Dramatic setting in a former
castle. €€€€

Évora
Pousada dos Lóios
Largo Conde de Vila Flor
Tel: 266 704 051
Fax: 266 707 248
Former monastery opposite the
Roman temple. Very popular, so
book early. €€€€
Évora Hotel
Quinta do Cruzeiro, EN 114
Tel: 266 748 800
Fax: 266 748 806
Modern and comfortable. €€
Hotel da Cartuxa
Travessa da Palmeira, 4
Tel: 266 739 300
Fax: 266 739 305
Luxury hotel inside the city
walls. €€
Hotel D. Fernando
Av. Dr Barahona, 2
Tel: 266 741 717
Fax: 266 741 716
Well appointed modern hotel. €€
Pensão Policarpo
Rua da Freira de Baixo, 16
Tel: 266 702 424
The most atmospheric place to
stay in Évora. An old noble's
house with a courtyard for
breakfasting. Plus a car park. €€
Pensão Riveira
Rua 5 de Outubro, 47–49
Tel: 266 703 304
Fax: 266 700 467
Small, old-fashioned; near the
centre. €€

Solar de Monfalim
Largo da Misericordia
Tel: 266 750 000
Fax: 266 742 367
A lovely converted palace in the
centre of town. Homemade
breakfast on the terrace. €€
Hotel Sta Clara
Travessa da Milheira, 19
Tel: 266 704 141
Fax: 266 706 544
Good value, very central. €€
Pensão Diana
Rua Diogo Cão, 2
Tel: 266 743 113
Fax: 266 743 101
Between the main square and the
cathedral, a good choice mid-price
lodging €€
Pensão Monte das Flores
Monte das Flores
Tel: 266 749 680
Fax: 266 749 688.
In the countryside just south of the
town with horses, tennis and a good
restaurant €€
Pensão Giraldo
Rua dos Mercadores, 27
Tel: 266 705 833
Friendly, inexpensive pension
around the corner from the
tourist office in the main square.
€

Marvão
Pousada de Santa Maria
Rua 24 de Janeiro, 7
Tel: 245 993 201
Fax: 245 993 440
Near Portalegre, within walled
town with border fortress.
€€€

Redondo
Hotel Convento de São Paulo
Serra de Ossa, Aldeia da Serra
Tel: 266 999 100
Fax: 266 999 104
Gorgeous furnishings and beautiful
gardens set in a national forest.
€€€€

Sousel
Pousada de São Miguel
Tel: 268 550 050
Fax: 268 551 155
Small country-house style with
facilities for hunting parties.
€€€

LOWER ALENTEJO

Santa Clara-a-Velha
Pousada da Quinta da Ortiga
Tel: 283 882 250
Fax: 283 882402
On the Algarve–Alentejo border,
overlooking a reservoir. €€€

Santiago do Cacém
Pousada da Quinta da Ortiga
Tel: 269 822 871
Fax: 269 822 073
Situated in peaceful surroundings
a few kilometres east of Sines.
€€€

Serpa
Pousada de São Gens
Tel: 284 544 724
Fax: 284 544 337
A modern hotel near the Spanish
border, overlooking the small town.
€€€

Vila Nova de Milfontes
Castelo de Milfontes
7645-234 Vila Nova de Milfontes
Tel: 283 996 108
Fax: 283 997 122
The best address in this seaside
town is this seven-bedroom castle
entered over a drawbridge, with
views down over the river estuary to
the Atlantic. Dress for dinner. €€€

Vila Viçosa
Pousada de Dom João IV
Tel: 268 980 742
Fax: 268 980 747
Located in a 15th-century convent
in the historical area of the town.
€€€€

ESTREMADURA

Batalha
**Pousada do Mestre Afonso
Domingues**
Tel: 244 765 260
Fax: 244 765 247
Right next to the abbey. €€€

Obidos
Albergaria Josefa d'Obidos
Rua Dom João d'Ornelas
Tel: 262 959 228
Fax: 262 959 533

Near the old town, very comfortable. €€€

Mansão da Torre
Tel: 262 959 247
Fax: 262 959 051
Modern hotel, 2 km (1 mile) out of town on the road towards Caldas da Rainha. €€

Pousada do Castelo
Paço Real
Tel: 262 959 105
Fax: 262 959 148
In the castle, within the walled town. €€€€

Porto de Mós
Quinta do Rio Alcaide
Tel: 244 402 124
A small group of houses set within an active *quinta* in the Parque Natural das Serras de Aire e Candeeiros. €€

Santarém
Casa da Alcáçova
Portas do Sol
Tel: 243 304 030
Fax: 243 304 035
Rooms all in splendid 19th century decor. €€

Quinta da Vale de Lobos
Azoia de Baixo
Tel: 243 429 264
Fax: 243 429 313
Secluded and restful. €€

Tomar
Hotel dos Templários
Largo Cândido dos Reis, 1
Tel: 249 321 730
Fax: 249 322 191.
Modern hotel in extensive grounds, with balcony overlooking the river Nabao. €€€

Estalagem de Santa Iria
Parque de Mouchão
Tel: 249 313 326
Fax: 249 321 238.
In the park, with an acclaimed restaurant. €€

Residencial União
Rua Serpa Printa, 94
Tel: 249 323 161
Fax 249 321299
Central and popular, set around a courtyard. €

Price Categories

Price categories are based on the cost of a double room for one night in high season.
€€€€ = above €200
€€€ = €120–€200
€€ = €60–€120
€ = up to €60

COIMBRA

Hotel Quinta das Lágrimas
Santa Clara
Tel: 239 802 380
Fax: 239 441 695
Eighteenth-century palace converted to a small, tasteful hotel, set in the park where Inês de Castro is said to have met her violent end. €€€€

Hotel Tivoli Coimbra
Rua João Machado
Tel: 239 826 934
Fax: 239 826 827
On the western outskirts, new and very comfortable. €€€

Hotel Astória
Av. Emídio Navarro, 21
Tel: 239 853 020
Fax: 239 822 057
A classic, Belle Epoque hotel on the river front a few metres from the tourist offfice. Good restaurant with Bussaco wines. €€

Hotel D. Luís
Santa Clara Coimbra
Tel: 239 802 120
Fax: 239 445 196
Tall, modern, on southern bank of the Rio Mondego with grand view of Coimbra. €€

Pensão Santa Cruz
Praça 8 de Maio 21
Tel: 239 826 197
Centrally located in a pedestrianised square, the pension has large, old-fashioned rooms. €

Dona Inês
Rua Abel Dias Urbano, 12
Tel: 239 855 800
Fax: 239 855 805
Modern hotel a few minutes from the centre. €

BEIRA LITORAL

Agueda
Pousada de Santo António
Mourisca do Vouga Serém
Tel: 234 523 230
Fax: 234 523 192
Very comfortable *pousada* 10 km (6 miles) north of Agueda. €€€

Aveiro
Hotel Afonso V
Rua Dr. Manuel das Neves, 65
Tel: 234 425 191
Fax: 234 381 111
Near the city centre. €€

Hotel Imperial
Rua Dr Nascimento Leitão
Tel: 234 380 150
Fax: 234 380 151
Very modern and central. €€

Hotel Moliceiro
Rua Barbosa de Magalhães, 15
Tel: 234 377 400
Fax: 234 377 401
Comfortable hotel overlooking the canal in the historic centre. €€

Pensão Estrela (Residencial)
Rua José Estevão, 4
Tel: 234 423 818.
One of a half dozen good pensions in this holiday town. €

Buçaco
Bussaco Palace Hotel
Tel: 231 937 970
Fax: 231 930 509
Luxury hotel in an old hunting lodge set in a forest. Nearby is the military museum featuring exhibits from the Peninsular War. €€€€

Leiria
Hotel Eurosol
Rua Dom José Alves Correia da Silva Leiria
Tel: 244 849 849
Fax: 244 849 840
Modern, with views over the old town and castle. €€€

Murtosa
Pousada da Ria
Torreira
Tel: 234 860 180
Fax: 234 838 333
Situated on an isthmus between the ocean and the lagoon. Peaceful setting overlooking the estuary. €€€

Oliveira do Hospital
Pousada de Santa Bárbara
Tel: 238 609 652
Fax: 238 609 645
Between Coimbra and the Serra da
Estrela. €€€

PORTO

Infante de Sagres
Praça D. Filipa de Lencastre, 62
Tel: 223 398 500
Fax: 223 398 599
The most splendid old hotel in
town, just off the main avenue; full
of character. €€€€
Hotel Ipanema Park
Rua de Serralves, 124
Tel: 225 322 100
Fax: 226 102 809
Excellent service and beautiful
views over the River Douro.
€€€€
Hotel Internacional
Rua do Almada, 131
Tel: 222 005 032
Fax: 222 009 063
One block west of the main
Avenido dos Aliados, this
handsome building dates from
the early 1900s and was
recently completely remodelled,
with single, double and triple
rooms. €€€
Hotel Apart. Tuela Torre
Rua Gonçalo Sampaio, 282
Tel: 226 071 800
Fax: 226 071 810
Modern; conveniently situated near
Boavista. €€€
Hotel Mercure da Batalha
Praça da Batalha, 116
Tel: 222 000 571
Fax: 222 002 468
Near the centre. €€€
Hotel Inca
Praça Coronel Pacheco, 52
Tel: 222 084 151
Fax: 222 054 756
Central; well-placed for shops.
€€€
Pestano Porto Carlton Hotel
Praça do Ribeira 1
Tel: 223 402 300
Fax: 223 402 300
Wonderfully situated hotel,
right on the quayside, with
all amenities. €€€

Price Categories

Price categories are based on
the cost of a double room for
one night in high season.
€€€€ = above €200
€€€ = €120–€200
€€ = €60–€120
€ = up to €60

Hotel Boa Vista
Esplanada do Castelo, 58,
Foz do Douro
Tel: 225 320 020
Fax: 226 173 818
Well located near mouth of the
Rio Douro. €€
Grande Hotel do Porto
Rua Santa Catarina, 197
Tel: 222 076 690
Fax: 222 076 699
Close to the main square. €€
Hotel da Bolsa
Rua Ferreira Borges, 101
Tel: 22 026 768
Fax: 222 058 888
Elegant hotel near the old stock
exchange. River views a few euros
extra. €€
Hotel Ibis Porto
Lugar de Chãs, Afurada
Tel: 227 720 772
Fax: 227 720 788
In Vila Nova de Gaia with
easy access from motorway.
€€
Hotel Peninsular
Rua Sá de Bandeira, 21
Tel: 222 003 012
Fax: 222 084 984
Tiled entrance, Art Deco
upstairs, this friendly hotel is
near the São Bento station.
€€
Holiday Inn – Garden Court
Praça da Batalha, 127
Tel: 223 392 300
Fax: 222 006 009
In the centre of town. €€
Residencial Vera Cruz
Rua Ramalha Ortigão, 14
Tel: 223 323 396
Fax: 223 323 421
Family-run hotel just off the
Avenida dos Aliados. Pleasant,
airy rooms, with a lift and
rooftop breakfast room.
€€

Pensão Pão de Açucar
Rua do Almada, 262
Tel: 222 002 425
Fax: 222 050 239.
Quiet location just west of
the main Avenue. €
Rex Pensão
Praça da República, 117
Tel: 222 074 590
Fax: 222 074 593.
A grand, central pension with
parking available. €

DOURO

Amarante
Pousada de São Gonçalo
Serra do Marão
Tel: 255 461 123
Fax: 255 461 353
In the Marão mountains, between
Amarante (24 km/15 miles) and
Vila Real (20 km/12 miles). €€€€
Casa da Lavada
Travança do Monte Amarante
Tel/fax: 255 433 833
There are superb rural views
from this 16th-century house. €€

Lamego
Quinta de Vista Alegre
Tel: 254 656 171
Fax: 254 656 180
Has good views – as its name
suggests. €€
Vila Hostilina
Tel: 254 612 394
Fax: 254 655 194
Samll *quinta* on Lamego–Porto
road. Pool and health facilities. €€

Pinhão
Vintage House Hotel
Tel: 254 730 230
Fax: 254 730 238
Beside the Douro in the heart of
port wine country with bougainvillea
dripping terrace, riverside gardens,
tennis court and pool. A Wine
Academy for tasting and first-
class restaurant. €€€
Residencial Ponto Grande
Rua Antonio Manuel Saraiva, 41
Tel: 254 732 456
One of two small hotels
in the town. Great home
cooking – just eat what
you're given. €

MINHO

Amares
Pousada de Santa Maria do Bouro
Tel: 253 371 970
Fax: 253 371 976
Splendidly converted 12th-century monastery. Conveniently situated for exploring the Peneda-Gerês National Park. €€€€

Arcos de Valdevez
Casa do Adro
Lugar de Eiró Soajo
Tel/Fax: 258 576 327
Fine old granite house in the centre of this mountain village, 15 km (9 miles) from Arcos. €€
Pensão Costa do Vez
EN 101 Silvares
Tel: 258 521 226
Fax: 258 521 157
Comfortable residencial situated half a kilometre out of town towards Monção. €

Braga
Hotel Elevador
Bom Jesus do Monte
Tel: 253 603 400
Fax: 253 603 409
Just 4 km (2 miles) from Braga; recently renovated. €€€
Hotel Turismo de Braga
Praceta João XXI
Tel: 253 060 000
Fax: 253 206 010
Near the centre; modern and comfortable. €€€
Albergaria da Sé
Rua Gonçalo Pereira, 39–51
Tel: 253 214 502
Fax: 253 214 501
Central, modern, not far from the cathedral. €€
Albergaria Senhora Branca
Largo Senhora a Branca, 58
Tel: 253 269 938
Fax: 253 269 937
Comfortable modern hotel in the centre of town. €€
Grande Residential Avenida
Avenida da Liberdade 738
Tel: 253 609 020
Fax: 253 609 028
Characterful old house in a central location. €€

Caniçada
Pousada de São Bento
Vieira do Minho
Tel: 253 647 190
Fax: 253 647 867
A restored hunting lodge on the edge of (and with fine views of) Peneda-Gerês National Park. €€€€

Guimarães
Casa de Sezim
Rua de Sezim, Santo Amaro
Tel: 253 523 000
Fax: 253 523 196
An estate near Guimarães with a splendid 18th-century façade. Well known for the high quality of its white wine. €€€
Hotel de Guimarães
Rua Eduardo de Almeida Guimarães
Tel: 253 424 800
Fax: 253 424 899
Modern; 10 minutes' walk from the city centre. €€€
Hotel Fundador D. Pedro (Residencial)
Av. D. Afonso Henriques, 740
Tel: 253 422 640
Fax: 253 422 649
One grade down from the next-door Hotel de Guimarães. €€

Ponte de Lima
Paço de Calheiros
Calheiros
Tel: 258 947 164
Fax: 258 947 294
Located 7 km (4 miles) outside Ponte de Lima, this is a splendid country manor house full of character. €€€
Casa do Antepaço
Lugar de Antepaço, Arcolezo
Tel: 258 941 702
Fine old Minho-style house overlooking the Rio Lima, on a farming estate. €€
Casa de Crasto
Lugar do Castro, Ribeira
Tel: 258 941 156
Fine granite kitchen and tower in a 17th-century house near Ponte de Lima. €€
Casa do Outeiro
Arcozelo
Tel: 258 941 206
Sixteenth-century country house, 2 km (1 mile) from town. €€

Casa das Torres
Facha
Tel: 258 941 369
Eighteenth-century house with fine views and impressive gateway. €€
Império do Minho
Av. Dos Plátanos
Tel: 258 741 510
Fax: 258 942 567
Very comfortable and near the town centre, but in a quiet position overlooking the river. €€

Viana do Castelo
Estalagem Caso Melo Alvim
Av. Conde Carreira, 28
Tel: 258 808 200
Fax: 258 808 220
Very comfortable estalagem installed in a restored period house near the railway station. €€€€
Casa Dos Costa Barros
Rua de S. Pedro, 28
Tel: 258 823 705
Fax: 258 828 137
An old town house right in the historic centre. €€
Hotel Aliança
Av. Combatentes da Grande Guerra
Tel: 258 829 498
Fax: 258 829 499
At the bottom of the main avenue, overlooking the River Lima, this is a good, mid-choice hotel. €€
Viana Sol Hotel
Largo Vasco da Gama
Tel: 258 828 995
Fax: 258 823 401
Near the old docks, 10 minutes' walk from town centre. €€
Pensão-Residencial Magalhães
Rua Manuel Espregueira, 62
Tel: 258 823 293
One of several inexpensive pensions just off the main street. €
Jardim (Residencial)
Largo 5 de Outubro, 68
Tel: 258 828 915
Fax: 258 828 917
By the river-front gardens, near the centre of town. €

Vila Nova de Anha
Quinta do Paço d'Anha
Lugar dos Penedos
Tel: 258 322 459
Fax: 258 323 904
Farming estate near Viana do Castelo, which produces its own

Price Categories

Price categories are based on the cost of a double room for one night in high season.

€€€€ = above €200
€€€ = €120–€200
€€ = €60–€120
€ = up to €60

vinho verde. Apartments in converted farm buildings. **€€€**

TRAS-OS-MONTES

Alijó
Pousada de Barão de Forrester
Rua José Rufino
Tel: (259) 95 92 15
Fax: (259) 95 93 04
Famous town house, a *pousada* since 1983. Near Vila Real. **€€€**

Bragança
Pousada de São Bartolomeu
Estrada de Turismo
Tel: 273 331 493
Fax: 273 323 453
Constructed in the late 1950s, recently refurbished. Overlooking the old walled town and castle.
€€€
Pensão Classis (Residencial)
Avenida João da Cruz, 102
Tel: 273 331 631
Fax: 273 323 458. **€€**
Pensão Bragança
Av. Sá Carneiro
Tel: 273 331 578
Fax: 273 331 242. **€€**

Miranda do Douro
Pousada de Santa Catarina
Estrada da Barragem
Tel: 273 431 205
Fax: 273 431 065
High above the Rio Douro with views across to Spain. **€€**

BEIRA ALTA

Almeida
Pousada da Senhora das Neves
Tel: 271 574 283
Fax: 271 574 320
East of the Serra da Estrela,

northwest of Guarda, within small fortress town. **€€€**

Caramulo
Pousada de São Jerónimo
Tel: 232 861 291
Fax: 232 861 640
A small *pousada* between Aveiro and Viseu. Swimming pool. **€€**

BEIRA BAIXA

Manteigas
Pousada de São Lourenço
Tel: 275 982 450
Fax: 275 982 453
High in the Serra da Estrela.
€€€

MADEIRA

Funchal
Reid's Palace Hotel
Estrada Monumental, 139
Tel: 291 763 001
Fax: 291 717 177
The most famous hotel on the island, still touched with Edwardian splendour. **€€€**
Quintinha Sao Joao
Rua da Levada de Sao Joao, 4
Tel: 291 740 920
Fax: 291 740 928
Set a little way back from Funchal, overlooking the bay, this is a lovely spot, with a rooftop pool.
€

AZORES

São Miguel
Hotel Estalagem de Camões
Largo de Camões, 38
Tel: 296 287 286
A reasonably priced 4-star establishment right in the heart of Ponta Delgada. **€€**
Convento de São Francisco
Vila Franca do Campo
Tel: 296 583 532
Fax: 296 583 534
There are 10 rooms in this 17th-century convent, which has been beautifuly renovated. Country walks and activities. Beach nearby.
€€

Where to Eat

What to Eat

Portuguese food is simple and fresh, abundant and filling, with few complicated sauces, but strong flavours and lots of garlic, olive oil and herbs. Canned and frozen foods are scorned. Portions are more than filling, and you'll often have to work hard to clean your plate. Shellfish is popular and is usually served by the gram: about 300 grams is enough for one. *For more details about Portuguese food, see pages 91–98.*

One word of caution: when you sit down for a meal you are often presented with a plate of appetisers – cheese, meat pastes, shellfish. These are not gifts of the house and you will be charged for anything you eat or pick at. Shellfish, in particular, can be expensive.

Meal times are relaxed: lunch is between 1 and 3pm; dinner usually between 8 and 9.30pm. *Menus* are set menus, which usually include a *prato do dia* (dish of the day) and are inexpensive. Eating out is generally cheap by European standards.

Favourite Foods

• *Caldo verde*, a cabbage and potato soup with *chouriço* (sausage)
• *Bacalhau* (salt-cod) is a national obsession. There are, supposedly, 365 ways to prepare it,
• *Carne de porco á Alentejana* (clams and pork with coriander) is a favourite meat dish.
• Sardines: fat, fresh and ubiquitous near the coast.
• *Doces de ovos*, or egg sweets, made with egg yolk, sugar and cinnamon and served at the end of a meal.

Restaurants in Portugal are rated on a scale of one to four stars, depending on expense, decor and service. The quality of food does not necessarily relate to the rating: there are plenty of 1- and 2-star neighbourhood places that serve great food.

Below are a few recommended restaurants, but there are, of course, many more. Some recommended restaurants are attached to hotels. *Pousada* dining rooms are of consistently high standard (and are also usually expensive).

LISBON

It is wise to reserve a table at the more expensive restaurants. Bairro Alto is the best place to head for to find intimate *tascas*, the typical restaurants of the city.

Expensive (€€€)
Casa do Leão
(in São Jorge castle)
Tel: 218 875 962
Portuguese cuisine at its best. A grand view.
Conventual
Praça das Flores, 45
Tel: 213 909 196
Pleasant decor, good food with interesting sweets.
Gambrinus
Rua das Portas de Santo Antão, 23
Tel: 213 421 466
In a pedestrianised street of restaurants; famous for seafood.
Tavares Rico
Rua da Misericelas Artes
Tel: 213 421 112
Lisbon's oldest and most sumptuous restaurant.
Terreiro do Paço
Lisboa Welcome Centre, Praça do Comércio
Tel: 210 312 850
Excellent Portuguese cuisine.
Torre Vasco da Gama
Cais das Naus, Parque as Nações
Tel: 218 939 550
International cuisine with views over the Tagus estuary.

Moderate (€€)
Adega do Tia Matilde
Rua do Beneficência, 77
Tel: 217 972 172
Friendly atmosphere.
Café Café
Rua de Cascais, 57
Tel: 213 610 310
One of the best of the trendy new restaurants around Alcântara docks. Live piano.
Doca Peixe
Doca de Santo Amaro, Armazém 13, Alcântara
Tel: 213 975 565
Serves fresh fish and seafood.

Price Categories

The restaurants are divided into the following price categories based on a meal for two:
€€€ (Expensive) above €35
€€ (Moderate) €15–35
€ (Inexpensive) below €15

Café Martinho da Arcada
Praço do Comércio 3, Baixa
Tel: 213 886 213
One of the city's oldest, full of atmosphere.
A Commenda
Praça do Império, Belém (inside Cultural Centre)
Tel: 213 648 561
International and Portuguese cooking.
Pap' Açorda
Rua da Atalaia, 57 (in the Bairro Alto)
Tel: 213 464 811
Modern, with an excellent reputation.

Inexpensive (€)
Bota Alta
Travessa da Queimada
Tel: 213 427 959
Popular restaurant in Bairro Alto.
Bomjardin
Travessa de Santo Antão 12
Tel: 213 427 424
Some say it's the best roast chicken in town.
Cervejaria da Trindade
Rua Nova da Trindade, 20c
Tel: 213 423 506
Classical wall-to-wall tiles – a large

and very popular restaurant. Go early at weekends.
Cosmos-Café
Doca de St Amaro – Armazém 6
Tel: 213 957 905
Mediterranean cooking.
Forno Velho
Rua do Salitre, 42
Tel: 213 533 706
Traditional food including goat roasted in the wood stove.
Malmequer Bemmequer
Largo de São Miguel, 25
Tel: 218 876 535
In the heart of the Alfama.
Solar dos Presuntos
Portas de Santo Antão, 150
Tel: 213 424 253
Hearty Minho food in the street-of-many-restaurants.
Sol Dourado
Rua Jardim do Regador, 19–25
(off Restauradores)
Tel: 213 472 570
Cheerful setting, tasty food.

AROUND LISBON

Cascais
Villa Albatroz
Rua Fernando Tomas, 1
Tel: 214 863 410
All the elegance of Cascais, with sunny terrace and sea views. Seafood specialities.
€€€

Sintra
Hotel Palácio de Seteais
Avenida Barbosa du Bocage, 8
Tel: (21) 9233200
Marvellous style, frescoed walls, a good meal.
€€€–€€€€
Café de Paris
Praça da República
Tel: 219 105 860
Delicious fresh fish and seafood dishes. €€

ALGARVE

Specialities *Ameijoas na cataplana* (clams with ham and sausage, flavoured with parsley and pepper); fried sardines; snails; seafood in general.

Albufeira
A Ruina
Cais Herculano
Tel: 289 512 094
Enjoy good food and good views
overlooking the ocean. €€
Fernando's Hideaway
Tel: 282 541 618
On the road from Albufeira to
Montechoro towards Ferreiras.
Family-run, serving excellent
traditional Portuguese food. €€
Os Arcos
Rua Alves Correia
Tel: 289 513 460
Roof terrace and traditional
Portuguese cooking. €

Almancil
A. Galeria
Estrada de Vale do Lobo
Tel: 289 396 234
Enjoy live piano music while dining
in Almancil's popular restaurant. €€
Sr. Frango
Estrada de Quarteira, Escanxinas
Tel: 289 393 756
Charcoal-grilled chicken to
perfection. €

Faro
La Réserve
Santa Bárbara de Nexe
Tel: 289 999 474
The best in the region, a few
minutes' drive inland from Faro.
It's the only *Relais & Chateaux*
establishment in Portugal. €€€
Dois Irmãos
Tel: 289 823 337
The oldest restaurant in Faro, in the
large and cheerful town centre.
Good rustic cooking. €€
Mesa dos Mouros
Largo de Sé
Tel: 289 878 873
Pleasant, near the cathedral.
Excellent cuisine. €€€

Lagos
Alpendre
Rua António Barbosa Viana, 17
Tel: 282 762 705.
Pleasing, dark-beamed place.
High-quality food. €€
O Galeão
Rua da Laranjeira, 1
Tel: 282 763 909.
Pleasant place to eat. €€

Price Categories

The restaurants are divided into
the following price categories
based on a meal for two:
€€€ **(Expensive)** above €35
€€ **(Moderate)** €15–35
€ **(Inexpensive)** below €15

Don Sebastião Restaurante
Rua 25 de Abril, 20
Tel: 282 762 795
Top quality restaurant serving fresh
fish and seafood cuisine. €€€
O Trovador
Largo do Convento D. Sra. da Gloria
Tel: 282 763 152
Friendly atmosphere. International
cuisine. €€
No Pátio
Rua Lançarote de Freitas, 46
Tel: 282 763 777
Quality food served in a pleasant
courtyard setting in old Lagos. €€

Loulé
A Muralha
Rua Martin Moniz, 41
Tel: 289 412 629
Varied menu including *cataplana*,
seafood and chicken piri-piri served
either in the secluded walled garden
or indoors. €€

Olhão
O Escondidinho
Rua José Leonardo
Tel: 289 702 674
In the delightful town centre. €€

Portimão
A Lanterna
East of the old bridge
Tel: 282 414 429
The nicest place to dine (no lunch).
The duck is home-grown, the
seafood excellent. €€
Dona Barca
Largo da Barca
Tel: 282 484 189.
A popular spot in the middle of
town. €€

Sagres
A Tasca
Tel: 282 624 177
A large and popular restaurant
above the fishermen's bay: its

---

shellfish is good and still sold at
reasonable prices. €€
Fortaleza do Beliche
Sagres to Cabo São Vicente Road
Tel: 282 624 225
Restaurant serving good food in a
converted cliff-top fortress. €€€

Tavira
Restaurant O Imperial
Rua José Pires Padinha, 22
Tel: 289 322 306
Freshly caught fish and seafood.
Special dishes include lobster
rice and clam *cataplana*. Dine
al fresco. €€
Patio
Rua António Cabreira
Tel: 281 323 008
On the east side of the old bridge,
serving Portuguese and French
food. Old house with roof terrace.
€€

ALENTEJO

Specialities *Açorda de alhos* (bread
soaked in broth heavily spiced with
garlic); *carne de porco á Alentejana*
(clams and pork with coriander).
Serpa and Beja cheeses.

Évora
Fialho's
Travessa das Mascarenhas, 16
Tel: 266 703 079
The Portuguese favourite for
classical regional food. €€€
Tasquina do Oliveira
R. Cândido dos Reis 45-A
Tel: 266 744 841
A small restaurant offering typical
Alentejan cuisine. €€

COIMBRA AND
BEIRA LITORAL

Specialities *Chanfana* (kid stew);
leitão (roast suckling pig); *pastéis
de Santa Clara* (pastries).

Aveiro
A Barca
Rua José Rabumba, 5
Tel: 234 426 024
Small family-run restaurant serving
excellent fish. €€

Centenário
Praça do Mercado 10
Tel: 234 422 798
Good Portuguese cooking. €€
O Mercantel
Rua António dos Santos 16
Tel: 234 428 057
Recently restored. Traditional
cuisine. €€

Coimbra
Colado & Colado
Rua Sota, 14
Tel: 239 827 348
A popular local in the restaurant
area. Try the *chanfana,* kid braised
in red wine, a Coimbra speciality.
Dom Pedro
Avenida Emidio Navarro, 58
Tel: 239 824 236
Coimbra's top restaurant, near the
tourist office. Serves *chanfana.* €€€
O Alfredo
Avenida João das Regras (south of
the river)
Tel: 239 441 522
Seafood; regional cooking. €€
Real das Canas
Vila Mendes, 7 Santa Clara
Tel: 239 814 877
South of the river, good food and
lovely view; very popular. €€

ESTREMADURA

Specialities Seafood, including
arroz de marisco (seafood and rice).
Ribatejo wines.

Santarém
O Mal Cozinhado
Campo de Feiras
Tel: 243 323 584
Busy small restaurant with weekly
fado and beef from the bullring. €€

Tomar
Bela Vista
Traversa Fonte Choupo, 6
Tel: 249 312 870
Excellent, inexpensive restaurant
by the river. €€

PORTO

Specialities Port, of course, plus
tripas á moda do Porto (tripe with

butter beans) and *presunto* (ham)
from Lamego.
Portucale
Rua da Alegria, 598
Tel: 225 370 717
Fine restaurant with a view. €€€
O Escondinho
Rua Passos Manuel, 144
Tel: 222 001 079
High quality food in traditional
surroundings. €€
Gambamar
Rua do Campo Alegre, 110
Tel: 226 092 396
Informal, very pleasant, excellent
seafood. Open late. €€
Mercearia
Cais da Ribeira
Tel: 222 004 389
One of the best typical Portuguese
places in Porto. €€
Tripeiro
Rua dom Passos Manuel, 195
Tel: 222 005 886
Good food and huge portions. €€

MINHO

Specialities Source of the great
caldo verde (cabbage soup). *Arroz
de sarabulho com rojões (*rice and
pork), lamprey, *vinho verde.*

Braga
Hotel Elevador
Bom Jesus do Monte
Tel: 253 603 400
Fax: 253 603 409
Excellent regional cuisine in a
hotel at the sanctuary *(see page
369).* €€–€€€

Coffee Choices

Coffee connoisseurs have a wide
variety to choose from:
● **bica:** a small cup of strong
coffee.
● **galão:** the same amount in a
large glass filled with milk; you
can have *galão escuro* or *galão
claro,* strong or weaker coffee.
● **meia de leite:** a regular cup
of coffee with milk.
● **garoto:** served in a smaller
cup.
● **italiana:** an espresso.

Inácio
Praca Conde S. Joaquim, 4
Tel: 253 613 235
Regional food, very pleasant. €€

Viana do Castelo
Estalagem da Boega
Quinta do Outeiral, Gondarém,
near Vila Nova da Cerveira
Tel: 251 700 500
Distinguished Minho cuisine.
Best to book. €€€
Pousada de Monte Santa Luzia
Monte de Santa Luzia
Viana do Castelo
Tel: 258 828 889
Fax: 258 828 892
This hilltop hotel with a grand
view serves international food.
€€–€€€
Os Três Potes
Beco dos Fornos, 9
Tel: 258 829 928
Traditional setting; regional food. €€

TRAS-OS-MONTES

Specialities *Chouriços de sangue*
(blood sausage); *feijoada* (bean
stew); goat; rabbit; trout; lamprey.

Bragança
Ogeadas
Rua de Loreto, 4
Tel: 273 324 413
Regional cooking. €€
Lá em Casa
Rua Marquês de Pombal, 7
Tel: 273 322 111
Regional cooking. €
Solar Bragançano
Praça da Sé, 34
Tel: 273 323 875
A cosy place, rustic decor, popular
among the locals. €€

Chaves
Carvalho
Alameda do Tabolado
Tel: 276 321 727
Typical Portuguese food. €€

Macedo de Cavaleiras
Estalagem do Caçador
Largo Manuel Pinto de Azevedo
Tel: 278 426 354
Fax: 278 426 381
Good food in a delightful inn. €€

Price Categories

The restaurants are divided into the following price categories based on a meal for two:
€€€ **(Expensive)** above €35
€€ **(Moderate)** €15–35
€ **(Inexpensive)** below €15

Mogadouro
A Lareira
Av. Nossa Senhora do Caminho
Tel: 279 342 363
A large restaurant in a small town, owned by a French-trained chef. Excellent value. €€€

BEIRA ALTA

Covilhã
Solneve
Residencial Solneve, Rua Visconde de Coriscada, 126
Tel:/Fax: 257 323 001
Large and cheerful. €

Guarda
Hotel de Turismo
Tel: 271 223 366
Fax: 271 223 399
Well-maintained old hotel with good cooking and service. €€

Seia
Hotel Camelo
Avenida 1 de Maio
Tel: 238 323 001
On the main street. Large, with a pleasant atmosphere and good food. €€
Vicente
Rua Cardeal Mendes Belo, 14
Gouveia
Tel: 238 492 336
Regional cooking. €€

Viseu
Muralha da Sé
Adro da Sé, 24
Tel: 232 437 777
In the heart of the old city near the cathedral. Regional cooking. €€

Drinking Notes

Port, the country's major gift to the wine world, is drunk as an *aperitif*

as well as a *digestif*. The best places to try it are the clubby Port Wine Institutes in Lisbon, at Rua São Pedro de Alcântara in the Bairro Alto, and the Solar do Vinho do Porto in the pleasant Jardim do Palacio de Cristal in Porto.

Madeira can be an *aperitif*, generally when it is dry (Sercial) or medium (Verdelho). A sweet version, Bual or Malmsey, is best for dessert.

Wine is red (*tinto* or *maduro*, mature), white (*branco*) or slightly sparkling *verde* (literally "green", but *vinho verde* can be either white or red). Always try to drink the local wines. *Vinho verde* should be sampled in the north of the country, Ribatejo wines in the centre and Alentejo and Algarve wines in the south. (*See Wine feature, pages 103–108.*)

Adegas are wine cellars, the equivalent of Spanish *bodegas*. These can also be small restaurants

Cervejarias are bars specialising in beers, but they are often indistinguishable from other bars. Beer (*cerveja*) is served by the bottle (*garrafa*), glass (*imperial*) or mug (*caneca*).

Ginginha or cherry brandy is a speciality of Lisbon and there are several tiny *ginginha* bars selling nothing else. A ration in a small paper cup, usually with a few black cherries, costs less than a euro.

Aguardente, the local *eau de vie*, is widely available, as is **brandy**.

Nightlife

After Dark

Portugal's nightlife is liveliest in Lisbon, and Lisbon's nightlife – from *fado* to great bars and discos – throbs in the Bairro Alto, an odd mix of the historical and the trendy; in a small, smart area behind the Avenida 24 de Julho; and around the reclaimed dockside at Alcântara.

Look out, too, for events in the **Fundação Calouste Gulbenkian** and the **Centro Cultural de Belém**. The **Coliseu dos Rocreios** in Rua das Portas de Santo Antão is the main venue for popular music performance. Major theatrical events are staged in the **Teatro Nacional Dona Maria II** in Rossio Square and in the Casino-Auditorio in Estoril. The **Teatro Camões** in the Parque das Nações is the main home of La Companhia Nacional de Bailado, the national ballet compay.

The **Teatro Nacional São Carlos** in Chiado is the city's opera house with a winter season. The **São Luz Teatro Municipal** is the capital's principal classical music venue, but look out for concerts in romantic settings, such as the São Roque church, and at Sintra and the palace at Mafra.

Tickets for many events can be obtained from the fifth floor of the Fnac department store in Chiado.

The **Orquestra Nacional do Porto** is a major national orchestra with its base at the former monastery of Mosteiro de São Bento da Vitória. Porto's other classical music venue is **Auditorio Nacional Carlos Alberta**, and popular music is staged at the Coliseu de Porto.

The **Orquestra do Algarve** holds concerts throughout the year and there are a number of festivals along the coast. Loulé has jazz and early music festivals.

There are a number of music festivals around the country throughout the summer, but towns otherwise tend to go to sleep after 10pm, and you'll find very little to do apart from a long, slow dinner or a disco. There are two exceptions: the tourist towns and resorts in Algarve, where summer visitors like to stay up late; and any town or village on the night of a festival. In particular Guimarães, Braga, Évora and Caldas da Rainha are full of fun in the evenings.

For a list of what's going on where, look for one of the many free listings magazines, such as *Agenda cultural Lisboa*, a free monthly magazine which is available at the airport and tourist centres. Even if you can't read Portuguese, the listings are comprehensible.

Music

Music, in *fado* houses, concert halls and nightclubs alike, tends to start fairly late, around 10pm.

The Portuguese musical tradition is much broader than simply *fado*. Folk music, very different from *fado*, is surprisingly vibrant in Portugal, too. Rock music ranges from the mediocre to the superb.

FADO HOUSES

Fado (literally "fate") is a nostalgic – though not necessarily woeful – music, a popular art with a long and mysterious history. Once associated with working-class neighbourhoods, when its most famous figure; Amália Rodriques, died in 1999 there were three days of mourning in Alfama. It is now of mixed appeal, and tourists are often a primary commercial target.

The *fadista*, a powerfully voiced singer, is usually backed by *guitarras* – the twelve-stringed Portuguese version– and *violas*, what we would call a guitar. Sometimes more charming, if less skill-ful, is *fado vadio*, or spontaneous amateur singing.

Fado is a performance, not a sing-song, and you are expected to

World Music

In Portugal you can hear local music played on strange instruments and rooted in deep traditions, and you can hear world music, brought in from the former colonies in Africa and Latin America.

Fiestas have kept alive local folk groups, which see no signs of dying out, and modern musicians often turn to these roots for inspiration, from the Arabic-inspired songs of Alentejo to the bagpipe wails of Trás-os-Montes. There is a rich variety of instruments, notably the *guitarra portuguesa*, a 12-string instrument which has several versions, and the four-string *cavaquinho*, the ancestor of the ukelele. There is also a strong *a capella* tradition, and you may hear student groups break into song in the streets of Porto or Coimbra.

Brazilian music has come to the fore in recent years, and Portugal is a place to hear it. You can seek out venues with music from Africa, or from Cabo Verde, a small Atlantic island and former colony with a disproportionate number of talented singers, such as Cesaria Évora. The Festival das Músicas e dos Portos in Lisbon in February has local *fado* and music from port cities around the world.

be quiet and listen. The *fado* of Coimbra is usually taken far more seriously than that of Lisbon The Portuguese say it takes more than a good voice to become a *fadista* – it takes soul as well.

There are also *fado* houses in Algarve, in Albufeira, Lagoa, Loulé and Silves.

Lisbon

Many of Lisbon's *fado* houses are located in the Bairro Alto. There are others in the older neighbourhoods – the Alfama, Alcântara and Lapa. They usually serve dinner (optional) and often charge a fairly steep

entrance or minimum consumption charge. Singing starts around 10pm. It's best to book in advance.

Adega Machado
Rua do Norte, 91
Tel: 213 224 640

Adega Mesquita
Rua Diário de Notícias, 107
Tel: 213 219 280.

Arcadas do Faia
Rua da Barroca 54–56
Tel: 213 421 923

A Sévera
Rua das Gáveas, 51–61
Tel: 213 428 314

Lisboa à Noite
Rua das Gáveas, 69
Tel: 213 462 603

Senhor Vinho
Rua do Meio, 18 (in Lapa)
Tel: 213 972 681

Coimbra

This is a university city, full of young people, so there is lots in the way of nightlife. But best of all is the enthusiasm for their own brand of *fado*. Among the best places are:

Aeminium
Nr. Largo da Portagem (only Friday)

Diligência Bar
Rua Nova

Trovador Restaurant
Largo da Sé Velha

The **Teatro Gil Vicente** usually has a bright weekly programme of concerts and other events.

Discos and Clubs

Bars with live music – and often dancing – are called *boîtes*. *Discotecas*, or discos, occasionally have live music as well. "In" places can be "out" very quickly, as fashions change. Try to check what is still open and still popular when you visit.

Lisbon

Most are in or near the Bairro Alto, Rato and São Bento – areas west and up from the Avenida da Liberdade – or in a cluster off the Avenida de 24 de Julho.

Frágil
Rua da Atalaia, 128
Tel: 213 469 578
Among the trendiest discos in town.

Right in the Bairro Alto. Good music.
Hot Clube
Praça de Alegria 39 (just above
the Avenida da Liberdade)
Tel: 213 467 369
The best place in town for jazz.
Jamaica
Rua Nova do Carvalho, 6 (near Cais
do Sodré railway station)
Tel: 213 421 859
American music and dancing with
DJs. In the city's red-light district.
Kremlin
Rua das Escadinhas da Praia, 5
Tel: 213 957 101
Also in the Alcântara area; lively.
Lux-frágil
Avenida Infante D. Henrique
Armazem A
Santa Apolónia
Tel: 218 820 890
Very trendy and popular, this club in
a converted dockside warehouse
near Santa Apolónia station has
great sounds and an easy-going
atmosphere. You can eat here, too.
Open till very late.
The Plateau
Rua das Escadinhas da Praia, 7,
Alcântara
Tel: 213 965 116
The most prestigious disco and
current attraction.
Ritz Club
Rua da Glória, 57
Avenida da Liberdade
Tel: 213 425 140
Good African music.
Salsa Latina
Gare Marítima de Alcântara
Tel: 213 950 555
As its name suggests it has a
Latin American flavour.
W
Rua Maria Luísa Olstein, 13,
Alcântara
Dancing all through the night.

Porto
Postigo do Carvão
Rua Fonte Taurina, 26–34
A restaurant and piano bar.
Aniki-Bobo
Rua Fonte Taurina (next door to the
Postigo do Carvão)
No food but good music.
Indústria
Av. do Brasil, 843
One of the trendiest places to be.

La Movida Beach
Matosinhos
The place to be seen.
Swing
Praceta Engenheiro Amaro da Costa
Another two-level disco/pub,
where the smart set hangs out.
Twins
Rua do Passeio Alegre, 1000
(at Foz do Douro, to the west)
Swing to the music of the 60s
and 70s.
Mal Cozinhado
Rua do Outeirinho 13
Dancing and traditional folk music.
Listen to Fado at this popular
restaurant.

Cinema

All films in Portugal are subtitled,
not dubbed, so they're accessible
to non-Portuguese speakers. There
are dozens of cinemas in Lisbon –
14 in the new El Corte Inglés
department store alone. In towns
elsewhere there are also plenty
of cinemas.

The Great Outdoors

National Parks

*Parque Nacional da
Peneda-Gerês*
The Peneda-Gerês *(see page 302)*
park extends over some 70,000
hectares (270 sq miles) and is
located in the far north of the
country. The highest peak in the
Peneda-Gerês is 1,544 metres
(5,065 ft), with a view of the Minho,
Trás-os-Montes, and across the
border into Galicia.
    The lush plant life is fed by heavy
rainfall. The park is home to 17
species of plants which are found
nowhere else, as well as extensive
forests of oak and pine. Wild
ponies, deer, wolf, golden eagles,
wild boars and badgers, as well as
many other animals, live within the
boundaries.
    You may fish, go horseriding,
hike and mountain climb amid the
breathtaking scenery in the park.
You can also visit picturesque
ancient villages. There are dolmens,
perhaps 5,000 years old, and
milestones that once marked the
old Roman road to Braga.
    Entrance to the Peneda half of
the park – the northern section – is
from Melgaço, at the Galician
border, and Ponte da Barca. The
entrance to Gerês is off the
Braga–Chaves road (take the turn
off to Caniçada). There is a
pousada at the edge of the park,
in Caniçada.
    Tourist offices in the Minho,
especially in Braga, can provide
information about the park.

Parque Natural Montesinho
In the far northeastern corner of
Portugal, Montesinho lies between
Bragança, Vinhais, and the Spanish

border *(see also page 316)*. As in
Peneda-Gerês, many varieties of
flora and fauna abound. There is
not only wild, heath-like scenery but
also ancient villages preserving
their age-old customs. Access is
from Bragança or Vinhais.

Parque Natural Serra da Estrela
Granite peaks, glacial valleys and
streams, lakes and boulders lie
within the natural park of the Serra
da Estrela *(see page 325)*. The
highest peaks in Portugal are also
quite accessible by car (though in
winter roads may briefly be
blocked). The prettiest season, with
wild flowers everywhere, is spring.
There are places to stay in the
larger towns in or near the Serra,
which include Gouveia, Seia, Covilhã
and Guarda. There is a *pousada* in
Manteigas. The Serra is about two
hours by car from Coimbra.

Serra da Arrábida
Just south of Lisbon, the Serra da
Arrábida's natural beauty is
accessible to anyone with a car
(see page 191). The steep hills,
with a wide variety of flowers and
trees, and the blue ocean for
contrast, are beautiful. The Serra
da Arrábida provides wonderful
views all along the highway 379–1,
west from Setúbal.
A good map will show you
Portugal's several other protected
areas. These include Algarve's
southwestern coast, and a coastal
wetland, the Parque Natural da Ria
Formosa, important to migrating
birds. Rural areas outside parks are
also astonishingly beautiful and rich
in birdlife.

Sport

Participant Sports

GOLF

The standard of golf courses in
Portugal is very high. Those in the
Estoril/Sintra area and in Algarve
are particularly popular. This is just
a selection of around 60 clubs in
the country.

Lisbon
Sil Golf
Quinta da Aroeira, Monte de
Caparica (south of the Rio Tagus)
Tel: 212 971 314
Estoril Golf Club
Avenida da República, Estoril
Tel: 214 680 176
Fax: 214 682 796
Estoril-Sol Golf Club
Estrada da Lagoa Azul, 3, Linho,
near Sintra
Tel: 219 232 461
Fax: 219 232 461
Lisbon Sports Club
Casal da Carregueira, Belas, near
Queluz
Tel: 214 310 077
Fax: 214 312 482
Penha Longa Club
Near Sintra
Tel: 219 249 011
Praia d'El Rei
Between Óbidos and Peniche, easily
accessible via the A8 motorway
Tel: 262 905 005
Fax: 262 905 009

Setúbal
Tróia Golf Club
Torralta, Tróia
Tel: 265 494 112
Fax: 265 494 315

Costa de Prata
Vimeiro Golf Club
Praia do Porto Novo, Vimeiro, about

65 km (40 miles) north of Lisbon
Tel: 261 984 157
Fax: 261 984 621

Porto
Miramar Golf Club
Praia de Miramar, Avenida Sacudura
Cabral, Valadares, near Porto
Tel: 227 622 067
Fax: 227 627 859
Oporto Golf Club
Lugar do Sisto, near Espinho
Tel: 227 342 008
Fax: 227 346 895

Algarve
This is a selection from a large
number of excellent courses:
Palmares Golf Club
Meia Praia, near Lagos
Tel: 282 762 953
Fax: 282 762 534
Penina Golf Club
Penina, near Portimao
Tel: 282 420 200
Fax: 282 420 300
Quinta do Lago Golf Club
Almancil, near Loulé and Faro
Tel: 289 390 700
Fax: 289 394 683
Vale do Lobo Golf Club
Vale da Lobo, near Loulé
Tel: 289 353 464
Fax: 289 353 003
Vilamoura-1 Golf Club
Vilamoura, near Loulé
Tel: 289 310 333
Fax: 289 310 349

TENNIS

In Lisbon, the **Marinha Golf Club**
and **Lisbon Sports Club** *(listed
above, under Golf)* have tennis
courts. Try also:

To ski or to *scu*?

The Serra da Estrela is the place
for the little that Portugal has to
offer in the way of winter sports.
Visitors ski here, but mostly they
scu – a combination of the words
ski and *cu*, which means rear
end in Portuguese. To *scu*, you
grab a plastic bag, sit on it, and
slide downhill.

Club Internacional de Ténis
Campolide Tel: 213 882 084
Club de Ténis de Monsanto
Tel: 213 648 741
Club de Ténis do Estoril
Tel: 214 662 770

In Porto, the **Miramar Golf Club** has facilities for tennis.

In Algarve, there are courts at the **Quinta do Lago**, **Vale do Lobo**, **Vilamoura Ténis Centre** and at many hotels. Several towns have their own municipal courts.

WATERSPORTS

There are few facilities for renting equipment outside Algarve. In the Lisbon area you'll find surfboards and other equipment for hire at the beaches. For sailing, there's the **Cascais Naval Club**. Windsurfers head for the long beaches and wild waves at Guincho, further out. For deep-sea fishing, check with the local tourist office.

In Porto, the **Porto Golf Club** (tel: 227 342 008) has skin-diving facilities. You can also try the Leça da Palmeira Beach (to the north) for sailing.

In Algarve, all the larger tourist beaches and towns have some facilities. Near Lagos, there are windsurfing and waterskiing facilities at Luz, São Roque (Meia Praia) and Alvor beaches; the latter two also have sailing facilities. Praia da Rocha has sailing, windsurfing and waterskiing facilities; sailing and windsurfing are practised at Armação de Pera, near Albufeira. Vilamoura has extensive watersports facilities, as does Vale de Lobo.

Spectator Sports

FOOTBALL

Football dominates Portuguese sports life. From the 10-year-olds playing in the street to the hundreds of professional, semi-pro and amateur teams, to the massive coverage the sport is given on TV and in the papers, football in Portugal is inescapable.

The three most important teams in the country are FC Porto, from Porto (the 1987 European champions), Benfica and Sporting, the latter two from Lisbon. Every Portuguese, no matter where they are from, are loyal fans of one of the three.

The football season stretches from September or October to July. Tickets for the big three teams are difficult to get, as there are many season-ticket holders. In Lisbon, try the ticket kiosk located in Praça dos Restauradores; elsewhere, try the stadiums themselves. Games are usually held on Sunday afternoons.

2004 European Cup Final

Ten stadiums around the country were picked for the games in the 2004 European Football Championships. Some have been upgraded, some are entirely new. The new ones include the flagship, 65,000-seater Luz Stadium – the Stadium of Light, on the site of Benfica's existing club in Lisbon. This is where the finals will be held. Lisbon's other club, Sporting, also has a revitalised home, in the José de Alvalade stadium. FC Porto gets a new stadium, Das Antas, while the town's other team, Boavista, has an update. The other new stadiums are the Estádio Municipal at Coimbra, home of Academica, Estádio Municipal in Aveiro, home of Beira-Mar, Estádio Municipal in Braga, home of Sporting Braga and Farense/Louletano's Estádio Intermunicipal de Faro/Loulé in Algarve.

Vitoria de Guimarães' Estádio D. Afonso Henriques had a makeover, as did Leiria's Estádio Municipal Dr Magalhães Pessoa for União de Leiria.

BULLFIGHTING

Portuguese bullfighting is different from the Spanish variety. It is considered less violent because the bull is not killed in the ring (although, naturally, it is killed later, out of public view). Nonetheless, it is bloody enough to upset the sensibilities of many people. The star Portuguese bullfighters are on horseback, the horses beautifully bedecked and highly trained. A striking aspect of the Portugese *corrida* is the team of *forcados* – eight unpaid local heroes, colourfully dressed in short coats, tight pants, waistband and stockings – who face the bull bare-handed in an exhibition of pure *machismo*.

Bullfighting is popular primarily in Ribatejo (just outside Lisbon) and in Lisbon itself. The season runs from spring to autumn. In Lisbon, *corridas* are held in the Campo Pequeño bullring. There is also a ring in Cascais. The most famous bullfights, however, are held in Santarém and Vila Franca da Xira, northeast of Lisbon. (Take the train from Santa Apolónia.)

Ribatejo festivals, which are frequent in the summer, almost always feature bullfighting and the freeing of bulls in the streets.

Shopping

What to Buy

Portuguese handicrafts range from hand-carved toothpicks to wicker furniture to blankets and rugs. The most famous items are ceramic tiles *(azulejos –see pages 170–1)* and pottery, Arraiolos rugs, embroidery and lace *(see pages 236–7)*. The beautiful Vista Alegre porcelain and Atlantis crystal bear comparison with the best in the world.

Pottery Different varieties of ceramic work are produced all over the country; in Alentejo, for example, you'll find examples of *barro* pottery, a simple brown clay, sometimes decorated, sometimes glazed. Decorations on ceramics tend to be paintings of fruit or flowers, or sometimes scenes of rural life. Fine pottery from around Coimbra often carries animal motifs, and looks quite intricate in comparison with the simple Alentejano decorations. Farther north, blue-and-white glazed pottery appears.

Rugs Arraiolos rugs, by contrast, come from only one place: Arraiolos, in Alentejo. (They are, however, sold in other parts of the country, especially Lisbon.) The art of designing and stitching these rugs probably goes back to the Middle Ages.

Where to Shop

Lisbon

Lisbon, as befits the capital, has several good shopping areas – in central Baixa, around Rua Garrett and in Avenida da Roma; there are also many small exclusive malls throughout the city. It also has an abundance of large shopping centres. Colombo, Iberia's largest shopping mall, to the north of the city; Amomeiras – Lisbon's first; the sleek Vasco da Gama in the Parque das Nações and the recently opened El Corte Inglés, the city's largest department store. Near Cascais, Cascaishopping is just off the new expressway.

But while many regional crafts are sold in Lisbon, there is usually a much wider and more authentic selection in the provinces. The following is a list of the traditional crafts produced in particular areas:

Alentejo

Cane and wicker work, cork products (baskets, coasters, sculpture), wool blankets, Arraiolos rugs, ceramics *(barro)*, traditional hand-painted furniture, copper goods and lace.

Algarve

Palm and wicker work, copper and brass articles, candles, earthenware pottery.

Coimbra and the Beiras

Ceramics (colourful animal motifs from near Coimbra; elegant Vista Alegre porcelain from the Aveiro region; black clay pottery from the Viseu region); woven rag quilts (from the Serra da Estrela); as well as lace and embroidery.

Douro and Minho

Ceramics, wickerwork, straw baskets and hats; embroidery, crochet, and regional costumes (especially from the Viana do Castelo area), religious art (from Braga). The Thursday market in Barcelos, north of Porto, has lots of handicrafts for sale.

Trás-os-Montes

Blankets; weaving and tapestries; crocheted bedspreads; black pottery from Bisalhóes (near Vila Real).

Language

Getting By

If you speak Spanish you will be able to read Portuguese and understand some, but certainly not all, the spoken language. There are also slight similarities with written, but little with spoken, French. For most English speakers, however, Portuguese, which has many nasal sounds, is not easy to follow.

Many Portuguese speak a second language, and most have the tolerance and courtesy to help resolve problems or queries. At the tourist offices and in virtually all hotels and many restaurants you'll find the major European languages are spoken. Yet learning just a few simple words and phrases in Portuguese will certainly enhance your visit.

Questions

Where is...? *onde é...?*
When...? *quando...?*
How much...? *quanto custa?*
Is there...? *há...?*
Do you have...? *tem...?*
At what time...? *a que horas...?*
What time is it? *que horas são?*
Do you have a...? *tem um...?*

Basic Communication

yes *sim*
no *não*
thank you *obrigado/a*
many thanks *muito obrigado*
all right/okay *de acordo/está bem*
please *faz favor, por favor*
excuse me *faz favor*
(to get attention)
excuse me *com licença*
(to get through a crowd)
excuse me *desculpe* (sorry)

wait a minute *espere um momento*
can you help me? *pode ajudar-me?*
certainly *com certeza*
can I help you? *posso ajudálo/a?*
can you show me? *pode mostrar me?*
I need... *preciso...*
I'm lost *estou perdido/a*
I'm sorry *desculpe-me*
I don't know *não sei*
I don't understand *não comprendo*
do you speak... *fala...*
English *inglês*
French *francês*
German *alemão*
please speak slowly *faz favor de falar devagar*
please say that again *diga outra vez, se faz favor*
slowly *devagar*
here/there *aqui/ali*
what? *o quê?*
when/why *quando/porquê/onde?*
where is the toilet? *onde é a casa de banho?*

Greetings
hello (good morning) *bom dia*
good afternoon/evening *boa tarde*
good night *boa noite*
see you tomorrow *até amanha*
see you later *até logo*
see you soon *até já*
goodbye *adeus*
Mr/Mrs/young lady/girl *senhor/ senhora/menina*
pleased to meet you *muito prazer em conhecê-lo/lá*
I am English/American *sou Inglês/Americano (a)*
I'm here on holiday *estou aqui de férias*
how are you? *como está?*
fine, thanks *bem, obrigado*

Telephone calls
I want to make a telephone call *quero fazer uma chamada*
the area code *o indicativo*
the number *o número*
can you get this number for me? *podia fazer-me uma chamada para este número?*
the line is engaged *está ocupada*
no one replies *ninguém atende*
the operator *a telefonista*
hello? *está lá?*
may I speak to... *posso falar com...*

hold the line please *não desligue, faz favor*
who is that? *uem/onde fala?*
may I leave a message? *posso deixar um recado?*
I will phone later *ligarei mais tarde*

At the hotel
do you have a room available? *há algum quarto disponível?*
I have a reservation *tenho uma reserva*
single/double room *um quarto individual/duplo*
twin/double bed *camas individuais/cama casal*
with bathroom *com casa de banho*
for one night *para uma noite*
two nights *para duas noites*
how much is it per night? *qual é o preço por noite?*
with breakfast? *com pequeno almoço incluindo?*
does it have air conditioning? *o quarto tem ar condicionado?*
it's expensive *é caro*
can I see the room? *posso ver o quarto?*
what time does the hotel close? *a que horas fecha o hotel?*
dining room *sala de jantar*
what time is breakfast? *a que horas será o pequeno almoço?*
please call me at... *acorde-me às...*
the bill please *a conta por favor*
can you call a taxi please? *chame um táxi por favor?*
key *a chave*
lift *elevador*
towel *toalha*
toilet paper *papel higiénico*
pull/push *puxe/empurre*

Eating and Drinking

IN A RESTAURANT

can we have lunch/dinner here? *podemos almoçar/jantar aqui?*
we only want a light meal? *podemos almoçar/jantar aqu*
a table for two/three... *uma mesa para dois/três...*
may we have the menu? *a ementa se faz favor*
we should like... *queríamos...*
what do you recommend? *que recomenda?*
what is this? *o que é isto?*

do you know what this is in English? *sabe o que é isto em Inglês?*
what wine do you recommend? *qual é o vinho que recomenda?*
not too expensive *não muito caro*
I'll have that *quero aquilo*
Is it good? *É bom?*
well cooked/rare *bem passado/ mal passado*
grilled *grelhado*
fried *frito*
boiled *cozido*
vegetables *legumes*
spoon/fork/knife *colher/garfo/faca*
would you like some more? *deseja mais?*
no thank you – no more *obrigado – não desejo mais*
yes please *sim – mais faz favor*
I enjoyed that *gostei muito*
we have finished *acabámos*
the bill please *a conta se faz favor*
toilets (ladies/gents, men/women) *serviços (senhoras/senhores, homens/mulheres)*

Menu Decoder

Entradas (Starters)
amêijoas ao natural *clams with butter and parsley*
camarão *prawn*
gambás *langoustines*
pasteis de bacalhau *dried cod fishcakes*
presunto *smoked ham*
rissois de camarão *shrimp pies*
santola recheada *dressed crab*

Peixe (Fish)
arroz de polvo *octopus with rice*
atum grelhado *grilled tuna fish*
bacalhau á Brás *fried dried codfish with fried potatoes and scrambled eggs (there is an almost endless variety of dishes with dried codfish)*
caldeirada de peixe *fish stew*

Sopas (Soups)
caldo verde *finely chopped cabbage and potato soup*
canja *chicken broth*
creme de marisco *seafood soup*
sopa de coentros *coriander, bread, and a poached egg*

Drinks

coffee (black and strong) um café
coffee with milk um café com leite
large, weak coffee with milk um meio de leite/galão
tea (lemon) um chá (de limão)
orange juice (bottled) sumo de laranja
orange juice (fresh) sumo de laranja natural
mineral water (still) agua sem gás; (fizzy) agua com gás
chilled/room temperature fresca/natural
red/white wine (mature/ "green") vinho tinto/branco (maduro/verde)
bottle/half bottle garrafa/meia garrafa
beer cerveja
milk leite
cheers! saúde!

ensopado de enguias eels with fried bread
lagosta lobster
linguado sole
lampreia lamprey
lulas recheadas stuffed squid
robalo sea bass
rodovalho halibut
salmão salmon
salmonete red mullet
salmonetes á moda de Setubal grilled red mullet
sardinhas grelhadas com pimentos grilled sardines and peppers
savel shad
truta trout

Carne (Meat)
arroz à moda de Valência kind of paella
arroz de pato duck with rice
cabrito assado roast kid
carne assada roast beef
churrasco pork cooked on a spit
coelho à caçadora rabbit stew
cozido à portuguesa variety of boiled meats and vegetables
feijoada dried beans with rice and various smoked meats
frango de carril roast chicken with a hot sauce

frango na pucara chicken casserole
leitão assado roast sucking pig
peru turkey
porco pork
tripas à moda do Porto tripe with dried beans
vitela veal

Salada (Salad)
alface lettuce
cebola onion
cenoura carrot
pepino cucumber
tomate tomato

Doces (Desserts)
arroz doce sweet rice
fruta fruit
gelado ice cream
laranja orange
leite creme type of custard
maça apple
marmelada quince marmalade
papos de anjo small butter cakes with syrup
pasteis cakes
pera pear
pudim flan cream caramel
queijo cheese
uvas grapes

Basic Commodities
açucar sugar
alho garlic
azeite olive oil
azeitona olive
manteiga butter
pão bread
pão integral wholemeal bread
pimenta pepper
sal salt
vinagre vinegar
sandwich (ham/cheese/mixed) sande (fiambre/queijo/misto)

Sightseeing

what should we see here? o que podemos ver aqui?
what is this building? que edifício é este?
where is the old part of the city/town? onde é a zona antiga da cidade/vila?
when was it built? quando foi construída?
what time is there a mass? a que horas há missa na igreja?

when is the museum open? a que horas está aberto o museu?
is it open on Sunday? está aberto no domingo?
how much is it to go in? quanto custa a entrada?
admission free entrada gratuita
can I take pictures? posso tirar fotografias?
photographs are prohibited é proibido tirar fotografias
follow the guide siga o guia
we don't need a guide não precisamos de guia
where can I get a plan of the city? onde posso obter um plano da cidade?
how do I get to...? como se vai para...?
can we walk there? podemos ir a pé?

Shopping

what time do you open/close? a que hora abre/fecha?
can I help you? posso ajudar?
I'm looking for... procuro...
we are just having a look around queremos ver o que há
how much does it cost? quanto custa?
do you take credit cards? aceitam cartões de credito?
have you got...? tem...?
can I try it on? posso experimentá-lo?
this is not my size não é a minha medida
too small/big é muito pequeno/muito grande
its expensive é caro
I like it/don't like it gosto/não gosto
I'll take this levo isto

Shops
bakery padaria
barber barbearia
bookshop livraria
butcher talho
chemist farmácia
department store armazém
dry cleaner lavandaria a seco
fishmonger peixaria
grocer mercearia
hardware store drogaria
optician oculista
post office correios

shoe shop *sapataria*
shopping centre *centro comercial*
stationer *papelaria*
tobacconist *tabacaria*

Travelling

airport *aeroporto*
arrivals/departures *chegadas/partidas*
boat *barco*
bus *autocarro*
bus station *centro camionagem*
bus stop *paragem*
car/hire *carro/a lugar*
customs *alfândega*
driving licence *carta de condução*
flight *voo*
motorway *auto-estrada*
railway station *estação de comboio*
return ticket *bilhete de ida e volta*
single ticket *bilhete de ida*
smokers/non-smokers *fumadores/não fumadores*
taxi *taxi*
ticket office *bilheteria*
toll *portagem*
train *comboio*

Health

is there a chemist's nearby? *há uma farmácia aqui perto?*
where is the hospital? *onde é o hospital?*
I feel ill *não me sinto bem*
it hurts here *tenho uma dor aqui*
I have a headache *tenho dor de cabeça*
I have a sore throat *dói-me a garganta*
I have a stomach ache *tenho dores de estômago*
I have a fever (temperature) *tenho febre*
call a doctor *chame um médico*
take this presription to the chemist *leve esta receita para a farmácia*
take this note to the hospital *leve esta carta para o hospital*
danger! *perigo!*
look out! *cuidado!*
help! *socorro!*
fire! *fogo!*

Days of the Week

Sunday	domingo
Monday	segunda-feira
Tuesday	terça-feira
Wednesday	quarta-feira
Thursday	quinta-feira
Friday	sexta-feira
Saturday	sábado

Numbers

1	*um/uma*
2	*dois/duas*
3	*tres*
4	*quatro*
5	*cinco*
6	*seis*
7	*sete*
8	*oito*
9	*nove*
10	*dez*
11	*onze*
12	*doze*
13	*treze*
14	*catorze*
15	*quinze*
16	*dezasseis*
17	*dezassete*
18	*dezoito*
19	*dezanove*
20	*vinte*
30	*trinta*
40	*quarenta*
50	*cinquenta*
60	*sessenta*
70	*setenta*
80	*oitenta*
90	*noventa*
100	*cem*
200	*duzentos*
1,000	*mil*

Further Reading

Portuguese Works

Although the Portuguese have a long and rich literary tradition, few books have been translated into English. The following writers and books should still be in print:
Luís de Camões Author of Portugal's best-known piece of literature, the epic poem *The Lusiads* (Penguin Classic), written in 1572 and celebrating the Portuguese Era of Discoveries.
Eça de Queiroz (1845–1900) is one of Portugal's best-known and most enjoyable authors. His most popular work is *The Maias*, about a wealthy Lisbon family at the beginning of the 20th century. Other titles in print include *The Tragedy of the Street of Flowers*, *The Crime of Father Amaro* and *The Sofa and Other Stories*.
Eugénio Lisboa has edited a number books of poetry and short stories, including *The Anarchist Banker and Other Portuguese Stories*, which takes its title from a Pessoa tale, and *Professor Pfiglzz and His Strange Companion*. Both are from **Carcanet Publishing**, based in Manchester, which has a specialist book series: Aspects of Portugal. You can view their titles on www.carcanet.co.uk
Fernando Pessoa (1888–1935) is second only to Camões in the long list of illustrious Portuguese poets. Many of his poems have been translated into English; others were originally written in English. He wrote under other names including Alberto Caeiro, Ricardo Reis and Álvaro de Campos; not simply changing from pseudonym to pseudonym, but transforming his style with each persona as well. His *Book of Disquiet*, a Penguin Classic, contains his disturbing meditations around Chiado.
José Saramago was born into a

family of landless peasants in Ribatejo in 1922,and received the Nobel Prize for Literature in 1998, hastening the translation of his works into English, published by Harvill Press. *Journey to Portugal* is a good place to start, a wonderful travelogue full of detailed insight. *Baltasar and Blimunda* and *The Year of the Death of Ricardo Reis* are also recommended.

Miguel Torga's autobiography, *The Creation of the World*, recalls his childhood in Trás-os-Montes and a boyhood in Brazil before returning to qualify as a doctor and practise in his native village, where his *Tales from the Mountain* and *More Tales from the Mountain* are set. Carcanet Press

Books about Portugal

Backwards Out of the Big World: A Voyage into Portugal by Paul Hyland, Flamingo, 2001. Following in the steps of Henry Fielding from Lisbon to the Spanish border, Hyland brings a new insight into the country.

Birdwatching Guide to the Algarve by Kevin Carlson, Alequin Press, 2000. Where to go and what to see.

A Concise History of Portugal by David Birmingham, Cambridge University Press, 2nd edition 2003. A solid standard, with many illustrations.

In the Lands of the Enchanted Moorish Maiden, edited by Mandi Gomez, Art Books International, 2003.These 11 'Exhibition trails' on Moorish Portugal cover mosques that were 'Christianised', palaces, fortifications and urban settlements between Coimbra and the Algarve.

Journal of a Voyage to Lisbon by Henry Fielding, Penguin (also available as a download from Amazon). Accounts of the last days of the author of Tom Jones who went to Portugal for his health in 1754 and expired in the 'dreariest City in the World'.

The Last Kabbalist of Lisbon by Richard Zimler, Arcadia Books, 1998. This international best-seller is set in Lisbon in 1506, when 'New Christians' converted from Judaism were being murdered.

Prince Henry The Navigator: A Life by Peter Russell, 2001 Yale. A portrait of the king as Renaissance man.

Portugal's Struggle for Liberty, by Mário Soares. Allen and Unwin, 1975. By Portugal's most eminent political figure – a long-serving president and a key personality in post-Revolution events.

The Portuguese: The Land and Its People, by Marion Kaplan. Penguin, 1992. Revealing, readable and entertaining.

A Small Death in Lisbon by Robert Wilson, Harper Collins, 1999. An excellent read as novel and description of life in Portugal.

Portuguese Voyages 1498–1663: Tales from the Great Age of Discovery, edited by Charles David Ley, Weidenfeld & Nicholson, 2000. Contemporary accounts of the great sea voyages.

Requiem: A Hallucination, Antonio Tabucchi, New Directions, 1996. A fan of Pessoa (he has written a biography), the Italian writer here meets his ghost haunting the Tagus.

The Taste of Portugal by Edite Vieira, Grub Street, 2000. Revised and updated, this is an important book of recipes, history and folklore.

They Went to Portugal by Rose Macaulay, Penguin. First published in 1946, this is a classic anthology of the visitors to Portugal, from Beckford and Robert Southey to obscure military types.

Other Insight Guides

The award-winning 190-title Insight Guide series covers destinations on every continent. **Insight Guide: Lisbon** provides further insight on the delights and historic sights of this city. **Insight Guide: Madeira** gives a full account of Portugal's Atlantic island.

Insight Pocket Guides
There are more than 100 Insight Pocket Guides, designed specifically for travellers on short visits. The carefully timed itineraries, compiled by local

writers, help to make the visit memorable. The books also contain an easy-to-use, full-size pull-out map. **Insight Pocket Guide: Algarve** brings to life this beautiful and fascinating area of the country, with its whitewashed churches and peaceful fishing villages. The pull-out map and timed itineraries help to make the most of a short stay. There are also Pocket Guides to Lisbon and Madeira.

Insight Compact Guides
More than 70 Compact Guides offer visitors a highly portable guide packed with detailed and cross-referenced text, photographs and useful maps. **Insight Compact Guides: Lisbon**, **Algarve** and **Madeira** highlight the best places to go and what to do when you get there.

Insight Travel Maps
Fleximaps on durable, coated paper are available for Portugal, Spain and Portugal, Madeira and Algarve.

For the complete list of Insight Guide titles, visit our website: www.insightguides.com

ART & PHOTO CREDITS

INSIGHT GUIDE
PORTUGAL

Cartographic Editor **Zoë Goodwin**
Design Consultants
Carlotta Junger, Graham Mitchener
Picture Research
Hilary Genin, Monica Allende

Map Production
Colourmap Scanning Ltd
© 2004 Apa Publications GmbH & Co.
Verlag KG (Singapore branch)

Index

Numbers in italics refer to photographs

INSIGHT GUIDES

The classic series that puts you in the picture

Alaska
Amazon Wildlife
American Southwest
Amsterdam
Argentina
Arizona & Grand Canyon
Asia's Best Hotels
  & Resorts
Asia, East
Asia, Southeast
Australia
Austria
Bahamas
Bali
Baltic States
Bangkok
Barbados
Barcelona
Beijing
Belgium
Belize
Berlin
Bermuda
Boston
Brazil
Brittany
Brussels
Buenos Aires
Burgundy
Burma (Myanmar)
Cairo
California
California, Southern
Canada
Caribbean
Caribbean Cruises
Channel Islands
Chicago
Chile
China
Continental Europe
Corsica
Costa Rica
Crete
Croatia
Cuba
Cyprus
Czech & Slovak Republic
Delhi, Jaipur & Agra

Denmark
Dominican Rep. & Haiti
Dublin
East African Wildlife
Eastern Europe
Ecuador
Edinburgh
Egypt
England
Finland
Florence
Florida
France
France, Southwest
French Riviera
Gambia & Senegal
Germany
Glasgow
Gran Canaria
Great Britain
Great Gardens of Britain
  & Ireland
Great Railway Journeys
  of Europe
Greece
Greek Islands
Guatemala, Belize
  & Yucatán
Hawaii
Hong Kong
Hungary
Iceland
India
India, South
Indonesia
Ireland
Israel
Istanbul
Italy
Italy, Northern
Italy, Southern
Jamaica
Japan
Jerusalem
Jordan
Kenya
Korea
Laos & Cambodia
Las Vegas

Lisbon
London
Los Angeles
Madeira
Madrid
Malaysia
Mallorca & Ibiza
Malta
Mauritius Réunion
  & Seychelles
Melbourne
Mexico
Miami
Montreal
Morocco
Moscow
Namibia
Nepal
Netherlands
New England
New Orleans
New York City
New York State
New Zealand
Nile
Normandy
Norway
Oman & The UAE
Oxford
Pacific Northwest
Pakistan
Paris
Peru
Philadelphia
Philippines
Poland
Portugal
Prague
Provence
Puerto Rico
Rajasthan
Rio de Janeiro

Rome
Russia
St Petersburg
San Francisco
Sardinia
Scandinavia
Scotland
Seattle
Shanghai
Sicily
Singapore
South Africa
South America
Spain
Spain, Northern
Spain, Southern
Sri Lanka
Sweden
Switzerland
Sydney
Syria & Lebanon
Taiwan
Tanzania & Zanzibar
Tenerife
Texas
Thailand
Tokyo
Trinidad & Tobago
Tunisia
Turkey
Tuscany
Umbria
USA: On The Road
USA: Western States
US National Parks: West
Venezuela
Venice
Vienna
Vietnam
Wales
Walt Disney World/Orlando

INSIGHT GUIDES

The world's largest collection of visual travel guides & maps